MANAGIN   ENT

This book sets out to explore   pment co-operation. Its argument is essentially ا

> How can relationships between organizations ں۔ ۔ ۔د so as to build the public action and outcomes desired from development interventions?

This book takes up the tale of the potential and real challenges and opportunities presented by the current wave of interest in the partnership approach to development co-operation. It does this by casting the net far wider than 'partnership' and 'co-operation'. It explores the diversity of inter-organizational relationships which exist in reality, and the somewhat bewildering, and at times contradictory, array of relationships which are being promoted by policymakers. For, at the same time as 'co-operation' is on the tip of the policymakers tongue, so too are words related to market efficiency, and competition and co-ordination.

In this book, partnership is taken to be just one form of inter-organizational relationship amongst many. Other forms of engagement between organizations are captured by terms such as alliance, network, federation, coalition. And there are also important forms of non-engagement or dis-engagement such as fragmentation, atomization, parallel responses and opposition. The fact is that forces of competition, co-ordination and co-operation are constantly at play, and any particular inter-organizational relationship or organizational arena may be more or less shaped by some combination of the principles and practices of these forces.

The book has been motivated by a recognition that changing institutional imperatives, terminology and political agendas have indeed created spaces for new types of relationships to emerge and extend between groups and organizations. Its primary concern is to make sense of these opportunities, both by analysing the underlying concepts and agendas, and by thinking explicitly about what these mean for management practice – and how these opportunities can be acted upon.

THE EDITORS

Dorcas Robinson is Programme Co-ordinator for Health Projects Abroad in Singida, Tanzania. Tom Hewitt is a Senior Lecturer in the Development Policy and Practice discipline at the Open University, Milton Keynes, UK and John Harriss is Reader in Development Studies at the London School of Economics.

ABOUT THE CONTRIBUTORS

Jon Bennett is an independent consultant with over 20 years' management experience in relief and development in Africa and Asia. He was OXFAM's Regional Representative in Sudan, Executive Director of the ACBAR NGO Co-ordination Body in Pakistan/Afghanistan and more recently directed the Global Internally Displaced People Survey. He has four published books on aspects of food aid, NGO co-ordination and governance and is a Research Associate at Queen Elizabeth House, Oxford University.

Teddy Brett is currently Programme Director for the MSc in Development Management at the London School of Economics. He has taught Political Science and Development at Makerere, Uganda, Sussex, and the LSE. He has published extensively on East Africa, International Political Economy, and Institutional Theory and has carried out major consultancies for the World Bank, ODA (now DFID), and DANIDA.

Joanna Chataway is a Lecturer in Development Management at the Open University and recently chaired the team working on an OU course in Institutional Development. She previously worked as a Senior Consultant for Segal Quince Wickstead, a Cambridge-based consultancy firm. As an academic and consultant she has worked on small business and institutional development projects in Southern Africa and Central and Eastern Europe.

Helena Dolny has a first degree in agricultural economics from Reading and PhD on the land question in South Africa from the Open University. She has worked in the co-operatives unit of the Ministry of Agriculture in Mozambique and the Centre for African Studies in Eduardo Mondlane University in Mozambique. In South Africa she was a member of the Land Commission and since 1997 she has been Managing Director of the South African Land Bank.

Joseph Hanlon is a Visiting Senior Research Fellow at the Open University and a freelance journalist on southern Africa, development, and economic issues. As a journalist in Africa, he has written for the BBC, *The Guardian*, *New Internationalist*, *The Economist* and other organizations. He is the author or editor of more than a dozen books on the political economy of southern Africa. His activities range from being editor of a newsletter, the *Mozambique Peace Process Bulletin*, to being policy advisor to Jubilee 2000, the campaign to cancel poor country debt.

John Harriss is currently Reader in Development Studies at the London School of Economics. He was formerly Dean of the School of Development Studies at the University of East Anglia, and Head of the Regional Office for South and Central Asia with Save the Children Fund (UK) 1994-96.

Tom Hewitt is Senior Lecturer at the Open University where he teaches and researches on development with particular interests in organizational life, technology, development policy and communications. He has been closely involved in the production and delivery of the Open University's MSc in Development Management. He has previously co-edited the books *Industrialization and Development* and *Development Policy and Public Action* both published by Oxford University Press.

Mick Moore is Professorial Fellow at the Institute of Development Studies at the University of Sussex. He researches, teaches and consults on the politics and management of development policy and practice.

Angela Penrose is Policy Director of Save the Children Fund. She has over 25 years' experience in the field of development, including work in developing countries in teaching, research, rural development and management of famine relief and emergencies. She has published work on children's issues, emergencies, humanitarian response, refugees, famine and environmental issues. A principal area of interest is the realization of children's rights through greater consideration of children in social and economic policy formulation.

Dorcas Robinson has worked as development advisor to the NGO, Health Projects Abroad, in support of two community based health care programmes, and is currently Programme Co-ordinator of the programme in Singida Region of Tanzania. She was also involved in the development of a number of courses in the Open University's MSc in Development Management.

Paul Taylor is Professor of International Relations, and Chair of the Department, at the London School of Economics. He has published on the history and theory of international organization, on the economic and social arrangements of the United Nations and on the politics of the institutions of the European Union. He was editor of the *Review of International Studies* between 1994 and 1997.

Gordon Wilson is a Senior Lecturer in the Development Policy and Practice (DPP) discipline at the Open University, where he chairs the University's undergraduate and postgraduate courses in Development Studies. He has a current research interest in institutional sustainability, or how norms and practices of participation and partnership can become entrenched in development initiatives and lead to social learning for sustainable development.

This book is one component of the Open University course TU872 *Institutional Development: Conflicts, Values and Meanings*, a core course in the postgraduate Global Programme in Development Management. It was produced in conjunction with the TU872 course team and the contribution of the following course team members in the development and production of this book is gratefully acknowledged:

Carolyn Baxter (Course Manager)

Philippa Broadbent (Print Buying)

Joanna Chataway (Course Team Chair)

Daphne Cross (Print Buying Co-ordinator)

Debbie Dickinson (Secretary)

Sue Dobson (Graphic Artist)

Gill Gowans (Copublishing Advisor)

Tom Hewitt (Academic)

Hazel Johnson (Academic)

Jane Moore (Editor)

Dorcas Robinson (Academic)

Jane Sheppard (Graphic Designer)

Claire Street (Secretary)

Alan Thomas (Academic)

Dave Wield (Academic)

Chris Williams (Project Controller)

Gordon Wilson (Academic)

Details of this and other Open University courses can be obtained from the Course Reservations Centre, PO Box 724, The Open University, Milton Keynes MK7 6ZS, United Kingdom: tel. +44 (0)1908 653231, e-mail ces-gen@open.ac.uk

Alternatively, you may visit the Open University website at http://www.open.ac.uk where you can learn more about the wide range of courses and packs offered at all levels by the Open University.

For information about the purchase of Open University course components, contact Open University Worldwide Ltd, The Berrill Building, Walton Hall, Milton Keynes MK7 6AA, United Kingdom:
tel. +44 (0)1908 858785; fax +44 (0)1908 858787; e-mail ouwenq@open.ac.uk; website http://www.ouw.co.uk

EDITED BY

DORCAS ROBINSON
TOM HEWITT
JOHN HARRISS

SAGE
Publications

The Open University

London • Thousand Oaks • New Dehli

SAGE PUBLICATIONS IN ASSOCIATION WITH THE OPEN UNIVERSITY

The Open University
Walton Hall,
Milton Keynes
MK7 6AA

First published 2000.

SAGE Publications Ltd
6 Bonhill Street
London EC2A 4PU

SAGE Publications Inc.
2455 Teller Road
Thousand Oaks
California 91320

Sage Publications India Pvt Ltd
32 M-block Market
Greater Kailash - I
New Delhi 110 048

11884371

British Library Cataloguing in Publication Data
A catalogue record for this book is available from the British Library

Library of Congress catalog record available

Edited, designed and typeset by The Open University.

Printed and bound in the United Kingdom by T.J. International, Padstow, Cornwall.

ISBN 0 7619 6479 7 (pbk)

ISBN 0 7619 6478 9 (cased)

CONTENTS

PART 5
CONCLUSIONS

INTRODUCTIONS

1 WHY INTER-ORGANIZATIONAL RELATIONSHIPS MATTER

DORCAS ROBINSON, TOM HEWITT AND JOHN HARRISS

1.1 INTRODUCTION

The government believes that genuine partnerships between poorer countries … and the donor community are needed if poverty is to be addressed effectively and in a coherent way.

We shall:
- Work closely with other donors and development agencies to build partnerships with developing countries to strengthen the commitment to the elimination of poverty, and use our influence to help mobilize the political will to achieve the international development targets.
- Pursue these targets in partnership with poorer countries who are also committed to them.
- Put in place new ways of working with the UK private and voluntary sectors, and the research community, towards the international development targets.

(DFID, 1997)

In its 1997 White Paper on International Development, the British Government's Department for International Development (DFID) makes extensive use of the language of partnership and co-operation. This language has become the hallmark of policy and practice in development and social policy circles internationally – as is apparent in print, online and in the buzz of discussions at workshops and meetings. High hopes are being pinned on the capacity of different groups and organizations to work together, co-operatively and in partnership, in the name of human development. But what does this all mean?

As the statement quoted above indicates, the discourse of co-operation implies some commonality of view can be, and indeed may already have been, reached. There is an implicit assumption that a shared perspective about the purposes and processes – about the 'what' and 'how' – of development exists, which in turn enables partnerships and concerted action in the name of common goals.

The international aid business, an organizational arena which has in the past tended towards practices which could be referred to as serial monogamy, has been indulging in more complex and polygamous behaviours. One-off and private relationships between bilateral donor and government department are developing in many places into forms of concerted donor action around commonly agreed approaches. This can be seen as a shift from aid-based to rules-based development, which requires the involvement of many parties and in which skills of negotiation become more significant. The emphasis on aid projects and disbursement of aid funds has not disappeared, but has taken more of a backseat as donors, governments and increasingly, other 'partners', turn their attention to defining sector-wide programmes and stimulating macro-level change. In inter-organizational terms, this might be described as a move from interaction generated by operational needs and requirements, to attempts to build more enduring relationships stimulated by an appreciation of more strategic issues.

Major challenges lie in making sense of the politics which underly the rather cuddly notion of co-operation, the real conflicts of interest and agenda which persist in all areas, and the processes through which both self-interest or short-sightedness, as well as genuine conflict over values, are constantly being managed.

1.1.1 DEFINING THE INTER-ORGANIZATIONAL ARENA

In setting out to make sense of the inter-organizational arena, this book is under-pinned by particular understandings of three linked concepts:

- development;
- development management; and
- public action.

In the first case, we understand 'development' to mean – following Amartya Sen – the expansion of capabilities. In other words, increasing the possibilities for more people to realize their potentials as human beings through the expansion of their capabilities for functioning. According to Sen's 'capability approach', development should be about the enrichment of human lives, not in the sense of 'having more things' particularly, but rather of having the freedom to choose between different ways of living. Human life is seen as

> ... a set of 'doings and beings' – we may call them 'functionings' –
> and ... evaluation of the quality of life [is related] to the assessment
> of the capability to function ... Capability reflects a person's
> freedom to choose between different ways of living. The
> underlying motivation – the focusing on freedom – is well captured
> by Marx's claim that what we need is 'replacing the domination of
> circumstances and chance over individuals by the domination of
> individuals over chance and circumstances'.
>
> (Sen, 1990, pp. 43-4)

'Development management', then, as Alan Thomas has argued (Thomas, 1996), is distinctive as a type of management because it is about the management of interventions aimed at external social goals. These goals are themselves directed at the expansion of 'capability to function', and thus of freedom – in contexts which are characterized by value-based conflict and multiple actors (Thomas, 1996). The key aims of development organizations and of development action are externally directed to the public sphere rather than, as in most organizations, being principally internal. They are goals which have to do with the quality of people's lives rather than simply with production or profits. 'Value-based conflict' is inevitable, therefore, because different people have at least somewhat different values and aspirations. There has to be negotiation between these people and around their differences – rather than the imposition of one particular set of values and goals – in order to achieve the best possible outcomes for everyone. The basic task of all managers is to bring about the kind of co-ordination of activities and co-ordination between people – who themselves have different or only partially overlapping goals – which is necessary to achieve their own objectives. But for development managers the task is especially challenging because the external, social ends which they are trying to realize are particularly complex. This view of development management is based on an understanding that it is necessarily a complex and contested process which is influenced by a multiplicity of interests, both within the state and outside it.

The process of negotiation over development lies at the heart of the idea of 'public action'. Public action is understood to mean more than just action by the state:

> Public action is not ... just a question of public delivery and state initiative. It is also a matter of participation by the public in a process of social change.
>
> (Drèze and Sen, 1989, p. 259)

Mackintosh (1992a) builds on this notion of public action, suggesting that it needs to be broadened to incorporate action of behalf of sectional interests. Public action is, then, collective, purposeful manipulation of the public environment by a range of actors, including state, community, non governmental organizations (NGOs) and private commercial agencies. This book uses this conception of public action in place of the more familiar idea of 'collective action'.

All of this means that the management of interactions between different organizations, and between different types of organizations, can fairly be seen as the essence of how development takes place. The multiple actors involved have at least partially differing values; usually no single individual or organization can control the process; nor can the outcomes be very clearly set in advance.

1.1.2 EXPLORING INTER-ORGANIZATIONAL RELATIONSHIPS

This book sets out to explore the policy and practice of development co-operation. Its argument is essentially a question:

> How can relationships between organizations be managed so as to build the public action and outcomes desired from development interventions?

This is an action-oriented question which arises from the fundamental philosophical, value-based and ethical issues that public action processes contend with and seek to address. These are captured in questions like:

> Who does what for/with/on behalf of whom? Why and how do they do it?

Managing in the multiple-actor contexts which confront development managers involves:

1 considering when and how to choose between various possible inter-organizational strategies, such as collaboration, advocacy, direct opposition, or organizational growth in order to achieve development ends; and

2 developing the practical skills for working with competitive, co-ordinated, or co-operative strategies for dealing with inter-organizational relationships.

1.2 COMPETITION, CO-ORDINATION AND CO-OPERATION

The starting point of the book is that there are three *'ideal types'* or modes for structuring inter-organizational relationships – using the sociologist Max Weber's term for a theoretical construction which emphasizes certain traits of a given social item which do not necessarily exist in reality. 'Ideal', here, does not mean 'what is most desirable' but rather something like a 'pure form'. 'Ideal types' are tools for thinking with. What we are suggesting is that there are basically three ways in which people or groups relate to each other, though in reality all sorts of different combinations exist. Referring to the 'ideal types' of competition, co-ordination and co-operation (the 3Cs) will help us to make sense of more complex realities, and to make judgements about how best to manage in different situations. These ideal types are the currency of international policy debate, research and ideology, and are proposed as different institutional frameworks for addressing the problems of public action.

Each ideal type is explored on three levels, being commonly associated with particular: institutional frameworks (guiding sets of norms, values, rules and practices); ways of organizing (forms of interaction); and organizational types (see Table 1.1).

TABLE 1.1 COMMON ASSOCIATIONS OF COMPETITION, CO-ORDINATION AND CO-OPERATION			
	Institutional framework	Ways of organizing	Organizational type
Competition	Market	Suppliers and consumers through price mechanisms	Firms
Co-ordination	State	Government and citizens through voting mechanisms hierarchy; rule-based administrative control	Government offices, from central to local
Co-operation	Civil society	Voluntary initiatives and social movements through identification of common goals, values and needs	NGO, trades unions, community groups, etc.

There are various and often contradictory definitions of the terms used to describe inter-organizational relationships. There are also a wide array of terms which are applied, including words such as conflict, collaboration, and coercion. In the rest of this section we establish the ways in which we use the terms competition, co-ordination and co-operation in the book. These are only a starting point, however. What is of greater interest is the complexity of practice, the ways in which the three forms or 'ideal types' combine in different institutional and organizational arenas.

Each of the 3Cs (competition, co-ordination, and co-operation) is generally attributed with certain characteristics which distinguish it from the other forms, and which appear to make it more or less suitable for tackling different types of collective problem. Thus, the state tends to be seen as the ideal form for ensuring legal systems and law and order. However, practice is more complicated than the ideal type suggests. Often there are significant overlaps between what might be considered state, market and voluntary organizations. It is not always clear what the differences are. And there are numerous situations in which different types of organization are working together in various arrangements, to resolve collective problems. For example, in the case of law and order, the government system may be responsible for the creation and management of laws (through legislative bodies, the judiciary and the police system), but private security systems of various kinds may also exist (including registered security firms and informal processes of justice).

1.2.1 COMPETITION

Compete: 'to strive for something together with another'.

Competition: 'the action of endeavouring to gain what another endeavours to gain at the same time; the striving of two or more for the same object'.

(Shorter Oxford English Dictionary)

At its simplest, competition as a way of organizing is based on the use of price criteria, by both suppliers and consumers of goods and services, to determine their behaviour. The common organizational type associated with competition is the firm, which maintains competitiveness (survives) through price competition. The institutional framework for organizing competition is provided by the market. Thus, one of the principal proponents of competition as the basis for development, the World Bank, puts it this way:

> In most circumstances ... the primary objective of public policy should be to promote competition among providers – including between the public and private sectors (when there are public providers), as well as among private providers, whether non-profit or for-profit.
>
> (World Bank, 1993)

In its positive connotations, the market provides a desirable institutional framework for organizing public (collective) action because it enables the exercise of choice by individuals. On the negative side, competition is often associated with conflict over scarce resources. For example: 'in competition people believe their goals are negatively related, so that one's success interferes with the others; one's successful goal attainment makes others less likely to reach their goals' (Thompson *et al.*, 1991).

Why might we choose competition as a way of organizing inter-organizational relationships?

Competition has become the dominant ideology about 'how to do development better'; but in development practice, there are numerous instances of conflict over resources, either head-on or through duplication. Our use of the term competition in the book is broad. Not only do we use it in the sense of 'competition for scarce resources' but also to reflect competition over ideas, constituencies, values and definitions of needs. Market-led, competition-based reforms of state structures have important implications for inter-organizational management; but we should remember that there may still be inter-dependencies between organizations, even when they are in competition with each other.

1.2.2 CO-ORDINATION

Co-ordinate: 'to place in the same order, rank, or division; to place things in proper position relatively to each other and to the system of which they form part; to act in combined order for the production of a particular result'.

Co-ordination: 'the action of co-ordinating; harmonious combination of agents and functions towards the production of a result'.

(Shorter Oxford English Dictionary)

The most common notion of co-ordination is as rule-regulated and hierarchically organized, generally associated with the state as a legitimate controller and coercer. This view of co-ordination has strong resonance with traditional views of management where the role of the manager is seen as being 'to plan, to organize, to command, to co-ordinate and to control' (Fayol, 1916).

In its positive senses, co-ordination by the state is based on the notion of a liberal state deriving its legitimacy through systems of elected representation. The state promotes the concepts of national unity and universality, the protection of which justifies its central role and that of other publicly accountable bodies in co-ordination of an array of social and economic activities. Co-ordination is a way to bring together disparate agencies to make their efforts more compatible (in the interests of equity, effectiveness and efficiency). Without co-ordination, the danger is of lapsing into chaos and inefficiency.

However, co-ordination, generally associated with hierarchies, is a relationship of power (which can be used and abused) and the co-ordinator (be it the state or other agent) can be monolithic and coercive against the wishes of those being co-ordinated.

Why might we choose co-ordination? Co-ordination has been a key form for organizing development practice: co-ordination between government, NGOs and donors has been important for a long time. However, the context in which co-ordination occurs has been changing. The role of the state in development has changed, from that of the state as the all encompassing provider, to that of the state as regulator. This change has implications for the areas in which the state can legitimately be seen to have a co-ordinating role.

As a form of practice, co-ordination tends to involve relationships based on hierarchy. However, this hierarchy can be either imposed or constructed voluntarily, where one actor is given the task of leading. This is highlighted for example, by the distinction made between co-ordination of a recipient *by* aid donors and co-ordination, by the recipient, *of* aid donors (Wield, 1997). These two arrangements imply very different things about the use of power and resource, about who controls agenda-setting and management, and about who is accountable to whom.

Our use of the term in this book is to describe relationships which are ordered by the exercise of authority through hierarchy and rules, rather than by the 'hidden hand' of competition or by solidarity based on trust and reciprocity.

1.2.3 CO-OPERATION

> Co-operate: 'to work together; act in conjunction with another person or thing, to an end, or in a work'.
>
> (Shorter Oxford English Dictionary)

There are few common understandings of the term 'co-operation' beyond a rather broad notion of voluntarily working together based on consensus, camaraderie or solidarity, community or compromise. Even then, the differences in the philosophy and practice of co-operation are immense. For example, the US 'communitarian' movement and the European co-operatives both invoke the importance of community and co-operation, but do so in different ways. In political terms, forms of co-operation are advocated both by the reactionary right-wing, defining 'community' to exclude others, and by the radical left wing, advocating solidarism (which can, in its way, be equally exclusionary).

Co-operation tends to be associated with voluntary organizations, as non-hierarchical and with all parties involved on an equal basis with each other. In this sense, it can be distinguished from co-ordination on the basis that co-operation assumes power based on knowledge, expertise, and/ or contribution, rather than power derived from role or function in a hierarchy. Co-operation is also often seen as the opposite of competition. On its positive side it is seen as a process of consensus-building and sharing in public action. However, as already indicated talk of co-operation frequently disguises power relations in the name of equality. In George Orwells' exposition of the practices of radical socialism, *Animal Farm*, we are reminded that 'All animals are equal, but some are more equal than others'. Terms commonly associated with co-operation, such as community or partnership, can in practice be little more than a smoke screen for many other kinds of relationship.

Why, then, might we choose co-operation as a strategy for building inter-organizational relationships? For many people and organizations, their philosophy or vision leans in this direction, for example those interested in the notions of 'participation', 'process management', and 'learning organizations'. Co-operation is also a potentially strong device for managing diverse interests. Rather than leaving these interests to compete in the financial, political and social 'markets', or seeking to homogenize and consolidate these interests through co-ordinated action, co-operation as a concept offers the possibility for diverse interests to be brought together and to be built into a whole new idea or approach. In practice, co-operative processes have often assisted organizations to move from crisis to vision-building to problem-solving by stressing the common ground and interdependencies rather than the differences.

1.3 DESCRIBING INTER-ORGANIZATIONAL RELATIONSHIPS

We started this chapter with a quote from the UK's Department for International Development which stressed 'partnership' as the way forward for international development initiatives and for the alleviation of global poverty. Questioning the widespread use of the term in current development discourse was the initial impetus for writing this book. Our interest (and disquiet) was centred on the ways that language can take twists and turns over time which can either enlighten or obfuscate our appreciation of real world events and processes. In compiling this book, our intention has been to take a more nuanced approach to the language of development and to the importance and variety of ways in which development organizations relate to each other.

A short discussion here of the language of 'partnership' and 'co-operation' serves to illustrate the broader purpose of the rest of the book. Even such a brief review of language and the way in which the relationships between organizations are described, underlines what we have said about their importance. It also clarifies the ideas behind the three ideal types from the complexities and the confusions of language.

The idea that development interventions involve relationships between development agencies is not particularly novel. Relationships have formed the substance of action and debate since the era of 'modern' development intervention began in the post-war years. Such relationships include those between:

- governments (donor agency and recipient government);
- northern NGO (NNGO) and southern NGO (SNGO);
- NGO and 'community';
- central government and local government;
- bodies within the UN system.

These relationships have long been described using words like 'partnership' and 'development co-operation', a term which, for example, has been used to describe the European Commission's aid programme for a number of years. Similarly, for NNGOs, many of which have built their activities around support for international solidarity movements such as anti-apartheid groups and women's rights organizations, 'partnership' has become a standard part of their vocabulary:

> Fighting poverty through partnership: ... Save the Children is
> working to fight poverty on all fronts from the UK to Africa, Asia
> and beyond. Support is rarely a simple question of finance. It
> involves building long-term partnerships and programmes which
> bring lasting improvements to children's lives.

(Save the Children, Annual Report, 1995-6)

> World Vision is an international partnership of Christians seeking
> to facilitate and empower the poor and oppressed ... World Vision
> Tanzania consults with and co-operates with other development
> agencies working in the area to avoid both duplication and conflict.
>
> (World Vision Tanzania, promotional brochure)

As a number of commentators have noted:

> The idea of 'partnership' has been knocking around in the
> development business for years ... [It] stems from the 1970s ... In
> the 25 years since then, the term has been used and abused as a
> blanket covering all sorts of relationships between all sorts of
> development agencies. Not only has this eroded the usefulness of
> the term, current trends towards contracting in the aid system are
> turning NGDOs [non governmental development organizations]
> away from the concept ...
>
> (Fowler, 1997, p. 107)

Fowler points to a phenomenon which exhibits aspects of both the old and
the new: old in the sense that this language has indeed been used for years,
and often inappropriately applied, masking relationships which would be
better described using other terms (such as co-ordination). This has been
noted by critics:

> Northern NGOs are becoming locked into a private world of
> discourse with its own 'development dictionary' ('empowerment',
> 'process', and 'animation') ... And 'partnership', that polite myth
> so obtrusive in NGO rhetoric, often disguised Northern
> manipulation of Southern NGOs.
>
> (Tandon, 1990)

and, with reference to donor aid giving to developing countries:

> ... assistance is given to make the partnership look plausible, but as
> it is worked out, the proletarian countries get poorer and the
> technological gap widens.
>
> (Ake, 1978)

But there *is* something new in the sense that this language is being used
more widely, and in areas where it has not been heard before, for example,
through the inclusion of business in development partnerships (Tennyson,
1998). Fowler refers to NGDO disquiet when the term with which they
have become so uncritically comfortable in their own circles, now acquires
rather sinister connotations because it is applied to their relationships with
donors, which are increasingly based on contracts. The word 'contract'
does not convey the sense of intimacy, understanding and equality that is
commonly associated with the term – if not the practice of – 'partnership'.
It is no doubt for this reason that there is a preference for talking about

'public–private partnerships', a term which somewhat sanitizes the fact of crumbling and/or dismantled government services and the increased reliance on private provision of social services:

> Private Health Care providers (both for-profit and not-for-profit) are now PARTNERS rather than opponents or competitors for the demise of each other.
>
> (Government of Tanzania, 1994, p. 8)

The range of contexts across which this language of partnership and co-operation is now being applied, gives the impression of a new consensus. This apparent consensus is expressed through the sharing of a vocabulary across diverse development agencies, which have in the past tended to reveal their differences through their different 'development dictionaries'. This is a common vocabulary around:

1   the desirability of 'partnership' as a focus for development intervention and support; and

2   the purposes of that partnership; and

3   the nature of the relationship.

1.3.1   THE FOCUS ON PARTNERSHIP

Over time there appears to have been a shift in emphasis from a focus on aid giving to that of development partnership. This is clearly captured by a 1996 report produced by the Development Assistance Committee (DAC) of the Organization for Economic Co-operation and Development:

> The record of the last fifty years, from Marshall Plan aid to the network of development partnerships now evolving, shows that the efforts of countries and societies to help themselves have been the main ingredients of their success.
>
> (OECD, 1996)

The report sets out goals for development to the year 2015, and identifies the strategies for achieving those goals as being: 'partnership in support of self-help efforts, improved co-ordination and consistent policies':

> To give substance to our belief in local ownership and partnership we must use channels and methods of co-operation that do not undermine those values. Acceptance of the partnership mode ... is one of the most positive changes we are proposing in the framework for development co-operation. In a partnership, development co-operation does not try to do things for developing countries and their people, but with them. It must be seen as a collaborative effort to help them increase their capacities to do things for themselves.
>
> (OECD, 1996)

The Department for International Development (DFID) in Britain, endorses these views; a recent speech by Clare Short, the Secretary of State for International Development, charts the history of development assistance in a similar way:

> Priorities in the early 1960s ... focused very much on support for ... infrastructure that had been developed in the colonial period. There was a significant shift in the mid 1970s, spearheaded by Robert McNamara at the World Bank ... towards support for the poorest people in the poorest countries ... There was a further shift in 1980 when the last government said it would take greater account of political and commercial factors in taking decisions about the allocation of aid resources ... Now is the time for another major shift ... I am very impressed by the approach outlined in the report of the DAC 'Shaping the 21st century'... The report proposes measurable targets ... It suggests that developing countries, international financial institutions and donor countries agree on openly prepared partnership plans for meeting these targets ... Our role is to support and complement – and not to do so in such a way as to suggest that we have all the answers ... We must share the lessons we learn and this must be a two way process ... Partner governments must be committed to the creation of the right economic and political environment – which includes dealing with corruption – if sustainable development is to thrive.
>
> (Short, 1997a)

1.3.2 THE PURPOSES OF PARTNERSHIP

Statements such as those above indicate some agreement over the purposes of partnership – what development intervention is about. It is *not* about giving aid, but about building capacities and local ownership – doing things *with* people not *for* them. It is about helping to create the 'right economic and political environment'.

The ostensible purpose of development partnerships in the late 1990s is 'institutional development' or 'institutional transformation', two more key terms in the current shared development dictionary. This is based on the idea that institutional weakness or decay is the main obstacle to the achievement of the development vision. Commissioner Pinheiro, in UK discussions on the future of European Union–ACP (African, Caribbean, Pacific) relations says:

> ... closely connected to the theme of reviving growth, is the question of institutional change and development. There is increasing evidence that growth prospects are seriously impaired by weak, ineffective, unpredictable and arbitrary administration and by governments which have no will to tackle the sources of inefficiency, waste and corruption, to confront problems, to practice

sound management in public finances and to achieve results. *As a large and significant partner in development the EC can help to strengthen government's political will to reform* … Institutionally strengthened governments are in much better shape to tackle the fundamental development problem of reducing poverty.

(Pinheiro, 1997; emphasis added)

This is a view shared by the World Bank amongst others:

An effective state is vital for the provision of the goods and services – and the rules and institutions – that allow markets to flourish and people to live healthier and happier lives … Many said much the same thing fifty years ago, but then they tended to mean that development had to be state-provided. The message of experience since then is rather different: that *the state is central to economic and social development, not as a direct provider of growth but as a partner, catalyst, and facilitator.*

(World Bank, 1997, p. 1; emphasis added)

1.3.3 THE NATURE OF THE RELATIONSHIP BETWEEN ORGANIZATIONS

The language of partnership and co-operation is also intimately connected with language used to describe how agencies work with each other. The *World Development Report* (World Bank, 1997) suggests that the state's role is to act as a partner, meaning as a catalyst and facilitator. Similarly, in other extracts used above, there is talk of donors supporting governments, helping them to strengthen their political will. This language suggests that everyone is now participating in a common enterprise – partnerships are being built through facilitative networks of development organizations, this process itself producing synergistic complementarities and enabling environments. The language of this last sentence, however, may mean different things to different people – or nothing at all to some!

In short, the language of 'partnership' often masks a complex reality, which is that relationships take many different forms, and that these vary widely in terms of the ways in which power, interests, substance and so on are organized.

1.4 THE IMPORTANCE OF INTER-ORGANIZATIONAL RELATIONSHIPS

As the quotes in the last section indicate, there is a strong message that development agents and organizations should be working more closely and with common purpose. However, there is a range of views on what this means. Some appear to take it as a given fact that agencies are doing so already; others are more explicit about the practical difficulties; and still others are advocating or discussing relationships between certain groups in order to challenge the agenda of others.

The central concern of this book, as we stated earlier is

> How can relationships between organizations be managed so as to build the public action and outcomes desired from development interventions?

This question assumes that inter-organizational relationships do matter. They particularly matter when it comes to working towards broader, collective outcomes and they require conscious nurturing or 'management'. Such assumptions are not exclusive to development interventions. For example, the significance of relationships between organizations is now recognized in the practice and research around business or commercial organizations. These relationships are explained in a variety of ways, depending on the perspective of the observer. Some of these explanations could be characterized as in Box 1.1.

BOX 1.1   SOME PERSPECTIVES ON WHY INTER-ORGANIZATIONAL RELATIONSHIPS MATTER

Evangelism: collaboration is a 'good thing', which should be aspired to for that reason. A view particularly strong amongst those concerned with community organizations (for example, NGOs, with experience of working at the 'grassroots'; or proponents of communitarianism in the US).

Pragmatism: in recognition of the fact that the world is becoming both smaller and more complex, and that societies and organizations are increasingly interdependent. A good example of this is the spotlight which has been turned on NGOs working in emergency or relief situations, and the need for them to work more closely together. International concerns over the environment, too, have brought diverse organizations together in negotiations.

Market imperatives: as the world of business organizations has become increasing specialized (characterized in the move from Fordist production models to the Japanese model), inter-organizational arrangements are seen as key to efficiency and competitiveness (co-operation for competitiveness).

Synergy: the idea that working with other organizations enables an organization to better achieve its objectives; that is, the achievement of the whole is greater than the sum of the parts. It strongly informs advocacy networks and also efforts to build NGO 'sectors' in developing countries.

Whatever the specific justification, the prevailing notion is that 'inter-action is best'. Although the language is not all new, current development discourse assumes that

- interagency collaboration is key to the success of development interventions;
- building such collaboration will produce new and more desirable (read 'effective') institutions; and
- this can be achieved through facilitation and support of a variety of relationships or arrangements between agencies.

Despite the positive story which is widely repeated about the benefits of inter-agency collaboration, discussion about the policy and practice of such relationships is limited. There is seldom consistent policy from development agencies which sets out what they mean by words like 'co-operation' or how they intend to promote it in practice. Nor do they describe the contexts and circumstances in which 'co-operation' is likely to be more efficient, effective and accountable than 'co-ordination' or 'competition'. There is perhaps even less systematic treatment of the issues which are involved in attempts to implement and manage the inter-organizational arena. Yet it is recognized by many practitioners that this area is very difficult. This book aims to address these gaps.

1.5 STRUCTURE OF THE BOOK

The book treats the three ways of organizing and managing inter-organizational relationships in what appears to be a linear way, rather as if there were a continuum from competition to co-operation. However, this structure is intended only as a way of organizing material and arguments, and throughout, the complexity and overlap in real life is drawn out. This is one of the main arguments of the book: no particular form of inter-organizational relationship is inherently 'better' than any other. 'Co-operation' is not necessarily more desirable than 'competition'. Both popular debates and policy discussions are often set up in such simplistic ways. We believe that it is important to challenge the assumptions which are rather commonly made – whether about the inherent virtues of competition and of market organization (which has been a central tendency in debates over international development in the last decade and more) – or about the virtues of co-operation (which have often led would-be 'community developers', for example, wildly astray). We also want to challenge the idea that competition, co-ordination and co-operation are alternatives; real organizations will often display elements of all three forms.

The book is in five parts. The first part introduces some of the conceptual and discourse issues relating to organizations and the divisions of roles by setting out conventional thinking around our three ideal types and by examining some contemporary thinking about inter-organizational relationships. The next three parts address the 3Cs (competition, co-ordination, and co-operation) in turn, setting out:

1 *Theory, concepts and definitions*: commonly associated with each ideal type and their alternative, more complex definitions.

2 *Inter-organizational arrangements and forms of practice*: using case studies, examples and interview material, to introduce the types of inter-organizational arrangements which emerge around each institutional form, and the issues (of values, efficiency, effectiveness and accountability) that arise.

Each of the parts has a short concluding section which draws out from the material some of the implications of each form for practice: how inter-organizational arrangements emerge or maintain themselves or change; who are key actors; how they are managed. The types of critical question include:

• What arguments are used when people promote one institutional form – competition, co-ordination or competition – as being most desirable for public action?

• What types of inter-organizational arrangements are commonly associated with each institutional form? How do the three forms overlap and interact?

• What are the implications of each type of arrangement in terms of values, efficiency, effectiveness and accountability?

The final part of the book provides two different types of conclusion.

Chapter 13 is a case study of inter-organizational relationships which reflects on the real world implications of concepts used throughout the book.

Chapter 14 explores ways of putting ideas in the book into practice, emphasizing certain generic skills that may be useful to practitioners and managers of inter-organizational relationships.

2 UNDERSTANDING ORGANIZATIONS AND INSTITUTIONS

TEDDY BRETT

2.1 INTRODUCTION

The last chapter introduced the ideas of competition, co-ordination and co-operation as *ideal types* of ways of organizing relationships – ways of establishing stable patterns of transactions between people and between organizations. Each of these distinct 'ways of organizing' is commonly associated with particular institutional frameworks – those, respectively, of the market, of hierarchy and of voluntary or reciprocal action. Also, in people's minds, each tends to be associated with particular types of organizations: respectively, firms, state organizations and voluntary associations. But as Chapter 1 demonstrated, in the real world 'ways of organizing' are combined in all sorts of ways.

Firms, which are key actors in markets, are themselves very often organized hierarchically as formal, bureaucratic organizations. Equally, one of the trends in contemporary management thinking argues the virtues of 'organization as (solidaristic) community', and of building greater degrees of co-operation, in place of co-ordinated hierarchical authority relations; while another urges the introduction of competitive, market principles into public management (Moore, Chapter 5). Similarly, organizations such as non governmental organizations (NGOs), which are often described as 'voluntary associations', and clearly are distinct both from private firms and from government departments, may nonetheless have hierarchical, bureaucratic management structures.

Claims are often made about the virtues of the market as opposed to the state – or vice versa – or about the merits of organization in civil society by comparison with either state or market. In this chapter I aim to counter this kind of fundamentalism which is characteristic of much policy advocacy. To achieve this, I will set out key ideas in organizational analysis with reference to the three stereotypes which appear throughout development policy literature:

- the market;
- the state;
- civil society.

I have chosen this approach because these stereotypes are often considered to be the most important institutional forms of competition, co-ordination and co-operation respectively. I also believe that it is important to understand the ways in which each of these types addresses the basic problems of social organization.

The idea that market, state and civil society each have distinctive strengths and weaknesses is explored. This is the explicit argument of the World Bank in its *World Development Report 1997* and marks a definite shift from the 1980s when the Bank embraced the virtues of market solutions to problems.

In different circumstances – and in relation to different kinds of problems – competition, co-ordination and co-operation may all have a part to play in establishing effective solutions. The chapter focuses then on the fundamentals of organizational life and is divided into the following sections:

Section 2.2 establishes why organizations and institutions matter and builds a framework for understanding inter-organizational relationships.

Section 2.3 examines the diversity of function and structure of organization in the economy, in the state and in civil society respectively.

Section 2.4 sets out from different perspectives the principles which govern relationships between organizations.

Section 2.5 examines in some details three key themes in understanding organizational life: scale, incentives and accountability.

Section 2.6 concludes briefly with an examination of some potentially contentious assumptions behind the approach adopted in the chapter

2.2 THE ROLE OF INSTITUTIONS AND ORGANIZATIONS

2.2.1 WHY DO INSTITUTIONS AND ORGANIZATIONS MATTER?

The approach to development management adopted in this book presupposes a clear recognition of the nature and role of institutions and their relationship to organizations. *Institutions* are sets 'of rules that structure social interactions in particular ways', based on knowledge 'shared by members of the relevant community or society' (Knight, 1992, p. 2). Compliance to those rules is enforced through known incentives or sanctions. In other words, institutions are the norms, rules, habits, customs and routines (both formal and written, or, more often, informal and internalized) which govern society at large. They influence the function, structure and behaviour of *organizations* – 'groups of individuals bound by some common purpose' who come together to achieve joint objectives (North, 1990, p. 4) – as actors in society. Institutions, by producing stable, shared and commonly understood patterns of behaviour are crucial to solving the problems of collective action amongst individuals.

Taking an institutional perspective transcends approaches which see society as composed of individuals making private choices on the basis of pure self-interest. The actions and attitudes of the people who run a hospital, a bank or a famine relief operation are not a matter of individual choice, but must be determined by the needs of the organization. Where complex activities are involved, people may even have to adapt their personalities to develop the skills and value systems required to perform their allotted roles. To become a doctor, an accountant or an administrator makes great demands on their technical competence, social commitment and personal identity. Hence 'human rationality', looked at from an institutional point of view, cannot be determined by pure self-interest. Instead they are determined at least partially by the 'higher goals and integrations (derived) from the institutional setting in which it operates and by which it is moulded' (Simon, 1957, p. 101).

Thus, effective organizations depend on the existence of institutions which create rules which everyone (including the managers) must accept, thus subordinating their personal needs and interests to those of the organization as a whole. This general requirement of all institutional systems is achieved in different societies using a wide array of rules, incentives and sanctions. These govern the internal relationships between managers and workers, and their external relationships with consumers or clients and with other agencies.

While institutions create the rules and value systems which sustain interactions, the activities they generate are carried out by organizations – defined earlier, as 'groups of individuals bound by some common purpose'. Behaviour in organizations (whether a government bureaucracy, a church, a family or a private firm) is governed by institutionalized rule systems. However, both the agencies and the individuals in them may well break these rules for private gain. In stable systems most individuals internalize rules, and obey them even when they would benefit from not doing so, but compliance still requires systematic enforcement. Where social norms and values are widely contested, however, or where they are threatened by political, economic or ecological crises, they may be systematically evaded, leading to organizational decay and possible transformation.

If appropriate services and products are to be available to meet as many social needs as possible, the organizations which provide them must be *effective* and *efficient*. It is important to distinguish 'efficiency' (in the conventional economists' sense of 'cost minimization'), and 'effectiveness'. And we should ask, for example, not just 'how can we create efficient health services', but 'what is the minimum cost at which we can run effective and accessible health services'. Measuring success in relation to effectiveness is difficult (Brett, 1993), but there is a real and important difference between agencies which do maximize their efforts on behalf of their consumers, and those which do not. Providing effective and appropriate services requires specialized agencies tailored to meet particular needs. The effectiveness of incentives within them depends on the extent to which providers (or 'agents') are made accountable to their consumers (or 'principals').

Thus key criteria which must be considered in evaluating different ways of organizing are those of *efficiency* and *effectiveness*, and *accountability*. These criteria are taken up in detail in Section 2.4.

2.2.2 A NORMATIVE FRAMEWORK FOR INTER-ORGANIZATIONAL RELATIONSHIPS

Inter-organizational management takes place in contexts where some agencies will be co-operating with each other for mutual benefit, others competing for the same voters, customers, or donors. If these co-operative or competitive relationships are to operate on a secure basis, all of those involved must accept the same values and rules. They must also recognize each other's rights and obligations. The analysis of organizational diversity in the next section will demonstrate that creating a recognized and enforceable system of values and rules in such circumstances is very demanding.

Peaceful interaction based on mutual agreement is only possible where each agency respects the rights of all of the others, and where viable institutions exist which embody and enforce the rules which allow them all to exchange scarce goods, services and payments on a secure and equitable basis. This, then depends on two things:

1   the existence of a normative framework and generalized morality to create the basis for mutual trust;

2   a system of efficient and accountable institutions for macro-organizational management.

Market societies assume that individuals and organizations should be free to pursue their own interests and preferences, within limits set by the rule of law, and be treated equally by the law (Mill, 1910, p. 75). These values of freedom and equality are rejected in command economies where autonomous agencies are suppressed, and in non-market societies where behaviour is constrained by hierarchical norms and institutions, for example patriarchy, religion, or inherited political and economic status. While neo-classical theorists ignore these constraints, they also exist in all market societies. Individuals are not equally free, but are effected by inequality and exclusion based on political power, inherited wealth and status, and by discriminatory belief systems based on ethnic, sectarian, or racial prejudice (see White, 1993). Thus even the most 'modern' societies are never exclusively driven by the principles of freedom of access and equality of rights. However, these principles do dominate ideological debate and policy theory in market societies, because people believe that they represent the only effective way of managing systems based on autonomous interdependence. The next sub-section will therefore consider the logic of these principles, and their implications for the creation of a viable system of social and political regulation for inter-organizational relationships.

2.2.3 MANAGING SYSTEMS BASED ON AUTONOMOUS INTERDEPENDENCE

In systems where agencies are interdependent yet free to do things which will impose serious costs on others, peaceful interaction is only possible if everyone accepts the rules which govern the competitive process, and does not resort to force or fraud when they lose. Ruling parties must give up power when they lose elections, and companies close down when they lose their markets. However these rules will only be accepted as legitimate and binding if they apply universally, and everyone has been able to participate in the key decisions through which they are made. Systems which excluded significant groups – like blacks in Apartheid South Africa, or workers in 19th century Europe – confronted systematic non-compliance with, and organized opposition to, their discriminatory rules.

Equally important, and even more difficult, such systems must also generate political and economic outcomes which produce a 'division of advantages' and 'distribute shares' which are considered to be fair and therefore just (Rawls, 1972, p. 4). If they do not, and if the competitive process leaves many people destitute, crime and violence may become endemic, imposing huge social and economic costs.

In our normative framework, inter-organizational relationships require a system of rules legitimated by the principles of freedom of choice, equality of access, universal participation, and, a fair distribution of resources. However, if the system is to operate securely, these values must be widely accepted, become a 'generalized morality' for the whole society and be embedded in formal institutional arrangements which will allow the rules to be known and enforced. This need for generalization and formalization increases with the scale and complexity of the social and economic arena in which interactions between organizations takes place.

In small societies, or in local economies in large ones, systems of values and rules often operate on an entirely informal basis. Property rights will be recognized and contracts fulfilled because everyone is dealing with people that they know and can therefore trust. Cheating is unlikely because they will want to do business again in the future, will have to meet each other in daily life, and because it will ruin their reputations with the rest of the community. Indeed, Granovetter persuasively argues that, even in complex societies, most exchanges depend on concrete social relations 'rather than institutional arrangements of generalized morality ... for the production of trust in economic life', since most managers depend on personal knowledge of the people with whom they deal (Granovetter, 1985, p. 61; see also Chapters 3 and 10).

The effectiveness of systems based on non-formalized morality and rules, backed up by personal knowledge and localized reputation, is confirmed by the success of parallel markets in many developing countries despite their lack of access to formal legal and judicial systems. However, the viability of informal values and rules decreases – but does not disappear – with the complexity and extent of the organizational system, and with the corresponding growth in the number of exchanges which have to take place between strangers.

To summarize, inter-organizational relationships depend on a generalized morality which accepts equality of access and obligations, and which has been formally institutionalized to provide a system of known rules and credible sanctions which will be imposed on all the agencies in the system. These institutions must also be based on the principles of openness and equality and be compatible with the diverse needs of the different kinds of organization that make up the system as a whole. This creates a very specific set of problems – how to create a viable relationship between state, private and voluntary sector agencies in large, complex and free societies?

2.3 DIVERSITY OF FUNCTION AND STRUCTURE IN ORGANIZATIONAL LIFE

Before approaching the question about how to create a viable relationship between state, private and voluntary sectors, we must take one step backwards in order to understand their characteristics. Different societies, at different times, have used different methods to produce appropriate and accountable organizations – with important implications for their citizens and managers. Recently 'fundamentalist' ways of thinking about these questions have been seriously questioned. In the 1980s, the ascendancy of neo-liberal ideas in both economics and politics meant that it was widely held that, on the whole, the provision of goods and services should be left to (the institution of) the free market, and it was argued that the role of (the institution of) the state should be the minimal one of providing for law and order and the security of contracts. These arguments represented a counter movement against earlier thinking in regard to development which held that, on the whole, the state should organize and manage the economy, so that economic growth and improved levels of living could be achieved through the most rational means.

Latterly a new fundamentalism has appeared, at least in the writings of some proponents of voluntary action, who hold that rather than organizing through either market or state, the task is to organize as far as possible through the institutions of 'civil society' – the sphere of voluntary association between the family (and wider units of kinship organization) and the state. A key proposition of this book is that such fundamentalist thinking is dangerous and misleading; for this reason it is important carefully to consider the requirements, strengths and limits of these different basic forms of organization.

Different kinds of organization are required in order to satisfy many different needs – for governance, material goods, social services, emotional and spiritual sustenance, sport and leisure. As was argued at the outset, policy models based on the ideal types competition, co-ordination and co-operation have emerged in response to these needs, producing the idea of three distinct systems of control and accountability:

Economy: an economic system to provide goods and services for individual consumers.

The state: a collective system of law and social management to create the conditions required to solve 'the problem of order' (Durkheim, 1964, p. 121) for society as a whole;

Civil society: a system of voluntary and solidaristic agencies where individuals develop the interpersonal relations required to meet their emotional, spiritual, physical or cultural needs.

The rest of this section will examine the commonly held characteristics of each in turn.

2.3.1 THE ECONOMY AS A COMPETITIVE SYSTEM

The economic system provides people with goods and services as consumers, and incomes and employment as workers. In a market economy these decisions involve individual rather than collective choices. Modern economic theory assumes that everyone must be 'free to choose' what to consume or do. Freedom of choice is now generally guaranteed through a system based on free markets and privately owned firms, so managers have to work within the limits set by the institutional arrangements of modern capitalism. Here there are two levels of analysis:

1   the macro level, relating to the organization of the market as a total system, in fact, as an institution; and
2   the micro level, relating to the firms and individuals who buy and sell goods and services.

Markets as institutions

Neo-classical economists do not think of markets as institutions where activities are planned and co-ordinated, but simply as places where individuals meet to buy and sell to maximize their personal self-interest. Where they do act 'rationally' in this way (and they often do), economics can make useful predictions about how supply, demand and prices will respond to changes in individual behaviour. However, while institutional theorists accept the value of this approach, they also recognize that a wide range of social conditions must be met if markets are to survive as open arenas where people will be 'free to choose'. Access must be open to all producers and consumers, prices must be set by individuals through competition, information must be freely available, no one must be forced to buy or sell to anyone else, everyone's property rights must be respected, and all legitimate contracts must be enforced. These conditions (which are rather rare in human history) presuppose the existence of a system of formal and informal rules which will be binding on all individuals and will ensure that no one uses force or fraud to gain unfair advantage over anyone else.

Thus, while institutional theory does not deal with the relationship between individual preferences and market prices, it does deal with the conditions which all individuals have to meet if the market as a whole is to operate as a viable social institution. This forces them to go beyond the level of purely 'economic' choices between individuals and come to terms with the political and cultural factors which have to exist if markets are to work effectively. Markets will only succeed where the state provides an adequate regulatory framework and infrastructure, and where people have been persuaded to internalize the necessary rules and obligations through the cultural, educational and family structures that operate in civil society.

Where this can be done, markets produce strong social benefits by putting managers as well as workers under heavy pressure to minimize costs and improve quality, allowing consumers to reject inferior products, and imposing a 'hard budget constraint' on all firms who are only paid for what they can sell. This, of course, has major implications for managers who are driven by very different sanctions and incentives from those that operate in the public sector where they are often protected by monopoly power. These benefits lie behind the recent shift from state- to market-controlled systems in policy theory, as seen in the collapse of socialism, upsurge in privatization and the attempt to introduce competition into the state sector by creating 'surrogate markets' (see Chapter 5).

Markets and firms

The neo-classical theory of markets excludes any understanding of organizational relationships that require co-ordination or co-operation because it treats economic activity as the outcome of short-term ('spot market') contracts negotiated between independent and self-interested individuals. However, everyone (including neo-classical economists) knows that in reality production does not depend on individuals, but on collective action organized through firms. These are organizations and institutions which operate on the basis of incentive and accountability systems determined by competitive capitalism. Externally this means that managers must respond to standards of performance imposed on them by international competition. This then has radical consequences for their internal organization, because it forces them to maximize the efficiency of their production processes. This depends in turn on the effectiveness of the rewards, sanctions and management systems which make joint production possible. Capitalist firms always involve hierarchical relationships between managers and workers, but such relationships can take very different forms comprising very different levels of coercion or consent.

The capitalist firm now dominates economic life in the modern world, but theorists still disagree about how their internal authority systems should be organized. This debate has generated an immense literature which cannot be adequately reviewed here; its key concern however has always been with the terms on which central authority is to be exercized. The first half of the twentieth century was dominated by large, vertically integrated and hierarchical corporations which placed immense authority in the hands of the central executive (Chandler, 1977; Miller, 1992). Problems of co-ordination, motivations and flexibility in such organizations have led subsequently to:

- decentralization of authority to different units within the firm (Williamson, 1985, ch. 11);
- the subdivision of large firms into smaller ones, linked together into networks (Alter and Hage, 1993); and
- the attempt to create increasingly participatory decision-making processes within firms (Kanter, 1984).

Thus, we immediately see components of all three ideal types under one roof – the market.

The appropriateness of any of these approaches will be a function of a number of things – the nature of the technology, the product, and the workforce; the availability of potential suppliers or competitors; the cultural attitudes and the skills of the society. Thus, learning to manage a capitalist firm is not a matter of learning and applying a standard formula, but of getting to know about the very wide range of methods that have worked well elsewhere, and finding ways of adapting the best of these to local circumstances. Such macro and micro characteristics are illustrated schematically in Figure 2.1.

2.3.2 THE STATE AND SOCIAL CO-ORDINATION

The state should represent the collective authority of society. It must be able to enforce its decisions over the whole of society to ensure that no single group can maximize its own benefits by threatening the rights of others. These powers should be used to promote people's welfare, but they can be used in an oppressive or predatory way, unless governments are accountable to their citizens. Pluralistic, representative democracy has been created to do this by organizing governance through an interrelated system of specialized agencies with clear boundaries, specific areas of authority and distinct systems of accountability.

Representative institutions and the budget constraint

The key objective of representative institutions is to ensure that governments serve the public rather than the needs of political or economic elites. Elected politicians are not expected to have technical expertise, but to know what their constituents want, and have a commitment to keep officials efficient and honest. Governments make decisions which are binding on the whole of society, but do so knowing that societies are made up of often conflicting groups. Social unity is then only possible where political institutions do not simply impose majority decisions, but allow all significant groups to exercise enough influence to ensure that policies represent an acceptable compromise rather than an imposition. Thus, effective political management depends on a number of conditions:

1 the incorporation of as many interests as possible in the political system;
2 the creation of inclusive decision-making processes which allow all the institutions to present their arguments and use agreed voting systems to validate outcomes;

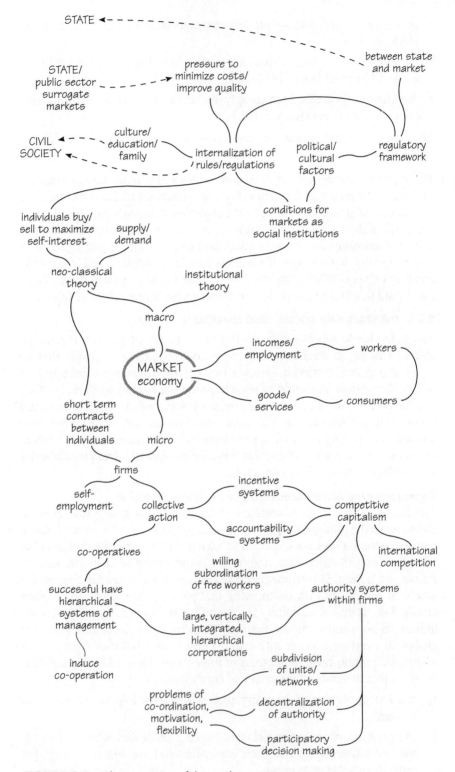

FIGURE 2.1 Characteristics of the market economy

3   the use of rigorous democratic procedures to ensure that representatives continue to enjoy public support.

It also has crucial financial implications. The state, unlike the economic
system which produces goods for individuals, is set up to meet collective
goals on behalf of the whole of society. While the role of the state has
varied dramatically in response to political and economic ideologies, even
neo-liberals concede that there is a wide range of functions which it must
perform for which it cannot be directly paid. It defends borders, regulates
access to common property resources (roads, parks, the air, rivers and seas),
and guarantees access to welfare services which people believe are essential for everyone, whatever their income. This costs money which usually
cannot be raised on a fee-for-service basis. Some goods, like defence or
street lighting, are 'non-excludable' and cannot be sold. In other cases,
fees would exclude the poor from services where it is felt universal access
is essential as with health and education. The state can only finance these
services by imposing a general charge on everyone, and it can only guarantee that everyone will make the appropriate contribution if it is allowed to
use its coercive powers to raise the taxes needed to provide them.

Thus the adequacy of any state, and its legitimacy in the eyes of its citizens, will depend on the way in which it exercises its power to tax, and the
adequacy of the services which it provides to citizens in return. So, while
democratic governments are constrained by the need to win elections, the
freedom of action of any government is a function of its budget constraint.
This will depend on many factors – the wealth or poverty of the community, the political commitment to support the state as opposed to private
action, the effectiveness of the tax authorities, and the state's real ability to
force people to pay.

Executives and bureaucracies

While politicians are elected to represent the public interest, officials (civil
servants) are appointed to implement policies on the basis of expertise.
Providing complex services like roads, health or education requires both
technical training and detailed 'time and place' knowledge relevant to the
particular service delivery system. The dominant agency developed to perform this function is the state agency based on what Weber called
'monocratic' or top-down bureaucratic authority (Weber, 1968, vol. 2,
ch. 11). Because officials must be expert and permanent, they are not elected
but selected on the basis of merit, and are guaranteed long-term security so
they can acquire the detailed knowledge needed to manage a complex
system. While politicians have to respect their expertise (since otherwise
services will fail), officials have to provide what the public want, so they
have to implement the decisions politicians (usually in the person of a minister) make. Hence orders have to emanate from the centre, and the role of
the official is not to make independent decisions about policy, but to
implement it.

Legal and judicial controls

More recently this centralized bureaucratic system has been strongly criti-cized for its hierarchical tendencies, its rigidity, secrecy, and its ability to hide errors and even encourage corruption. Wide-ranging experiments are now underway to achieve greater official efficiency, responsiveness and accountability under the general designation of the 'New Public Manage-ment' (see Chapter 5). These attempt to introduce 'results-oriented man-agement systems' which impose greater pressures on officials to perform, by setting them targets and relating their incomes to performance rather than seniority. Surrogate 'markets' are being created in which different public sector agencies compete with each other for clients, and 'contract-ing out' services to private or quasi-governmental agencies supervized by a regulatory authority. So, again, components of other ideal types are found within the stereotype of 'state co-ordination'.

These systems often weaken the direct control exercized by politicians, but effective performance in them does depend, in the last analysis, on the effective exercise of political authority and budgetary provision and con-trol. While politicians make laws and officials administer them, courts and the legal system are required to make binding decisions relating to the disputes which will inevitably arise under them. These can be disputes between individual citizens, between governments and citizens accused of crimes, or between citizens and governments accused of breaking its own laws. Thus creating a fair and accessible judicial system, and so establish-ing the rule of law, rather than arbitrary power, is crucial to the long-term legitimacy and stability of the state.

Political parties, pressure groups and the media

Citizens in a state of any size cannot take direct control over political and administrative processes, they monitor what it does, resist bad governance and produce alternatives. All individuals should take part in these pro-cesses, but in complex modern states the public interest can only be effec-tively represented when people operate through a permanent and differen-tiated system of political organizations. Such organizations must aggregate and articulate the interests and needs of a wide range of individuals, and represent them in the public sphere by dealing directly with government. Three distinct kinds of agency perform these functions.

1 *Political parties* produce policy programmes, support or oppose the government, and compete for public office.
2 *Private associations* (for example trades unions, employer's associ-ations, environmental organizations, religious groups) operate as press-ure groups which do not compete directly for power, but intervene to influence policy and programmes that affect their members or constituencies.
3 *An independent and critical media*: research agencies, individuals and groups are essential components in a democracy, to provide reliable information about what government is doing, and could do.

The main components of the co-ordinating role of the state are summarized in Figure 2.2.

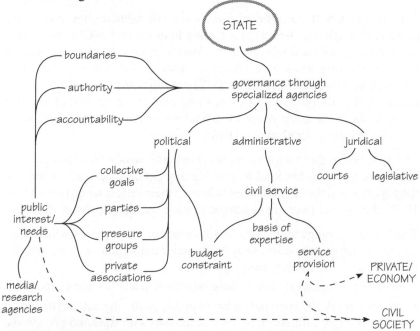

FIGURE 2.2 The state

2.3.3 CIVIL SOCIETY AND CO-OPERATION

In every society, many activities depend on voluntary relationships between individuals and groups, motivated by 'affectivity' (love, friendship), or ethical commitment. This may be called civil society and produces what is often called a *third sector* consisting of families, churches, clubs, professional associations, political parties, participatory organizations and NGOs. These organizations have different characteristics from those in either the state or the market. They are private in that they do not depend on the coercive power of the state; yet, unlike 'private sector' firms, they do not depend on self-interest where success is determined by 'the measuring rod of money'. Such *solidaristic* organizations have always existed, but were often not taken seriously as service delivery agencies with a major developmental role. This has changed for both practical and ideological reasons.

Policy theorists have come to recognize the importance of solidaristic agencies like families and NGOs in providing essential services and building the levels of trust and social awareness required to sustain a viable political and economic system. These views are now supported by conservatives as well as radicals: conservatives support them because they operate in the private sector, and do not depend on the state; radicals do so because they are non-profit (usually democratically) based, and can help promote social equality and empower marginal groups. Typically, this sector is characterized by participative democracy as distinct from the representative democracy that characterizes the liberal state.

This recognition of the imortance of solidaristic agencies has led to a significant expansion in the resources going to this sector. NGOs, in particular, are being increasingly used by donors in less developed countries (LDCs) with very weak state agencies. However, the authority and incentive structures through which agencies like families and participatory groups operate will only promote efficiency and empowerment if they are subjected to the same kinds of rigorous analysis as public and private sector agencies (Ostrom, 1990; Brett, 1996).

The agencies in this sector are so diverse that it would be impossible in a broad overview of this kind to provide any detailed account of the way they operate and the variables that influence their performance (see Uphoff, 1995). Many examples are discussed in the ensuing chapters of this book.

The functions, range and levels of autonomy of the agencies which make up civil society vary enormously, with major consequences for those that manage them and for the change process:

- *traditional societies*: little is done outside households and clans;
- *modern capitalist societies*: what happens inside the solidaristic sector is increasingly influenced by its relationship with state and private sector provision;
- *totalitarian or restrictive regimes*: states constrain the freedom of private agencies which might threaten the power and values of the governing elite, thus marginalizing civil society as an arena of autonomous social action;
- *pluralistic systems*: depend on the assumption that all agencies should be free to operate unless their activities systematically damage other members of society. Here civil society becomes a system of organized group activities through which individuals develop their skills and meet their personal needs in more and more complex ways. These agencies will only function well where they are linked into a broader system which allows them to maintain effective links with state and private sector organization.

Solidaristic organizations and the budget constraint

It is easy to underestimate the real costs of organizations in the third sector, and their need for resources. If we think of it as a 'voluntary' sector – as is often the case in the UK for example – where people participate in their 'spare' time without payment, we ignore the real costs incurred. The activities will only continue where members receive incentives which persuade them to do so. Some activities are truly voluntary – for example clubs, associations, religious movements, charities, trades unions or political parties. However, any group that operates on a significant scale must pay for staff, property and equipment, and have access to a stable income.

The staff might be primarily motivated by commitment rather than self interest, and accept lower wages than they would in the private sector, but there are significant limits to how little people will accept (Kanter, 1972).

Thus, solidaristic agencies also confront a budget constraint, though they meet it differently from those in the public and private sector. They depend on fees and labour inputs from members or donations from supporters; some sell goods and services on the commercial market, and many NGOs depend on government grants. The nature of the source of support and its stability imposes a major constraint on any agency's freedom of action. Donors, unlike taxpayers, cannot be forced to pay, so agencies will only survive for as long as they offer them a plausible return – some large NGOs now look less and less like charities and more and more like public sector subcontracting firms. While many agencies do have stable sources of support, the dependence on voluntary contributions and the competition for contracts from donors (the 'contract' culture) makes it much more difficult for this sector to guarantee a long-term and universal service equivalent to that provided by the state agencies on which the twentieth century welfare state has been built.

Figure 2.3 shows some of the salient characteristics of this sector.

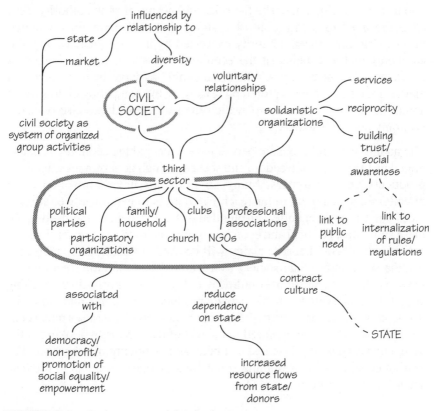

FIGURE 2.3 Civil society and the third sector

The characterization of the three sectors, market, state and civil society, in this section shows that they each have different answers to the question of organizing: inputs and outputs/outcomes, processes of production, accountability, resource use, incentives and sanctions and so on. Even in the stylised way that 'sectors' have been presented here, it is evident that elements of our three ideal types appear in all three. The different ways in which they are combined have a direct bearing on the different ways that social, economic and political life can be organized.

2.4 RELATIONS BETWEEN ECONOMY, STATE AND CIVIL SOCIETY

The last section looked at the organizations which exist to meet the economic, political, and social needs in a pluralistic society. It showed how they should be designed to meet our general desire for efficiency and accountability in ways that were consistent with the functions which they had to perform and the context in which they had to operate. Now the focus shifts from the principles which govern the structure and functioning of particular kinds of organizations, to those which govern the relationship between them.

The principles which underlie the rules and norms of state authority stem from the need to create control systems that will maintain a balance between the centralized authority exercized by its own agencies, and the autonomy and well-being of the economic and social agencies which it regulates. The means by which these problems have been resolved in market societies can be explored by reviewing the competing claims made about the nature of the control which the state should exercise over the economy and civil society.

The nature of the relationship between the state and the economy is determined by the degree of freedom and security which government extends to producers and consumers. Many governments have controlled them directly, subjected them to far-reaching controls to maximize welfare services and promote equality, or plundered them to benefit themselves. In these situations, political and economic power is fused to a greater or lesser extent, and, liberal theorists claim, will be used or benefit those who control the state, rather than society as a whole. They therefore recommend the separation of control over political and economic institutions by using competitive markets to enable *private* producers and consumers to make decisions without deferring to the government. This claim raises many contested issues which are explored in the rest of the section by looking at the competing arguments presented by liberal and interventionist theorists. The section concludes by examining some contemporary attempts to produce viable compromises between them.

2.4.1 STATES, MARKETS AND CIVIL SOCIETY IN LIBERAL THEORY

In market societies inter-organizational relationships between political, economic and social agencies operate on the basis of what Macpherson calls 'possessive individualism' (Macpherson, 1962). A market is a place where private buyers and sellers exchange goods or services on a voluntary basis. Each tries to maximize their own advantage, but neither can exploit the other because both can go elsewhere. Prices are set up by agreement and supply is determined by what any entrepreneur believes can be sold at a profit. If they are right, they become rich, if not, they go out of business.

A perfect market is thus a fully decentralized system governed by competition and co-operation. All decisions are made by individual agents trying to maximize their own benefits rather than to achieve any collective social purpose. Here firms and individuals co-operate when it suits them, but will also attempt to take business away from their competitors. Their only *social* obligation is to respect everyone else's property rights and to meet their own contractual obligations. The state should only specify and enforce the rules which allow everyone to know and do what is expected of them. The implications of market systems for the behaviour of firms and their managers will be considered later (Section 2.5). Here I am concerned with the way in which they relate to the state agencies with which they co-exist.

As already indicated, a minimalist approach to the role of government in market societies has dominated policy since the early 1980s. This will guarantee 'the efficiency of the property rights structure' (North, 1981, p. 17), and organizational autonomy in two ways:

- it allows associations of firms to operate without reference to the state; and
- it also protects private individuals from coercion by criminal private agencies like the Mafia.

Market competition also guarantees efficiency, because no one has to buy inappropriate or over-priced goods or services.

Liberal theorists claim that market freedom promotes political and social freedom as well as economic choice and efficiency. Friedman claims that all democratic societies have 'used something comparable to a free market to organize the bulk of economy activity' (1962, p. 9), because separating political and economic control reduces the power exercized by governments, and gives private individuals and groups independent access to the resources needed to check the exercise of political power (p. 15). In a command economy the state controls employment, production and technological choice. It can use this power to suppress opposition, control information, literature and culture, and deny private individuals and groups the resources required to finance political, cultural, religious or social organizations which it dislikes. Hence an autonomous sphere of 'civil society' cannot exist.

In 'mixed economies' there is enough private ownership to sustain private associations, and thus autonomous action in civil society. However, the government can still use economic patronage and access to benefits like health, housing and social security, to exercise a strong influence over private action. This, liberals claim, will allow members of the regime and their 'cronies' to extract 'monopoly rents' from society through the allocation of monopolies, import licences, or subsides (Krueger, 1974). It will also lead to economic inefficiency, and undermine the democratic process by encouraging corruption and allowing the government to buy political support by offering special favours to its supporters.

Thus, in a liberal state, the system of inter-organizational relations must be based on a particular combination of competition, co-ordination, and co-operation:

1 The degree of co-ordination imposed by the exercise of collective political authority over economic and social agencies should involve directives which do no more than guarantee their security and freedom of action.

2 The behaviour of producers and consumers will be mainly regulated by competition – they will not have to consider the welfare of others when they act, and must allow others to do the same to them.

3 Markets will produce co-operation as well as competition, since firms will need to enter into short- and long-term relationships to provide each other with inputs and services. These will lead to the creation of *networks*, or stable systems of voluntary co-ordination, which will co-exist with adversarial and 'arms-length' relationships. (Thompson *et. al.,* 1991, chs. 14-16, 20, 21.)

4 State intervention involving control rather than co-ordination should be minimized, and can only be justified where *market failure* makes it essential. Liberal theorists do offer a theory of market failure which justifies something more than pure laissez faire.

2.4.2 THE LOGIC OF STATE INTERVENTION

The Russian revolution in 1917, the great depression of the early 1930s and the Second World War gave rise to a long period dominated by Marxist, social democratic or structuralist theorists who claimed that un-controlled markets generate exclusion, insecurity, and monopoly power rather than efficiency and freedom. They claimed that capitalist competition did not create 'even' development, but led to markets domi-nated by a few economically powerful countries and transnational firms. The majority would lose their control over productive resources and become wage labourers, the small firms that did survive would be domi-nated by the market power of the large ones. These large firms would con-trol political power in the dominant countries, and use this to maintain a system of direct or indirect imperialistic exploitation over poor countries.

Competition in these circumstances will not guarantee freedom of choice and efficiency, but constantly reinforce the power of the strong over weak, thus demonstrating 'that capitalism [cannot] co-ordinate without coercion' (Macpherson, 1973, p. 146). Here freedom is confined to the ruling class in the countries and firms which dominate the state and social agencies. Economic power overrides political power because the state depends on the dominant firms to create jobs, and pay taxes, while they are also free to finance political parties, control the media and be increasingly important in supporting all forms of research and culture.

Thus, while socialists accept the need for democracy and personal freedom, they claim that these cannot be maintained in a *capitalist* market economy unless its inherent tendency to produce inequality, insecurity and exclusion, is brought under social control. This requires a state which will not only guarantee the rights of property owners, but also those of the majority who are too poor to compete on reasonable terms. The state then should represent the collective interests of society as a whole, manage its borders to suppress unfair foreign competition, control the activities of private firms to ensure that the economy develops in a stable and equitable way, and redistribute resources to eliminate poverty. These theories gave rise to a range of political movements whose policies imposed very different patterns of state–market relations in different countries.

- *Marxists* eliminated private ownership and created command economies in Eastern Europe and the third world.

- *Social democrats* in the West retained private ownership, but used state power to manage the relationship between supply and demand, nationalized public utilities and some dominant firms, controlled foreign trade, and introduced redistributive taxation to cut inequality and provide universal access to essential services and 'safety nets' (Held, 1987, chs. 5-7).

- *Structuralist* governments in developing countries protected their 'infant industries' from foreign competition, and used a variety of methods to shift resources from agriculture and primary production to industry. They set up state industries which they subsidized from public funds and gave monopoly powers, introduced planning, often in conjunction with foreign donors, to develop rational investment programmes in infrastructure, education and the social services. In more radical countries foreign companies were nationalized, in less radical ones close controls were imposed on them.

In these scenarios governments controlled rather than co-ordinated firms and groups. Competition was limited by the allocation of subsidies, licenses and monopolies. Co-operation between firms did not emerge out of free choices by autonomous agents, but in response to state control and directives.

The success or failure of these different systems still arouse intense political and theoretical controversy. Radicals still claim that all successful modern economies have developed through processes involving strong state intervention, and have only gradually been liberalized after the transition to capitalism had been completed. They justify this by pointing to the heavy controls used in the post-war reconstruction of Japan and Western Europe; and to the dominant role of the state in the successful development of South Korea and Taiwan in the 1980s (Wade, 1990). Liberals point to the clear evidence of economic failure in the states which adopted import substitution in Latin America and South Asia, and especially to the economic disasters produced by the statist experiment in most post colonial African states (Lal, 1984; World Bank, 1981).

2.4.3 MANAGING INSTITUTIONAL DIVERSITY: POLICY NETWORK ANALYSIS

Whatever the merits of these arguments, a decisive shift did take place in inter-organizational relationships during the 1980s. This change was initiated by the dominance of liberal theory in the wake of the political and economic crises of the mid-1970s to the late 1980s. Recessionary conditions prevailed in most interventionist states and this was seen as a failure of interventionist policies. The late 1980s also saw the comprehensive rejection of command planning in most Communist countries. The initial response by political reformers was an attempt to reduce direct state intervention to a minimum, but the ability to do this was constrained by many factors. The countries that they were working in were dominated by statist structures which could not be dismantled overnight, so they had to make many concessions to the groups which had a vested interest in maintaining these systems.

Further, as the reform process developed, most liberal theorists had to recognize the weakness of indigenous entrepreneurial classes and the reality of some of the problems of market failure identified by the radicals. It became clear that private firms could only operate effectively in contexts in which the state:

- provided an effective regulatory environment and controlled natural monopolies;
- supplied non-excludable public goods like roads and policing;
- dealt with marginalization and exclusion by guaranteeing essential social services; and
- where the resources were available, provided minimal access to 'safety nets' for the unemployed, the old and the disabled.

While few theorists still supported direct state production, and most accepted the need for the state to reduce protection and allow the price of foreign exchange and interest rates to be set by market forces rather than political decisions, it was clear that a 'strong' rather than a 'weak' state would still be needed to perform these functions. As a result the reform process which has been going on in most countries can be seen as a compromise between liberal and interventionist theory, where the original assumption that all that was needed was to 'get the prices right' has now been followed by a recognition of the need to 'bring the state back in'.

This renewed recognition of the importance of 'governance' has led to two major initiatives in the international policy debate:

1   First, a renewed recognition of the significance of democratization to reduce the tendencies to inefficiency and corruption which have clearly been largely responsible for the poor performance of state agencies during the interventionist period.

2   Second, a new recognition of the weaknesses of the centralized, hierachically co-ordinated and 'top-down' institutional arrangements which were used by both social democratic and command economies, and of the need for new forms of public, private and public–private management systems which attempt to address the problems associated with uncontrolled capitalism and the over developed state.

The problem of governance is closely associated with the institutional changes discussed at the start of this chapter – the recognition of the values of institutional diversity, the widespread recourse to privatization, the introduction of 'surrogate markets' within state controlled bureaucracies, the increasing use by the state of sub-contracting work to private agencies or NGOs. All of these changes also mark an important change in the kind of authority which the government can exercise over the agencies it relies on to ensure that its economic and social objectives are achieved. All of the changes noted above involve a shift from direct to indirect forms of control. The government has moved from a situation in which it can at least stand 'above society and ... "steer" it' (Kickert et al., 1997, p. 3) to one in which the relationship between state, private and solidaristic agencies is one of interdependence in which the government can at best operate as 'first among equals'. Chapter 13 is a vivid example of such changes.

The resulting changes in public management systems have led to a bewildering array of different kinds of solution to service delivery problems. In the past socialist theorists would have preferred health, educational or public transport systems based on state monopolies. Most are now willing to see complex combinations of state provision, state regulated private provision, for profit and market-driven private provision and provision by formal NGOs and grass roots organizations, all operating in the same sector. In some cases the organizations concerned may be performing the same function (for example providing hospital care) but offering it to different kinds of service which require different kinds of relations with consumers (for example curative as opposed to primary health care).

It is not possible to go into the very complex implications of this shift for both the efficacy and status of government, and for the managers of the different kinds of agencies which are involved. Some of these issues are taken up in Chapter 3. Indeed these experiments in institutional diversity and pluralism are all so new that we have yet to see whether they will withstand the demands of practice and actually deliver better services than the organizational systems they are designed to replace (Ostrum *et al.*, 1993). I will simply conclude this section by highlighting the usefulness of the notion of 'policy network' as the basis for the analysis of public policy making in this emerging pluralistic organizational environment.

> The government is no longer seen as occupying a superior position to other parties, but as being [on] an equal footing with them. Public policy making within networks is about co-operation or non-co-operation between interdependent parties with different and often conflicting rationalities, interests and strategies. Policy processes are not viewed as the implementation of ex ante formulated goals, but as an interaction process in which actors exchange information about problems, preferences and means, and trade off goals and resources. A success criterion for policy is the realization of collective action in order to establish common purposes or avert common threats.
>
> (Kickert, *et al.*, 1997, p. 9)

Most developing countries continue to operate on far more elitist principles than those which are increasingly dominating public management in developed countries. There is little doubt that these views dominate the approach of the powerful donor community in most countries, and they are being increasingly taken up by the leading elements in local political and civil society. They represent a new 'middle-ground' in which the old oppositions between 'right' and 'left' associated with an interventionist as opposed to a laissez faire approach to the state have become increasingly irrelevant. From a development management point of view they create a new and more open environment in which to operate. It is one however, which offers participants fewer certainties, and imposes much heavier responsibilities on them. In the past little more was expected of them than to take orders from their superiors and provide standardized services to voiceless clients.

2.5 SCALE, ACCOUNTABILITY AND INCENTIVES

Later chapters of this book give examples and discuss the changing ideas about competition, co-ordination and co-operation in some detail. In particular, they show the diversity of situations in which these ideal types appear on their own or, more usually, in combination. If you, the reader, are engaged in constructing relationships between organizations, the changing situation described at the end of the last section and at least some of the diverse experiences in the rest of the book might be familiar.

There are, however, some overarching themes that whilst not necessarily addressed explicitly have a bearing on all three institutional forms. These are *scale*, *accountability* and *incentives*. In this section, the relationship between the three and their relevance for inter-organizational relationships is examined.

2.5.1 IS BIG ALWAYS BETTER?

Size has often been equated with development, with theorists attributing growth in political and economic capacity to increases in the scale of both private and public sector agencies in the nineteenth and most of twentieth century. Big seemed to be better, since it allowed agencies to mobilize more resources, economize on management costs (economies of scale), increase specialization and innovation, and guarantee consumers stable and economic sources of supply. Giant firms like General Motors dominated business, and huge state bureaucracies such as the all-encompassing welfare state in the UK provided social and economic services.

More recently, however, consumers have found large agencies remote, unresponsive and rigid, and theorists have increasingly recognized the costs incurred in steep hierarchies, providing effective incentives in large bureaucracies, and controlling managerial overload. Small organizations are now thought to be more flexible, egalitarian, and closer to their consumers. Large organizations continue to dominate many sectors, greatly facilitated by ever-improving communications, but current thinking now favours systems which decentralize power in large organizations and increase scope and scale by building networks between smaller ones (see Chapter 3).

There are constant tensions between greater organizational size and needs for flexibility and responsiveness. Debates about the relative merits of scaling up or down have pointed to mechanisms other than organizational growth for scaling up, including advocacy and action to influence other organizational actors, and networking between a number of organizational units to produce goods and services.

This section takes up some of these issues, focusing in particular on the reasons why large organizations should or should not out-perform small ones, and the kinds of authority systems which are likely to produce the best results. A discussion follows of the benefits of centralized control in organizational systems, of the conditions which are likely to favour small-scale systems and, an issue of increasing importance, factors which are likely to favour the subdivision of large organizations into smaller ones through decentralization of various kinds.

Economies of scale

Many factors can influence the scale on which an agency operates – for example, technology, communications, function, managerial skills, access to resources, and relationships with consumers. Scale always imposes some costs on agencies, since concerted action involves planning, collective decision-making, and the ability to ensure compliance. Thus scaling up is only justified where the gains from additional numbers are large enough to offset these additional costs (or 'diseconomies of scale'). Policymakers have to consider both kinds of factors when they make decisions about the type of agency they should support.

In the public sector scale has often been preferred because of a desire to provide universal access to a standardized service, or because it is assumed that a large agency – a school or hospital for example – will be able to provide a more comprehensive service than a smaller one. Thus many governments create large centralized ministries to manage their health or education system, and subject all the agencies to the same management systems, salary scales, conditions of service and so on. Operating in this way may make it possible for access to be guaranteed, and for poorer or less well placed consumers to be subsidized by wealthier ones. Some services are also natural monopolies – for example, defence or justice – where competition is not considered appropriate.

Decentralization in organizations

Large bureaucracies, however, generate many problems. Workers may not share the organization's goals and have to be closely supervized, and the larger the organization the more levels of authority are needed, thus creating potential problems of evasion and incompetence (Tullock, 1987). Creating specialized departments can reduce communication and increase conflicts over resources and responsibilities. The need to guarantee workers' wages can be very costly, and the need to persuade large numbers of people, often with entrenched attitudes and rights, of the need for change can lead to inertia and tendencies to ignore the needs of consumers, constituents and clients. The attempt to overcome these problems, has usually led policymakers to adopt solutions which break up large centralized organizations into smaller ones. These are then linked together through the development of inter-organizational systems of various kinds – markets, networks and sub-contracting systems. These trends are visible in both the public and private sectors.

Many governments are trying to reduce the scale of public sector organizations through a variety of mechanisms – decentralizing control to local governments; contracting out services to competitive private or non-profit agencies; creating 'internal' markets in which, for example, doctors purchase services from hospitals or train operators buy access to rail lines through the owners of the track.

This process is paralleled by a growth in the importance of local agencies – local governments, small firms, grass roots organizations (GROs) – and there has been a widespread tendency to create local agencies where none existed before, and to increase the autonomy and resources available to

40

them where they do already exist. These changes have occurred in all kinds of organizations:

- In *government* there has been a shift from systems dominated by central government to those where local governments have wide responsibilities and, under fully developed federal systems, constitutionally guaranteed powers. Here the key issue is whether decentralization devolves real political authority to local councils, or is limited to the delegation of limited authority to local officials chosen and funded by central government.

- In *firms* there has been a movement from the centrally controlled and vertically integrated firm to 'multidivisional' structures involving 'the creation of semi-autonomous operating divisions (mainly profit centers) organized along product, brand, or geographic lines' (Williamson, 1985, p. 281). More recently, this tendency has been reinforced by moving from direct control to joint production systems based on long term (networking) relationships with semi-autonomous associates (Alter and Hage, 1993)

- In the *solidaristic sector* perhaps the most notable feature is the desire by international NGOs to increase local offices (often complemented by a desire to replace expatriate with local staff), and to hand control over projects to local NGOs and GROs, again through sub-contracting and joint ventures.

I cannot review all of the complex implications of these tendencies towards decentralization. However I can conclude by noting that the optimistic assumptions set out at the start of this section are all being brought into question as a result of experience. Many local communities may not have the skills and resources needed to manage complex programmes, and can be dominated by incompetent or even predatory local elites; ethnic or sectarian conflict can make local co-operation difficult; and regional economic inequality can mean that local agencies have very unequal access to taxes and skills. This suggests that local autonomy should be balanced by adequate support from national and international agencies.

2.5.2 ACCOUNTABILITY AND INCENTIVES IN ORGANIZATIONAL LIFE

Organizations differ in terms of function and scale, and in the ways in which they guarantee accountability and provide incentives. *Accountability* is a function of the leverage exerted over agencies by their principals – consumers, donors, owners, taxpayers. *Incentives* are the rewards and sanctions which are used to induce appropriate performance. These are distinct but related areas, since the resources which agencies use to reward their staff are usually derived in some form or another from the people the agency serves. Accountability works best when rewards depend directly on the quality of the service provided – failures occur when there is no direct relationship between the two. In the worst case perverse incentives can reward people more for providing a bad service than a good one. Thus a key issue in the debate over institutional change relates to the terms on which principals and agents interact to ensure that the latter are only paid what is required to elicit the necessary levels of effort and skill.

Creating effective incentives through strong accountability systems is a normative and political, rather than a technical, problem. Workers must be offered what is perceived as a just reward for their effort. This is difficult because of the inherent conflict between consumers and providers – the costs of the former represent the benefits of the latter – and because performance is difficult to measure and monitor. Both parties need each other, and must arrive at an accommodation, but the way this exchange relationship is organized has implications for organizational efficiency and the distribution of wealth and power in society.

- At the *macro level* this means that consumers should be able to exert some control over the costs and quality of any service – *the accountability problem*.

- At the *micro level*, within organizations, rewards should be directly related to performance – *the incentive problem*.

These are difficult tasks, and many different systems have been tried to solve them. The accountability and incentives problems provide another source of diversity in institutional arrangements, and another set of options which managers can explore when they wish to improve organizational performance and relevance.

Creating accountable organizations
Accountability exists when providers are rewarded only when they provide adequate services to consumers, and can thus be sanctioned if they fail. Managers must exercise authority and receive adequate rewards for doing so – accountability exists to ensure that they use this power to promote the general interest rather than their own. Thus analysing accountability systems is in fact the most important way of thinking about the problem of power and empowerment in society, because the terms on which resources are exchanged between those who depend on services and those who provide them can be specified with some exactness.

Much organizational theory focuses on internal accountability systems, which specify the way in which subordinates can be held to account by their superiors or within the hierarchy. This is undoubtedly important, since it is naive to assume that workers or managers will always want to maximize the interests of the agency rather than their own (Tullock, 1987). However, this alone will not guarantee good performance, because any agency with monopoly powers can fail its consumers or funders, either through self-interest or incompetence. Exploitative systems which allow governments to eliminate democratic controls, firms to operate monopolies, or men to dominate women, will benefit elites but block progressive development. Thus the key problem in institutional theory is not to show how supervisors can control subordinates, but to find ways of supervising the supervisors or guarding the guardians.

External accountability in organizations depends on a number of factors – their function, scale and relationship with other agencies of the same kind. For example state agencies which provide collective services develop different relationships with consumers from private firms which sell in competitive markets. Both differ from relationships within small groups – families, associations, clubs – which provide services for their own members on a reciprocal basis. Hirschman (1970) provides a useful way of understanding accountability systems and how they work, by identifying three key mechanisms: *exit*, *voice*, and *loyalty*. These relate directly to the role of democracy, markets and reciprocity in the state, economy and civil society.

Exit

Consumers have most power when they can change or *exit* from one provider to another without serious costs. This will force providers to provide an adequate service, and eventually raise standards to those of the 'best practice' of the most efficient provider. Exit is therefore a function of market competition, but it is important to recognize that it applies to any system where consumers choose between competing providers, not just to 'economic' markets. This is central to democratic political theory, which presupposes a market for votes where dissatisfied citizens can shift their support from one party to another. It also applies in civil society where private associations and NGOs have to ensure that their supporters do not shift to competing services.

Voice

Exit is not always possible or desirable where collective services are essential, and long-term relationships have to be sustained. Here consumers have to make their influence felt through participation or *voice*, where agencies have to implement decisions based on systematic discussion, enforced by some form of majority rule. These systems depend on the effectiveness of the representative systems, rules of debate and decision-making, and relationships with officials. As well as providing governance, these systems have to exercise control over authority in any hierarchical system, including large corporations. Strengthening voice is becoming an important element in institutional reforms in developing countries, as donors and government try to introduce a participatory element into programme and project management (UNDP, 1993; World Bank, 1994), and to improve democratic accountability by decentralizing power to lower level agencies.

Loyalty

Finally, many agencies are not only driven by fear of exit or voice, but also by the need to maintain the *loyalty* of their stakeholders. In many cases stakeholders do not support agencies in response to immediate gains or active participation but out of a generalized commitment based on belief in the value of what they do. In many solidaristic agencies like families and social networks, loyalty is in fact based on the willingness to support agencies, not in the expectation of immediate personal gain, but on the basis of ethical commitment or long-term affective relationships. Hence commitment can sometimes be based on pure altruism; more commonly this will take the form of reciprocity, whereby people do not make direct cost calculations as they do in markets, exiting whenever a better offer is available. Instead, they make long-term commitments, but continued loyalty will usually be negotiated through 'voice', and a failure to receive enough in return may eventually lead to exit (Brett, 1993, 1996).

2.5.3 CREATING EQUITABLE INCENTIVE SYSTEMS

Organizational efficiency and effectiveness depends on the ability to motivate managers and workers by ensuring that they receive the appropriate reward for what they do. This occurs automatically where individuals are involved in direct exchanges in spot markets or reciprocal economies, when effort is directly related to reward. However, it is not easy in complex societies and agencies where individuals take part in co-operative activities involving different levels of effort, skill and intrinsic interest. Appropriate rewards depend on the ability to determine the value of what people are doing, and to ensure that they have actually delivered what is expected of them. However, it is impossible to attribute an objective value to any service, and usually difficult to measure what each individual has actually contributed to most joint production processes. Despite this, all societies have to decide how much of their total production to allocate to each activity, and how much to pay each individual for their particular contribution. Whilst there are macro level issues concerning the allocation of social resources in any society, I will focus here on the micro level problems of how incentives are related to performance equitably.

Arguments about rewards inside organizations are dominated by the relevance of market-based as opposed to non-market-based incentives systems. Neo-classical theorists claim that rational rewards are only possible in open labour markets where incomes and conditions of work are not set by governments or unions, but are set in response to autonomous agreements between employers and workers. They feel this will produce just results because the workers need not work for anyone if they could do better elsewhere, and competition will stop employers from passing excessive wage costs on to consumers. Wages will rise where labour is scarce, fall where it is plentiful. High wages will discourage investment, low wages will encourage investment and increased employment. Keeping wages artificially high – for example, through minimum wage legislation – may benefit some workers, but reduce profits, investment, and employment and thus disadvantage those out of work.

However, this logic cannot be applied directly to public or voluntary sector workers whose incomes come from taxpayers or donors, or where monopoly powers allow firms to pay workers less or charge consumers more than the free market would allow. Here, employers may confront a soft budget constraint, and perverse incentives come into play. Employers will not benefit by increasing efficiency, but by raising wage and other costs to the point where they coincide with what the society can be made to pay. Such practices were a major factor in discrediting the state-managed economies prior to 1989. The response by neo-classical theorists to this problem of public sector wages was to compare them with those for similar skills and tasks in the private sector and such arguments are becoming influential everywhere. Thus no manager can afford to ignore the market-determined wage entirely, but a number of 'non-economic' variables enter into this area as well.

In both the private and the public sectors, employers have found it unwise to pay no more than a market-determined minimum and to treat employees as no more than energy machines. This has been driven by the need to establish long-term relationships with workers to encourage high levels of loyalty and commitment, and the difficulties associated with measuring and monitoring performance. Historically, the most obvious challenge to market theory comes from socialist theorists, who have seen wage rates as the outcome of an antagonistic struggle between owners and workers, leading to state control in the east and to political and union struggle for better wages and conditions in the west. During the early post-war era social democratic parties in Europe were able to introduce legislation laying down minimum wages, hours and working conditions in many countries, and to set up unions to increase wages and job security for the best organized workers in most developed countries, and in the protected, large-scale industrial sectors of developing countries.

It has rarely been possible, however, to maintain all of these gains, because they depended on the full employment created by the post Second World War boom, and the ability to insulate national economies from international competition. In the 1980s governments were forced to deregulate labour markets, and tried to reduce union membership and industrial militancy. Management has responded directly to market pressures by 'downsizing' labour forces, and demanding greater performance measured against 'benchmarks' derived from the 'best practice' in similar firms (Womack et al., 1990).

Thus market competition continues to force employers to maximize performance by intensifying labour discipline, yet many of them also recognize that workers will be most productive when they believe that the company is committed to their welfare and gives them as much responsibility as possible. This view is reinforced by evidence which suggests that many workers do not respond best to unequal incentive systems where everybody is paid in exact proportion to their contributions, because they feel that group solidarity is more important (Deutsch, 1985). This is especially so where, as is commonly the case, tasks are so interdependent that it is impossible to measure the actual contributions made by any particular worker (Ouchi, 1980). Thus employers cannot retain workers unless they offer them competitive conditions, or cannot motivate them effectively unless they respect their autonomy and the need to build team solidarity.

Market forces dominate wage determination in the private sector, but public and non-profit agencies have been more concerned with the desire to build long-term loyalty, and make use of a sense of 'duty' based on a belief in the intrinsic value of the tasks being performed. While the importance of reasonable wages can never be ignored, 'value driven' incentives are very often equally or even more important. For example well-educated priests work for little more than subsistence wages or managers will sacrifice high private sector wages in exchange for the opportunity to run 'worthwhile' projects which contribute towards a social goal that they support.

In some contexts people may even resist the notion that their incomes should be directly related to their own performance relative to that of their colleagues, and prefer instead systems based on job security, where wages and promotions are determined by job classification and seniority rather than competition. With strong motivation and supervision, such systems can generate high levels of service at relatively low wages, but they can also produce perverse results since tenure can be abused, and seniority can produce mediocrity. Thus where accountability systems are weak, traditional bureaucratic incentive systems have often led to apathy, rigidity and lack of concern for clients.

These problems have led to a variety of attempts to introduce 'results-oriented systems', which weaken tenure and relate incentives to performance. These again depend on the ability to identify appropriate 'success indicators' and to find comparable examples of 'best practice' against which to measure performance. Such problems are difficult enough in the private sector, but are even worse in the public or voluntary sectors because agencies are commonly implementing projects (for example, the empowerment of rural women) whose output cannot be priced and is very difficult to observe. Thus these agencies will perform effectively only where managers know that citizens or donors are able to keep a critical eye on what they are doing, and to withdraw support when they are dissatisfied. This, of course, is to affirm yet again the critical role of accountability systems in producing just and efficient incentives.

2.6 CONCLUSIONS

This chapter lays out a theoretical framework which addresses some of the normative and technical issues which confront development managers by considering the implications of using different kinds of institutional and organizational systems to provide the goods and services which people require. The result has been an interdisciplinary exercise which recognizes that different kinds of agency – 'political', 'economic' and 'social' – are required to meet the full variety of needs that people seek to achieve. It suggests that choosing one set of institutions rather than another will have decisive consequences for the organization of the social system – for the way the division of labour operates and power is exercised, for levels of inequality and exclusion, and for possibilities of growth and human development. It sees that the primary objective of management theory is to create organizations which offer service providers adequate levels of autonomy and incentives, while allowing consumers to exert enough leverage over them to ensure that they do not abuse their authority and privileges. This approach rests on some possibly contentious assumptions.

The first assumption is that we can distinguish between 'developed' or 'advanced' systems and less developed ones. Crucially, the former involve more complex systems and knowledge, can operate on a greater scale, and offer more autonomy to managers and to their subordinates, and greater accountability to their customers and beneficiaries than the latter. As a result they not only cater for a much wider range of personal and social needs, but also create non-oppressive social and working environments in which everyone is free to extend their personal capacities by building strong co-operative relationships. This implies that 'development' can be under-stood as a process of transition from societies based on less to more advanced institutional arrangements.

Second, trying to meet complex and diverse human needs requires us to use complex and diverse institutional arrangements. Institutions are systems of collective rules and practices which enable, or even force, individuals to work together for common purposes. They can do this by *co-ordinating* activities through hierarchies; by creating open systems based on private property where *competition* determines who will supply services and how; or by offering each other reciprocal benefits and thus creating systems based on voluntary *co-operation*. Conservative, socialist and libertarian theorists have tended to seek solutions which depend exclusively on one or other of these approaches. This pluralistic approach suggests that human potentials will only be fulfilled where all organizational possibilities are recognized and choices are based on the specific requirements of the service and the prevailing social and cultural conditions, which will differ from time to time and place to place.

'Top-down' systems may actually work best where factories are producing standardized products and workers are uneducated and inexperienced, but they will fail where there has to be continuous innovation driven by a highly educated workforce. Competition may be the best way to provide services in societies with predatory governments, but co-ordinated state provision offered by committed public servants may provide wider access and lower costs where democratic accountability is strong. Co-operative systems will succeed in groups with high levels of solidarity and social capital, but will fail where they do not exist and freeloading is common. Thus recognizing the benefits of diversity offers managers a wide range of creative options, but also imposes much heavier demands on their knowledge and adaptability than traditional co-ordinative bureaucratic systems. Here clear blueprints exist for every problem, and managers can rely on power rather than persuasion to secure compliance rather than consent.

Third, this approach emphasizes the significance of strong motivation rather than formal systems for organizational performance. Poor performance is often attributed to limited skills which can be remedied by teaching people the latest management system. However, experience suggests that people with strong motivation and limited skills will produce better organizations and results than highly educated and well-resourced groups who are more concerned to maximize their private interests than those of the clients they are supposed to serve. To understand the force of this claim, just compare the performance of the rebel groups that defeated powerful armies in Vietnam, Eritrea or Uganda with that of the well-funded but accountable governments they opposed.

This emphasis on motivation, then, forces us to identify the principles on which effective incentives need to be based. This determines the nature of the relationships which prevail within agencies and between agencies and their clients, where the key issue is not only what people receive, but the way in which they are made accountable for their performance. Here, yet again, I have argued that incentive and accountability systems must vary in response to varied needs and conditions – scale of operation, function, and social and cultural values and expectation. This chapter has illustrated that choosing between co-ordination, competition or co-operation is in fact a choice between different accountability mechanisms and incentive systems, since each of these systems makes different use of the possibilities of voice, exit or reciprocity (or loyalty).

Finally, it is important to emphasize that understanding the principles which lie behind the analytical categories developed here is crucially important to policy makers and managers who are concerned to improve institutional performance in developing countries. However, they will only produce effective results if they are combined with a detailed knowledge of the local situation – a knowledge of local resources, indigenous skills, and the cultural expectations that will condition the way in which people will respond to attempts to change existing practices.

3 A HYBRID OR A THIRD WAY? CONTEMPORARY THINKING ON INTER-ORGANIZATIONAL RELATIONSHIPS

TOM HEWITT

3.1 INTRODUCTION

A review of contemporary thinking about inter-organizational relationships unerringly trips over one word – networks. So widely used is the word from explaining the lubricant of individual social interactions (for example, Beres and Wilson, 1997) to depicting the current workings of the global economy (for example, Castells, 1996) that we might immediately conclude that it is a hollow term to which we can attribute any meaning that suits our purposes. There is some truth in this. There is also an irony. In its broadest sense, the term network as used to understand inter-organizational relationships means 'connectedness' (Easton 1996), dialogue or human interaction. And yet it is extraordinary how different peoples' minds work. To take two extremes, compare the articles by Marschak and Reichelstein (1998) 'Network mechanisms, informational efficiency, and hierarchies' and Lowndes *et al.* (1997) 'Networks, partnerships and urban regeneration'. Both have 'network' as the first word in the article title. The first is a mathematical modeling exercise on the costs of communications in a network and the second is an examination of social networks in an urban regeneration project. The connectedness between the two is negligible. The irony is that the users of the term network are frequently worlds apart. Therein lies the difficulty of dialogue between organizations (and the individuals they comprise) in order to reach mutually beneficial ends.

So let's start with a point of clarification over terminology. 'Network' in the context of this book is a particular kind of inter-organizational relationship. The focus of this book as a whole is in trying to understand inter-organizational relationships in function of three ideal types – competition, co-ordination and co-operation – which we argue map roughly onto the three organizational forms – markets, hierarchies and networks (after Thompson *et al.*, 1991). As the rest of this chapter will indicate, inter-organizational relationships can encompass all three ideal types. The confusion in terminology arises partly because the first two do not necessarily involve inter-organizational relationships whilst the last, networks, does by definition. Many authors, in fact, conflate the terms to inter-organizational networks.

In this short chapter, I will try to make some sense of the now large literature on inter-organizational relationships in a way that will inform the later chapters. To this end, I will try to move beyond, but not discard, the three sector model developed by Teddy Brett in Chapter 2 by looking at what the literature can tell us about the connectedness of the terms competition, co-ordination and co-operation. Subsequent chapters of the book take up some of the issues raised here in more detail, notably Chapter 5 by Mick Moore (on forms of competition under the New Public Management), Chapter 7 by Dorcas Robinson (on pluralism in the co-ordination of services) and Chapter 10 by John Harriss (on networks, partnerships and trust in co-operative relations).

Chapter 2 discussed autonomy and diversity (the commonly attributed distinctive competencies and functions of each 'sector' or ideal type) in organizational systems. This chapter will look at interdependence between organizations – its emergence, forms and management. This interdependence can be talked about in two important ways.

As already indicated, all organizations face common issues. For example, all organizations are engaged in forms of internal co-ordination. All organizations are confronted with matters of accountability, legitimacy, governance and so on. Whatever the 'sector', they are involved in relationships with customers/clients/constituencies which shape their responses to these issues.

Whether explicitly recognized or not, the organization of social, political and economic life involves a variety of inter-organizational relationships. The complexity of these relations depends on the degree of specialization and autonomy in any society. This depends on a system for structuring reciprocal rights and obligations which allow each agency to interact peacefully with all of the others. However, such systems are not static or uncontested. The boundaries commonly set around the three 'sectors' or ways of organizing – competition, co-ordination and co-operation – may serve some conceptual purpose at times, but are limited in their capacity to capture the nuances and dynamism of real organizational and institutional life.

Around the world policy discussions in recent years have shifted attention to the relationships which exist both within and across these 'sectors'. This has generated ideas such as 'public–private' partnership, debates about complementarily, co-production and synergy, and, as indicated above, much talk of networks.

This chapter has drawn mainly on literature from business and innovation studies, partly because the rest of the book focuses on other areas of social and economic co-ordination, particularly in the field development management, but also because the business literature is probably the most developed in this field. This provides opportunities to apply what is learnt from one context into another.

The following sections examine in turn

- the reasons for developing inter-organizational relationships (Section 3.2);
- different forms of inter-organizational relationship (Section 3.3); and
- some of the theoretical explanations for the existence of inter-organizational relationships (Section 3.4).

Section 3.5 concludes by looking at managing, learning and process in inter-organizational relationships as well as pointing to inter-organizational relationships in public policy and development by way of introduction to the rest of the book.

3.2 WHY DEVELOP INTER-ORGANIZATIONAL RELATIONSHIPS?

Inter-organizational relationships are of concern in all areas of social and economic life:

- in the way that firms build competitiveness;
- the manner in which government co-ordinates social and economic affairs; and
- the many co-operative interactions of civic life.

Inter-organizational relationships are an extension of the more usual understanding of the way that social and economic life is mediated, that is, through markets or through hierarchies. The distinguishing feature of inter-organizational relationships is that they imply more than the hermetically sealed perfect market or perfect bureaucracy. Indeed, inter-organizational relationships are often invoked as a response to market or bureaucratic failure. In this way, inter-organizational relationships 'are neither spontaneously co-ordinated by the price mechanism, like markets, nor authoritatively set by administrative fiat, like hierarchical forms of organization' (Lutz, 1997, p. 221).

3.2.1 TWO VIEWS ON THE DETERMINANTS OF INTER-ORGANIZATIONAL RELATIONSHIPS

The widespread diffusion of inter-organizational relationships in recent years can be attributed to two separate trends. On the one hand is the forced interactions between organizations that have come about through the policies of neo-liberal governments in the last two decades. For example, compulsory competitive tendering in local government was introduced by the Thatcher government in Britain in the 1980s. Such policies were intended to make the public sector emulate what was perceived as private sector behaviour and thereby increase the efficiency of service delivery. Large organizations such as the health and education sectors had their hierarchical (internally co-ordinated) structures broken down and contracts for services introduced. 'If in doubt, contract out' became the slogan. As a result, inter-organizational relationships became compulsory. Similarly in industry, large corporations in the US and Western Europe initially responded to the competitive challenge from East Asia by becoming 'leaner' through 'downsizing' (i.e. sacking staff – which is why many say 'leaner and meaner') and contracting in non-core activities, or, as one commentator calls it, 'sticking to the knitting' (Milne, 1997).

The other trend, visible in many sectors and at odds with the above, is towards co-operation through inter-organizational relationships as a voluntary and positive move towards creating greater efficiency and effectiveness in social and economic transactions. Whilst the free market policies of the 1980s (worldwide) were informed by one model of the way that competitiveness and efficiency were achieved (in both public and private sectors), the role-models themselves were behaving otherwise. Thus Deakin and Wilkinson note that in contrast to the institutionalized use of the principle of 'good faith' between firms in Germany and to some extent Italy, 'in the Anglo-American systems, deregulation has in many cases generated adversarial relations which are inimical to trust and co-operation' (1997, p. 155). Examining the trend towards greater co-operation in social and economic life is the substance of the rest of this chapter. However, notwithstanding the euphoria in some of the literature on inter-organizational relationships (see, for example, Lipnack and Stamps, 1994 or Castells, 1996 for engaging contributions in this vein), co-operation is not automatically positive, nor do co-operative arrangements necessarily dispense with questions of power or asynchronicity in relations between organizations.

3.2.2 WHY DO ORGANIZATIONS INTER-RELATE?

Inter-firm networking is increasingly important in economic life, because of its capacity for regulating complex transactional interdependence as well as co-operative interdependence amongst firms.

(Grandori and Soda, 1995, p. 183)

There is a long list that could be drawn up of why it is advantageous for organizations to co-operate with each other in one form or another. The reasons come from literature on business/management, economics, technological innovation, geography, the public sector, the voluntary sector and in the field of development. Of the many catch phrases characteristic of management literature, my favourite in describing the reasons for inter-organizational relationships is because of 'the strength of weak ties' (Granovetter, 1973). By this I understand that exchanges between organizations, whether based on market or hierarchical principles often contain hidden (or embedded) social relations that have a history and transcend the transaction under scrutiny. This is more than the hidden hand of the market (where price determines choices) and is beyond bureaucratic behaviour where formalized rules determine actions.

Two views amongst analysts of inter-organizational relationships as to why they occur have predominated until recently. The first is that they are an intermediate form between markets and hierarchies and, by implication, less effective than either and destined to be temporary (following transaction cost theory – see Box 3.3). The second views inter-organizational relationships, particularly networks, as a third form of organizing social, political and economic life (Thompson *et al.*, 1991; Hakansson and Snehota, 1994; Forsgren *et al.*, 1995). More recently, both tendencies have come under criticism for being either too temporary (the first view) and therefore not explaining the real world which is awash with such relationships or as being too rigid (the second) and therefore not explaining the wide diversity of practice in different kinds of relationship (Grandori and Soda, 1995; Salancik, 1995; Grandori, 1997).

Ebers (1997a) suggests that the reasons for entering inter-organizational relationships will be mediated by influences at three levels of analysis between which there are 'recursive influences':

1 the *actor level* (the networking skills and motivations of individuals and/or organizations);

2 the *level of pre-existing relations* amongst actors (the extent and history of social embeddedness between individuals and/or organizations); and

3 the *institutional level* (the social, economic and political context in which relations develop).

A non-exhaustive list of practical reasons for setting up inter-organizational relationships would include:

• gains in scale and scope (in research, products, service delivery, etc.);

• meeting flexibility of demand;

• information sharing;

• building complementary skills and resource synergy;

• strengthening competitive position;

• access to new technologies and/or new markets;

• protecting an existing resource base against competition;

• strengthening a group of organizations as a political lobby.

In a more generic fashion, Oliver, 1990 (cited in Ebers, 1997a, p. 7), proposes six motives for establishing inter-organizational relationships: *necessity* (when mandated through regulation or law), *asymmetry* (allowing one party control over another), *reciprocity* (in the pursuit of common or mutually beneficial goals), *efficiency* (where co-operation produces higher input/output ratios or economies of scale), *stability* (to overcome uncertainty through risk sharing) and *legitimacy* (by enhancing reputation, prestige of those co-operating).

Some of these motivations are illustrated in the field of technological innovation where inter-firm co-operation has been a feature for perhaps longer than in any other collaborative activity. Knowledge is the key commodity. Competition in technology and knowledge intensive industries (for example biotechnology, electronics, the auto industry etc.) depends not only on market share but on always keeping ahead through innovation (Liebeskind *et al.*, 1996). Such firms have opted to use co-operation for competitive purposes. As one author puts it:

The choice of a design configuration [i.e. with whom to make alliances] is among the most important that any firm ever makes ... Collaborative ventures are partly defensive innovations in that they are aimed at reducing or sharing risks and costs. They are also offensive innovations in that they extend the skill base of the firm and the range of knowledge available to it and thereby improve its ability to compete. Because specialist knowledge is produced, collaboration can be a source of sustained competitive advantage because it is difficult to imitate.

(Gibbons *et al.,* 1994, p. 121)

Co-operation in this instance requires a shift from the creation of knowledge to its configuration, that is, decisions about whom you co-operate with in order to put in place a particular set of knowledge and skills. Such configurations are increasingly through public–private partnerships and may involve pooling skills from firms, business units, universities, research centres, governments, customers and often stakeholders (Chataway, 1998, p. 14). The challenge then, and as with other forms of inter-organizational relationships, is how to manage such distributed knowledge systems. It is probably true to say that due to the open-ended nature of such co-operation, management is about increasing the permeability of boundaries between organizations and brokering the outcomes. However, the mode of management also depends crucially on the degree of symmetry in relationships which range from hierarchical control to mutual co-operation.

There is then a wide choice of reasons for developing inter-organizational relationships. The selection of quotes in Box 3.1 suggests, however, that inter-organizational relationships offer advantages that transcend reliance on either the market or on hierarchy, or at least can enhance their imperfect functioning. Much of course depends on the form that the relationship takes.

BOX 3.1 SOME IDEAS ON INTER-ORGANIZATIONAL RELATIONSHIPS AND NETWORKS

[Inter-organizational relationships are] ... co-operative efforts among business firms, governmental bodies or organizations, persons, or other entities that are interconnected in various ways. These connections permit them to be seen clearly apart from the environment in which they are embedded.

(Ring, 1997, p. 115)

Because inter-organizational networks establish recurring, partner-specific exchange relationships, actors ... develop contractually unspecified reciprocal obligations and mutual expectations about relation specific activities.

(Ebers, 1997a, p. 21)

A relationship often arises between two parties because of the inter-dependence of outcomes … As it entails mutual commitment over time, a relationship creates interdependence which is both positive and negative for the parties involved. A relationship develops over time as a chain of interaction episodes … It has a history and a future. In this way a relationship creates interdependence as much as it is a way to handle interdependence.

(Hakansson and Snehota, 1994, p. 25)

There is a division of work in a network that means that firms are dependent on each other. Therefore, their activities need to be co-ordinated. Co-ordination is not achieved though a central plan or an organizational hierarchy, nor does it take place through the price mechanism, as in the traditional market model. Instead, co-ordination takes place through interaction among firms in the network, in which price is just one of several influencing conditions.

(Johanson and Matisson, 1987)

As in a system, one assumes that there is more to the network than the sum of its interacting components. In other words, the network assumes positive – or negative – synergy … Networks must involve a positive-sum game, where some members may be losers some of the time, but most members are winners, most of the time.

(DeBresson and Amesse, 1991, p. 364)

The organization of social relations becomes a central concept in analysing the structural properties of the networks within which individual actors are embedded, and for detecting emergent social phenomena that have no existence at the level of the individual actor.

(Knoke and Kuklinski, 1991, p. 173)

… different trends in the organizational transformation of the infor-mational economy are relatively independent of each other … but they are all different dimensions of a fundamental process: the process of disintegration of the organizational model of vertical, rational bureaucracies, characteristic of the large corporation under the con-ditions of standardized mass production and oligopolistic markets … Networks are the fundamental stuff of which new organizations are and will be made. And they are able to form and expand all over the main streets and back alleys of the global economy because of their reliance in the information power provided by the new technological paradigm.

(Castells, 1996, p. 167-8)

3.2 FORMS OF INTER-ORGANIZATIONAL RELATIONSHIPS

Part of the appeal of inter-organizational relationships as a way of co-ordinating social and economic life is the diverse application of the form. Thus we find joint ventures, franchises, licensing, long-term contracts, strategic alliances, corporate interlocks, single sourcing arrangements, industrial districts, science parks, research consortia, networks and partnerships to name just a few.

As the list above shows there are so many forms of inter-organizational relationships that a chapter of this size could not do justice to them. Grandori and Soda (1995) have done a useful synthesis of the various mechanisms that co-ordinate forms of relationships found in business networks. A summary of this is produced in Box 3.2.

Management of such a diversity of business networks requires flexibility and understanding of what it is that is to be managed. Continuing with the review by Grandori and Soda (1995), they build a classification of inter-organizational forms which is useful when trying to distinguish different forms of collaboration and how they might be managed. There are three:

1   *social networks* which rely on individual and informal relations, often based on tacit understanding of common interests and on trust;

2   *bureaucratic networks* which have a degree of formality often with contractual back-up but left open as to the day-to-day running and management of the relationship; and

3   *proprietary networks* which are formal and specified in detail in contracts between parties.

3.2.1 SOCIAL NETWORKS

In symmetric social relations, personal ties are key. When organizations first link, they are often exploratory ties for the exchange of confidential information which has potential but unknown value. These are important as pools of trustworthy potential partners amongst whom to search for eventual network partners.

Such personal networks are important where there are problems of occupational mobility, resource mobilization, the configuration of skills and knowledge and the effectiveness of communication. Personal and confidential contacts may also be the only viable mechanism in delicate, volatile agreements.

Industrial districts are a form of social networking, where close family ties, active industrial associations and pooled resources are commonplace. Interlocking directorates are another, more formal type of social network. When social network relations are contractual, they will only specify goods and service exchange and not the organization of the relationship. Asymmetric social networks include: putting out and sub-contracting.

BOX 3.2 MECHANISMS OF INTER-ORGANIZATIONAL RELATIONSHIP IN BUSINESS

- *Communication, decision and negotiation*: low cost, always present to some degree, required to form alliances and to maintain long-term relations. Some based solely on these.
- *Social co-ordination and control*: all stable systems have some element of this. Often deep and stable relations based on group norms, reputation and peer control.
- *Integration and linking-pin roles*: horizontal roles and responsibilities, such as inter-organization project management.
- *Common staff*: some relations may be large and complex enough to merit dedicated staff for co-ordination.
- *Hierarchy and authority relations*: these still have their uses in networks, for example franchises require supervision, planning, etc. similar to that found within individual firms.
- *Planning and control systems*: one problem of co-operation is controlling the delivery of co-operative behaviour, so this is often mediated by control systems based on results rather than hierarchical supervision, for example in fast food franchises.
- *Incentive systems*: where performance is difficult to measure, e.g. in informationally complex activities, other mechanisms such as contracts, profit share or income share are used. A specification of property rights over the results of collective action can be a strong incentive to co-operate.
- *Selection systems*: relates to specificity of access. The broader the scope of co-operation, the stricter the rules of access. For example, a trade association requires only general conformity whereas a franchise chain has much stricter requirements for entry.
- *Information systems*: IT is a powerful mechanism for managing interdependence. The cost reductions of communication can be considerable and enable forms of co-operation that would otherwise be prohibitively costly.
- *Public support and infrastructure*: some forms of co-operation may not occur without public sector support, for example where the costs of R&D [research and development] are high relative to the appropriability of its benefits. The public investment for science parks is possibly another example.

(Grandori and Soda, 1995)

3.2.2 BUREAUCRATIC NETWORKS

These are inter-firm co-operations that are formalized in contractual agreements, that is, the agreement specifies the organizational arrangement. However, these are not watertight and therefore can only assist, not substitute, for a social network relation. Symmetric forms include trade associations, providing common services to co-ordinate behaviour among large numbers of similar firms where inter-firm dependency is not complex or specific. Cartels and federations act in this way. A more complex form is that of research consortia.

Asymmetrical forms include agency networks (such as the insurance service wings of banks), licensing (for which contracts increasingly have organizational clauses) and franchises.

3.2.3 PROPRIETARY NETWORKS

This is the most formalized kind of inter-organizational relationship. The most common being joint ventures and capital ventures. Joint ventures, symmetrical relations at least on paper, involve specific alliances between partners that generate enough surplus to cover the cost of the governance structure. Where they succeed, joint ventures use a range of co-ordinating mechanisms from effective communication to joint decision-making and negotiation processes.

A more asymmetrical proprietary relationship is capital ventures where capital is provided to risky or innovative undertakings. To cover the risk, this generally involves in-depth information about the partner, significant property rights and the setting up of joint decision-making and managerial know-how.

Understanding the form that a particular relationship takes gives us clues as to how it will function and how it is to be managed. But as usual in this area, there are many ways of doing this. Other useful and more practical ways of understanding the form of a particular relationship would include:

- assessing a combination of resource flows, information flows, mutual expectations, the distribution of property rights over resources and co-ordination mechanisms (Ebers, 1997a, p. 17);
- examining a combination of: activity links (technical, administrative, commercial, etc. that can be connected to those of another organization), resource ties (how to combine the technological, material and knowledge resources at the organizations' disposal), and actor bonds (the specific relationships of individuals between the organizations) (Hakansson and Snehota, 1994, p. 26).

In sum, the forms that inter-organizational relationships take and the changes in form of particular arrangements over time are varied but there are some general features as outlined above which help us to identify different forms and therefore to give some guidance on how to manage particular arrangements. The diversity of forms of inter-organizational relationships is also reflected in the literature on the functioning of inter-organizational relationships which I turn to next.

3.3 EXPLANATIONS OF THE FUNCTIONING OF INTER-ORGANIZATIONAL RELATIONSHIPS

The theoretical underpinnings of the functioning of inter-organizational relationships draw on several disciplines and, notwithstanding considerable overlap, there are disagreements over why inter-organizational relationships emerge and in how they function in theory as well as in practice.

From an initial survey of the literature, I was inclined to say that much of the writing on inter-organizational relationships was quite descriptive and under-theorized. However, a quick look at Box 3.3 perhaps shows the opposite; a great many theories and frameworks have been used or devised to understand inter-organizational relationships. So much so that disagreements are inevitable.

BOX 3.3 THEORIES AND FRAMEWORKS FOR INTER-ORGANIZATIONAL RELATIONSHIPS

Without wishing to over-simplify the extensive writing on attempts to theorize inter-organizational relationships, the following is a thumbnail sketch of the theories that underpin and have most influenced the area. There is at times considerable overlap of content between these approaches.

Transaction cost economics: attributed to the work of Williamson 1979; 1985) but subsequently used in variant form by many others, transaction costs revolve around the make-or-buy decisions of firms for a single transaction, that is, what are the relative costs of transacting in the market or within the firm? Transaction cost efficiency is the motivation for firm behaviour. The forms of governance of inter-organizational relationships in this school are asset specificity, uncertainty and frequency of transactions.

Other frameworks are closely related. They include:

- *Strategic alliance theory*: this is now part of orthodox management thinking, based on analysis of a firm's strategic core. Other companies – through formal contractual alliance – perform complementary activities whilst the main company focuses on those activities which have a high asset specificity, i.e. it sticks to the knitting. This is an extension of transaction cost economics as market and hierarchy are still viewed as the key forms of governance of transactions;

- *Industrial economics*: based on analysis of economies of scale, scope, specialization and experience to explain incomplete forms of vertical and horizontal integration in firms and in the process of internationalization of operations of firms;
- *Organizational economics*: stresses the reduction in costs of governance in inter-organizational relationships that hybrid forms of market and hierarchy can obtain under certain circumstances. Transaction cost economics is a specific subset of this.

Resource dependence view: tries to capture the strategic advantages of, particularly, alliances which transaction cost economics ignores, such as learning, creation of legitimacy and rapid market entry. In this view firms are bundles of tangible assets (financial, technological) and intangible assets (reputation, management skills). Alliances with other firms are driven by resource needs based on strategic and social factors (not just transaction costs) and on needs and opportunities (not just efficiency).

Inter-organizational relationships: as a framework this focuses on resource procurement and allocation and strategies (diversification, joint ventures, withdrawal, etc.) for coping with imbalances and dependency. It tells us (contrary to transaction cost theories) that when the environment is turbulent or uncertain, organizations will deal repeatedly and co-operatively for 'idiosyncratic' resources through network organizations even to the point of foregoing a better deal elsewhere.

Network theories: stress the importance of resource development over time, rather than the one-off arrangements of transaction cost theory, access to and use of information, learning and social capital. Network theories also examine the embeddedness of relations where economic exchanges are imbued with social exchange containing unspecified obligations based on trust.

Other theories that have been used to explain inter-organizational relationships include:

- *relational theory* stresses how pre-existing social relations between individuals are the foundations for building more relations between organizations;
- *evolutionary approaches* to innovation (such as in Dosi,1988) use inter-organizational relationships as a way of understanding the costs and learning problems associated with innovation;
- *social network theory* from psychology to understand the behaviour of small groups;
- *population/organizational ecology* which has been concerned with the survival rates of organizational arrangements based on economic efficiency criteria;

- *institutional economics* which has extended transaction cost theories by looking at inter-organizational relationships in terms of their institutional embededness (e.g. how arrangements fit with the legal system, labour markets and the political system, etc);
- *negotiation analysis* used to understand the form of inter-relation adopted and how this is negotiated between partners.

(After Hakansson and Snehota, 1994; Grandori and Soda, 1995; Eisenhardt and Schoonhoven, 1996; Park, 1996; Ring, 1996; Ebers 1997b)

Transaction cost economics – the starting point from which the other theories follow – concerns itself with make-or-buy decisions for a single transaction between two firms. The choice is whether to produce goods or services in-house or whether to buy them in the market place. Both have a price and both have an overhead (the transaction cost). Working in collaboration with another organization (a hybrid form between market and hierarchy, the theory states) also has a transaction cost. Making such choices, then, are based on a calculation of what is the least cost option.

What transaction cost theory usefully does is recognize that in the real world there is no such thing as a perfect market (as neo-classical economics assumes) and that any choice over transaction needs to take this into account. This is an important step forward, but real world transactions are even more complicated than simply a choice between make or buy. The hybrid transaction characterized by joint effort between firms is, in transaction cost theory, regarded as temporary and, ultimately, doomed to be replaced by market or hierarchy.

From this point flow most of the other theories or frameworks for understanding inter-organizational relationships. Why, they ask, is there such a prevalence of inter-relating if this is a sub-optimal form of organization? From my notes in Box 3.3, it is apparent that neither single transactions nor simply cost considerations are the only, nor the most important, parameters. Depending on the theory, and on the form of inter-organizational relationship, other longer term and often non-economic variables come into play. The starkest of these might be termed inter-organizational network theories, many of the component parts of which have been discussed in the previous two sections. These frameworks argue for a distinctive form – networks – to be added to the established forms of market and hierarchy.

What does this imply for our tripartite view of inter-organizational relationships based on competition, co-ordination and co-operation? We have already argued, after Thompson *et al.* (1991) that they map onto stereotypical notions of market, hierarchy and network. As argued in Chapter 2, each has a distinctive set of attributes and each contains considerable explanatory power for the way that social, economic and political life is organized. Taken individually they remain analytical constructs or ideal types, however the reality is much more complex. Thompson *et al.* (1991) use the analogy of each being like the beam of a torch, able only to pick out small, and different, segments of the whole.

Understanding inter-organizational relationships becomes a matter of understanding how the three ideal types combine and interact under different conditions and configurations – three torch beams intersecting to give a composite pattern of shades. The diversity of inter-organizational relationships is a reflection of these different configurations. Inter-organizational network theorists provide us with the key to understanding how either market or hierarchy are incomplete specifications of the real world, as exemplified by one of the principal theorists of business networks:

> It is common to think of competitiveness as a company's 'capacity to outperform others'. That assumes that the relevant dimensions of 'performance' are clear and common to different companies ... that is hardly ever the case ... what matters for a company's economy is to exploit the benefits of relationships and that means to produce value together with others and for others ... producing value for others is more than achieving efficiency in resource transformation and ... what is valued by others is subject to continuous change and always specific for the parties in a relationship. Value for others is not produced simply by economizing and saving on the costs of relationships, rather, it is achieved mainly by improving the pay-offs from relationship investment. It is achieved by managing the relationships benefits, by developing and exploiting the activity links, resource ties and actor bonds in business relationships, which in turn is improving the economic efficiency of the overall network structure.
>
> (Hakansson and Snehota, 1994, p. 397)

3.4 FINALLY...

In this final section, I will touch on three aspects of inter-organizational relationships that have not featured strongly so far but which are implicit in what has already been said:

1 the management of inter-organizational relationships;

2 the importance of process in inter-organizational relationships; and

3 inter-organizational relationships in other areas of social, political and economic life.

3.4.1 MANAGING RELATIONSHIPS

> We know much less about how inter-organizational networking relationships are built, developed and dissolved.
>
> (Ebers, 1997a, p. 13)

Several arguments have been put forward in the literature – for example, sequential phases of pre-networking, relationship building and solidifying or of network formation, development and testing. A more appealing approach than sequential models is one of cyclical development which

> ... involves an ongoing, repeated process of negotiation of mutual expectations, commitments for future action, and execution of commitments which is assessed in terms of equity and efficiency. Underlying these cyclical phases are formal and informal processes of sense making, understanding, committing and enacting.
>
> (Ebers, 1997a, p. 14. See also Ring, 1997 and Chapter 10)

This notion ties in with relatively new ideas about 'learning networks' (Larsson *et al.*, 1998; Bessant and Francis, 1999), and is of particular relevance in developing countries where knowledge resources are scarce (Hewitt and Wield, 1997). The benefits of shared learning between organizations, after Bessant and Francis (1999), can include:

- the potential for challenge and structured critical reflection from different perspectives;
- different perspectives can bring in new concepts or old concepts new to the learner;
- shared experimentation can reduce risks and maximize opportunities for trying new things out;
- shared experiences can be supportive, confirmational;
- shared learning helps explicate the system's principles, seeing the patterns – separating 'the wood from the trees';
- shared learning provides an environment for surfacing assumptions and exploring mental models outside of the normal experience of individual organizations – helps prevent 'not invented here' and other effects.

The chapters in the rest of this book give us a number of examples of how inter-organizational relationships are managed – or mismanaged – in practice.

3.4.2   PROCESS IN RELATIONSHIPS

In any consideration of inter-organizational relationships, the really important aspect is process (as opposed to, say, structure) and it is this aspect about which least in known (Ring, 1996).

However, one advantage of examining networks of institutions and firms is that it gives scope to move away from linear or blueprint policy approaches and 'solutions' to co-ordinating organizational life toward one which relies more on contingency and flexibility. Several metaphors have been used to describe this shift of emphasis – from 'policy as prescription to policy as process' (Mackintosh, 1992b) 'from mechanistic to organic policy' (Murray, 1992); 'from public policy to public action' (Wuyts, 1992) – but they add up to a similar approach.

This approach has also been implicit in the discussion so far – where frequent emphasis was placed on the long-term and socially embedded nature of inter-organizational relationships. The policy and management implications of viewing inter-organizational relationships as a process are substantial. As the last quotes indicate, policy becomes itself a multi-actor and iterative process.

3.4.3 INTER-ORGANIZATIONAL RELATIONSHIPS IN OTHER AREAS

Private sector inter-organizational relationships have their own specific characteristics but there is much to learn for other areas too. The rest of this book examines instances of inter-organizational relationships in diverse settings. In fact there is a good deal of convergence of views between the private, public and voluntary sectors on inter-organizational relationships. Recent work on policy networks illustrates this (Kickert *et al.*, 1997). Policy networks are being discussed as desirable forms, for their flexibility, capacity to organize pluralism and include wider participation. This was not always so. In the past, they have been cast in a negative light – viewed as closed, informal and therefore undesirable forms in a world which worked to the image of a rational, rule-based organization of the state. In other words, networks have existed, but have not been recognized because they did not fit prevailing images of desirable organization until more recently.

The policy network model is presented as an alternative approach to governance, whereby public policymaking and governance takes place in networks consisting of various actors '... none of which possesses the power to determine the strategies of the other actors. The government is no longer seen as occupying a superior position to other parties, but as being on equal footing with them' (Kickert *et al.*, 1997, p. 9).

Without denying the occurrence of such a trend in public policy, herein lies a weakness of much of the literature on networks, particularly that which is outside business concerns. Power relations are frequently glossed over in the rush to establish the novelty and effectiveness of inter-organizational relationships. Power asymmetries can remain even when reciprocity is invoked or when there are calls for partnership.

Nevertheless, the notion of policy networks in the public sector is a creative way of understanding the new and distinctively less hierarchical configurations and forms of governance which have emerged in the last two decades of public sector reform. Kickert *et al.* again:

> Because these interactions are frequently repeated, processes of institutionalization occur: shared perceptions; participation patterns and interaction rules develop and are formalized. The structural and cultural features of policy networks which come about in this way influence future policy processes.
>
> (Kickert *et al.*, 1997, p. 6)

As a result of these structural transformations in the public sector, the 'voluntary' sector has risen to a new prominence as part of a pluralist approach to service delivery. Inter-organizational relationships play a key role as the contributions to this book illustrate. The 'development business'– be it NGOs, the UK's Department for International Development or The World Bank – has many parallels with the business literature reviewed here. Contrary to recent policy thinking, formal contracts are not the only, nor by any means the most effective, inter-organizational arrangement. Informal and reciprocal ties, for which accountability depends on repeated transactions and trust, can have an equally sustainable effect. But the management of such ties is not straightforward. As one commentator notes, 'the fashioning of collaborative relationships of substance remains a job for talented practitioners' (Hudson, 1993, p. 375).

The literature cited in this chapter has at least one common theme. To build, maintain and manage inter-organizational relationships requires a high degree of organizational capacity in the first place. Frequently, the reasons for not relating with other organizations is that people do not have the expertise to do so. Even such seemingly simple tasks as sharing information happen relatively rarely. Not only does there have to be capacity, however, but also crucially, inter-organizational relationships will only succeed when the parties involved have a clear idea of what they want and more importantly are prepared to invest the resources into achieving that. Without such a convergence of goals, inter-organizational relationships will remain the hollow term identified at the beginning of the chapter.

4 THE PRIVATE SECTOR AND COMPETITIVE MARKETS IN DEVELOPMENT

JOANNA CHATAWAY

4.1 INTRODUCTION

Promotion of the private sector and competitive markets have gained ground as the recognized means of achieving efficiency in the provision of goods and services. This has been on the back of a strong ethical/political surge in the promotion of the private sector's involvement in delivering public services. There has been a wide acceptance of ideas of a more constrained role for the state and the rewriting of the boundaries between it and the private sector's domain.

But simple models used in public debate are not reflected in the complexities on the ground and the simple models rarely operate in practice as the theory supposes: not least in the case of the simplistic model of the atomistic competitive supplier to efficient markets. As the last chapter demonstrated there are, and have been for a long time, extensive co-operative behaviour patterns between individual firms and groupings of firms working alongside and even within competitive relationships. More co-operative forms of competition and positive synergistic relations between the public and private sectors are increasingly sought by policymakers. There is also increasingly a recognition that the private sector itself and the environment in which it is situated can benefit from engagement with broader social and economic agendas.

There are many different types of competition. Tender and prize based frameworks for promoting more efficient performance in both private and public sectors can take on a multitude of different forms. Moore (Chapter 5) writes mainly about competition within the public sector. This chapter focuses more on efforts to promote organizations and institutions which are competitive, private sector and market based. Examining the practice of private sector promotion and the different ways in which the private sector contributes to development enables us to provide some pointers to appropriate behaviour and management strategies for development oriented organizations.

4.1.1 STARTING POINTS

The analytic framework of private sector promotion and competitive markets have been used to promote open markets and private sector development through much of the developing world. The major multilateral and bilateral aid agencies have followed an agenda of structural adjustment and economic restructuring to cut back the state-owned economic sectors in most of their client states. The full range of Bretton Woods institutions have been brought into play and a market oriented International Monetary Fund (IMF)/World Bank push has ensured client states adopt the tight monetary stances demanded by the market logic. World Bank and IMF thinking during the 1980s and early 1990s pushed hard for privatization and liberalization of markets.

New institutions and agreements, spearheaded by the World Trade Organization, have concurrently been formed to push for a free trade agenda in an increasing range of goods and services. Again the evidence of the growth of world trade at a faster pace than overall world economic growth has been used to demonstrate the economic benefits of competitive markets. These have extended beyond the traditional commodities into the new knowledge-based industries and the area of intellectual property, both of which are seen as crucial to the future of world prosperity. Despite a recognized inequality of countries across the world economy there has been sufficient momentum to keep the pressure on all member states to accelerate the opening of their markets to international competition.

In parallel, there has been a damning critique of the inefficiency of the public sector. This has cited the inability of most state owned enterprises to match the efficiency performance of private firms – without necessarily undertaking a thorough analysis of the underlying reasons. Additionally, the widespread distrust in the general population of public bureaucracies and the levels of inefficiency with which many perform their duties has contributed to the hegemony of competitive market models for development.

This has led to moves to rewrite the boundaries of the public sector and the withdrawal of publicly managed agents from whole ranges of economic activity that has until recently been most frequently found in the public sector. It has led to attempts to maximize the active role of the competitive model in all markets. The utilities, such as water supply, once the preserve of public service provision because of their inherent characteristics of geographic monopolies, are now increasingly commonly found as private sector organizations working in supervised but competitive markets. Also a growing range of personal services as well as a range of executive administrative tasks now fall into the intermediate space where mixed provision is the norm. Continued encroachment by 'more efficient' private sector agencies has been confidently predicted to lead to additional benefits.

The appealing simplicity of the free market competitive model has added to its power in shaping thinking about its relevance to all aspects of resource management. However, in practice it has never been applied in its purest form and even on theoretical grounds it has been demonstrated to be less than tenable. In the last chapter, Hewitt discussed inter-firm relationships and more co-operative forms of competition rather than pure competition. Co-operation can occur because of technological interdependencies, shared externalities and a recognition amongst corporate actors that legitimacy and image are increasingly important and can often best be preserved by taking action against 'cowboy' and disruptive operators.

Also there are additional costs that have been recognized as associated with the pure competitive model that undermine its purported universal relevance. These arise from:

1 *Information costs.* In the information age these are expensive to assemble as well as notoriously inaccurate. This affects both consumers – who resist a bombardment of selective facts from suppliers and stick with wider criteria than economic efficiency in choosing purchases – and producers who must work with imperfect information to second guess both competitor and consumer behaviour.

2 *Fragmentation.* This increases the need for interaction rather than leading to independence or autonomy and increases the scale of the information costs mentioned above.

3 *Vulnerability and instability.* These arise through the transitory nature of contracts in both the product and labour markets, because of the supposedly relentless search for the holy grail of better economic performance. These are also exacerbated by the speed with which economic fashions and moods can sweep away rational analysis of underlying factors – seen most recently in market runs on world currencies that have added to the problems of Russia's adjustment to a market economy.

4 *Unaccounted externalities.* These arise from the conflicts inherent in the pursuit of individual welfare when we are organized socially and on occasions when the behaviour of one individual or firm affects others for which it has no responsibility to take any account of in its decisions. These include externalities ranging from the negatives of pollution to the positives of training for which there are common interests as well as individual responsibilities.

At a policy level, donors have also shifted their perspective and operations. The harsh anti-state line has to some extent been replaced by an approach which takes a more positive attitude towards partnership, both between private sector actors themselves and between private, public and civil society (World Bank, 1997a). Although there is debate about the extent of the change, donors have placed more emphasis on good governance amongst private sectors actors, environmental sustainability and in some cases on integrating social objectives.

Similarly there has been a growing realization that there are aspects of competitiveness that are not susceptible to narrow economic appraisal. Seeking to subject everything to the market undermines softer social conventions that have held society together successfully and compounds the instability inherent in short-term relationships. A whole series of interdependencies are increasingly being recognized as contributing to behaviour but lying outside the limited view of humans as economic rational beings.

None of this means that the strong commitment to private sector development has been diminished (World Bank, 1997a, 1998; OECD, 1994; Hewitt, 1999). However, some hybrid mix of collaboration and competition is now increasingly recognized as the reality in most instances and is favoured by policy makers. The variation amongst these hybrid models is huge and authors have analysed these models in various ways. For example, Fukuyama (1995) gives a very central role to levels of trust in accounting for variations on industrial and market structures in different countries. What is clear is that a complex interaction of economic and non-economic variables make up the different models. It is also clear that while globalization is a powerful force which is integrating markets and nations in fundamental ways, it is not a force which undermines national and regional difference. No single model will be applicable in all places, indeed, the strength of competitive market-based institutions can be related to the way they interact and are synergistic with non-market institutions.

4.2 FOSTERING PRIVATE SECTOR GROWTH

Some economists hold that markets will naturally throw up efficient private sector organizations. However, in many cases the most successful promotion efforts involve private, NGO and state sectors. Bilateral and multi-lateral donors are exploring more co-operative forms of market-based competition and are creating institutional infrastructures which foster mutual support and build on technological interdependencies and shared externalities. Building up institutional capacity in all sectors is vitally important both in creating new private sector organizations and in making the overall institutional environment more efficient. This is particularly true in efforts to promote new private sector enterprises.

Figure 4.1 gives an overview of some of the support services, institutions and programmes needed to facilitate small firm growth.

In this diagram, the business is the centre of attention. To succeed requires a number of internal (i.e. under the control of the firm) and external factors. These are grouped into four categories:

1   *Capital*: provided to the firm for a suitable duration at a viable cost and accessible to those short of collateral.
2   *'Know How'*: accessed through business professionals (at affordable prices and of good quality) and general skill and training programmes that encourage investment and ensure efficient markets for skilled labour.
3   *Information*: covering market needs and information sources in particular with more general elements relating to technology and standards and sources of assistance.

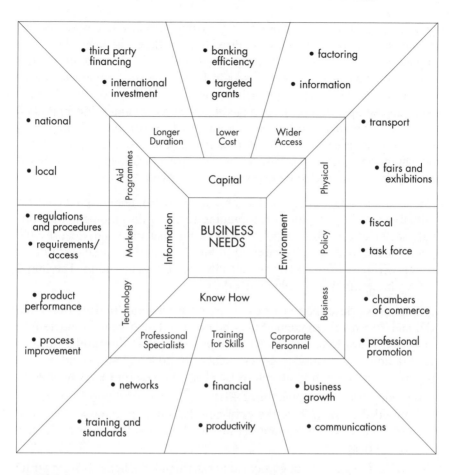

FIGURE 4.1 A framework for sustaining busines growth in small firms (simplified from Segal Quince Wicksteed Ltd., 1995)

4 *Environment*: including the legal and regulatory environment of public policy as well as the physical market infrastructure and the business advice and support institutions.

The outer layer of the diagram indicates the type of initiatives and programmes which may be needed to create an institutional framework which might provide the ingredients helpful to small business success. Programmes and initiatives may have private sector involvement but are unlikely to be totally supported in this way. This more holistic approach tries to address some of the limitations of the pure competitive model outlined earlier.

The promotion of institutions based on competition involves a range of different private sector and public sector programmes and institutions. Some of these services, infrastructure and programmes have their natural home in the state sector; the construction of laws, regulation and deregulation is predominantly a state led activity. The state may also play a prominent role in other areas, for example promoting good governance in businesses and business support organizations. Provision of financial know how and capital may all be taken on directly by the state or by the state in partnership with NGOs and the private sector. In many cases, initiatives may be started by the state and then transferred to the private sector. Box 4.1 provides an example of a project created in the early to mid-1990s in Poland which attempted to addresses a number of constraints of small and medium enterprise (SME) development and stimulate the supply of and demand for business support services. The project was explicitly designed to draw in private sector involvement as it evolved.

The example given in Box 4.1 is an attempt to combine a public sector initiative relating to quite broad-ranging regional development with private sector effort. This model tries to ensure that funds provided by the public sector will actually be used to build up market-based institutions which will prove financially sustainable over the longer term. The initial money hopefully has a 'snowball' effect.

The initiative described in Box 4.1 involved bilateral funds between the UK and Polish governments. Many bilateral and multilateral funders face dilemmas in working directly with the private sector. Most DFID finance, for example, is provided to government – for government to lend-on – or provide as equity to private enterprise. The rationale for this is twofold:

(a) It provides a mechanism for DFID to ensure that additional funds are provided to the private sector at non-distortionary rates so that some sectors and enterprises are not favoured through the terms of finance over others.

(b) As loans are repaid or equity earns a dividend, the benefits from DFID funds eventually end up with government for spending through the budget and so distribute the benefits more widely than to specific consumers or producers.

There are disadvantages however. Sticking rigidly to a policy of providing funds through government means that it retains a role in governing these funds. Some governments have a track record of extremely bad or inefficient corporate governance. It can also mean that projects to support newly privatized enterprises or those in the private sector lead to some form of 're-nationalization' through the use of aid funds.

The policy of providing funds via government is not the only mechanism used. More recently, substantial use has been made of NGOs in aid programmes as an implementation agency with independence from government. The fact that in the UK the emphasis is now being placed on government to government aid and 'partnership' should in no way obscure the vitally important role which civil society will play in aid and more generally in development policy. NGOs, as part of civil society, are in many cases able to ensure that funds get to grass-roots in a way that the state is

BOX 4.1 POLISH–BRITISH ENTERPRISE PROJECT

In two lesser developed regions of Poland – Lublin and Bialystok – an integrated enterprise development project was implemented. Included in the programme were:

1 *Institutional development*: strengthening of public/private regional development bodies to provide strategic overviews and initiate programmes, but *not* to deliver services.

2 *Small equity fund*: providing access to equity through private sector agencies, to new and growing small firms for reducing their cost of capital and introducing non-executive advisory inputs.

3 *Market development programme*: using local private sector consultants, part funded by the company and part by the project, to do market appraisals and develop marketing initiatives with individual firms of groups of firms.

4 *Loan guarantee fund*: designed to develop an independent private sector financial service to help local banks and businesses to overcome the collateral problem in SMEs so easing access to commercial funds.

5 *Professional advisor development scheme*: with shared funding to stimulate demand and skills updating to improve competence of local private professionals and NGO staff.

Design issues that proved crucial were:

(a) separating the strategic overview from service delivery which allowed for greater participation in service delivery from private sector providers;

(b) building widespread support which reduced factionalism;

(c) working with both the demand side and the supply side so encouraging a market to develop; and

(d) integrating commercial players to foster private solutions.

(ODA, 1996)

In practice, of course, implementation was not so straight forward, but the initial design of the project tried to maintain a degree of flexibility and encouraged local solutions to emerge.

Regional Development Bodies were strengthened in order to act as temporary 'owners' of the capital injected by the Overseas Development Administration (now Department for International Development, DFID) until the equity and loan guarantee funds – which were set up as incorporated private sector companies – could be sold to private sector owners. The Regional Development Bodies will then be the main beneficiaries of the concessionality of the aid funds when the assets are sold.

unable to do. As Robinson argues in Chapter 7, they are also vehicles for voicing the interests and concerns of people involved and engaged with them. In terms of building the private sector, NGOs often play a key role. Box 4.2 provides an example of a NGO-led business enterprise scheme.

In trying to identify good practice in fostering development of private sector competition-based organizations we can draw out some potential lessons:

- support for these organizations is multi-faceted;
- support is often built through private and public sectors and NGOs;
- building good working relationships between support organizations is a vital part of the work.

This of course is not a complete list, for example participation from clients and recipients is vital. Also, in any concrete situation, existing social and economic institutions will shape support policies and programmes in very different ways.

BOX 4.2   EXPORT MARKETING DEVELOPMENT PROJECT, SOUTH AFRICA

This project supported craft and small farm enterprises in the Western Cape in South Africa. Just Exchange, a local NGO set up with technical assistance through Traidcraft UK, assists SMEs and producer groups to participate more effectively in local, regional and international markets.

Project inputs consist largely of technical assistance and training, and the outputs expected are craft and agri-businesses operating on a commercially viable basis, and, in many cases, exporting increased volumes of projects abroad. As two examples, Just Exchange has assisted with the growth and development of a craft exporter, Africa Trading, and has also enabled the export of agriculture produce from Eksteen Farmers Association, a group of 117 small farmers.

Because successful enterprise support, particularly in the marketing field, requires the development of a wide range of commercial relationships and training materials, Just Exchange has also developed a Market Information Service, and publishes source material such as an Export Marketing Manual and Environmental Guidelines for small producers. Links with UK and European businesses are facilitated through Traidcraft UK or from direct contact through trade fairs and similar events.

(ODA, 1996)

4.3 A CHANGING PRIVATE SECTOR?

Recent reviews of regions and countries which have performed well economically have stressed the benefits of partnership and trust between state, private sector and civil society. Policies aimed at promoting the private sector have only just begun to incorporate these lessons. The latest analysis has focused on trust and social capital as underlying development (see Chapter 10). It is arguable that in some contexts at least, elements of the private sector have also begun to operate in ways that demonstrate an increased commitment to broader social and economic objectives.

Elkington and Burke, for example, argue that

> ... what we are seeing is the emergence of a new age of capitalism, appropriate to a new millenium, in which the boundary between corporate and human values is beginning to dissolve. It is now clear from the results who won the nineteenth century argument about capital and labour. Socialism, as an economic theory, though not as a moral crusade, is dead. The argument is about what kind of capitalism we want.

> (Elkington and Burke, 1987, quoted in Welford, 1995, p. 2)

Or, from Charles Handy

> As in the Renaissance, it will be an exciting time, a time of great opportunities for those who can see and seize them, but of great threat and fear for many. It will be more difficult to hold organizations and societies together. The softer words of leadership and vision and common purpose will replace the tougher words of control and authority because the tough words won't bite anymore. Organizations will have to become communities rather than properties, with members not employees, because few will be content to be owned by others. Societies will break down into smaller units but will also regroup into even larger ones for particular purposes.

> (Handy, 1995, p. 11)

The vision, then, is of a private sector driven economic growth based on more co-operative forms of competition delivering new opportunities for both industrially developed and developing countries. What is clear is that this sea-change, if indeed one is occurring, will be slow to bring benefits to the poorest. While the presence of the private sector and private sector capital flows has increased enormously (PWBLF, 1996, p. 36), the poorest are not touched by benefits which could accrue from some forms of economic growth. Whilst the 1997 United Nations Development Programme (UNDP) report notes that progress is very real – in the past 50 years poverty has fallen more than in the previous 500 – poverty remains pervasive. More than a quarter of the developing world's people still live in poverty as measured by the UNDP. About a third – 1.3. billion people – live on incomes of less than $1 a day (UNDP, 1997, p. 2).

Proponents of the view that a new capitalism can be based on social objectives as well as economic competitiveness point to the success of companies which have attempted to respond to social and environmental concerns. The Body Shop (a company producing cosmetics based on natural products) is an obvious example, but there are thousands of other examples of companies drawing up codes of behaviour, undertaking environmental and special audits and attempting to engage with broader societal goals (Welford, 1995; PWBLF, 1996).

The scope and meaning of these initiatives may be disputed, but what is clear is that in terms of the development agenda, the private sector's influence and presence is growing. The role of the private sector, and the potential role for the sector, have thus become of central concern to policy makers.

Companies can endeavour to change the way they operate to reflect development objectives and commitments to broader social, economic and environmental aims in a number of ways. Some would argue, however, that the most important changes in private sector activity and the way in which competitive markets operate is not the outcome of conscious decisions to change, but a response to the need to be more flexible. Some regions, such as 'The Third Italy' are often held up as examples of areas in which companies have developed new forms of capitalism. These new forms of more co-operative competition are more rooted in regional development, less about the performance of individual units and more the outcome of 'clusters' of firms, research institutes and universities. Another feature of the 'post Fordist' or flexible specialization competitive framework are the strong links between firms and their suppliers so that relations are built up over years. Firms, it is argued, tend towards 'self-organization' so that relations between them are based on mutual self-interest and a degree of co-ordination that goes far beyond 'arms length' market-based relations. There is a large debate about the nature of change and the applicability of these models to developing countries. It is relevant to this chapter that development projects and policy makers have begun to take on board the notion that encouraging co-operation and learning between private sector companies is important.

A project in Romania, for example, to help firms improve innovation and competitiveness, implemented in the late 1990s, tried to encourage firms to learn from one another. The approach draws on approaches of 'action learning' and experiential based learning. This 'learning network' approach encourages broader development in the sense that firms based in a region begin to see that their development can actually be enhanced by the strength of other firms, research institutes and support units in the region. There is a mutual interest in supporting regional efforts. John Bessant and David Francis, already referred to in Chapter 3, summarize some of broader implications and dimensions of the approach in Box 4.3.

BOX 4.3   CLUSTERING, NETWORKS AND INTER-FIRM LEARNING

... there is a growing interest in inter-firm learning and there is a valuable convergence with studies being carried out of networking and clustering as an alternative mode of economic development. For some time it has been recognized that particular configurations of firms in particular regions have been able to achieve what Schmitz calls 'collective efficiency' that is, together a group of small firms can overcome the traditional economic barriers to development (Schmitz, 1997). Examples abound, but include the 'industrial districts' of Italy, Spain and other European countries and the significant clustering observed in Brazil and Pakistan around particular regions but also concentrated on particular sectors or product groups (Piore and Sable, 1982; Schmitz, 1995).

These models have become a focus of interest amongst policymakers, and efforts to stimulate the clustering and networking of firms are underway in a variety of countries. One element of such clustering is that the process of learning and capability-building is enhanced and supported arguably through action learning/experience sharing ... For example, in the case of the textile industry cluster in Italy one outcome of the networking was the setting up of shared R&D (learning) amongst the many small firms. This led, over many years to the formal establishment of a shared technology institute (CITER) and to the development of a rich and robust learning network, the result of which is a technologically strong and highly competitive export-oriented industry (Murray, 1993).

(Bessant and Francis, 1999)

4.4   ASPECTS OF THE CORPORATE SECTOR'S CONTRIBUTION TO DEVELOPMENT

A study by the Prince of Wales Business Leaders Forum (PWBLF) in collaboration with the World Bank and UNDP looks at the way the private sector contributes to development (PWBLF, 1996). The study focuses to a large extent on the role that larger multinational firms have to play and the following section draws heavily on examples from the study. The study is undoubtedly aimed at promoting engagement between public and private and is a largely uncritical account of private sector activity. Nevertheless, it provides a wealth of detail. It sees the companies influencing stakeholders and managing their wider roles and responsibilities in society in three overlapping ways:

1   through its core business activities;
2   through social investment or philanthropic activities;
3   through relations with government and engagement with public policy dialogue.

4.4.1 PROMOTING DEVELOPMENT OBJECTIVES IN CORE BUSINESS ACTIVITIES

Corporate policy and strategy

The challenge here is to encourage the alignment of objectives promoting sustainable development and creating value not only for shareholders, but also other stakeholders.

One way in which many companies choose to express their intentions and commitments is through a public statement of their corporate policy and 'code of conduct'. These may be general, or as in the case of the Swiss pharmaceutical company Ciba, choose to design targeted policies towards developing countries. Ciba's statements are given in Box 4.4.

The outcome of statements is difficult to evaluate. However, its clear that what matters is not so much the statement itself, but the way in which it is followed up and implemented in practice. Significant culture change in companies is necessary if statements are to come alive. An increasing number of companies undertake social and environmental audits in order to give weight to paper commitments. Important developments in the area of social auditing include significant increases in the number of companies undertaking audits and the efforts to establish agreed methods for evaluation. In relation to the second point, NGOs – including the Catholic Institute for International Relations, Christain Aid, the Fair Trade Foundation, the New Economics Foundation, Oxfam and the World Development Movement – and companies are active in trying to agree systems for monitoring and auditing company performance. The New Economics Foundation's research director, Dr. Simon Zadek believes the growth in social auditing is based on companies' need 'to earn and sustain "licenses to operate" by demonstrating their practice of responsible corporate citizenship'(PWBLF, 1996, p.86). He says:

> The most innovative experiences have moved beyond fragmented reporting towards more systematic, comprehensive, rigorous, and externally verified methodologies for exploring, disclosing, and improving social performance. The 'social audits' carried out by The Body Shop, Traidcraft in the UK and now Ben and Jerry's in the USA, the 'ethical accounting' undertaken by Sbn Bank and other companies in Denmark, and the 'social balances' of Co-op Italia, all offer practical, powerful, lessons for the corporate sector. For example, the social audit method developed and practised by the New Economics Foundation and others has drawn from best practice in benchmarking, stakeholder dialogue, management and quality assurance systems, external verification procedures and the principle of continuous improvement.
>
> (PWBLF, 1996, p. 86)

BOX 4.4   BASIC PRINCIPLES FOR CIBA'S ACTIVITIES IN DEVELOPING COUNTRIES

Ciba has set forth its own principles in its policies for business activities in developing countries.

1   Ciba acts in partnership with developing countries to advance their economic potential in the interest of both partners. It fully observes the rights and duties arising out of such partnership.

2   In making business decisions (for example about products, services, technologies, and investments), Ciba considers the impact on the development of the host country in addition to economic criteria. Ciba is prepared to take a long-term view of profit in developing countries.

3   If a developing country adopts measures to protect its economy (for example, import restrictions, export obligations, or conditions of ownership) Ciba co-operates as long as partnership and adequate returns are not jeopardized in the long-term.

4   Ciba considers it a duty to advise its partners against undertakings of doubtful benefit (for example prestige projects) even if such a move proves detrimental to our economic interest.

5   Ciba has progressive social and personnel policies in developing countries, adapted to local conditions. In particular, Ciba trains employees locally if possible, and abroad if necessary; allows capable staff to gain international experience in the company; and considers nationals for executive positions.

6   The quality of Ciba's products is the same in all countries.

7   In environmental protection and safety, Ciba pursues the same objectives in all countries. Through the transfer of technology, Ciba helps make chemicals more environmentally sound and safer.

8   Information and advice are based on the same scientific knowledge in all countries, Ciba thus pursues safe and proper use of its products.

9   The prices of Ciba products are determined by particular national market and competitive conditions.

(PWBLF, 1996, p. 181)

Operations and production activities

Social and environmental audits cover operations and production activities (and other aspects of company activity outlined below). Questions which might be asked include: How safe are the company's operational processes and equipment? Is it developing policies and practices to promote cleaner production, focusing on both the inputs and outputs of the production process? What type of quality controls and assurance procedures are in place? Is the company investing management time and money in gaining quality standards such as ISO9000 and ISO7500? What are the social and environmental implications of the products being produced? What is the average product life, performance and packaging requirements? (PWBLF, 1996, p. 58).

Different types of standards aimed at improving companies' environmental and management performance are being developed at national, regional and international levels. They are becoming increasingly important to firms, particularly those firms trying to enter new markets or attract foreign investment. Many firms in Central and Eastern Europe for example have found it essential to work towards meeting international standards in order to compete and partner their western European counterparts. Thus, competition tends to drive companies to comply with codes.

Purchasing and supply chain management

Recent high profile campaigns pressuring companies to look carefully at conditions amongst suppliers have succeeded in some cases at least in encouraging companies to publicly commit to investigating suppliers. Labour conditions, including pay and safety conditions are principal concerns. Setting social, environmental and financial standards and helping suppliers, particularly small scale suppliers to meet them are also key components of many companies' codes. Sometimes companies will commit to using a certain percentage of supplies from local companies, even where foreign owned companies may be cheaper.

Distribution and retailing

The issues of distribution and retailing are becoming increasingly important to environmental campaigners. Richard Welford writing about green marketing says that:

> ... preference should be given to transportation systems which have reduced environmental costs in terms of energy consumption and pollution ... distribution channels should be established between the producer, wholesalers, retailers and customers which minimize transportation and packaging needs. These same systems can also be used to ensure that used products and packaging can be recycled.
>
> (Welford, 1995, p. 156)

In addition to these concerns which focus predominately on the environment, companies concerned with promoting themselves as good corporate citizens also make efforts to work with small-scale retailers.

Sales, marketing and customer relations

Committing a company to providing high standard goods and services in all parts of the world is a starting point. Is advertizing culturally sensitive? Do marketing efforts take on board the needs of customers in places without a powerful economic voice?

Social marketing is becoming increasingly popular and is potentially powerful in raising awareness amongst customers about development issues. Business in the Community (a UK business forum) defines social marketing as follows:

> Social or cause-related marketing is a commercial activity by which a company with an image, product or service to market, builds a relationship or partnership with a 'cause' or a number of 'causes' for mutual benefit. When it works well, everyone wins, the company, the charity and the consumer.
>
> (PWBLF, 1996, p. 59)

Examples of social marketing include:

- banks operating credit card schemes in partnership with environmental and humanitarian NGOs;
- retailing companies, such as Body Shop, Pick n' Pay in South Africa and B&Q in the UK running in-store educational and awareness-raising campaigns about environmental and social issues;
- the Canadian IMAGINE campaign where the Canadian Centre for Philanthropy mobilized hundreds of companies to endorse the value of volunteering through the country's television, radio and print media.

The PWBLF report highlights the growing importance of social marketing but also warns of the dangers.

> This is an area of great potential, but there are dangers for all partners involved if the different goals and approaches used to communicate different messages are not clearly understood by each party, and there is not a sincere and long-term commitment to creating accurate messages
>
> (PWBLF, 1996, p. 59)

4.4.2 SOCIAL INVESTMENT AND PHILANTHROPY

An enormous range of social investment vehicles are used by companies. Sometimes these activities are run through public relations or corporate affairs departments, but increasingly larger companies have dedicated community relations functions or work through social foundations. The PWBLF reports a significant change in the way companies organize their social investment programmes. Corporations are becoming less ad-hoc and undertaking more 'proactive impact assessment and stakeholder management more closely aligned to core business objectives'

(PWBLF, 1996, p. 65). This change is put down to increased pressures on corporate competitiveness and corporate governance.

> Global competitiveness is placing intense pressure on business to be more productive, efficient and innovative, and essentially to deliver 'more with less' whereas the increasingly sophisticated demands of a growing number of external stakeholder groups is putting intense pressure on business to be more responsive and responsible, and essentially to deliver 'more to more'.
>
> (PWBLF, 1996, p. 65)

Companies are creating much more sophisticated management infrastructure for their social and community investment programmes. The aim is to get maximum benefit from resources deployed both for the communities but also for the businesses themselves. As social investment programmes grow, it is becoming a higher priority for companies to try and 'add-value' to core business. Partnerships with the NGOs, local, regional and national governments and donor agencies are becoming much more common. According to the PWBLF report, companies are paying increased attention to:

- developing a more strategic approach to philanthropy and in some cases removing the term altogether and replacing it with terms such as community investment or partnership;
- creating win-win situations and mutual benefit, which offer the company a return on its investment, rather than ad hoc charitable donations;
- applying the core competencies of the business to social investment, especially the skills and energy of its employees, but also products and services, instead of simply making cash donations;
- linking corporate community investment to mainstream business strategy and interests, instead of it being a 'bolt-on'. This is most noticeable in the growing emphasis being placed on education, training and human resource development (which are the major focus of CCI activities in most companies, be they in the USA or South Africa, UK or the Philippines); and
- global strategies with localized delivery, reflecting a similar trend in the core business functions of many multinational companies.

Table 4.1 shows different 'waves' of corporate social and community investment styles.

The last of these styles (4th Wave), if translated into meaningful integration of broad social, economic and environmental goals, clearly concurs with the image of a 'new capitalism' talked about at the beginning of the section. Thus, the demarcation between philanthropy and good core business practice becomes blurred. The example given in Box 4.5 appears to be in line with this 4th Wave model.

TABLE 4.1 STYLES OF CORPORATE SOCIAL AND COMMUNITY INVESTMENT

	1st Wave	2nd Wave	3rd Wave	4th Wave
Purpose	Philanthropy	Strategic philanthropy	Community investment	Healthy business environment
Motive	Morality	Long-term self-interest	Long-term/ direct self-interest	Direct self-interest
Strategy	Ad hoc	Systematic	Strategic	Organization ownership
Staff	Administrator	Manager	Entrepreneur/ consultant	Ingrained at all management levels
Structure	Detached from business activities	Detached, but linked to business interests	Part of line structure	Integrated with business functions
Initiative	Passive	Responsive to requests in target areas	Initiating	Integrated into daily decision-making
Contribution	Mainly goods	Cash and donations skills and cash	Business resources	Embedded in profit and growth goals
Drivers	Chairman's whim	Guidelines in place	Business-linked guide-lines in place	Part of business strategy
Sustainability	One-offs	Assistance on specific issues	Nurturing and capacity building of NGOs	Ongoing part of business management/ goals and appraisals

BOX 4.5   HINDUSTAN LEVER IN INDIA

The Integrated Rural Development Programme (IRDP) was established by Hindustan Lever (HL; part of the Unilever Group of companies) in 1976 as a last effort to improve milk yields from its dairy factory. The company had purchased the factory in 1963, in response to the Indian government's call for rural industrialization. Milk was supplied by local villagers, but after ten years of co-operation, despite efforts to introduce better cattle and livestock management practices, the milk supply was so poor and erratic that the plant was operating at 50% capacity and incurring substantial losses. HL realized that the problem could only be overcome by taking a more integrated approach to tackling not only livestock management, but the underlying poverty in the area. The IRDP was therefore launched to address the following activities:

- improved dairy production through better animal husbandry and milk collection practices;
- diversification to pigs, poultry, complementary crops and dual use crops;
- development of other income generation projects;
- improved health care, especially immunization for mothers and children;
- infrastructure development, especially improving access for women and girls; and
- establishment of village development committees.

Since 1976 milk collection has increased from 15,000 to 86,000 tonnes per annum and the dairy at Etah is now one of HL's most profitable business units. Over 10% of the dairy's pre-tax profit is currently invested in the IRDP which has also attracted increased government funding. It employs over 60 staff – mostly field officers who work with the village committees and the young [Unilever Group] managers [who come on] six week secondments. From an initial six villages the programme now covers over 400, and planned to reach 700 by 1998. Not only has milk and factory production increased dramatically, but a 1991 evaluation also found improvements in other sources of village income, increased employment, literacy, health and leisure time. The company recognizes that there is still room for improvement. PLAN International recently assessed the project against the following criteria – empowerment, gender equality, sustainability, quality and learning – and found a number of shortfalls, especially in the first two criteria. The company's willingness to participate in such an evaluation indicates its commitment to continuous improvement, and increased attention is now being focused on these areas.

There can be little doubt, however, that the villagers are enjoying a better quality of life now than they were in 1976. The on-going investment of Hindustan Lever, in terms of money, management secondments, technical expertise, budgetary discipline, senior management support and influence with local government departments, has played a critical role. The fact that the company is also benefiting from the programme, both directly through increased milk yield to its factory, and indirectly through the development of its young managers, is more likely to ensure long-term continuity and sustainability of the initiative, than if it was driven purely by corporate philanthropy.

(PWBLF, 1996, p. 205)

4.4.3 PUBLIC POLICY DIALOGUE

Companies attempt to influence governments in all sorts of ways for all sorts of reasons. However, an element of this lobbying is set within the context of dialogue between different sectors of society and is directed towards defining approaches and solutions which, whilst not undermining industry, have broader concerns. Examples of this include South Africa's National Economic Development and Labour Council (see Box 4.6).

BOX 4.6 SOUTH AFRICA'S NATIONAL ECONOMIC DEVELOPMENT AND LABOUR COUNCIL (NEDLAC)

Launched in February 1995, Nedlac is a formal vehicle for dialogue on social and economic policy between the South African government, business, labour and community interests, aimed at jointly pursuing goals of growth, equity and participation. Despite a number of difficulties and disagreement on certain issues, by June 1996 Nedlac had been able to conclude seven formal agreements, including the labour relations bill, mine health and safety bill and agreements regarding the establishment of small and medium-sized enterprises. It operates through an 18 person Executive Council which meets monthly, with members drawn from all sectors, and an annual National Summit for about 300 delegates. Four chambers cover the issues of public finance and monetary policy; trade and industry; the labour market; and development, and meet on a frequent basis.

(PWBLF, 1996, p. 74)

In all areas of private and public sector agreements, there is a danger that power relations will distort outcomes so that private interests dominate to the detriment of public interests – or vice versa. This is particularly so in the area of policy dialogue. There is potentially a very fine line between private sector efforts to lobby in the interests of their commercial activities, which can have a cost to society, and efforts to engage in broader dialogue.

Conflict over these issues is important in defining the rules of the game. It is not necessarily indicative of fundamental incompatibilities between private and public sector agendas.

4.5 PROBLEMS IN PARADISE: PARTNERSHIPS, POWER AND CONFLICT

The previous section outlined ways in which public/private sector partnership can have positive outcomes. However, it is clearly important to remember that not all attempts at partnership have these positive outcomes and indeed, that the whole conceptual framework which advocates partnership needs careful consideration. There are numerous critiques, for example, of corporatist approaches, whereby powerful alliances between large business, government, unions and other key elements of civil society dominate policy making and development. Corporatism can and often has resulted in forms of development which cater to a very narrowly defined agenda.

It could be argued that conflict actually plays an important role in constructing successful partnerships. If trust is, as many argue, the linchpin of constructive engagement between different elements of society, it is almost certainly true that the space to disagree and be heard is equally vital. Hirschmann's (1970) thinking around voice, exit and loyalty is a useful tool for thinking about this (see Chapter 2).

Development management, Alan Thomas (1996) has argued, is characterized by the need to manage in the context of different and often conflicting value systems; conflict is to a large extent inevitable and should not be viewed necessarily as sign of failure. It is an integral and necessary part of the world of development and a necessary outcome of real participation by individuals and groups with different interests. Conflict, if it takes place within a context where some recognition of democratic rights exist and the need to provide responses to different interest groups is acknowledged could be viewed as a cornerstone of successful partnership. If success in promoting stable competitive market based structures often seems to rest in the ability to foster competition through co-ordination and co-operation, the role of conflict should not be forgotten.

However, there are clearly situations in which this context does not exist and in which neither constructive partnership nor healthy conflict is possible. Creating good inter-organizational practice in ways which I have outlined above is important. Good management in this sense can make an enormous difference. Understanding why and how good practice takes root in some environments and not others cannot however simply be explained by a style of management. The issue here is about how public action does or does not produce results which satisfy local, regional and national demands. One important thing to realize is that there is not simply a single universal ideal way in which private and public actors interact to achieve results (see Chapter 7).

Harriss in Chapter 10 writes about the importance of trust and social capital. Another way of thinking about conditions which facilitate productive public action is with the concepts of synergy, complementarity and embeddedness developed by Peter Evans (1996). Synergy is based both on complementary actions by government and citizens and on 'embeddedness' which refers to ties that cross the public–private divide. However, there are clearly many contexts in which synergy between public and private sectors is impossible or leads to unhealthy outcomes.

4.5.1   CONSTRUCTING COMPLEMENTARITY AND EMBEDDEDNESS; OVERCOMING 'UNRULY COMPETITION'

Central planning in the Former Soviet Union (FSU) no longer exists, but it is not clear that efforts to promote a liberal capitalist system are even managing to deliver basic economic goods to the majority of people. Particularly following the financial crash of 1998, the future of a cohesive capitalism which provides an acceptable standard of living for people looked doubtful. In Chapter 5, Moore refers to 'unruly competition' as being something which can reduce the scope for co-operation. Unruly competition can 'exacerbate bad relations between people, thereby reducing the scope for future co-operation'.

During the years of reform in the FSU, unruly competition has existed at various levels; corruption and unfair practice existed on a large scale at macro, meso and micro levels, undermining levels of social capital. Levels of social capital will clearly influence the extent to which synergy between different public and private actors can be created. In large part, unruly competition in the FSU, and elsewhere, can be related to the disintegration of co-ordinating structures which (however imperfectly) both regulated and represented actors (Burawoy, 1996). This severely limits the scope for synergy.

The FSU is, of course, far from being the only area of the world with limited prospects of creating synergistic activities on any grand scale. Writing about Africa, Brett observes

> Economic and political failure in Africa has reduced most countries to foreign dependence and many to civil war. Millions have been killed, tortured, displaced or dispossessed. Economic policy is made in Washington then inefficiently implemented by unaccountable national governments. Little now remains of the vision of an autonomous and prosperous democratic state system which legitimated the decolonization process in the 1950s and 1960s.
>
> (Brett, 1995, p. 200)

'Unruly capitalism' may not be the best framework for facilitating more equitable or sustainable forms of market based growth, but a harsh macro environment does not preclude beneficial action at the meso or micro levels. Some micro-finance initiatives illustrate this point. In the 1990s micro-finance schemes became a key strategy for poverty alleviation and in particular as a tool to increase women's income and have in some cases managed to unite private and social development targets. Micro-finance initiatives provide very small loans to people in order that they might set up as self-employed or start their own 'micro' businesses, usually defined as employing under 10 people. Well known schemes such as the Grameen Bank which lends to small groups mainly of women in Bangladesh and Banco Sol (Bolivia), have been widely replicated in the South. Such schemes are also increasingly being used as part of poverty alleviation strategies in the North. The idea is that by providing financial assistance directly to people they are able to organize themselves so that they can fit income generation into their lives. Micro-finance schemes often incorporate social development components such as training and child-care provision in order to provide more comprehensive assistance. Their ability to generate capital without recourse to donor funds gives them an independence from public structures through which most funds are channelled.

4.6 CONCLUSION

Development partnerships involving the private sector and, based on competitive markets, are an important component of development efforts. The economic presence of the private sector, the increase in capital flows to industrially developing nations and lessons from relatively successful developing regions point to the need to draw in private sector actors and for the state, private sector and civil society to act in synergy.

There are no simple correlations to be made between local programmes and initiatives and the emergence of a broader development-friendly mix of institutions based in co-operation, co-ordination and competition. Neither are there universal principles. But there clearly are ways in which micro and meso level initiatives can have broader institutional impacts and contribute to 'synergy'. The other implication of what I have said here is that in situations where official government institutions are unable or unwilling to promote more sustainable forms of markets, international donor agencies can try and support initiatives that can work around macro level constraints. Current emphasis on partnership and government to government collaboration is unlikely to totally overshadow the potential benefits of this manner of working. However, current research and analysis (Evans, 1996; Burawoy, 1996; Fox, 1994) points to the importance of institutions which can 'scale up' local efforts as being key to creating the synergistic relations necessary in creating stable market based competitive organizations. 'Scaling up' is likely to include local, regional and/or national governments. Looking at the various ways in which the public sector, at all levels, and civil society organizations can act to facilitate synergistic activity and encourage stable competitive markets is currently a key area for development policy makers.

5 COMPETITION WITHIN AND BETWEEN ORGANIZATIONS

MICK MOORE

5.1 INTRODUCTION

Recent developments in the theory and practice of public management include the increasing importance of 'competition' – typified by what is often termed the New Public Management (NPM). This is a movement to change the organizational and policy framework within which public agencies operate. Decisions about how public agencies provide services are shaped by market-like considerations of efficiency, cost-saving, the danger of being out-competed by rivals, etc. NPM also involves a radical extension within the public sector of the scope of competition, material incentives, contracting to service-providers, and similar market-like practices. It developed in the 1980s, mainly in the United Kingdom and New Zealand, where it has been promoted consistently (Schick, 1996, provides an excellent summary of NPM in New Zealand). NPM has been especially attractive to governments of anglophone countries, but it is gradually making converts in many other parts of the world, and has for example, been extensively introduced into the management of the health, education and social security sectors in Chile (Angell, 1996; Larranaga, 1997; and Rounds Parry, 1997). NPM is *the* big new idea in public management. The same concept also goes by other names such as 'managerialism', 'market-based public administration', or 'entrepreneurial government'. There is an extensive literature on this topic. Hughes (1994) for example, provides a very useful introduction to the principles and historical context (but see also Hood, 1991; Lane, 1995; and Chapter 7).

The notion of inter-organizational competition lies at the core of NPM. So it would make sense for a chapter dealing with competition to focus on the nature, strengths and weaknesses of NPM. Indeed this chapter pays considerable attention to the NPM concept of inter-organizational competition – competition for 'contracts' to provide public services with government funding. However, this type of competition, called *tender-competition* represents only one of two major forms of competition to which we should be looking as means of improving the effectiveness and efficiency of public organizations. The other type, *prize-competition*, involves the recurrent award of prizes, both material and non-material, to organizations that perform particularly well in terms of such criteria as efficiency, service, enterprise or innovation. Prize-competition is found widely, in both public and private organizations. However it has not as yet received as much attention from scholars and theorists as tender-competition.

Prize-competition and tender-competition are distinct in principle. In practice, each comprises a diverse menu of options rather than a standard package. Some variants of the one form have much in common with variants of the other. Elements of tender-competition and elements of prize-competition are often complementary: the one can reinforce the other. The challenge for practitioners is to find workable mixtures of the two forms.

We will look at these forms in more detail in later sections. First however, in Section 5.2, I will briefly dispose of a couple of issues of formal definition: the meaning of the terms 'inter-organizational' and 'the public sector' respectively. Section 5.3 contains much more meat: a conceptual exploration of the various dimensions of the competitive process, and the analytical basis for the distinction I have drawn between tender-competition and prize-competition. In Section 5.4 we come down to earth, looking at the kinds of inter-organizational competition that are actually found in the public sector in developing and transitional economies. The benefits of competition in the public sector are discussed in Section 5.5, and the costs in Section 5.6. We will look at the scope for introducing tender-competition in Section 5.7 and for prize-competition in Section 5.8. Section 5.9 draws together some conclusions about competition within and between organizations and the form it takes.

5.2 SOME FORMAL DEFINITIONS

What is meant here by 'inter-organizational competition'? Organizations are not discrete, homogenous entities. All large organizations have other organizations 'nested' within them. The 'military' may comprise an army, an airforce and a navy. The army in turn may comprise a number of battalions; battalions are formed from regiments; regiments are divided into smaller units, down to a platoon. Civilian public organizations are 'nested' in the same way, often with more ambiguity about the legal and authority relations between different units and levels. A ministry might have a number of departments under its direct control, and some authority and responsibility over a number of 'boards', 'authorities' or 'agencies' that are also partly independent or answerable to other organizations. Within each department, board or agency are nested divisions, directorates, bureaux, sections, ranges, circles, offices, etc. The basis of these divisions may be function (e.g. highway construction versus transport planning) or it may be territory (provinces, regions, districts etc.). Inter-organizational competition may take place at any level: between ministries; between 'divisions' (functional or territorial) within the same ministry or in different ministries; between 'units' in the same division, etc. The meaning of 'organiz-ation' in this chapter is therefore dependent on context. For example in some cases, the Ministry of Labour is an organization. At other times we may consider as separate organizations (a) the Employment Agency and (b) the Vocational Training Department, both of them components of the Ministry. For yet other purposes, local Employment Offices under the Employment Agency may be treated as separate units. (I am not dealing here with the question of how far it is feasible to combine high levels of competition inside organizations with high levels of competition between them, see Hood, 1996, p. 217-8).

What do I mean by 'inter-organizational competition in the public sector'? I mean any competition in which public sector organizations are involved. In some cases, all major roles in a competitive process might be performed by public sector organizations: for example, where the Ministry of Education offers all public universities and polytechnics the opportunity to tender for contracts to retrain unemployed graduates as maths and science teachers. It remains 'competition in the public sector', by my definition, if (a) the Ministry also opens the tender to private colleges or companies, or even, (b) if it restricts bidding to these private sector organizations. We are still dealing with attempts to use inter-organizational competition to improve public services, and a public agency is involved in policy-making and financing roles.

5.3 WHAT IS COMPETITION?

Competition is all around us. It takes many different forms and occurs in many different contexts. Yet we seem to lack general conceptual frameworks to help us think about varieties of competition. Most of the ideas about competition that influence public sector reformers come from economics. The economists' conception of competition is narrow. It relates almost entirely to competition in markets, and involves some very restrictive assumptions about the means used by competitors to make the market work in their favour. The most fundamental conceptual distinction that economists make between types of competition is between (a) a situation where all competitors ('firms') use the same technology (so-called 'neo-classical competition'); and (b) one where they compete mainly by seeking technological superiority over rivals (so-called 'Schumpeterian competition'). Both are variants of market competition. Although we normally assume that economics embodies a relatively advanced understanding of competition, it has been plausibly argued that standard economic theory 'is less a theory of competition than a theory of decentralization – that is, a theory of how atomized decisional units, without any mechanism of central co-ordination other than the free market system of prices, can produce outcomes that are optimal for the collective (Moe, 1984, p. 741). Rather than starting from economists' ideas on the subject, let us instead begin with a set of concepts to help us think about varieties of competition in the broad sense of the term. I initially developed these concepts in response to a lack of anything suitable in the literature.

A standard definition of competition is 'rivalry between two or more actors over a limited resource or reward'. 'Competition is a rivalry between individuals (or groups or nations), and it arises whenever two or more parties strive for something that all cannot obtain' (*New Palgrave Dictionary of Economics*, p. 531). That is very abstract: it places on the same level the manoeuverings of Microsoft and a small number of rival companies to dominate the world market for Internet software; squabbles between two toddlers for the attentions of their parent; the strivings of thousands of firms to increase their share of the US garment market; a friendly snooker match; continuing contests between gangs for control of the drugs trade; and a host of other behaviours that appear to have little else in common beyond 'rivalry'. We need some general concepts to distinguish different categories of competition. To do this, we need to focus not on *behaviour*, but on differences in the *context* within which competitors act out their rivalry. One could list dozens of types of competitive contexts. It is easiest to explain the significance of context by describing four standard, abstract roles that may be performed in competitive processes: *competitors*; *referees* (who enforce the rules); *judges* (who rank the competitors); and *prize donors* (who determine the rewards for success). The conclusion, to anticipate, is that some types of competition are more complex than others: market-competition (the inspiration for tender-competition) requires only *competitors* and *referees*, while tender-competition requires *competitors*, *referees* and *judges*, and prize-competition requires the performance of all four roles.

There are by definition *competitors* in any competition. Most competitive situations involve a *referee* role – a person, institution or set of persons/institutions that decide whether or not the rules of the competition have been broken, and can sanction offenders. In the case of a football match in the UK, the front-line *referee* role is performed by the referee and the linesmen, with back-up from Football Association disciplinary committees for serious offences (in cricket the front-line *referees* are called umpires). In the cases of market competition or democratic electoral contests, sets of legal and regulatory institutions perform the *referee* role in a diffused and decentralized fashion. For example, market competition is regulated by

(a) civil and criminal law (involving legislatures, judiciaries, lawyers, police, etc.);

(b) specialized institutions of economic regulation, such as anti-monopoly bodies, stock exchange councils and associations of insurance companies; and

(c) public and private arbitration organizations.

Where there are effective *referees*, we may talk of *ruly competition* – competition that follows accepted rules, and is therefore to some degree predictable and controllable. *Unruly competition* is not only unpredictable and uncontrollable, but may also be violent and generate continuing bad feeling to a greater extent than ruly competition. Unruly competition is rarely productive or desirable, for example, civil wars; the rivalry between siblings for parental attention; or competition between the Zonex Oil Corporation and GasCo Inc. for control, through bribery, over the government of Oilrichstan.

Many competitions require only *competitors* and *referees*. No further roles need to be performed if two functions – ranking the competitors, and determining the reward(s) for success – are fully determined within the competitive process (always assuming *ruly competition*). Let us take first the ranking function. In the case of 'ideal' market competition, the rankings are made automatically, in the form of relative profit levels, as a result of the interaction of competing firms and their customers. Democratic electoral competition involves the same kind of automaticity, as does a football match, whose outcome reflects simply the interaction of two teams on the field. The *judge* role is required where the ranking does not follow automatically from the behaviour and interaction of the *competitors*; *judgement* is required. This is true of design competitions; talent contests; 'employee-of-the-month' awards; and, most relevant to present purposes, both tender-competition and prize-competition in the public sector. The *judge* role is distinct in principle from that of the *referee*, although the two may be (partially) combined in practice. For instance, in boxing matches, the referee in the ring enforces the rules, and the panel of judges allocate the points that normally determine the result. However, in the case of a knock-out, the referee takes over the *judge* role and declares the winner.

All competitions are for a *reward* of some kind. There is a continuum in the extent to which the nature and level of the rewards are set in an automatic or a discretionary fashion. In 'ideal' market competition, this process is automatic: no agent outside the market process can affect the distribution of rewards. At least, not without making some radical institutional changes, e.g. in taxation systems or anti-monopoly policy, to the extent of changing the 'system'. At the other end of the scale, some rewards are necessarily set on a discretionary basis, i.e. are subject to recurrent decisions by an external agent. What will be the prize this year for the winner of the Grand Prix motor race? How will we award the 'employee of the month'? A bonus? A day's leave? Or just the honour? Let us call these more discretionary rewards *prizes*. In such cases there is by definition a *prize donor* role – a person or organization that determines the nature or level of the prize for varying degrees of competitive success. There is no *prize* and no *prize donor* in market-competition, or in tender-competition, where the nature of the *reward* – the contract to perform the service – is intrinsic to the competition. A *prize donor* is required, by definition, in the case of prize-competition. This distinction between *prizes* and other types of reward is in practice very nuanced: there are *prize* elements in many rewards.

Table 5.1 helps to summarize the ideas presented above and to illustrate some of the implications. The most important is that market competition according to the economists' model – that provides much of the inspiration behind NPM and tender-competition – is distinctive in two related senses: (a) it involves only two main roles (*competitor* and *referee*, not *judge* or *prize donor*), but (b) is generally assumed by economists to be ruly, although there are frequently strong temptations for competitors to break the rules. Firms do not generally go to the extremes of unruly competition. They do not assassinate the chief executives of their rivals, sabotage their

TABLE 5.1 ROLES REQUIRED IN VARIOUS TYPES OF COMPETITION				
	Competitors	Referee	Judge	Prize donor
Civil war	✔			
Market competition, or friendly tennis match	✔	✔		
Tender-competition, or friendly boxing match	✔	✔	✔	
Professional tennis match	✔	✔		✔
Prize-competition	✔	✔	✔	✔

computer networks, or bribe banks suddenly to cut off their credit (such things do happen in the commercial sector, notably in some of the successor states to the Soviet Union). However, there are many less drastic ways in which firms in practice can and do break the rules of market competition. Tender-competition and prize-competition in the public sector are more complex than market competition in terms of the number of roles to be performed. A larger number of roles suggests a greater possibility of the competitive process producing adverse consequences if it becomes *unruly* (see Section 5.6).

5.4 FORMS OF INTER-ORGANIZATIONAL COMPETITION IN THE PUBLIC SECTOR

This chapter is about the productive uses of inter-organizational competition. We need to ground the discussion in types of inter-organizational competition that actually exist. I have listed below seven types of inter-organizational competition frequently found in the public sector. I begin with those that are (a) often more harmful than useful and (b) more widespread in developing and transitional countries than in wealthy nations. The list is not intended to be exhaustive. It serves rather to:

- illustrate the range of types of inter-organizational competition that exist;
- demonstrate that some forms are definitely undesirable; and
- show that some have consequences that are mixed and difficult to determine.

Note that only at number seven (Section 5.4.7) do we begin to discuss types of inter-organizational competition that are at all similar to those advocated by supporters of NPM (i.e. tender-competition) – and prize-competition does not enter into this list at all. The point is that there is much more inter-organizational competition in the public sector than we tend to assume; most accepted concepts and theories assume that the public sector is – or ought normally to be – co-ordinated in a hierarchical fashion. Competition is assumed deviant – but as the following list shows it is not!

5.4.1 COMPETITION FOR CASH

It is inevitable that public organizations should compete for financial allocations when government budgets are being drafted. However, in many poor countries there is considerable competition for public money in a more direct sense of the term: for the actual cash or bank credit that public managers need to pay staff salaries, purchase equipment, and generally perform the activities expected of them. I am talking of situations where, say, municipal finance officers cannot expect to obtain their quarterly cheques from the provincial government unless they (a) go personally to the provincial finance office, perhaps accompanied by influential local politicians, and find some means of persuading the officials there to issue a cheque; and then (b) go to the bank and negotiate the conversion of the cheque into cash. At each point they will find other municipal finance officers competing for the same scarce money; some may have to wait long to get a cheque, and others may have to wait until there is sufficient money in the provincial government's account for the bank to honour the cheque. This type of competition can become acute due to a mixture of circumstances: weak budgeting procedures; shortage of public revenue; and the acceptance of the practice that public money is released only in return for bribes. It encourages public officials to depend on private business, especially government contractors, to advance money to pay urgent bills, and is likely to be accompanied by corruption. The consequences are clearly malign. They include: general uncertainty about the timing of government programmes; long delays in the completion of capital projects; and reduced morale of public servants who can never be sure when they will receive their salaries.

5.4.2 COMPETITION FOR COMPETENT SENIOR STAFF

In many of the poorest countries, a high proportion of government expenditure is financed by foreign aid. Within individual recipient countries, aid is disbursed by a large number of different donors – national (bilateral), multilateral (UN agencies, World Bank, regional development banks, European Union etc.), and NGOs – that each have their own objectives, policies, procedures and, above all, their 'own' projects. In 1991-5, the 48 countries that (a) were classified by the World Bank as 'low income econ-omies' and (b) had populations of a million people or more, received aid amounting to an average of 17% of gross domestic product (GDP) from an average of 29 official aid donors per recipient country (figures from OECD, 1997). Individual donor agencies are generally concerned that their own projects should receive attention and priority from the recipient government: good quality senior staff; timely release of the matching funds allocated to the project by the recipient government; and the patronage and support of senior politicians and public servants to solve problems. To achieve these objectives, they are willing: to pay generous 'allowances' of various kinds (including various kinds of meeting, travel and posting allowances, and paid overseas visits for study or education purposes) to competent and influential local public servants attached to their projects; to employ these same people directly, on high salaries, as project staff; or give them jobs as programme officers in local aid offices because they have much better local knowledge and local contacts than expatriate aid management staff, who typically change posts every two years. In countries where (a) public service salaries are low; (b) educational levels are poor and there is a scarcity of competent senior public servants; and (c) aid donors fund a significant fraction of government activities, there can be intense competition between different government agencies and aid donors for the services of competent local senior public servants. These excess demands are partly met by the rapid transfer of staff between posts. While this system might provide senior public servants with some incentives to perform well by some criteria, the negative effects are more evident. They include: the instability of public policy and practice that results from continuous, rapid turnover of senior staff; national policy incoherence arising from influence of diverse aid donors; and the strong implicit incentives to design and manage aid projects such that they become attractive to senior public servants (Wilson, 1993).

5.4.3 COMPETITION FOR FOREIGN AID (DUAL COMPETITION)

Even where foreign aid does not lead to excessive competition for the services of senior public servants, it tends to promote competition between government agencies in the recipient countries for aid funds. The poorer the country, the more valuable aid funds are and the more intense the competition for them. This is not the same as the 'normal' competition between government agencies for larger budgets – and, sometimes, the enlarged responsibilities to justify those budgets. There is no doubt that such competition takes place. However, the evidence suggests that it is less intense in practice than is assumed in some of the more hostile critiques of public bureaucracy. Public organizations frequently decline opportunities to expand their scope of operations and budgets (Gibson, 1990). Where foreign aid is involved, the key difference is that spending agencies have scope to obtain funds from more than one source. Although aid is nominally allocated only at the request of one central agency within recipient governments (normally in the Ministry of Finance), in practice all aid donors have some capacity to stimulate and promote the kinds of activities and projects they prefer to fund. In some situations, notably those sketched out in the previous paragraph, where governments do not exercise coherent central control over policy, budgets or personnel, individual aid donors may have considerable autonomy to pursue their own goals. Similarly, spending agencies within recipient governments may have scope to do the same by trying to obtain funds from both the central treasury and several aid donors. There is a *dual competition* going on: between funders for good projects to fund, and between spending agencies for funding sources. Other interested parties, such as local or foreign companies interested in procurement or construction contracts, may play important roles in promoting and organizing these competitive processes.

At the national level, this kind of dual competition means, for example, that the Ministry of Health may be able to obtain the national network of cold stores for vaccines that it wants because, if the Americans will not fund them as part of their Health Care Rehabilitation Project, and the Danes will not include them in their Primary Health Development Programme, the Japanese will be willing to fund them under their Virulent Disease Eradication Initiative. It is easier for spending agencies to play this game if aid is given as a grant, with no local financing contribution expected. Then the main obstacles to be overcome may be simply the abstract policy concerns of the Ministry of Finance about the overall level of public spending or the wisdom of particular expenditures. Such abstract concerns may carry little weight in the face of a spending agency supporting a project, an aid donor willing to finance it, and one or more companies promoting it in the expectation of receiving contracts to help implement it. Note that this kind of competition can be relatively *unruly*, especially in poorer countries with many aid donors who are poorly co-ordinated and see themselves in competition for good projects.

A more ruly form of dual competition takes place in more restricted territorial arenas, notably in the context of what are most commonly termed IRDPs (Integrated Rural Development Programmes). IRDPs involve block funding, normally from an aid donor, for a range of activities in one territorial jurisdiction, often a district. IRDP funding is additional to normal government funding, and typically may be allocated and re-allocated flexibly between different activities and sectors. Much of the justification for the IRDP model lies in the institutionalization of flexible funding arrangements that are adaptable to local circumstances and experience. Arrangements for allocating IRDP funding among different local activities vary widely. There is always the potential for competition between funders – normal government and IRDP channels respectively – for activities to support. Both the IRDP authorities and the Ministry of Agriculture may want to increase funds for the agricultural extension service if it is likely to make good use of money. More important, there is scope for competition among the local offices of government agencies for IRDP funding. Most local offices will want to make a case for IRDP funding to top up their normal allocation from sectoral ministry sources. This competition may be ruly and productive if IRDP funds genuinely are allocated on a 'performance' basis. That will normally involve a relatively independent IRDP office, that has some autonomy from the recipient government and local politics, and is responsive to, and to some degree protected by, the donor agency. Such arrangements have often been derided as 'rent-a-district' and condemned for 'bypassing' normal government structures and hindering the development of effective, coherent central policymaking in weak states. These criticisms are valid in some circumstances. At the same time, this kind of competition has been observed to encourage district-level government offices to find ways of becoming more innovative and of better serving the needs of the rural poor in a cost effective fashion. For example, I found in Sri Lanka in the 1980s that, through these competition mechanisms, IRDPs were at the forefront of implementing several rural development innovations, including low-cost feeder roads, effective sanitation systems for resident plantation workers, social forestry and effective procedures for rehabilitating small scale irrigation systems (Moore, 1992). There is a discussion in Section 5.5 of the ways in which line managers can take advantage of these situations to stimulate inter-organizational competition on an informal basis.

5.4.4 NGO COMPETION FOR FUNDING

It is often said that, especially in some of the poorer developing countries, NGOs (non-government organizations) are 'replacing the state', i.e. increasingly performing roles often thought to be the responsibility of government: education, health care, and agricultural extension. This is possible only because NGOs are publicly funded, either by national governments or, more frequently, through official and unofficial aid agencies. To the extent that funders make some kind of conscious choice between funding (a) NGOs rather than state agencies or (b) one NGO rather than another, these processes do involve inter-organizational competition. The competition is however mainly implicit and informal. It is unusual for funders to call for tenders in a formal fashion. NGOs tend to espouse the values of co-operation and complementarity, and rarely have been willing to enter into explicit competitions for contracts. They are also typically free of strong pressures to practice efficient and transparent corporate governance: governments regulate NGOs largely with political considerations in mind, and collective self-regulation is almost unknown. NGOs practice a wide range of accounting short-cuts in their financial reporting to donors (Fowler, 1997). Insofar as NGOs are funded partly through processes of inter-organizational competition, this competition is generally weak and probably not very effective.

5.4.5 GOVERNMENTAL COMPETITION FOR GENERATING FUNDS

In China in particular – and to a lesser extent in some states of the former Soviet Union – government agencies have considerable freedom to generate their own incomes by using their resources to attract customers in completely new economic activities. To the extent that military units, county governments, and branches of the Ministry of Labour are all trying, for example, to go into the property development business, they are all competing against one another. Such competition may be more efficient in an economic sense than similar 'public entrepreneurship' under more monopolistic conditions. Similarly, a 'competitive corruption' system, where several state agencies or individuals effectively bid against one another to take advantage of corruption opportunities, is probably more in the public interest than monopolistic corruption (see Doner and Ramsay, 1997, p. 250-3). However, there are grave doubts about the political consequences of permitting state agencies to bypass in this way any kind of political accountability for the resources that they obtain and use. Such accountability is a central principle of democracy; its absence encourages the centralization and abuse of political and economic power.

5.4.6 REGIONAL COMPETITION FOR PRIVATE INVESTMENT

There is a form of inter-organizational competition in the public sector that is steadily becoming more intense in most countries, largely as a result of changes in the global political economy, and partly independently of the policies or preferences of governments: competition between territorial jurisdictions for private investment. Several factors interact to intensify this competition, notably: active public policies to reduce barriers to international trade and capital movements; continuing reductions in the costs of transport, communications and data processing; increasing competition from foreign goods and services in 'national' markets; and the growing willingness of the people who control capital to use their enhanced bargaining power by relocating – or threatening to relocate – production activities. Competition to attract capital takes place at both national and sub-national levels. At the national level, Brazil competes with South Africa, Vietnam and many other countries to attract new foreign investment and to retain the investment it has. The threat to Brazil is not simply that Ford, for example, will establish its new Latin American vehicle assembly plant in Peru or Uruguay rather than in Brazil. It is also that Brazilian companies manufacturing sports shoes will begin to 'out-source' some components from Belize or Honduras, rather than producing them in Brazil. However, it is increasingly questionable whether this kind of competition should be viewed as mainly taking place between *nations*. What is often at stake is, for example, the question of whether companies will maintain or expand their production facilities in one *city* or *region* rather than another. The real competition is increasingly between the São Paulo and Recife industrial regions within Brazil, the Johannesburg area of South Africa, the industrial regions of Illinois, etc. It is at the level of cities and regions that companies make known their interest in investing in new plant or in closing down existing factories. It is here that negotiations take place, bluffs are offered and called, and decisions are made. The government of Dearborn County, Illinois agrees to exempt MotorParts Company from local taxes for five years if it will promise not to reduce employment below current levels. The Recife Industrial Authority offers tax exemption and a tailor-made industrial training programme for local workers to bring them up to the skill level required by the company if it will relocate there. The Welsh Development Authority offers all this plus an excellent living environment for executives and immediate access to the European market. It is increasingly difficult for local territorial authorities to avoid being drawn into this bidding process: as more authorities and companies play the game, those who stand aside are likely to be the losers. There are clearly benefits to such competition: municipal, city, metropolitan and regional governments are paying increasing attention to providing the physical infrastructure, human capital, physical and human environment and administrative efficiency needed to attract and retain private investment. At the same time, this type of competition is especially likely to produce what we might call *disabled competitors:* competitors who are unable to stay in the competition because they lack the resources to do so. In the case of market competition, economists assume that the *disabling process* is generally positive: it eliminates unfit firms and allows their resources (capital, employees) to be used by more efficient enterprises. In the case of investment compe-tition between territorial jurisdictions, we cannot be so confident that the net result is positive. *Disabled* industrial areas that fail to get new investment – and therefore lack the economic base (a) to raise sufficient taxes to invest in infrastructure or (b) to retain their skilled, educated and enterprizing people – still contain large numbers of poor people who may find it very difficult to obtain housing and jobs elsewhere. A city in decline cannot be liquidated as if it were a bankrupt firm.

5.4.7 TENDER-COMPETITION

All governments routinely issue tenders, i.e. invitations to other agencies, public or private, to bid to provide a specific service: to extend the airport runway; rehabilitate a section of road; re-equip the electricity generation stations; re-stock the Government Supplies Office with pens; provide ammunition for the armed forces; import scarce or rationed foods, etc. Bids are normally sealed. After they are opened, decisions about awarding the tender are made according to some mixture of cost and quality criteria. This is tender-competition. In market economies, governments depend relatively heavily on tendering. It is less common in statist or state socialist systems. Under statism/state socialism, individual public agencies (a) are relatively self-sufficient; (b) obtain external services from other public agencies on a non-competitive, administered basis; and (c) if they do tender out for services, accept bids only from other public agencies. For example, urban water supply companies in Vietnam normally have a large 'in-house' capacity to do construction work; and, insofar as they contract construction services from outside, they have little or no choice among a small number of state construction companies. NPM theorists advocate a system of political economy for the public sector that is the complete opposite of statist/state socialist arrangements: one that involves substituting contractual relations for relations of hierarchy or command within and among public organizations. More concretely, the NPM ideal involves three key *organizational* principles: (a) public organizations should be divided into relatively small, discrete, independent units on the basis of clearly-defined core functions; (b) management, evaluation and incentive systems should encourage each unit to focus on the efficient performance of its core functions; and (c) public agencies should depend as far as possible on market transactions and limited term contracts to obtain the resources and services they need to perform their tasks.

5.4.8 NPM AND TENDER-COMPETITION

NPM may be seen in part as a set of arrangements to promote tendering. It involves more tender-competition than is currently practiced in market economies – and much more than has been the rule, at least until recently, in most developing and transitional economies. NPM also involves expanding tender-competition into areas where it has so far been little practiced. Readers of British newspapers are becoming used to seeing invitations to tender, for example, to provide education services in prisons. These advertisements would appear shocking in many countries. There is a great deal of variation between national and local governments in the kinds of activities for which they routinely issue tenders. Some governments have their own construction companies that undertake large and small public construction projects on a negotiated basis; other governments depend heavily on tendering. Some have central workshops that make school furniture; others procure from private firms through tenders. However, there are some basic similarities in the kinds of public functions that are rarely tendered out in any country: those that involve (a) large, permanent labour forces undertaking standardized, routine activities and (b) control and use of extensive physical assets, especially buildings. These may be thought of as 'post office' functions: post offices were typically the earliest big civilian public employer in most states, and have been models for the organization of civilian public services generally. Other contemporary examples of 'post office' organizations include education, agricultural extension, pension payments and social security administration generally. By contrast, tendering has been more common in the case of temporary, sporadic or short-term activities that involve putting together very specific resources: large specialized construction projects; the supply of more complex manufactured products (pens rather than school furniture); and irregular imports of foodgrains to meet unpredictable shortages. NPM has had a significant impact in those countries where governments have taken it seriously because it has involved the extension of tender-competition into 'post office' activities where it has rarely been practiced before. It involves not only office cleaning and hospital laundry, but also the ownership and management of physical office facilities, the maintenance of military vehicles, the provision of payroll services, the issuing of driving licences, the paying of pensions, and the provision of job placement services for the unemployed. The extension of tender-competition in developing and transitional countries need not be so radical, at least initially. There are good reasons why it should be tried first in relatively peripheral activities like office cleaning and hospital laundry. They include above all issues of honesty, fairness and corruptibility. The award of government tenders is already one of the prime sources – often *the* prime source – of large scale corruption in developing and transitional countries. Any proposal to extend the scope of tender-competition has to be assessed in the light of the danger of creating more corruption opportunities.

5.5 THE BENEFITS OF COMPETITION

The conceptual arguments about potential benefits of inter-organizational competition are straightforward. They concern the ways in which competition might lead to improved organizational performance, through two different kinds of mechanisms: *incentive mechanisms* and *intelligence mechanisms*.

Incentive mechanisms are the most familiar and the most important in practice. They are all variants of the case that organizations will generally perform better when faced with competition because (a) the consequences of losing are unwelcome or (b) the prospects of winning a prize are attractive. In what ways do organizations attempt to achieve better performance in the face of competition? We can usefully categorize their responses along a continuum. The least fundamental response is simply to try a little harder. For a city waste disposal service, this might include, for example, paying closer attention to maintenance schedules for waste collection vehicles so that they are out of service less frequently and collection schedules are better observed. A more substantial response is to reallocate the resources available to improve overall performance. In the waste disposal case, this might mean introducing a separate 'on-demand' service with purpose-built vehicles for large commercial and industrial firms that have special needs, or introducing a night collection service in the town centre to make more continuous use of equipment and avoid traffic delays. The most radical response is to introduce a different technology to deal with the problem: for example, a shift from using waste for landfill to a combination of mandatory recycling and incineration. Note that, for *incentive mechanisms* to work in the case of tender-competition, it is not always necessary that competition should be taken to the stage of actually issuing a tender, and calling for bids. The *credible* threat this will happen unless the (monopoly) service provider improves its performance may be sufficient in itself. The emphasis is however on the word *credible*: some attempts to introduce competition-like mechanisms into the public sector in poor countries have failed because they were formally accepted by governments to satisfy the demands of international financial institutions, and were not credible locally: the people involved did not expect anyone else to take them seriously. Shirley and Xu (1997) explain that this has been a major reason why 'performance contracts' between governments and public enterprises in poor countries rarely have been effective in improving public enterprise performance.

Incentive mechanisms bear directly on competitors. *Intelligence mechanisms* rather operate indirectly through organizations that are 'purchasing' services from other organizations and face problems in discovering whether their suppliers are efficient and cost-effective. Purchasers face these problems when they are engaged in long term, monopolistic relations with suppliers who provide customized services or products that are not generally available on the market. The problems arise in both private and public sectors. Suppose that Truck Manufacturers Ltd. buy all their supplies of high performance carburettors from one sub-contractor, CarbCo. Even if CarbCo won the original tender by being the most efficient, how does Truck Manufacturers Ltd. know, four years later, that CarbCo still gives them the best deal available, and has carefully kept up with all recent advances in materials and engineering techniques for high performance carburettors? Since only CarbCo makes this particular kind of carburettor, there is no market price that can be used as a reference point. Similarly, Christchurch City Council purchases park maintenance services from its own Parks and Gardens Department. How does it know what represents a reasonable annual budget? The Council may try to apply some national norms of annual costs per hectare. But the Director of the Parks and Gardens Department might explain that costs appear high in Christchurch because its gardens are highly fragmented and dispersed and therefore costly; because he works to an unusually high standard, at the request of the City Council, in the interests of the local tourist industry; because the semi-tropical plants that he grows in this marginal climate are unusually expensive to purchase and maintain; and because experienced, qualified workers are unusually scarce and expensive locally. Who is to judge these and the many other arguments that suppliers will advance to explain their apparent high costs? In this situation of what economists call bilateral monopoly, information on costs and alternatives is a scarce and valuable commodity that suppliers try to keep secret from purchasers.

Purchasers may try many ways of obtaining independent information on costs and alternatives. One of the more powerful means is to create *intelligence mechanisms* through organizing competition among actual or potential suppliers. This can be achieved by allocating supply contracts among several suppliers simultaneously, so that performances can be compared; or by engaging more frequently in open tendering to give new suppliers an opportunity to compete.

5.6 THE COSTS OF COMPETITION

The benefits of competition have been summarized under two terms: incentive and intelligence mechanisms. By contrast, the costs of competition are more diverse and are incurred through a wider range of mechanisms. We can classify them into five main categories, but the impacts of each depend very much on specific circumstances:

5.6.1 RESOURCE WASTAGE

Competition can lead to the waste of resources through four main mechanisms:

1 *Unruly competition* in particular leads to the direct destruction of resources: in war or when, for example, two rival lawyers diminish their professional reputations by spreading rumours about one another.
2 Other resources may be used fruitlessly when too many people or organizations invest in trying to win a competition in which very few

will achieve success. This is especially likely in the case of tender-competition, for those who are not awarded the tender get nothing for their effort. However, to the extent that they are then better equipped to compete for other similar tenders, they might be said to obtain some benefit – and society as a whole to obtain even more. Note that prize-competition generally leads to a more positive outcome. To the extent, for example, that many police stations try to work better with local communities in the hope of achieving the top grade in the city's annual community relations assessment. Nothing is wasted and society is better off – provided that undue effort has not gone into achieving a good community relations score at the expense of more important but less visible police work.

3   Other resources may be wasted when *competitors* use unintended or illegitimate means to influence *judges* and *referees* in their favour. The mildest and most common cases involve competitors concentrating on 'assessable' activities to the neglect of other important functions, e.g. police working to establish good relations with local communities by ceasing to monitor local criminals who commit their burglaries else-where. However, every performance assessment system potentially re-sults in this kind of 'goal displacement' effect; one should not identify it as a specific cost of competition. A 'goal displacement' effect more specific to competition would be, for example, the financing of a major public relations and image-building campaign by a company that held a local healthcare contract, and wanted to bring political pressure to ensure its renewal. In practice, the most serious kinds of 'goal displacement' involve *competitors* bribing *judges* or *referees*; this is much more likely to be a problem in the case of tender-competition because the potential rewards are much higher than in the case of prize-competition.

4   Compared with more traditional public service systems, competition – especially tender-competition, and NPM more generally – involve higher 'transactions costs', i.e. the costs of defining clearly the pur-poses of public agencies; of measuring and evaluating performance; of organizing and awarding contracts and tenders, etc. Indeed, in econ-omists' terms, *the* main question about NPM is whether it produces efficiency savings that outweigh these increased transactions costs.

5.6.2 DISTORTING THE RULES

The openness of *judges* and *referees* to bribery may have wider conse-quences beyond the particular awards that are made corruptly: the encour-agement of corruption in general, and the implicit incentives for those in authority make the (tender) competition process non-transparent so that they might more easily benefit from bribes. This kind of process can negate the potential efficiency gains from introducing competition, and is the major problem to be faced in most poor countries.

5.6.3 UNDERMINING TRUST AND CO-OPERATION

1   Competition – especially *unruly competition* – can stimulate jealousies and exacerbate bad relations between people, thereby reducing the scope for future co-operation. This is especially the case if competition is perceived not to have been fairly refereed or judged. If it is believed that the annual award and bonus for the best local tax office was actually given on political rather than merit grounds, the entire Revenue Service may be demotivated. Prize-competition has a particularly high moral component, and is therefore especially likely to have perverse consequences if *judges* or *referees* are believed not to have behaved honestly.

2   Competition can also undermine trust and co-operation in a more diffuse way, by generating a fear that the information gained about one organization in the course of co-operation with another may be used against it in some way. For example, the staff of a municipal water company may not share with the provincial water resources agency its research on projected local patterns of water demand if it anticipates that the two organizations will become competitors for a contract to manage the local water supply system. Such problems of commercial secrecy are routine in the private sector; in the past there has been a general expectation that information is widely shared in the public sector.

3   The standard employment contract in the public service in most countries has in recent history given public employees a high degree of job security and some assurance of promotion on the basis of years of service and of overall competence rather than specific job performance. This has been justified on the grounds that this (a) creates loyalty to the public service; (b) generates a public service *esprit de corps*, involving among other things considerable co-operation and adherence to a common, understood set of norms and procedures; and (c) increases the chances that public servants will act in the long term public interest in cases where this conflicts strongly with their short term private interests. The introduction of competition tends to reduce expectations of a guaranteed career and creates a more diverse public service culture. The advocates of NPM believe that these changes will improve public service performance. There are however costs, and the overall balance is not clear.

5.6.4 DESTABILIZING EFFECTS

Competition can impose costs by inducing uncertainty where certainty is valuable. For example, if contracts to supply computer services to public employment agencies are too competitive – i.e. broken up into a large number of small contracts that are re-tendered frequently – then no computer company will feel sufficiently secure to invest in developing the software and expertise needed to manage employment agencies more efficiently.

5.6.5 INEQUITY AND INEFFICIENCY

Competition may simply be unfair. For example, members of some poor, marginal social groups might be able to use political influence to obtain public sector jobs and thereby contribute to the long term integration of their community into the nation. If those same activities are tendered out, the new managers may have no concern for long term national goals, and not hire members of these minority groups. In some cases, the burdens imposed on groups that lose a competition may also result in economic inefficiency and waste from a broader societal perspective. An example is the kind of competition between cities for private investment discussed in Section 5.4, where losers may be permanently *disabled* from re-entering the competition.

It is relatively easy to construct a case in principle against tender-competition (in particular), along the lines used by early opponents of the introduction of NPM: that it leads to short-term self-interested behaviour in the public service; the demoralization of public servants; an obsession with measurable performance indicators rather than underlying purposes; high 'transactions costs', etc. The extent to which these fears will be realized depends on a wide variety of factors: local circumstances; the nature and performance of the public service before the introduction of competition; and the degree of learning from experience. We have limited experience of *intentional* inter-organizational competition in the public sector, especially in poor countries. Such conclusions as we can draw derive mainly from recent experiences in a few rich countries where conditions are very different.

We need to be sceptical of gut reactions against competition in the public sector. But we should be equally suspicious of the highly ideological, simplistic critiques of existing public services that are made by the advocates of NPM and competition: the alleged conservatism, control-focus, rigidity, insularity and self-interested character of 'traditional bureaucracy'. These critiques are almost a mirror-image of the ideas about 'modern bureaucracy' developed by Max Weber almost a century ago. Many of the features of the modern bureaucratic *machine* (his word) that Weber celebrated – notably lifetime careers, standard routines and procedures, insulation of the public service from social influences, clear allocation of responsibilities and duties to posts, and hierarchical authority – are the target of the NPM critique. To Weber, the modern bureaucratic machine was a clear advance on previous systems of rule where the public treasury was not clearly separable from the private purses of rulers and public officials; officials were recruited on the basis of social position and personal contacts; their authority depended on their individual identities and connections, not the posts they occupied; procedures were arbitrary, etc. In the eyes of critics of contemporary bureaucracy, the system that Weber viewed as a fine-tuned machine has become a noisy, inefficient, smoky old contrivance. There is no surprise in that, Weber was writing in different world, where the internal combustion engine was a novelty. NPM has developed in the informatics era, in part because new, cheap, rapid information processing and information transfer capacity opens up new options for monitoring, structuring and managing public activities. Weber's ideas on what makes public services effective – that have no place for inter-organizational competition – have lost some of their authority. One can no longer say to students of public management: 'Start with Weber for a summary of basic principles'. However, Weber's principles are not out-dated. They continue to embody much fundamental wisdom. A public service system driven by ideas of inter-organizational competition cannot replace a 'traditional' (Weberian) bureaucracy. Competition of any kind will only work within a Weberian framework characterized by a substantial degree of discipline, honesty, accountability, predictability and coherence. For this reason, the scope for using inter-organizational competition to improve the public service is relatively small in many of the (poorer) countries facing a deficit of these public sector basics. The main priorities in such circumstances are to find ways of paying public servants realistic salaries; reducing corruption; and reintroducing standard procedures, accountability and discipline. Where these 'basics' are absent, there may be considerable inter-organizational competition of a perverse and unproductive kind.

5.7 TENDER-COMPETITION

One *may* think of tender-competition in the public sector as a component of a broader NPM package that has been developed in a few OECD countries under the aegis of governments deeply wedded to free market ideas. To think in those terms, especially in relation to developing countries, is to begin with a strong bias against the idea. One can more fruitfully think of competition (in general) as a typical, albeit often informal, unrecognized *dimension* of many inter-organizational relations. Tender-competition, in particular, can be thought of as an *extension* into new areas of the practice routinely followed by all contemporary governments to procure many goods and services, i.e. 'tenders' in the literal sense of the term – for extending the airport runways; re-stocking the Government Supplies Office with pens; providing ammunition for the armed forces, etc. (Section 5.4). There is scope to use tender-competition to improve public sector performance in many poor countries. There are three important general points discussed in Sections 5.71 to 5.7.3, relevant to deciding what the scope is in any particular context.

5.7.1 TENDER-COMPETITION WILL NOT WORK UNLESS ADEQUATELY REGULATED

If contracts are not properly prepared, awarded competitively and transparently, adequately monitored etc., then actual and potential bidders (*competitors*) are motivated to put their energies into corruptly obtaining and retaining contracts, not into providing a good service. In these circumstances, the attempt to use tender-competition could easily result in a worse outcome for society than the traditional methods for public service delivery. The standard of regulation of these kinds of activities is low in many countries: the major single source of corruption in the world is probably government tenders. It is likely that the extent of this form of corruption has increased appreciably in developing and transitional economies over recent years as they have become more market-oriented and made greater use of the tender procedure. The adequate regulation of tender-competition is partly a technical issue, where the experience of countries like the UK and New Zealand may be relevant. However, the dominant factors affecting the adequacy of regulation are political. There are two main policy implications. One is that the development of effective tender-competition is likely to go hand-in-hand with the (re-)establishment of an effective senior public service, recruited on meritocratic principles for a career of public service, well paid, characterized by a strong *esprit de corps*, and insulated from political pressures in the implementation of public policy. For a statement of this case, see the World Bank's *World Development Report 1997*, chapter 5. The second is that there are two important criteria for deciding which public activities previously managed in a 'traditional' fashion should first be opened to tender-competition. It will be best to begin with (a) relatively low budget activities that are unlikely to attract a great deal of corrupt interest and (b) activities that will tend to generate automatic non-formal regulation, i.e. vocal, organized and influential client groups who will complain to the political authorities if contractors are not providing them with a good service. These activities are more likely to be urban than rural. Street cleaning and urban solid waste disposal tend to be good places to start (Moe, 1984, p. 760).

5.7.2 POLICIES THAT APPEAR DESIRABLE FROM A PUBLIC INTEREST PERSPECTIVE MAY NOT BE POLITICALLY FEASIBLE

In practice, political considerations are likely to play a major role in the design of programmes to introduce and extend tender-competition and, in the light of those considerations, the previous paragraph might appear naive. Especially when the idea of tender-competition is new, it is likely to generate little positive support from citizens, and active, often virulent opposition from existing public sector employees and their trades unions. It may be possible to generate adequate political support from potential contractors only by offering them scope to make high profits by tendering out relatively high budget public services. This increases both the risk of corruption in the tendering process and the likelihood of major political conflicts with public service trades unions. Not all governments wish to avoid these conflicts. An important motivation for the governments of the UK, New Zealand and Chile to pioneer tender-competition – and NPM generally – was to generate conflicts they could win and thereby break the power of public service trades unions and, in the British and Chilean cases, to undermine an important organizational base of the democratic political opposition. By fragmenting the public sector among a wide range of employers, each under strong competitive pressure to minimize wage costs and to use temporary (and part-time) employment contracts, tender-competition and NPM represent a major threat to public service trades unions, as well as a significant profit opportunity to contractors. The introduction and extension of tender-competition is intrinsically a conflictual and political process.

5.7.3 THE DISJUNCTURE BETWEEN THE 'IDEAL' AND REALITY

There is a routine disjuncture between:

1   what researchers know about the functioning of organizations and multiorganizational systems; and

2   the way in which they, and policy advisers, frame discussions about reforming public management.

Research shows not only that inter-organizational relations in the public sector are often highly informal, but also that it is often these informal links and connections that make for good co-ordination in situations that might otherwise be chaotic (e.g. Chisholm, 1989). By contrast, policy debates – and most of this chapter – focus on ways of changing formal rules and structures. This is inevitable: public policy cannot be based on an acceptance that government organizations operate very differently in practice than in the rule book. But line managers have different concerns. They cannot formally make policy or change the structures of public agencies and the rules governing their interaction. They can however sometimes exploit informality and the discretion this brings them to create informal, productive inter-organizational competition for funds. This is most likely to be possible in the kind of situation outlined in Section 5.4: where the existence of an aid project or some other source of non-routine funding gives managers the leverage to switch money between agencies, and thus to establish informal performance competitions. The scope to do this productively is greater where the activities involved do not require great expertise or highly specialized, expensive equipment. For example, when the water supply agency in Bahia, Brazil was reluctant to get involved in constructing small scale irrigation facilities in a rural development project, the project managers switched the money to a rural co-operative, that 'borrowed' the engineer they needed from the water supply agency. This case illustrates in an interesting way the potential benefits of inter-organizational competition that was both informal and short term. The engineer finally returned to work in the water supply agency, and the competition between the agency and the co-operative was ended. However, the engineer then was able to 'convert' the water supply agency to do what it had previously resisted: use its expertise to construct low technology, low cost irrigation facilities that brought little professional prestige but were needed by the farmers (Tendler, 1993, p. 19-22). This story illustrates the economists' contention that a little competition sometimes goes a long way.

5.8 PRIZE-COMPETITION

Tender-competition appeals to the tough-minded. It can be a means of breaking the power of public service unions, radically reorganizing the public service, and generally making an imprint on the world. It is supported theoretically and ideologically by economists, economic theory, and the 'tough' economistic assumption that people are motivated mainly by individual material self-interest. Prize-competition, by contrast, is for the more tender-hearted. It is an instrument to support gradual change, by bringing out, publicizing, rewarding and encouraging the best of what already exists. As with all competition, individual self-interest plays an important driving role. However, to a much greater extent than for tender-competition, the scope for prize-competition derives from the more 'social' motivations for human action: the sense of satisfaction derived from being a member of a winning *team*; and the pleasure that we experience when we feel that we have done a good job and made a contribution to society or a useful cause, and when other people, especially those in authority or whose opinions we respect, tell us the same thing.

Tender and tough can complement one another. The British Conservative governments of 1979-97 introduced some very tough restructuring of the public service along NPM lines. However, in 1992 they also announced the introduction of a new prize-competition: the award of the Chartermark to public organizations for excellence in public service. The first award was made in 1995, and the scheme has become widely recognized and popular, despite the fact that additional work but no material reward is involved. Organizations are nominated by the public, inspected and, if successful, awarded the Chartermark for three years. The American equivalent differs in predictable ways: the emphasis, as on the whole public service reform programme in the United States, is on *innovation* (see Osborne and Gaebler, 1992); and an 'Innovations in American Government' award is worth $100,000 to an organization that receives it. The involvement of the Ford Foundation and Harvard University helps to guarantee the reputation of the award and protect against political interference.

There are many ways of organizing prize-competition in the public sector alone. For example, the prize can be material or non-material; the competition can be routine or unusual; entry can be automatic or limited; if limited, it can be by nomination or application; *judges* can be from within the supervising organization or external; and the criteria can be general ('good performance') or specific ('innovation', 'dedication'). The variety of potential types of prize-competition is so large that it is not possible even to begin to map them out here. There are five important general points about prize-competition:

1   There is typically a very wide scope for introducing or extending prize-competition.

2   It is a tool for gradual rather than radical change.

3   Prize-competition is a means of motivating employees. It is most likely to be effective where lack of effort on the part of individuals or small groups is a significant constraint on organizational performance. It is not a tool for tackling deeper problems rooted in organizational structures or financing.

4   Prize-competition can be closely integrated into routine organizational activities, including performance monitoring, inspection, and the payment of performance bonuses. It may be an extension of existing practices. This is illustrated in a summary description of the use of prize-competition in a very successful primary health care programme in Ceara State in Northeast Brazil:

> ... the state awarded prizes to the municipalities achieving the best immunization coverage. By 1992, 43 of the state's 178 municipalities had received prizes for the best DPT-III coverage (diphtheria, pertussis, and tetanus). The prizes were set up partly with the goal of getting program personnel to take seriously the collection of health data – always a problem in rural health programs. At the same time, the fanfare surrounding the granting of the prizes, as well as the program's broader publicity and its language of 'mission', bestowed substantial recognition on the agents and their supervising nurses, and enhanced their prestige in the communities where they worked and lived.
>
> (Tendler and Freedheim, 1994, p. 1778)

5   When it works well, prize-competition can generate additional 'commitment' among public sector agencies and staff on a large scale at very little resource cost. Because it is rooted in morality and values as well as self-interest, it is very vulnerable to the suspicion that the *judges* and *prize donors* are not themselves behaving morally. If casualty departments in British hospitals struggle to raise their work to a standard worthy of a Chartermark and then come to believe that the key to success is actually to have a local MP who has influence in the right quarters, the net effect on morale and commitment is likely to be negative.

5.9 CONCLUDING COMMENTS

The current interest in inter-organizational competition in the context of development management stems from the New Public Management ideas that are increasingly setting the agenda for public sector reform worldwide. The New Public Management paradigm is founded on a concern about *incentives*: that 'traditional bureaucracy' does not provide adequate incentives for public servants to be efficient, and to innovate, in a world where their tasks are often complex and 'traditional' methods of making them accountable are ineffective. Inter-organizational competition is part of a New Public Management menu of options to sharpen performance incentives. It is not the only item on the menu. Many factors bear on the incentives that shape the behaviour of public servants. If lack of adequate incentive is seen to be the problem, the quickest solution may simply be to improve incentives directly, without worrying about inter-organizational competition. For example, if tax collection is low and collectors are corrupt, the best move may be to select the most effective of them, establish a new high powered tax collection agency, and give staff a share of proceeds from collection (Klitgaard, 1989, p. 453; Thorp, 1996). One can worry later about the possible benefits of establishing rival taxation agencies, or tendering out the tax raising role.

Inter-organizational competition is simply one possible means to an end. It is often a powerful and appropriate means to improving public sector performance. *Intentional* inter-organizational competition will almost certainly become more widespread in the public services of developing and transitional economies. In the best possible circumstances, it will spread alongside the revival of 'public sector management basics', in a complementary, not a competitive relationship. It is more likely to spread productively if we can avoid a polarizing debate that identifies inter-organizational competition with NPM and rich countries, and invites poor countries to reject the very idea of competition for that reason. There is no need for poor countries to copy the rich. There are already many kinds of inter-organizational competition in the public sector in poor countries. We need to focus on developing, improving and extending the useful kinds, and suppressing the others.

CONCLUSIONS

There are five main conclusions in this chapter about inter-organizational competition in a development context:

1   We should be thinking about the potential for both prize-competition and tender-competition: both have a great deal to offer.

2   Development line managers need not necessarily wait for policymakers to restructure the public service along NPM lines before the potential benefits of tender-competition can be reaped. Relationships within and between public sector organizations are typically informal in many respects, and are often very different in reality than they appear in constitutions and organization charts. Managers able to influence the allocation of funds between organizations can create informal but productive competition, that may be no less useful for being short-lived.

3   No form of inter-organizational competition is a substitute for the kind of public sector management 'basics' – governmental systems characterized by a substantial degree of discipline, honesty, accountability, predictability and coherence – that are absent in many developing and transitional economies.

4   Where these basics are absent, the immediate priority task is to try to establish them, and this may involve reducing inter-organizational competition, not extending it.

5   It is often possible to improve public sector performance by introducing more *incentive*, without at the same time initiating inter-organizational competition.

6 TWO DECADES OF COMPETITION OVER HEALTH IN MOZAMBIQUE

JOSEPH HANLON

Provision of health services in Mozambique has been a highly managed process. Over a period of two decades, managers, agencies, goals and agendas shifted dramatically and often came into sharp conflict. The changing international political and economic environment played a central role. In this case study, we look at health in Mozambique between 1975 and 1995. We try to assess the success or failure of development actors in satisfying both overt goals and hidden agendas. This discussion is divided into four overlapping periods, each with very different issues:

1 **Independence: 1975-82**. Development of a new health service and primary health care.

2 **War: 1982-92**. Health becomes a battle zone in a particularly brutal war.

3 **Foreign aid: 1985-94**. Donors with their own goals and agendas play a larger role, making issues much more complex.

4 **Stabilization and reconstruction: 1990-96**. Health is dominated by the policies of the International Monetary Fund and, with the end of the war in 1992, the need for rapid reconstruction.

Finally we look at the strategies adopted by the main players over this 20 year period — a mix of competition, co-ordination and co-operation — in response to the changing environments and see what lessons can be drawn from them.

6.1 INDEPENDENCE: 1975-1982

When Mozambique became independent, Frelimo (Frente de Libertação de Mocambique) was the only liberation movement and it was widely popular. Thus it was unopposed when it established a one-party state. High government officials were also high party officials, so party congresses set overall Mozambican policy. Health was always high on the agenda of the leadership. 'The hospital is the only contact many people have with the state', commented President Samora Machel, himself a former nurse. It 'touches their most sensitive point: health, well-being, and their very life'.

This high priority was explicitly political. The new socialist government had to show that it could improve the well-being of ordinary people. A vaccination campaign in the first years of independence covered what at that time was a world record 95 per cent of the population. As well as launching a new preventive health strategy, it showed that Frelimo was doing something. It reached people whose only knowledge of Frelimo was hostile colonial propaganda which painted Frelimo as bloodthirsty 'terrorists'.

6.1.1 PRIMARY HEALTH CARE

In 1970 in colonial Mozambique, there were 500 doctors, two-thirds of whom were in the capital. At independence in 1975 at least 400 of those doctors left.

In 1975 the new Frelimo government with its great emphasis on health had two major goals: keeping the health service running despite staff flight, and providing basic health services to rural people and the urban poor who had been ignored during the colonial era.

On coming to power the government immediately 'nationalized' health care, ending all private medical practice. In 1977 it further 'socialized' health care by cutting fees to a low level that made services effectively free and adopted 'primary health care' (PHC) as the national policy in order to fulfil its goals. This involved shifting emphasis and resources to a broader-based, but less sophisticated health care system (see Box 6.1).

Following this strategy, of the 4,500 health workers trained between independence and 1982, only 100 were doctors; most of the rest had only two or three years training, but were competent to deal with 90 per cent of cases of illnesses and injuries, most mother and child health problems, and preventive care. Expenditure rose from £0.80 per capita in 1975 to over £2 in 1981. This allowed a rapid expansion of the rural health network; the number of first level health posts increased from 326 at independence to 1,122 in 1983.

In 1982, a World Health Organization (WHO) survey found that 81 per cent of rural children had been seen at least once by a health worker. The World Bank concluded that 'since independence Mozambique has been in the vanguard in the development of broad-based primary health care and in the implementation of an essential drugs program ... Mozambique has done much better than other African countries' (World Bank, 1989, pp. 71-2).

6.1.2 TENSIONS OVER HEALTH CARE STRATEGY

From the outset, Frelimo faced conflicting political and medical goals. Although there was widespread support within Frelimo and the government for the new strategy of primary health care, the remaining urban doctors (although now working for the new national health service) and a politically outspoken middle class demanded that the new government provide what they saw as a sophisticated and high quality care which had been available to the urban elite under the colonial regime. By 1982, half of all doctors were in the capital and doctors in rural areas were often foreigners working in Mozambique as part of aid or solidarity projects; a calculation in 1979 showed that while health spending in the capital was £7 per head,

BOX 6.1 PRIMARY HEALTH CARE

The Frelimo Third Party Congress in 1977 set out a health strategy to:

- extend the health service to all parts of the country, and as a priority establish health posts in rural areas;
- give priority to preventive medicine, especially environmental sanitation, mother and child health, and vaccination and other methods of combating preventable diseases;
- define a national policy with respect to endemic diseases such as malaria, tuberculosis, and diarrhoeal diseases;
- extend curative care to rural areas.

For any health ministry, the two most expensive areas are staff and medicines. In carrying out this strategy, the Ministry of Health put its emphasis on one- to three-year training of lower and middle level health workers such as nurses, midwives, and auxiliaries. There was also a six month training programme for village health workers. At the same time, the medicines policy was revised; private imports were banned and the Ministry of Health set up a state company which imported a restricted list of just over 300 drugs for the entire country. Bulk buying led to a sharp fall in prices and to sharp increases in imports of essential drugs.

The emphasis on lower and middle level health workers and basic medicines made it possible to carry out the rapid expansion of health services and provide care for the first time ever in many rural areas.

This strategy is commonly known as 'primary health care' and reflects the knowledge that 80 to 90 per cent of all illnesses and injuries do not need doctors and can be treated by paramedical workers with a small range of drugs and simple equipment. This applies in particular to the endemic diseases and maternal health. For example, vaccination can prevent killer diseases such as measles, while health education can both reduce the incidence of diarrhoea through improved sanitation and limit its impact when it occurs by showing mothers how to use oral rehydration.

Finally, the Ministry of Health set up a referral system. Indicators were introduced to identify those women most likely to have problem births, who were to be referred to maternity hospitals. People with complex illnesses or needing surgery were to be referred to district health centres or urban hospitals, which had better facilities, more sophisticated medicines, and the few doctors.

(Adapted from Walt, 1983; Hanlon, 1984)

it was only £0.40 for each rural resident (Hanlon, 1984). Nevertheless, the World Bank was able to argue that 'the common problem of excessive concentration on referral hospitals has been avoided, with nearly all investment directed to lower level facilities' (World Bank, 1989, p. 72).

Within the Ministry of Health and within Frelimo, the tension between primary health care for the masses and sophisticated care for the urban elite has continued up to the present. It means that decision-makers always face two conflicting goals, and the balance between them is constantly changing.

6.1.3 FOREIGN AID AND THE HEALTH SERVICE

Mozambique was left very poor by its Portuguese colonizers, and from independence in 1975 it received significant foreign aid. During the first decade, the largest donors were the Nordic states and the eastern European states of the socialist bloc, although European Community countries and the United States were also significant. Annual grain donations were more than 100,000 tonnes. During this period, however, Mozambique maintained tight control of aid. Donations and loans all went through government ministries. Colonial policy had been to limit education of Mozambicans, so the new state was desperately short of skilled staff. The socialist bloc (including Cuba), United Nations agencies and 'solidarity organizations' in western Europe sent hundreds of technicians and experts to Mozambique.

More than two-thirds of doctors and many Ministry of Health trainers and staff were foreign. Many of those foreigners reflected the then progressive thinking about 'primary health care' and had a strong influence on government policy. But all senior officials were Mozambicans, decision-making remained firmly in Mozambican hands, and nationalization meant there were no private health workers of any kind. This allowed Mozambique to carry out its transformation of health services despite the lack of skilled people of its own. The model was one of co-ordination by senior party and health ministry officials, and the health minister.

6.1.4 SUMMARY

Mozambique came to independence in a favourable international climate. There was wide discussion about a possible New International Economic Order which would transfer money from the industrialized countries to poor ones. The US defeat in Vietnam and the presidency of Jimmy Carter led to a lull in the Cold War. Socialist and state-led development was seen as acceptable (Abrahamsson and Nilsson, 1995). Internationally, primary health care was coming into vogue, and Mozambique had adopted it a year before the United Nations World Health Organization (WHO) began to promote the idea internationally. Mozambique's progressive health policy was seen in this context and received widespread kudos and some financial support (see Box 6.2).

BOX 6.2   GOALS AND RESULTS: INDEPENDENCE (1975-1982)

International context

- Consensus for primary health care strategies.
- Widespread support for 'third world' development.

Goals

- Government and Frelimo, health goals: (a) introduce primary health care and extend services to rural areas and unserved people, while (b) still satisfying urban demands.
- Government and Frelimo political goal: use improved health care to enhance the popularity of Frelimo and show the potential of socialism.

Were the goals met?

In general, yes. Mozambique did transfer health resources to rural areas. Mozambique's primary health care programme won high praise from the WHO. Frelimo was popular and peasants often cited improved health care as a reason. However, resources transferred to rural areas were not as high as claimed publicly, and urban and hospital services were also maintained and improved.

6.2   WAR: 1982-1992

The favourable international climate turned suddenly hostile in 1980. The 1979/80 oil price rise was linked to a sharp rise in interest rates and a fall in international terms of trade, causing balance of payments problems in most developing countries. Ronald Reagan was elected president of the United States and there were radical policy changes. Economically, proposals for a New International Order and transfer of wealth from north to south were replaced by the global free market and financial transfers the other way – from south to north to fund a growing US balance of payments deficit. Politically, the Cold War was reactivated with a new ferocity. In southern Africa, the new US administration backed the apartheid South African government as an anti-communist bastion against the socialist majority-ruled neighbours. The South African military attacked Mozambique for the first time just ten days after Reagan took office. South Africa began heavy backing for an anti-government guerrilla force, Renamo (Resistencia Nacional Moçambicano).

6.2.1   EFFECTS ON THE HEALTH SERVICE

The health service became a particular target of Renamo and the South African military precisely because it was seen as a source of Frelimo popularity. The government had been encouraging women to have babies in special maternity hospitals, and the number of births in health units rose sharply. Renamo specifically attacked these maternity hospitals. On 18 July 1987 Renamo guerrillas massacred 424 people in the town of Homoine, going through the local hospital killing staff and patients, including mothers with new-born babies.

Thus the health service became a battlefield, with Renamo trying to close health units and make people too frightened to use them and work in them, while the government tried to keep as many open as possible. During the war, Renamo closed or destroyed 500 health posts; by the end of the war, fewer than 900 were still open. Although the Ministry of Health tried to keep the rural health service operating wherever access was still possible, it increasingly concentrated on serving the displaced people who flooded into towns; new health posts were built in periurban areas and staffed by health workers who had fled with the people they were serving. The number of contacts with the health service peaked at 7.5 million in 1981 and fell to 4 million in 1988, rising again to 5.6 million in 1990.

BOX 6.3   GOALS AND RESULTS: WAR – 1982-1992

International context
- The Cold War.

Goals
- Renamo/South Africa political/military: reduce use of health service to cut off a perceived benefit of the Frelimo government.
- Government political/military: (a) keep people away from Renamo, and (b) maintain services in government controlled-areas.
- Ministry of Health: obtain maximum coverage by targeting services to the largest concentrations of people.

Were the goals met?
Renamo succeeding in destroying large parts of the rural health service and by 1988 almost halving use of the health service. The government however did maintain an effective health service in towns and cities.

The government was also successful in keeping people away from Renamo. Renamo controlled few towns and the intensity of the war, the harsh life under Renamo, and government military strategy led most people to flee Renamo-controlled rural areas. An estimated one-third of the country's entire population fled to neighbouring countries or to towns. When the war ended in 1992, the United Nations estimated that Renamo controlled 23 per cent of the land area but only 6 per cent of the population. (*Mozambique Peace Process Bulletin*, Amsterdam, Feb 1995).

6.2.2 SUMMARY

From 1982-1992, of Mozambique's 14 million people, 1 million died, 1.7 million were refugees in neighbouring countries, and 3.2 million fled from rural areas to the relative safety of the towns because of the war. Some in the US government encouraged covert support for Renamo, but in 1988 the US Deputy Assistant Secretary of State for African Affairs, Roy Stacey, accused Renamo of carrying out 'one of the most brutal holocausts against ordinary human beings since World War II' (Hanlon, 1991, p. 47).

Box 6.3 provides a summary of how the health service fared during this period.

6.3 FOREIGN AID: 1985-1994

In 1984 in an attempt to stop Mozambique being a Cold War battlefield, the government made its 'turn to the west' and signed a number of agreements, in particular joining the World Bank and International Monetary Fund. This did not stop the war or US support for South Africa. But it did sharply increase aid, which rose from £80 million in 1981 to £325 million in 1986 and £500 million in 1988. This huge flow of aid gave donors an increasing share of power within Mozambique. In 1993, for example, donor 'projects' covered 58 per cent of Ministry of Health recurrent expenditure (Wuyts, 1995). In the remainder of this section, we look at four examples of this new aid relationship. The first involves a form of partnership and co-operation, while the other three show different types of competition.

6.3.1 UNICEF: SYMBIOSIS

Because of the international consensus in the late 1970s supporting Mozambique's development approach, the United Nations had one of its largest budgets in Africa in Mozambique. United Nations agencies normally support the government in power. UNICEF, the UN Children's Fund, concentrates on the major causes of death and disease of children under five years old. It is unusual (but not unique) in the UN family in that is has little money of its own and must fundraise from UN member governments and through non-governmental organizations and national UNICEF committees. This gives UNICEF two clear goals: the social goal of improving the health of children, and the institutional goal of increasing its income and prestige. In Mozambique it succeeded spectacularly well by working closely with the government. UNICEF's Mozambique budget jumped from £1.6 million in 1984 to £17.5 million in 1989. Marta Mauras, who became UNICEF head in Maputo in 1984, was rewarded with a promotion to be head of UNICEF's Africa Section in 1989.

Two examples will show how UNICEF and the government were able to co-operate to satisfy their separate and collective goals and to support each other. In the second half of the 1980s the war intensified and there was a growing campaign in the west (including some parts of the US government) to argue that Renamo was fighting a civil war against a Marxist government. Mozambique and its allies emphasized the well documented proof that this was a war of destabilization promoted by the apartheid government in South Africa. But the ambivalent attitude of the US and intensifying Cold War led many of the smaller governments who were giving the most aid, as well as UN agencies, to help the Mozambican government but not challenge the war itself, because it was seen as a battle between the superpowers.

In 1987 UNICEF took a very public stand with a report 'Children on the Front Line – the impact of apartheid, destabilization and warfare on children in southern and South Africa' (UNICEF, 1987). This chronicled the devastation being wrought by Renamo and South Africa in Mozambique, and was published at a time when the international campaign against apartheid was growing. This helped to prevent the United States giving public support to Renamo, as it had to Unita in similar circumstances in Angola. It put Mozambique into the spotlight as a victim of apartheid, which was politically useful. It was published as part of a UNICEF fund-raising campaign and played a large part in the ten-fold increase in money for Mozambique, because it put UNICEF firmly in the front line of the anti-apartheid struggle and as a safe recipient of anti-apartheid funds from governments.

By putting its priority on children, and by providing the funds to back up that priority, UNICEF was able to shift the balance of priorities with the Ministry of Health. Thus, although the total number of patients seen by the health service nearly halved, the number of contacts with children under five rose to 1,150,000 in 1990. Similarly, vaccination levels rose rapidly in the late 1980s. For example, measles vaccinations fell from 309,000 in 1981 to 220,000 in 1986, but then rose to 313,000 in 1990, an estimated 59 per cent of all children. As noted in Section 6.1, vaccination was always a high priority for the Ministry of Health, and the ministry and UNICEF developed a mutually useful relationship on this issue. UNICEF provided vehicles and vaccines that the government could no longer afford to buy. The government provided a highly motivated workforce and allowed UNICEF to take the credit and gain the publicity. This was shown in the capital, Maputo in 1986. By February the ministry had already vaccinated 84 per cent of all children and would surely have reached its 90 per cent target by the end of the year; UNICEF jumped in and gave cars, refrigerators and funds sorely needed by the city health department (although not for vaccination, which was already adequately equipped). UNICEF was then allowed to proudly take credit when the 90 per cent target was reached (Hanlon, 1991, p.197).

6.3.2 MEDICINES

Medicines policy was an early Mozambican success. In colonial times pharmaceutical imports were largely unregulated and more that 13,000 products were in circulation. The government moved quickly to establish a new policy with a short national formulary of only 316 drugs and a corresponding therapeutic guide. Expensive drugs of dubious value were dropped. To reduce costs, this limited range of drugs was purchased and prescribed by generic rather than brand name. Although Mozambique was one of the first countries to follow this path, it was part of an international trend backed by the World Health Organization.

The next step was to set up a single state company to do all national medicine buying through international tender. Up to 200 companies in 15 countries bid on parts of the tender; western European companies remained the main suppliers, but selling for prices as low as one-third of what they had charged before independence.

The final step was to double the national drugs budget, from £2.9 million in 1977 to £5.9 million in 1981. The result was that for the first time in Mozambican history, there were enough basic medicines for common illnesses. Even remote health posts had essential drugs. But the financial crisis meant imports fell to £2.6 million in 1984. After that, medicines imports were paid almost entirely with aid money which brought about significant changes in the way medicines were obtained.

Major donors for medicines were the western countries with pharmaceutical industries. They had three goals: support Mozambique's health service, end competitive tendering (because this forced down the selling price of medicines), and provide direct support to the donor country's industry. Western donors tied their aid, either to purchases from their own domestic firms, or to purchases through UNICEF. Both were much more expensive. By 1988 medicine imports were £8.2 million, but the volume of imports was less than had been purchased for £5.9 million in 1981.

Because of the higher cost of imports from the major transnational drug companies, donors were unable to satisfy Mozambique's entire needs, so donors imposed an even more restricted list. Donors even excluded as inessential some items for treating war wounds.

This is the first example where donors' non-aid-related goals – support of politically important domestic industry – came into direct conflict with government and aid related goals, leading to poorer health care.

6.3.3 THE UNITED STATES AND PRIVATIZATION

The United States had an explicitly and openly political agenda in Mozambique. For its 1989 aid year, for example, the United States Agency for International Development (USAID) had three official 'short-term objectives' in Mozambique: 'humanitarian assistance', 'to promote the development of the private sector', and 'to promote privatization' (USAID, 1987).

Politically, as part of the Cold War, the US wanted to weaken the Marxist Frelimo government and reduce its links with the socialist bloc. More concretely, it was promoting a neo-liberal agenda which involved a sharply reduced role for the state and a much larger role for domestic and foreign businesses and charities. This reflected both the attitudes of the Cold War-riors, who saw everything in East–West terms and simply wanted to defeat Frelimo, as well as committed aid workers who held the curious US view that the state cannot be the best provider of health services.

As part of negotiations leading to the 1984 'turn to the west', the United States demanded that the Mozambican government allow NGOs to under-take work which had previously been the exclusive role of government, notably distribution of relief food and provision of health services.

This opened the way for a number of NGOs, some related to conservative churches, which were openly hostile to the socialist government and wanted to provide alternative and competing services. This led to a sharp division, with many NGOs working with the government, following its primary health care strategies and often providing assistance to the Ministry of Health, while other NGOs took particular pride in ignoring the Ministry and even opposing its treatment regimes and reporting requirements. One large NGO, for example, conducted surveys of child malnutrition but refused to give the results to the government in a way that would be compatible with sur-veys being done in other parts of the country. For some agencies working in Mozambique, an important or even primary motivation was to challenge the socialist government and convert people to the free market and/or Chris-tianity. Providing health services (and distributing food, seeds and agricul-tural implements) was a means to that end, rather than an end in itself.

The conflict between a donor's health and political goals was shown quite clearly when the USAID Maputo office in 1987 proposed a project 'to seek to improve primary health care delivery by strengthening the Ministry of Health' in Zambézia province. This was rejected by USAID headquarters in Washington, which did not wish to 'strengthen' the government. Instead, it contracted a French NGO, Médecins Sans Frontières-France (MSF-F), to carry out this work. This was an unusual choice, because MSF-F is best known for flying doctors; USAID admitted that MSF-F was 'biased to-ward curative services' and had little primary health care experience. Fur-thermore, MSF-F was not a US NGO so USAID had to register it in the US before it could give it money. The main reason for the choice was that MSF-F had a reputation as the health NGO in Zambézia which was most hostile to the Ministry of Health and had gone farthest to create a parallel system in competition to the Ministry.

Later USAID reports noted a second reason for wanting a programme independent of government. The project included a large number of study visits by US officials and academics, and USAID later said it was intended as a pilot project and study as to how the US should be involved in the health sector in Mozambique (Hanlon, 1991, p.181).

In 1990, the US was able to again link humanitarian and political goals. Because of growing political crises in Italy, the Italian government on short notice said it was unable to provide £5 million for the essential drugs programme. With drugs due to run out within months, Mozambique looked for an alternative donor. USAID said it would fill the gap – on the condition that the Ministry of Health accept another USAID project which would mean direct involvement of USAID with health ministry management. The government had already rejected the project, which was designed entirely by the US and could not be changed to satisfy Mozambican needs; in the end, the ministry needed the money for medicines and had no choice but to accept (Hanlon, 1996, p. 129).

6.3.4 CONTRACTING

By 1990 there were 180 foreign NGOs working in Mozambique, mainly on emergency relief relating to the war. Some raised money on their own, but NGOs were mainly contractors for other, larger, donor agencies; 87 per cent of the money NGOs spent on emergency work in Mozambique in 1989 came from other sources and the two most important NGOs (both US-based) were 100 per cent contract funded.

The European Union has a wide range of 'budget lines' for work in former European colonies (under the Lomé agreement) and in southern Africa and Mozambique (notably under anti-apartheid budgets). Some are specifically for European NGOs and some are available both to NGOs and recipient governments. Many NGOs maintain lobbyists in Brussels to ensure that such money goes to them and not, for example, to the Mozambican Ministry of Health.

With the end of the war in 1992, there were very high levels of contract spending in 1993 and 1994 to assist returned refugees and begin rebuilding health facilities. At its peak spending in 1994, the European Commission gave ECU 71 million (£56 million) (Hanlon, 1997, p. 28) to European NGOs for work in Mozambique, of which a substantial amount was for work in health. Commission-funded NGOs did health work in more than half of Mozambique's districts. Several NGOs had health contracts worth more than £2 million per year. The MSF family of organizations spent £10 million in 1994. By contrast, the state budget for recurrent health expenditure for the entire country that year was less than £6 million. When the contracts ran out at the end of 1994, many of the NGOs moved on to the next country with a disaster, leaving little behind in Mozambique.

NGO managers, then, have goals not dissimilar to those of any business manager: competing to win contracts and fulfil them as profitably as possible. In the field, the target was a particular group of refugees or building a particular health post.

It was here that the contrast in goals was sharpest. Mozambique as a whole and the national health service had no place in the goals of the contract NGOs. The Ministry of Health complained that many NGOs went directly to the field without even contacting the ministry, and left behind expectations that could not be fulfilled – health posts in the wrong place that could not be staffed because the ministry had no budget and small populations which had grown to expect very high levels of service that could not be sustained by the government.

NGOs also had very high overheads paid by the EC, in some cases requiring several cars, computers and up to four support staff for each front-line health worker. Government argued that it could have made more efficient use of the money than the NGOs, in part because it had an administrative structure in place. The contract NGOs tended to respond that they were better at reaching target populations in an emergency, in this case when 1.7 million refugees were returning from neighbouring countries in just two years. European Commission officials stressed the political importance at home of supporting European NGOs as part of the aid process.

6.3.5 SUMMARY

The mid-1980s to the mid-1990s saw a huge inflow of foreign aid to Mozambique both in cash terms and in the number of aid organizations which set up operations in the country. This period was characterized by a steep reduction in the government's co-ordinating role in the provision of health services and an increase in fragmented health service provision by contracted agencies, often in competition with each other and with the Ministry of Health. Box 6.4 gives a summary of goals and results in the ten years to 1994.

BOX 6.4   GOALS AND RESULTS: FOREIGN AID (1985-1994)

International context
- Victory for the West in Cold War, with imposition of free market policies.
- Growing international support for anti-apartheid struggle led to majority rule in South Africa.

Goals
- Ministry of Health: use aid to maintain broad coverage and support state-run national health service.
- Most donor agencies: target specific groups for aid based health services rather than general population.
- Many donor agencies: (1) privatization and weakening of state health system, and (2) support of companies and NGOs at home.
- UNICEF and contracting NGOs: increase funding and win profitable contracts.

Were these goals met?
Most goals were partly met. Health care was provided, albeit at a high cost. Foreign contractors had a higher income than the Ministry of Health. The government health service was weakened, but not permanently bypassed.

6.4 STABILIZATION AND RECONSTRUCTION: 1990-1996

The 1990s brought a whole new set of challenges to the health sector in Mozambique. The war ended in 1992. This was followed by a massive return of more than three million refugees and displaced people, as well as the demobilization of 78,000 soldiers. In successful internationally monitored elections in 1994, Frelimo was re-elected and Renamo became the parliamentary opposition party.

The Ministry from 1990 had seen that the war was coming to an end and began planning for rebuilding and the return to previously inaccessible rural areas. In particular, it was seen as an opportunity not simply to restore physical infrastructure but to redefine development priorities. The hope was to improve quality while further redressing imbalances inherited from colonial rule. Better use was to be made of existing resources, and increased emphasis was to be put on fairness and equity. Rural coverage had to be improved, with emphasis on the worst served provinces.

A December 1990 policy paper by Deputy Health Minister Igrejas Campos said that the Ministry of Finance had already ruled that the total number of health workers could not increase. The Ministry of Health had also decided not to increase the number of health units, and to cope with expected increased use by upgrading staff through retraining and replacing retiring unqualified people such as cleaners with newly qualified health workers. Better staff could use facilities more intensively and efficiently. Health workers who moved from rural to urban areas during the war must return to the countryside; reopened health posts would be staffed by relocated or replacement staff. To compensate for the decision to not expand the network of rural health posts, more voluntary village health workers would be trained and there would be substantially increased use of mobile health brigades.

The policy called for two phases. In the first, coverage would be restored to pre-war levels within four years. In the second, facilities would be upgraded, for example to add a rural maternity hospital to each health post.

Campos noted that even without an increase in the number of staff, costs would rise significantly. More highly trained staff would earn higher salaries, while mobile brigades need fuel and vehicles. Within four years, spending would return to pre-war levels.

Donor-driven fragmentation of the health system had made planning and control virtually impossible. By the early 1990s the big players were already trying to reassert control. This took two forms. First, both the World Bank and the government were anxious to control the whole aid process under the guise of co-ordination. Second, the International Monetary Fund (IMF) wanted to impose stabilization and control government and aid spending. These adjustment and stabilization packages (see Box 6.5) had very different effects on health policy and decision-making.

BOX 6.5   ADJUSTMENT AND STABILIZATION

The World Bank and the IMF are the two main international financial institutions. Bilateral aid is usually 'conditional' on a developing country having agreed programmes with both institutions. They both follow the 'free market' dogma fashionable in the 1980s, which calls for a reduction in the role of the state and uses market forces as the engine of development. The two work together and impose an identical set of measures on all developing countries:

- rapid devaluation;
- deregulation of domestic and international trade;
- ending subsidies;
- fees for social services such as health and education; and
- privatization of parastatal industries and, often, services.

This package is usually known as structural adjustment and is often administered by the World Bank. In a 1987 report on Mozambique, the Bank said that 'inherent' in structural adjustment 'is the recognition that the closer integration of the Mozambique economy into the international economy is essential'.

The World Bank's goal is to create the conditions under which the free market will increase production. The Bank backs up its conditions with loans, both to improve infrastructure such as roads, and to help newly privatized industries invest. The success of adjustment is subject to considerable debate, but there is broad agreement that throughout the developing world, structural adjustment has led to a sharp increase in income differences between the better and worse off and has caused a sharp increase in poverty, at the least in the short term. This led the Bank in the late 1980s to introduce its 'Social Dimensions of Adjustment' programme which tried to provide a 'safety net' for the poorest; this did not help much in Mozambique since an estimated two-thirds of the population was below the poverty line.

Meanwhile, the IMF concentrates much more narrowly on reducing inflation and balance of payments deficits. The IMF is strictly 'monetarist', which means that its single goal is to control the money supply. Its policy is known as 'stabilization' and imposes three types of conditions:

1 sharp cuts in government spending (including that funded by foreign aid);
2 increases in taxation to curb consumer spending; and
3 reductions in the total amount of bank credit available to the private sector.

In Mozambique, this led to sharp falls in civil service wages and delays in repairing damage caused by the war.

The goal of both bodies is to balance supply and demand. The World Bank tries to increase 'supply' by encouraging the free market to produce more, while the IMF tries to reduce 'demand' as a way of curbing inflation and reducing balance of payments deficits. In theory, the two policies should be complementary and lead to a balanced and stable economy. In practice, this does not happen. Mozambique's economic crisis is a result of colonialism and of the long war, so its economic instability is at least partly externally caused. The Bank argues that adjustment must take priority and that there must be a substantial increase in production. The IMF argues that there will be no investment while inflation remains high, so that long term growth requires that inflation be cut first, even though this means a reduction in consumption in what is already the world's poorest country. This led to open conflicts between the Bank and IMF in 1995, with the IMF forcing Mozambique to not take up reconstruction loans being offered by the Bank.

(Adapted from Hanlon, 1991, 1996)

6.4.1 ENDING PROJECT PROLIFERATION: A NEW SYMBIOSIS

The 'Wild West' atmosphere of the late 1980s with hundreds of agencies running around doing 'their own thing' did not peak until 1994, when there were 405 different donor-funded projects in health. Each had its own administrative costs of up to 40 per cent of total project funds, and each required separate administrative support within the Ministry. The then Minister of Health, Dr Leonardo Simão, appealed to donors to allow him 'to move away from a Ministry of Health Projects and toward a Ministry of Health Services'. The World Bank argued that 'the only way to ensure a more equitable allocation, rationalizing and keeping track of public expenditures and of external funding' was through 'strong co-ordination' (World Bank, 1995a, p. 7).

The World Bank clearly expected to do that co-ordination. Its 1995 'Country Assistance Strategy' sets seven 'necessary conditions' for World Bank support (and thus for most other aid which is conditional on Mozambique having a World Bank programme). Two are 'Formulation of medium-term sector policy frameworks and investment programs (particularly in the agricultural and social sectors)' and 'Improved budget management, in accordance with targets agreed in sector policy frameworks'. The key word is 'agreed' – a new condition of virtually all international aid to Mozambique is the World Bank must 'agree' health policy, investment programmes, and budgets. After more than two years of negotiation, the health policy was approved by the Bank at the same time, 7 November 1995, as the Country Assistance Strategy.

Together, these make clear a central World Bank goal. Through the need for its 'agreement', the Bank must play a central role in health policy formulation and implementation; through its new role in 'co-ordination' it will take some control of other donors' funds.

The Bank, however, started from a weak position. It admitted that its first health project had been 'unsatisfactory' partly because there had been 'little participation (and sometimes even little consultation) by implementing institutions.' (World Bank, 1995a, p. 18). In other words, the Bank had failed in 1988 to impose a project written in Washington without discussion with the Ministry. Thus an implicit and institutional goal was not to have a second failure. This required working closely with the Ministry.

A third institutional goal is that Mozambique take a substantial loan from the World Bank. Bank officials privately allege that 'task managers' in Washington, such as those responsible for health loans to Mozambique, are judged mainly by the size of their loan portfolio.

Effectively acknowledging its weak position in health, the Bank decided to form an alliance with government to 'co-ordinate' and control donors. The Bank eventually accepted the government's late 1970s emphasis on primary health care and the 1990 post-war reconstruction strategy as a basis of agreed policy.

But the Bank itself admitted that 'donors felt they were not sufficiently consulted' during the preparation of the health policy, 'and were invited to join an already completed program' (World Bank, 1997b, p. 38). Donors had already been collaborating to support the Ministry of Health, in what many saw as a genuine 'partnership', and they were not pleased at what they saw as a World Bank take-over. In the end, the Bank agreed that the Health Ministry and not the Bank would have final say over donor funds. And a 1997 evaluation by the Bank itself recommended that in 'the social sectors' the Bank should 'defer to other donors' because they already have a 'major presence' and 'a comparative advantage'. (World Bank, 1997b, p. 66).

In exchange, Mozambique took a £66 million loan from the Bank, probably somewhat larger than was needed. In particular, the Ministry agreed to use Bank loan funds to pay some recurrent expenditure and other things which donors were prepared to fund with grants. This meant higher costs to Mozambique, because the loan must eventually be repaid.

In the end, the Bank gained its second and third goals – a policy success and a substantial new loan – only by conceding substantial ground on the first. Whereas in many ministries it gained the right to 'co-ordinate' the sector and other donors' funds, in Health it was forced to defer to the government which kept control over donor funds. And its policy rule was limited.

The World Bank entered into three policy debates – medicines, the urban-rural divide and health charges. Unexpectedly, World Bank support for keeping spending down led it to side with the government and oppose USAID with the World Bank calling for an increase in 'centralized procurement of generic drugs.' The Bank used its power to block the construction of a hospital in Nacala, a major port and the largest city with no hospital; the government argued that the concentration of people and economic importance made it cost effective, while the Bank insisted the money go to rural areas. The Bank initially appeared to accept Mozambique's line that there was very limited potential for increased cost recovery, which is normally one of the Bank's neo-liberal priorities. But the Bank proved to be just biding its time. In 1998, it unexpectedly made reduction of Mozambique's debt conditional on a five-fold increase in health service cost recovery, and further demanded the Mozambique's parliament approve 'new user fees legislation' (World Bank and IMF, 1998, p. 19 and p. 36).

6.4.2 STABILIZATION

In 1990 Mozambique signed an agreement with the International Monetary Fund for an 'Enhanced Structural Adjustment Facility'. This is a type of loan granted only on very rigid conditions which, in effect, give the IMF total control over national macro-economic policy. IMF policy is known as 'stabilization' and is strictly monetarist – the single goal is to reduce inflation by reducing the money supply. To do this, the IMF imposes sharp cuts on public spending and credit to the economy. Cuts began even before the war ended, and have accelerated since the 1994 election.

Cuts hit civil service pay particularly hard. Nurses earned £70 per month in 1990. This fell to £40 in 1993 and below £25 in 1996. Nurses and virtually all other front line health workers are now well below the United Nations-defined poverty line. The result was widespread demoralization and corruption, with patients being forced to pay informal fees to health workers.

At first, despite the fall in salaries, overall health spending increased from 1990 through 1993, but it fell again in 1994 as the IMF imposed further government spending cuts. The World Bank explicitly calls for salaries of health personnel to be restored to 1980 levels, but the IMF spending cap will not permit it. In 1996, the Deputy Minister of Health, Dr Abdul Noormahomed, asked: 'Is it worth extending the health system if staff are not motivated and provide bad service, and have no fuel and too few medicines?' (personal communication).

Meanwhile, IMF policy was not working. Instead of falling, inflation increased steadily from a low of 21 per cent in early 1991 to 78 per cent in mid 1994. In response, the IMF imposed tighter restrictions each year. Finally in 1994 it decided that foreign aid to Mozambique, by then the poorest country in the world, was such a large part of public expenditure that aid would have to be cut. This meant significant cuts in reconstruction of war damage. In 1995 the Ministry of Health was forced to delay reconstruction of health posts and cut back its proposed World Bank loan from £89 million to £66 million. The revised health strategy now assumes per capita spending in 2002, 10 years after the end of the war, will still be below pre-war levels. The number of primary health care facilities will not be restored to pre-war levels until 2005, 13 years after the end of the war instead of the 4 years planned by the ministry.

6.4.3 SUMMARY

Post-war reconstruction of health services were compromised by the conflictiong requirements of the two principal donors – the World Bank and the IMF. Nonetheless, a negotiated agreement between the Bank and the Ministry of Health succeeded in reducing the proliferation of health projects and returned some co-ordinating powers to the Ministry. Box 6.6 summarizes the period of reconstruction and stabilization.

BOX 6.6 GOALS AND RESULTS: STABILIZATION AND RECONSTRUCTION (1990-96)

International context

Widespread acceptance by industrialized and donor countries of conservative economic policies, notably monetarism and of IMF stabilization

Goals

- Government and most donors on health: rapid restoration of health services after the war; restore wage and service levels; restructure.

- IMF political/fiscal: bring health within spending cuts.

- Ministry of Health: end proliferation of donor and NGO contract projects; reassert control of health projects, policy and spending.

- World Bank bureaucratic/institutional: gain control of health projects, policy and spending; agree a large loan.

Were these goals met?

Proliferation of health provision agencies was ended and a compromise led to joint control by the Ministry of Health and the World Bank, based on policies set by the ministry.The World Bank made a large loan for health.

Health spending was capped. Restoration of health services is to be spread out over 13 years instead of four; spending to remain below pre-war levels with most wages kept below the poverty line.

6.5 MANAGING THE COMPLEXITY: LESSONS FOR DEVELOPMENT MANAGERS

Up until the start of the war in 1982 the health service in Mozambique was co-ordinated by the government. The effects of the war, global economic and political changes since then have forced the government away from the direct management of health service provision. Box 6.7 summarizes some of the complex and changing environment with which the health service in Mozambique has had to contend.

BOX 6.7 GOALS AND RESULTS: 1985-1995 OVERALL

Global political goals

- IMF, US and some other donors: weaken government, encourage free market, draw Mozambique into western orbit, impose stabilization.
- IMF: bring health within ambit of stabilization, restrict spending and delay rebuilding.

Health goals

- Government and donors: maintain service during war and rebuild after the war.

Health political goals

- Many donors: encourage private health care delivery.
- Government: maintain national health service.

Were these goals met?

The global political goals were all successfully met. The health service was maintained during the war, but post-war reconstruction will be significantly delayed.

Private medicine was legalized in 1991. Unexpectedly, there has been little entry of the private sector into health care. Outside the capital, Maputo, there are few private clinics. There are very few non-profit (church, NGO or other voluntary) health care providers. Thus the national health service remains the overwhelmingly dominant provider.

Perhaps the most notable point for development managers to draw from this case study is the way in which growing complexity meant that while everyone claimed that improving the health of Mozambicans was their main goal, in reality other covert and overt agendas dominated. In the first years after independence, health decision makers were able to focus more directly on health issues; expanding and improving health care was seen as actually supporting the political agenda of the time.

But in the following years, managers spent less and less time considering health issues. The aid process itself, and its political and bureaucratic goals, came to become more important than goals relating to health care. For many foreign decision makers, health was the means to an end; for many Mozambican decision makers, managing and increasing aid became a goal in itself. Four phrases capture this:

1 **This will hurt now but it will be good for you in the long run**. Foreign development managers have explicitly chosen to sacrifice the health of Mozambicans in the intermediate term for what are seen as broader and more important goals, which they believe will benefit Mozambicans in the long run. At an international policy level, health was made subordinate to Cold War agendas, for example by destroying health posts to reduce support for Frelimo – in the often genuine belief that people will only be healthier if communism were defeated. Later, health has been subordinated to international fiscal goals, by preventing rebuilding in the name of stabilization.

2 **Help now at all cost**. The opposite is the view taken by some donor decision makers that saving a few lives immediately overrode all other considerations. This usually meant using flying doctors and other foreign staff to bypass all Mozambican systems. Mozambican government officials who had a longer term view and proposed more integrated approaches were dismissed as misguided, incompetent, and worse.

3 **Doing well by doing good**. For many donor decision makers, Mozambique could only be 'helped' if the donor also gained extensive benefits, in order to keep the money flowing. Governments would provide aid in support of political goals, such a privatization or protecting the pharmaceutical industry. The survival of agencies providing services brought to the fore bureaucratic goals, such as winning contracts and ensuring salaries for headquarters staff.

4 **Keep the money flowing**. For Ministry of Health officials, the priority became obtaining funds which were essential to keep the health service operating. This required managing aid and increasing it.

The complexity of the aid process meant that not only were development managers juggling their own mixed goals, they also had to co-operate with other managers who had their own bag of mixed priorities.

Negotiations can be complex and difficult; some agencies saw their goals being advanced most by being competitive and non-co-operative. But in most cases, some negotiated agreement was necessary and often fruitful; Ministry of Health managers needed aid money to keep the health service running, while donors needed access and co-operation from the Ministry if their political and policy goals were to be met. The UNICEF cases show how this occurred when both sides shared a goal of improving health care. The example of USAID funding for medicines shows the importance of knowing the other side's goals and 'bottom line' in negotiations – Ministry officials knew USAID wanted increased influence in the Ministry of Health and would pay for it, while USAID officials knew that the top priority of health managers was to provide medicines and that, when the crunch came, that would override their dislike for US officials and their demands.

I think the most successful development managers were those who were able to decide what was the highest priority while also keeping secondary goals within their sights. Thus several donor agencies, such as UNICEF, did expand substantially, fulfilling the priority institutional goal, while providing genuine help to the Mozambican health service; others met institutional goals but did not help Mozambique. Some Ministry of Health officials did see health as the priority while accepting that aid was essential to achieve it; others became so lost in the aid process that they forgot about health.

Thus, for those with a development or health objective, some balancing of goals and collaboration was more effective. But for those with political goals, single-mindedness was most useful. Those who took winning the Cold War or weakening Frelimo and the Mozambican state as an absolute priority were successful; those who tried to fight the Cold War and help with health in Mozambique were generally unsuccessful at both.

Thus if there is any single lesson from this case study, it is the importance of deciding what is the genuine objective, and not be caught by rhetoric (about improving health care) or competing institutional pressures.

KEY CONCEPTS AND PRINCIPLES OF COMPETITION

WHAT IS COMPETITION?

All too often the idea of competition has been dominated by the narrow conception put forward by economists, in which competition is explored through models which make very restrictive assumptions about behaviours and incentives. As Moore writes, this has led to a theory of decentralization – of how firms as atomized units relate to others around a market system based on prices and determined through the free interaction of demand and supply – rather than to an adequate explanatory theory of competition.

The three chapters in this section highlight the unsatisfactory nature of this conceptualization in different ways. They indicate that competition is not simply about price-mechanisms. As Moore points out there are material and non-material benefits to be had in the real world. Therefore competition can be over financial resources, competent senior staff, good projects to support, and takes place between NGOs, government departments, regional administrations and commercial organizations. Hanlon writes about political agendas and imperatives towards organizational survival which also provide an impetus for competitive behaviours. The chapters also show that building competition-based systems, or more effective markets for the efficient allocation of resources, is not simply a question of giving free reign to atomized and independent actors. Chataway argues that effective market-based competition also involves important forms of inter-organizational relationship. Firms often work together as a means to overcoming problems of access to know-how, or to share externalities, or to ensure a reliable supply of inputs. Bizarre as it may appear at face value, co-operation can make firms more competitive, more efficient, more effective! As Chataway shows, there are many ways in which firms are relating to other types of organizations and to the agendas they are setting, in order to be more competitive in the market. These include initiatives to demonstrate concern with, and performance in, social and environmental arenas. At the heart of moves to adopt voluntary codes of conduct or social auditing procedures may lie a competitive interest in terms of meeting the perceived demands of the market and expanding market-share. But the imperative to do so arises from the various forms of organizational and inter-organizational action which have placed these issues ever higher on the agenda – from campaigning groups lobbying companies to governments instituting legislation governing competitive practice.

WHY COMPETE?

The underlying rationale or justification for competition is that it leads to an efficient allocation of resources. But if competition is not just about price-mediated action in markets, and if it commonly involves forms of inter-organizational relationship, why compete? One answer is that where competition is *ruly* it can still lead to a greater efficiency in allocation of resources than might be the case without competition. It is just that far more needs to be done than simply 'leaving things to the market' if competition is not to become *unruly*. Moore identifies three types of ruly competition – market competition, tender competition, and prize competition. Each of these involves a different combination of the roles of competitor, referee, judges and prize donors. The essence of ruly competition is effective referees who ensure that competition follows accepted rules, and that it is therefore predictable and controllable to some degree.

But what are the differences between ruly and unruly forms of competition? Hanlon describes fragmented and contradictory actions as 'unhealthy competition' and Chataway refers to the kind of 'wild capitalism' emerging in many liberalizing economies. From the position of an external observer, these look simply like unruly competition. Ironically, however, although these forms of competition may look unruly and dysfunctional in terms of outcomes, they are the entirely rational outcome of the particular institutional factors which shape the given competitive arena. For example, the apparently unruly processes and outcomes discussed by Hanlon are taking place in a context in which those involved are party to explicit and implicit rules (such as how to obtain funding or forms of support). They are more than capable of effectively managing their roles as they perceive them.

Competition is about achieving your goals – which might be increased profit, increased market share, or increased influence over agendas. Unruly competition can be less effective for all those involved, lending itself to conflict. On the other hand, ruly competition might lead to more effective outcomes and greater choice, and its existence may encourage more constructive inter-organizational engagement. In a world where what is defined as ruly may be more about predominant values than it is about some objective or economistic notion of 'rational' behaviour, it seems that building ruly competition is about effectively managing ruly means for ruly ends.

MANAGING MEANS AND ENDS

Each of the chapters makes important points about *means* and *ends*. In the Mozambique case, the intended end is ostensibly improved health, yet Hanlon indicates that the means used to achieve that end can actually hinder its achievement. In this case, the existence of different agendas (both covert and overt) and the imperatives of organizational survival, lead to very

different ideas about appropriate means – and in some situations to contradictory or incompatible ideas about ends. This contributes to forms of
inter-organizational competition in which the end – improved health – get
somewhat sidelined as the means – the aid process itself – takes on a life of
its own.

Moore writes about the expectation that inter-organizational competition
is the means to 'improve public services'. Although this is only one possible means of working towards this end, it is a strategy which has captured
the imagination of 'reformers' world-wide during the 1990s. The language
of inter-organizational competition introduced to the public sector carries
with it connotations of 'entrepreneurialism' in the market-place. It resounds
with exciting terms such as 'efficiency' and 'cost-saving', and implies death
to obsolete (read unresponsive and inefficient) organizations through out-
competing them.

Building ruly competition and markets, however, is not an end which is
easily attained, as Chataway indicates. Even in the world of commerce and
private enterprise, the supposed home of effective competition, there are
many obstacles to the achieving this end. Information costs, unaccounted
externalities, instability, and fragmentation are factors which fundamentally shape the ways that firms and markets function. In the 'real world'
these, and other factors, may lead towards another end – unruly competition or 'wild capitalism' with all the attendant economic and social costs.
The challenge for builders of competitive markets is to look closely at their
means. As Chataway discusses, firms need capital, know-how, information, and a supportive environment to flourish. Action at one level, such
as macroeconomic policy, may well not be a sufficient means to achieve
the desired end.

Finally, there are real conflicts over what constitutes means and ends.
Chataway talks about the promotion of the 'model' of market competition
as a means to development. Ideas about state-led economic development
may have become highly unfashionable, but there are plenty of concerns
about what kinds of 'end' the capitalist market 'means' are leading to – not
least the exclusion of whole sections of society. And one person's means
can be another's ends. For example, inter-organizational competition might
be seen as a means to 'improving' a state-co-ordinated health system. But
it might be seen as an end in itself – a competitive private health system.
These fundamental differences of view help to explain some of the non-
material aspects of competition, where organizations are setting, and
competing over, different agendas for supporters, votes and other forms of
influence. Gaining and demonstrating 'market-share' can be as important
as a means to levering change for a campaigning organization, as it is an
important means and end to a successful commercial enterprise.

TAKING ACTION: TURNING PRINCIPLES INTO PRACTICE

Moore points out that there are plenty of potential downsides to competition as a means to allocating and managing resources, not least waste through unruly competition. These downsides derive both from existing institutionalized behaviours and practices, and from limits imposed on the scope for change such as access to information and capacities. So how do you build functional as opposed to dysfunctional competition? How do you manage to be ruly in an unruly context? How do you build on principles of choice, effectiveness, innovation, and efficiency, and avoid falling into forms of conflict and even anarchy?

INSTITUTIONAL FRAMEWORKS: THE RULES OF THE GAME

It is clear from all these chapters that the characteristics of the arenas in which competition takes place will shape the forms of competitive practice which result. Market-building reforms of the kind described by Chataway and Moore, have required reforms at the macro-level which both enable and enforce certain types of practice. Reforms aimed at creating a more conducive institutional context for competitive practice clearly cannot simply focus on the components of the macro economy – such as interest rates and exchange rate controls. Ruly competition also requires the existence of legal frameworks which help to provide the broader rules of the game, and of referees such as regulatory bodies to act as the monitors and enforcers of these rules. As Moore points out, the key issue is establishing the credibility of the roles required for ruly competition to operate. This means developing the settled certainty within the given institutional context that competitors, referees, judges and prize donors will function in certain ways and not in others.

WAYS OF ORGANIZING: INTERDEPENDENCE

Competition involves organizations, whether they work in an atomized way, in parallel, or in concert. As Moore indicates, in the absence of immediate reforms in the institutional set-up, organizations can initiate certain practices in the name of building ruly competition at the inter-organizational level. This can be done, for example, through existing informal relationships, perhaps restructuring these relationships through a different allocation of resources. This type of action is tackling what Moore refers to as *incentive* and *intelligence* mechanisms.

The notion of atomized organizations behaving competitively may not be at all useful, particularly in contexts where some of the basics identified by Moore – discipline, honesty, accountability, predictability – do not function effectively. There are important 'health' warnings in each of these chapters about the rapid introduction of 'competition' and an over-emphasis on the scope for markets to deliver effectiveness and efficiency in resource allocation. It may be more useful to think in terms of creating a competitively structured set of incentives which also involve organizations in co-operative ways of organizing in the interest of building competition. Strategies for this range from chambers of commerce which support and promote local businesses to bringing firms together in industrial districts where they can share services and other resources.

The importance of action at this meso level – between the macro and the micro – is emphasized by one private sector development consultant:

> ... I'm not a top-down person, but equally I'm not a grass roots person. I think you've got to work from both and most of my work I would define as being work at a meso level, which is work somewhere between the macro level and the micro level ... It is often at the meso level that things start to go wrong.

> ... at the micro level you are more often than not dealing with a single organization ... with its effectiveness in achieving its ... very specific objectives. At the macro level you're dealing with some systemic changes but you are trying to do it in a way that creates the environment and conditions for independent actors to achieve their objectives. Hopefully there's sufficient commonality that they'll come together and achieve the national objectives. But you're not actually working with individual institutions or with individual people or individual sources of power and contribution, you're just [suggesting] this has got to work because we say it has to work from a national level. It's at the meso level, intermediate level, where these two forces can come together and that's where I think the most effective institutional development work happens.

ORGANIZATIONS: THE BUILDING BLOCKS

Hanlon suggests that it is vital that development managers recognize their own mixed goals, and that they understand that they are engaging with others who also have their own mix of priorities. In other words, at the level of the organization and individual manager, managing competitively in a competitive environment requires a good knowledge of your 'market' and of means to exploit it effectively to achieve your ends. This implies a need for skills of *appreciation* on two levels. The first, as Hanlon writes, is knowing or appreciating what your own goals are, and not getting caught up in an attempt to manage too many, or being distracted by your own rhetoric. This should increase your chances of achieving the outcomes you aim for – a solid entrepreneurial principle! The second aspect of appreciation is getting to know what others are doing, and what their priorities are, in order to be able to compete more effectively against them, or to compete more effectively with them.

Many managers tend to know a great deal about their own organization and its internal linkages, but have comparatively limited information about their environment and other organizations in it. Over the years management teaching and training have also been lacking in their development of tools which assist managers to look outwards and to analyse their environment. Yet the environment is a rich source of opportunity. Inskip (1994) writes about the importance of 'network agents':

> The start-up of network agents generally begins when a cosmopolite leader recognizes trends in the macroenvironment or a community problem that cannot be solved by one organization and starts scanning the environment for similar problems or possible solutions.

There are individuals and organizations which perform an important role in constantly scanning the environment, identifying problems or opportunities, communicating the problem, identifying potential organizations which share the same problem or interests, and then mobilizing these organizations. Such a function can be central to building and maintaining competitiveness, and a very different strategy to believing in conflict.

ENDNOTE: ORGANIZATIONAL LIFE AND DEATH

In the idealized version of competition, firms have to be efficient and only the fittest survive. In the real world, however, it seems that many organizations do not die. Instead they find ways to survive, and ways which are not based on any obvious comparative efficiency. In the complex web of material and non-material forms of competition, it is not always clear when an organization has become defunct. And as Hanlon proposes, the very process of existing and being can in fact take over from the achievement of stated ends.

CO-ORDINATION

7 REFORMING THE STATE: CO-ORDINATION, REGULATION OR FACILITATION?

DORCAS ROBINSON

7.1 REDEFINING THE ROLE OF THE STATE

International debate about the role of the state – what the state *should* do – has shifted over the last fifty years. The original idea of the welfare state, with the state as the lead actor, implementing and *co-ordinating* development was replaced by the idea of the *regulatory* state (the so-called 'rolled back' state), allowing for more private enterprise and competition. This has in turn been replaced by the more recent idea of the *facilitative* state, where the state provides an 'enabling' environment. This debate reflects changing ideas about the nature of co-ordination: a function in social, economic and political life with which the state has commonly been associated.

An important argument for direct state co-ordination of basic social services has been its potential for building *universality* of coverage and *equity* of access which neither the market nor voluntary action could offer. For many newly independent countries in the 1950s and 1960s, the imperative to 'modernize', to meet expectations raised by independence movements, and to unify societies, all suggested a need for direct state co-ordination.

By the 1980s, however, international debate was shifting away from a focus on the state as the central mechanism for changing economies and societies, to the state as the central problem (Mackintosh, 1992b). Negative views of the state – on the one hand portrayed as 'weak' and 'disintegrating', characterized by economic crisis, collapsing services, and civil conflict; and on the other as 'predatory' and 'corrupt' – began to provide a strong impetus for its reform.

The idea that the state could be more of a hindrance than a help in some aspects of development found allies across the political spectrum. Diagnosis of the problem varied: on the left the critique was of the 'unresponsive but invasive' state, and on the right of the 'inefficient but restrictive' state (Mackintosh, 1992b). However, both shared the view that the state is not necessarily a unitary or benevolent actor operating in the public interest, or capable of responding effectively to forms of market failure. The state might produce equally problematic distortions in itself – forms of 'government failure'.

Reform – social sector reform, civil service reform, local government reform, to name just a few types of current reform package – has been a dominant theme in the 1990s. Reform has connotations not simply of change, but of change for the better. 'Better' in the international agenda for reform in the 1990s has not meant 'better' access and equity (an important issue in the 1970s) so much as 'better' management – 'leaner and meaner' management for more efficient and effective services. Reform, change, improvement, are of course not new ideas. What is quite new is the approach. Reform programmes of the 1990s have been based on reducing the role and size of state services, through privatization and increasing the scope for both for-profit and not-for-profit service provision, and decentralizing decision-making to other actors. This idea of reform is not about small modifications to parts of a system. It is concerned with wholesale change – a fundamental reorientation of whole sectors of activity and the principles on which these operate.

This type of reform has two major implications for the co-ordinative function of the state and for a variety of inter-organizational relationships:

1   between central and local governments (the basis of a renewed interest in decentralization); and

2   between the state and other actors, including for-profit businesses, NGOs and community groups (the substance of debates about 'gap-filling', public-private partnership, collective action and synergy).

This chapter discusses these two aspects of the reform agenda. The first in terms of what it means for the role of the state as co-ordinator. The second in terms of what it means for the roles of other actors – non governmental organizations (NGOs), private business, communities and users, local governments – and the management of the relationships between these actors and the state. The chapter explores these two aspects of the changing role of the state by looking at health sector reform in Tanzania.

7.2   THE ROLE OF THE STATE: WHAT DOES IT MEAN TO CO-ORDINATE, REGULATE AND FACILITATE?

Tanzania's health sector reform programme seeks to address the ideological, managerial, financial and organizational problems identified in existing policy. As in many other countries currently reforming their health sectors, these reforms involve reversals of, or significant changes to, past policy. A key change which has been proposed is in the role of government:

> To meet all these challenges the government has decided to *change its role from that of main provider to facilitator* of health services.

> (Government of Tanzania, 1994, pp. vi-vii, emphasis added)

This has far-reaching implications for the 'what?' and 'how?' of the government's involvement in health services.

7.2.1   THE STATE AS CO-ORDINATOR (THE WELFARE STATE)

co-ordinate: to bring the parts into proper relations and to cause to function together or in proper order.

Whilst this definition of co-ordination does not preclude activity by a plurality of 'parts' (such as community organizations, NGOs, private clinics and so on) the story of the welfare state tends to assume that the state is policy-maker, funder *and* direct provider of social services. In other words, not only does the state determine what the 'proper order' is (i.e. policy), *and* manage the relationship between the 'parts', it also provides most of these parts itself.

This is exactly the role which Tanzania's single-party government began to adopt after the Arusha Declaration of 1967, in which it laid out its commitment to socialism and self-reliance. Free government provision of health and education services became a key pillar of Tanzania's development strategy, in the name of equity and the development of people.

The health system inherited by the newly independent Tanzanian government in 1961 was largely urban-based, serving 'Grade A' patients (which included expatriates and senior civil servants), and focused on curative medical services (Coulson, 1982). These government hospitals accounted for 58% of beds in 1958, with the rest being located in the private sector. NGOs, predominantly religious agencies, provided 81% of dispensaries, many of which provided services in rural areas (Munishi, 1995).

In the 20 years since the Arusha Declaration, the Tanzanian government set out firstly to extend basic medical services by increasing levels of spending on health in real terms, initiating programmes to construct government dispensaries and health centres, and training large numbers of government medical staff. Secondly, it attempted to shift the focus of the government health system away from a bias in expenditure to curative and urban facilities which served a few, towards primary health care, with an emphasis on health promotion for the benefit of the rural majority. By the time that Primary Health Care (PHC) was adopted internationally in the World Health Organization's Alma Ata Declaration of 1978, Tanzania was a flagship for the movement. The government had managed to extend support so that 72% of the population was now within 5 kilometres of a health facility, over half of which were providing mother and child health services aimed at tackling high levels of maternal and infant mortality and morbidity (Jonsson, 1986).

In most discussions of PHC the emphasis is placed on district health care provision as the best means for tackling the goal of 'Achieving Health For

All'. This model is usually based on the premise that government is the main provider of health services, that the health service system runs in a straight line from district to centre, and that therefore the task is one of direct co-ordination by the state, of itself:

> The district health offices will supervise their network of health centres; district hospitals will provide logistical support for priority health interventions; other sectoral institutions will collaborate with the health centre staff in implementing health-related interventions. Intermediate (regional) health institutions will provide backup – referral of patients, selection of health technologies for the package as well as training and research. Central level institutions will ensure that health policies, strategies and plans are supportive of the District Health Package.

> (Monekosso, 1994)

This is the approach which the Tanzanian Ministry of Health had adopted, and in the process it had made arrangements with 17 mission-owned hospitals, nominating these as government district-designated hospitals in return for government inputs for staff and material costs. In the process of increasing its commitments to the health system the Tanzanian government also took action with regard to other actors. This included the nationalization of two major church hospitals, turning these into government zonal referral hospitals. It also included a ban on private medical practice on the basis that private activity in certain key areas was not compatible with the commitment to socialism. Health service provision outside the government system was restricted to approved organizations such as religious missions. The Ministry of Health extended its role as policymaker, taking over all national projects and responsibility for providing policy direction for overall sectoral co-ordination in 1972.

By the mid 1980s however, with economic crisis and later, structural adjustment, the health sector was taking its share of budget cuts. In 1982/3, the health budget was 57% in real terms of what it had been in 1977/8 (Kahama, 1995). Despite the stated commitment to rural health (with a rural population representing 85% of the total) and PHC, hospitals were receiving increasing shares of government spending, and in 1989-1993, only 4% of the government's recurrent budget went to prevention (Government of Tanzania, 1994). Donor-funded vertical programmes, such as the Essential Drugs Programme, were introduced, but were only intended to provide temporary support measures to the system. By the late 1980s it was clear that the government could no longer maintain its ideological commitment to free health care – there were constant shortages of drugs and other material supplies, deterioration of physical structures, limited training and supervision contributing to low staff morale. The gaps between stated intentions and reality were widening dramatically.

7.2.2   THE STATE AS REGULATOR AND/OR FACILITATOR

The Health Sector Reform proposal and action plans developed by the mid-1990s emphasize finance and management. Cost-recovery schemes were introduced into government hospitals, in many cases formalizing a *de facto* situation in which users had been paying for services informally for some time. Whilst the proposed extension of cost-recovery to lower level facilities such as health centres has been halted for the time being, pilot Community Health Fund schemes which generate funds through a form of health insurance, have been introduced. In addition, to help shift the financial burden from the government as the 'main provider and sole source of health financing, supplemented by non-profit NGOs', for-profit health services were re-legalized in 1992, allowing for 'tapping of private sector potential' (Government of Tanzania, 1994).

Now positively advocating pluralism in health service provision, the Tanzanian government faces important questions about the roles of different actors, and the nature and management of relationships between them:

> Private health care providers (both for-profit and not-for-profit) are now PARTNERS rather than opponents or competitors for the demise of the other.
>
> (Government of Tanzania, 1994, p. 8)

This statement indicates a need to find mechanisms which go beyond the unhealthy forms of competition which are hinted at here. But is direct co-ordination by the state the way forward?

Not according to the World Development Report of 1993, *Investing in Health*:

> In most circumstances, however, the primary objective of public policy should be to promote competition among providers – including between the public and private sectors (where there are public providers) as well as among private providers, whether non-profit or for-profit.
>
> (World Bank, 1993)

This view of the role of 'public policy', as promotion of competition, has dominated recent international reform agendas. It is associated with the idea, now in vogue, of the state as *indirect* co-ordinator of parts – the regulatory or facilitative state.

The underlying rationale for this position is that private organizations are more effective and efficient direct providers of services than governments, that their activities are best mediated through competition, and that the appropriate role for the state is therefore as promoter of a market-based environment which 'enables' a plurality of parts to function effectively. There is naturally substantial debate however, over just what type of environment is enabling (and enabling of what sort of activities and outcomes), and disagreement over the desirability of the market-based, competitive approach.

But how does a state provide an 'enabling environment'? What do 'regulation' and 'facilitation' actually imply for a state and its co-ordinative function? Given that the notion of the 'enabling environment' is common both to the regulatory and facilitative roles of the state, it would seem that there is little distinction between them. However, the dictionary definition does indicate a clear difference, with implications for *how* the state promotes an enabling environment:

To regulate: to control by rules or to subject to restrictions.

To facilitate: to make easy or to promote.

In the definition of regulation there is reference to 'control by rules', which could include, for example, determining national health policy and the rules for operation in the health sector.

The definition of facilitation shifts away even from indirect co-ordination, with somewhat vague reference 'to make easy or to promote'. This is reminiscent of the idea of an 'invisible hand', which has often been used to describe the market. It suggests a situation in which a facilitative government supports an enabling environment, in the sense of ensuring the necessary legal, economic and political conditions are created. But this does not necessarily mean that the state is determining specific policy or engaging in any co-ordination of parts. Taking this idea to its logical conclusion, the state may not even be directly formulating the rules (policy) or have a monopoly on this, but rather, be supporting other actors to develop these (for example, encouraging professional associations to develop shared standards) and providing the systems whereby these become legal and protected.

In the Tanzanian case, as no doubt in most others, references to the government as 'facilitator' are probably better expressed as 'regulator', as this is certainly what practice indicates is aspired to. The Ministry of Health maintains its role as central policymaker, determining the rules by which various actors operate, as well as making the necessary legislative changes which will enable private practice and district government management in all areas of health service provision. Whilst it has begun to move away from a perception of itself as direct co-ordinator of a government health system, it is a long way (and many would argue, should continue to be a long way) from simply promoting the activities of other actors. At the same time, as the Ministry moves from direct co-ordination towards regulation, it faces significant challenges – in obtaining and managing information, developing the required management capacities, and in making sense of the huge diversity which exists in reality. The next section looks more closely at three arenas of action which provide some ideas about what forms of state co-ordination might be appropriate and feasible in this context.

7.3 MANAGING THE ROLE OF OTHER ACTORS: WHAT AND HOW DOES THE STATE CO-ORDINATE ?

7.3.1 THE 'PRIVATE' SECTOR

Most policymakers discussing the reform of social services tend to refer to both for-profit and not-for-profit organizations as the 'private' sector. Given the relatively recent re-legalization of for-profit private health practice in Tanzania, this section focuses primarily on not-for-profit organizations, or NGOs. The Tanzanian Ministry of Health's documentation suggest two things about the 'private' sector. Firstly that, although for-profit provision was banned in 1977, there is a history of relationships between the state and other providers. Secondly, that the nature of those relationships may not always have been amicable.

Recognition of NGO activities in health service provision is comparatively recent, both in international policy agendas and within Ministries of Health (Green and Matthias, 1994), even though the story of the welfare state as almost monopolistic provider of health services has not been true of practice in many countries. In Tanzania, NGOs, largely religious organizations, own 56% of hospitals (Mujinja *et al.*, 1993), provide 30% of all health service points (Government of Tanzania, 1994), and even at the peak of government financial support to health care in 1976, accounted for between 37% and 43% of total health expenditure (Mujinja et al, 1993). This level of NGO involvement in health care is not dissimilar to other African countries (DeJong, 1991).

As governments have turned their attention to health sector reform, the level of NGO involvement in health care has made it apparent that adequate regulatory frameworks are needed to guide their operations. Where government policy and implementation frameworks are already weak, and where NGOs are in receipt of increasing amounts of donor funding, a lack of direct contact between large numbers of NGOs and government planning systems may be contributing to the fragmentation of the health sector (Green and Matthias, 1994). Gilson *et al.* (1994) propose that Ministries of Health have four options when it comes to dealing with NGOs. They can:

1 restrict NGO operations;

2 maintain the current situation;

3 increase government regulation, co-ordination and supervision; and/or

4 actively promote NGOs.

Making decisions between options like these must depend however on a careful assessment of what NGOs are currently doing and why, what government policy seeks to achieve, and what is feasible in the given institutional context. The problem all to often is that whilst the significance of NGOs has now been noted by ministries (and donors), this is yet to be followed through with a comprehensive approach to assessing what they do and how best the state can relate to them. The reality of practice is all too often a situation in which NGOs and government officials report good informal relationships with each other, but also identify problems such as lack of information-sharing and dialogue, for which they blame each other (Green and Matthias, 1994).

The evidence in Tanzania is that large numbers of NGOs active in health are not conversant with changing government health policy. With a few important exceptions, such as the Christian Social Services Commission which formed specifically to co-ordinate and represent the concerns of the churches working in health and education, neither NGOs nor the central ministry have made systematic and formal efforts to liaise with or inform each other. Part of the problem is obviously the diversity and geographic spread of NGOs, many of which relate most appropriately to local governments. On the other hand, governments themselves may not be clear how they perceive their role, let alone how they plan to manage it:

> The role of the private sector in health care must be encouraged and private providers should be facilitated to provide complementary services. Once the Government has determined its role in the provision of equitable health services and has liberated private practice, the public will have access to a health service mix it can afford, and can then make a choice between public and private services depending on the quality, affordability and consumer satisfaction of such services.
>
> (Government of Tanzania, 1994)

The implication is that other organizations will fit in once the government has determined its position. But, in the process of reforming the state, it needs to be recognized that other actors are already engaged in health services, shaping the system, and not always with reference to specific government policies coming from the centre.

Exploring the idea that NGOs are 'gap-fillers' in deteriorating government health systems, Cannon, (1996) effectively provides a critique of the idea that NGOs simply fit into government-determined health systems. In the case of Uganda, Cannon notes that some aspects of donor, government and NGO behaviour are consistent with this idea of gap-filling – the Ugandan health sector is heavily dependent on external support, donors increasingly contract NGOs to implement programmes, and some NGOs are concerned that they are effectively enabling the government to withdraw from its responsibilities in health. However, many government and NGO staff take exception to the idea that NGOs are gap-fillers, with statements like:

> The missions are part of us, even if they are external. They are not doing somebody else's work. They were pioneers in the fields of health and education; the government came in later.
>
> (local government official quoted in Cannon, 1996)

and:

> NGOs are partners in the services of health care, given the history,
> the churches etc. They were the first people to start offering health
> services in this country. It wasn't gap-filling. They felt the service
> was needed and they continue to exist. It's not that the gaps
> continue, but the NGOs are established and continue in their own
> right.
>
> (quoted in Cannon, 1996)

Cannon goes on to note that NGO-government relationships are described
using familial language, often referring to them in terms of a marriage
partnership:

> Using the imagery of marriage, an official in the Ministry of Health
> explained, 'The government has learned a great deal from missions.
> In cost-sharing, we have borrowed a lot of ideas to build up our
> system. I hope the marriage grows stronger and stronger to improve
> the health of people'. In a classic marriage analogy, an official of a
> Ugandan NGO explains: 'The man of the family is supposed to be
> responsible for everything. In the same way, the government has
> the responsibility. The NGOs are like a wife. The husband and wife
> supplement each other and work together, sharing, complementing
> each other. The government is the overall co-ordinator, and it is
> accountable, but the wife is too'.
>
> (Cannon, 1996)

and:

> ... an Oxfam staff member chided Ugandan NGOs at a conference,
> saying that their competition for resources and recognition
> resembled the fighting of co-wives.
>
> (Cannon, 1996)

What emerges from this research is that whilst NGOs have been operating
in health service provision for some years, there are a number of issues still
to be addressed if a pluralistic health sector is to function effectively. These
include a perceived need to move from informal, 'gentleman's
understandings' to memorandums of understanding between organizations,
not just individuals. The Ugandan government is also challenged to find
ways of co-ordinating health services so as not to lose credibility in the
eyes of its citizens, but in a situation in which it is highly dependent upon
external sources in funding. As one Ugandan researcher explained:

> Government has a mandate to look after the country but not the
> machinery to influence what other actors are doing.
>
> (quoted in Cannon, 1996)

In this case, NGOs, as a set of actors, may also have an interest in coming together with the government to help ensure that co-ordinated action, not fragmentation, is the outcome for health services.

It is increasingly evident that NGOs have not simply been filling minor gaps in government systems, but have been the pioneers in many areas, undertaking activities which are often later adopted by governments. Whilst current reform discourse depicts NGOs as 'private sector' organizations, there is plenty of evidence that NGOs are long-term actors in the *public* health system, engaged both in defining as well as meeting needs (Robinson, 1999). The Ugandan case provides an interesting insight into the importance of meaning in inter-organizational relationships – the way in which different parties construct their understanding of their roles. The language used indicates that interdependence is both recognized and positively celebrated by NGOs and government.

On the other hand, institutional contexts are complex and constantly evolving, and where tensions arise, this language may also be an important tool for managing changing relationships. Where a government is challenged to contend with the implications of growing NGO (and for-profit) health sectors (in the interest of national health policy and outcomes), the husband and wife analogy clearly reminds the parties involved of the nature of their interdependence – the 'husband' or government is the legitimate co-ordinator, whilst NGOs are partners not leaders.

In some situations, such language may seem to be doing no more than paying lip-service, and obscuring more complicated and contradictory realities. However, no matter to what extent it reflects actual practice, it is an important statement of intentions. It is these intentions which may allow NGO and government relationships to survive shifts in policies and politics over time. These broad intentions are reproduced on different levels, often depending on informal social links, whether through direct person-to-person contact or through social and professional groups in which people share and maintain similar backgrounds, training and concerns. This is a point emphasised by Sivalon (1995) when discussing the relationship between the Roman Catholic Church and the Tanzanian state. He notes that contrary to some expectations, the government's nationalization of church schools in the 1970s did not create tensions (indeed, this relieved the church of a great resource burden). Instead the relationship between church and state around social service provision has essentially been one of co-operation. Sources of tension were more to do with a perceived move of the state towards a more Marxist approach to development (Sivalon, 1995). He notes that, in fact, many of the same people have been involved in both 'church' and 'state' groups either personally, through familial ties or through other social relationships, such as shared educational background, to the point where the relationship between the 'bureaucratic class' and the churches has heightened tensions between Muslim and Christian communities (Sivalon, 1995).

In the future this is an important factor to remember. It hints at how foreign sources of aid can affect the relationship among different organs of civil society and how, in turn, these will affect their relationships with government. It is highly conceivable that alliances will be formed between particular political parties and organisations of civil society, with access to outside funding being the main bargaining counter.

(Sivalon, 1995)

This work illustrates that even where pluralism has not been promoted by government (Tanzania was a one-party, socialist state until 1992), other independent actors have existed, and have been initiators and maintainers of relationships with the state. In this case, there is a significant history of interdependence, built in part on social relationships which develop across and beyond 'the state' or 'the church'. However, organizations are also independent, and they have a certain autonomy in developing and expressing their own organizational agendas. For example, the nature of government co-ordination (its focus and approach) has altered over time, as indicated by the policy to nationalize social services, an attempt at direct co-ordination. At the same time, it is clear that the Church also has its own changing agendas, which interact with government agendas, and which affect relationships. These are not only shaped by the actions of the state but other factors too:

> ... of which the most important was the changing internal understanding of church personnel concerning the social ministry itself. In the 1960's tremendous emphasis was placed on rural and socio-economic development ... Similarly, in the 1970s there was another shift emphasising a more critical stance towards the structural obstacles to development ... Furthermore, in the late 1970s and 1980s, the church was much more inward-looking as it strove to become self-supporting and self-governing.
>
> These shifts had an effect on how the church responded to the call to provide social services. However, at no time did the church remove itself from the provision of social services. Nor was the church at any time completely replaced by the state in the provision of traditional social services like health and education. Rather, the primary factor in the relationship of state and church in the provision of social services has been an attempt to co-operate ...
>
> (Sivalon, 1995)

In most situations there will be constant tensions between attempts to control and organizational autonomy; tensions which increase when organizational agendas do not coincide. Managing these tensions requires some understanding not just of individual relationships, between two organizations, but also of the broader institutional context. For example, whilst a Ministry of Health may be legitimately concerned about its capacity to control NGOs, and whilst it seeks more formality in relationships, its ideas about what NGOs should be doing may not be realistic. This is an import-ant issue in current privatization initiatives. 'Private sector' organizations may simply not have the capacity, or the desire, to provide the 'parts' to the system which the co-ordinating, regulating or facilitating government is anticipating. For example, in the early 1960s, the Tanzanian government's Titmuss Commission recommended that the voluntary agencies concentrate on curative services with some preventive activities. Yet there has been, and continues to be, major involvement by NGOs in PHC and activities related to health development.

In situations in which 'donors contribute 90% of the Development Expenditure on health services' (Government of Tanzania, 1996, p. 6), where there are many hundreds of NGOs and private practioners, the direct control approach to co-ordination by government is not a realistic option. But is simply providing regulatory frameworks enough or is more active building and maintenance of inter-organizational relationships required to ensure effective forms of co-ordination?

7.3.2 DECENTRALIZATION

The World Development Report of 1993, setting out the agenda on Health Sector Reform which forms the basis of World Bank financial and technical support to health sectors in countries like Tanzania, proposes certain components to a reform package:

- that governments reorient themselves from being policymaker, provider and funder of health services and move towards the state-as-regulator position;
- that cost recovery and Community Health Insurance schemes be introduced as strategies for financing services; and
- that state provision be focused on 'basic essential health care' (this is specified as a limited and targeted safety net, providing immunization and micro-nutrient supplement programmes, school health programmes for worm treatment, family planning awareness programmes, and AIDS and Sexually Transmitted Diseases prevention).

The reformers have revisited 'decentralization', offering this as the big idea, or the pin which can hold together these proposed components with some coherence:

> Decentralization of government services is potentially the most important force for improving efficiency and responding to local health conditions and demands. It will be successful only when local agencies and hospitals have a sound financial base, solid administrative capacity and incentives for improving efficiency – when they are accountable to patients and local citizens.
>
> (World Bank, 1993)

The Tanzanian Ministry of Health also recognizes that 'the district is the most important administrative and implementation level because planning, budgeting and resource command takes place there' (Government of Tanzania, 1994). Tanzania's Health Sector Reform programme sets out to clarify co-ordination within government. Problems have accumulated over the years. For example, at the district level, local government and the central Ministry of Health have been responsible for different aspects of local health services, often resulting in the under-utilization of resources, and an improperly functioning referral system. Similarly, the existence of several vertical health programmes, managed at the local level by managers responsible to the Ministry of Health and within their own budget lines, has meant that generic functions, such as purchase and distribution of supplies, or training of staff, are duplicated. In order to address such problems, the reforms have set out to hand all aspects of local health service delivery to the single authority of local government, whilst defining the Ministry of Health's role as policy, legislation and regulation.

Such changes are logical attempts to rationalize the government's co-ordination of itself. However, there is a great deal more implied in the idea of 'decentralization' as currently associated with these types of reform package. Given that the policy and practice of decentralization has been notoriously fraught with difficulties, mostly arising from gaps between stated intention and actual implementation, it is important to be clear about what is actually meant by decentralization – what outcomes are looked for, and what co-ordination mechanisms are being proposed.

The term 'decentralization' in fact masks different meanings and set-ups, each with its own implications for the distribution of powers of decision-making and of resource mobilization and usage. It is important to remember that the traditional notion of decentralization has been administrative decentralization or the re-distribution of powers within an organization (such as a company, or the state) itself. These forms of decentralization can be divided into three categories (Mills, 1994):

1 *deconcentration*: the transfer of some administrative responsibilities (but not political authority) to the locally based offices of central government ministries;

2 *devolution*: the creation and strengthening of sub-national levels of government that are substantially independent of the central government, often with clear legal status and authority to raise revenue;

3 *delegation*: the transfer of managerial responsibility of defined functions to organizations outside the central government structure and only indirectly controlled by it; this is often a nationalized company or parastatal.

Recently, the somewhat chaotic idea of 'decentralization to the market' has come into reform debate. This is about liberalizing business and social service systems, involving the privatization and deregulation of state-run concerns (Rondinelli *et al.*, 1989). Decentralization to the market is not about decentralizing within government, but about the market being 'free', supposedly allowing various actors to operate flexibly at all levels, unencumbered by centralizing forces or control. In its use of language such as 'participation' and 'empowerment', this idea of decentralization as providing greater consumer choice in a market-based system has become implicitly connected with another more organic or bottom-up version of decentralization. Where forms of local or grassroots action (community based organizations, NGOs, traditional leaders) are making decisions and managing resources. Of course, for many of the proponents of community participation, the intention is to create space for increased participation in relations with government policy and practice, not the market.

From these various perspectives, it is clear that 'decentralization' can imply different forms of co-ordinative relationships depending on its focus. It might emphasize:

- vertical relationships, for example, between central and local government;
- or horizontal relationships, for example, across local government departments; or
- between local government and other local actors.

Tanzanian health reform appears to match the devolutionary form of administrative decentralization, within government. The reforms provide for greater emphasis on District Health Management Teams. But in practice, such initiatives face two significant problems. The first is resourcing. Whilst expected to take on more of the responsibility for co-ordinating development at the local level, district governments are not being given the funding needed to perform this task. When funding does arrive, it has often already been allocated to a particular activity by central government. It is therefore not uncommon to hear District Medical Officers complain that they have been sent money for training, but that their most pressing need is money for drugs and material purchases. Secondly, in the context of such resource constraints, the relationship with other local actors can be tense, as district governments attempt to gain some control over what these agencies do. It is not uncommon to hear NGOs complain that district governments are insisting that they channel their funds through government, or that they only conduct projects put forward by governments. The guidelines issued under Health Sector Reform are not helpful for those ostensibly managing a multi-actor health system at the local level. For example, the District Health Management Guidelines are based on the assumption that health system managers are organized in a clear hierarchical line within the government system. Whilst the language of policy is about decentralized power and the promotion of 'private' health providers, in the guidelines, reference to working with other actors is limited to statements like:

> In areas where there are 'special' programs financed partly or in total by external donors or NGOs, these *might* be represented in the District Health Planning Team.
>
> (Government of Tanzania, 1995, emphasis added)

Or:

> All NGOs/Managers of vertical programmes will integrate their planning process and execute programmes together to allow cross-fertilisation of ideas and efficient utilisation of resources and quality standards maintained ... in both public and private practice.
>
> (Government of Tanzania, 1996, p. 2)

This rather directive language does not invite or support local-level government managers to adopt a facilitative approach to co-ordination, or encourage non-government managers to engage. For many managers, there is a long way to go before they could say of themselves:

> I am just a facilitator. I am neither a manager nor a teacher. I am just an animator and facilitator who enhances people to think forward.
>
> (Government health co-ordinator, Tanzania, 1998)

Yet where government and non-government managers have little knowledge of each other, or have to manage genuine organizational differences over goals and outcomes, a facilitative approach to relationships may be an important place to start. All too often in practice, government and non-government managers are either effectively ignoring each other, or are involved in long and often difficult processes of negotiation over autonomy and control. The end result can be frustration and fragmentation, not the coherent District Health Plan which is desired. From this scenario it is evident that effective co-ordinative relationships are not simply about form (vertical, horizontal) but about the organization of power:

- ensuring that district governments are actually given the power to do what the centre has 'decentralized';
- appreciating that independent actors are autonomous and may not respond positively to attempts at control;
- acknowledging that a key actor like the state often has a legitimate role in laying out the ground rules.

7.3.3 CO-ORDINATION AT THE MICRO-LEVEL: GOVERNMENT, COMMUNITIES AND NGOS

Nowhere are the 'managerial' problems identified in current health sector practice more evident than at the micro-level. In the Tanzanian case, the idea of decentralization is connected to the promotion of Primary Health Care (PHC) which has been retained as the overarching framework for health development, despite the World Bank's recommendation that governments focus on more limited public health packages. In a PHC

approach to health, community action is key, and therefore decentralization means more than government reorganization – it is also about
intersectoral, interagency collaboration at the local level:

> ... the Government needs to create an environment that will enable
> communities, households in particular to improve their health
> status. It also has to redirect resources to support the implemen-
> tation of cost-effective health interventions. Since the focus of
> Primary Health Care implementation is at the district, district health
> services management including the district hospital should be
> placed under the Local Government. This will facilitate effective
> management and streamline accountability.

(Government of Tanzania, 1994, pp. 5-6)

However, the government acknowledges a major challenge, namely that:

> ... the concepts of decentralization and primary health care (PHC)
> are not well understood by some policy makers, implementors and
> community members.

(Government of Tanzania, 1994, p. vii)

It is problems such as these that initiatives like the Community Based Health
Care (CBHC) approach to PHC set out to address. Originally developed by
the African Medical Research Foundation (AMREF) in Kenya, CBHC is
the complement to the more familiar Institution Based Health Care (IBHC)
approach to Primary Health Care. It is now also widely promoted by NGOs
and governments in Tanzania and Uganda. CBHC is primarily focused on
individuals and households within the community setting, and beyond the
context of health services delivery units. It is concerned with the basic
PHC problem: that the majority of cases presented at village health facilities are 'home-preventable'. They tell the tale of poverty – in income, environment (sanitation, water supply, housing), education, power and
organization. The CBHC approach recognizes that these are issues that no
health facility alone can tackle, even where that facility is well-resourced
and has the capacity to deliver quality health education. Therefore, CBHC
seeks to develop health awareness and healthful practice within a framework of empowerment. It focuses on community, on local needs and
understanding, on local organization and resource, and on making
linkages between the network of organizations which interact with
communities.

CBHC is therefore about collective action at all levels. In implementation,
it encourages CBHC-trained community members, village health workers,
traditional birth attendants, religious and political leaders, and government
extension staff to work together at the village level. In order to move
beyond duplication of work, or single, vertical programmes, CBHC
programmes also attempt to build intersectoral and multi-actor awareness
and committees at other levels, from ward to district to region, drawing
together government and NGOs.

CBHC has to date been largely implemented by NGOs. The approach taken varies according to the history and size of the NGO. For example, local church development offices often focus primarily on training parish educators, drawn from their own village congregations. Other NGOs work across groups of villages, which tend to fall within existing government ward and district boundaries. This approach commonly involves the training of trainers at ward or district government level, who are then supported by the NGO in their regular interaction with village health workers, committees, and village CBHC groups. These programmes may be part of integrated development projects (also concerned with education, water, agriculture and income-generation) or may grow out of earlier health education projects which had focused on single issues such as Mother and Child Health or reproductive health. Many NGOs, particularly the church organizations, have developed CBHC programmes out of old PHC outreach projects which were operated from their own health centres or hospitals. Therefore, CBHC is promoted both by health service providing NGOs working in the formal health system, and NGOs which support broader community development programmes.

These are all efforts to build up micro-level co-ordination activities. Yet whilst NGOs may be the main initiators and implementors of CBHC with community level groups, they also generally seek to build the approach into government systems, with a view to government undertaking the on-going regional and national co-ordination of CBHC. For example, in 1988 AMREF began a CBHC programme in Rukwa Region of Tanzania in collaboration with the Ministry of Health and local governments. The agency trained and supported relevant government staff, eventually pulling back its own direct input in the mid-1990s. A similar example is provided by the Community Based Health Care Council (CBHCC), which grew out of an earlier multi-agency (NGO and government) PHC Co-ordinating Committee, and registered as an NGO in 1992. Initially funded by Oxfam, the Council's first plan of work involved CBHC training of key government staff in the hospital and regional/district structure in 9 regions. Subsequent diversion of Oxfam's funding in the wake of the Rwandan refugee crisis severely limited the Council's capacity to continue these activities, but it has left behind trained government personnel, a number of whom are now supported in their CBHC work by other NGOs.

NGOs also link their CBHC activities with other health support services they provide. For example, many NGOs are involved in the delivery of government vertical health programmes, such as family planning, childhood vaccination and malaria control. They tend to integrate this with CBHC programmes, for example, developing social marketing schemes for bed-nets or condoms, or providing information at village-level prior to vaccination campaigns, as well as logistical support (transport, drugs and funds) for those campaigns.

These implementation-related activities reveal a significant level of inter-dependence between NGOs and government. Not only do NGOs train and support government staff, they often have government staff seconded to them. This mirrors a long-standing reciprocal situation in the provision of curative services, where government provides inputs to mission-owned hospitals which have been designated as the district hospital.

In the 1994 Proposals for Health Sector Reform, the Ministry of Health notes its relationship with AMREF, and identifies CBHC as one of its strategies for promoting PHC. This document explains that previous initiatives, such as the village health worker programme, or the establishment of PHC committees at all levels from region to district to village, have not been hugely successful. However, it believes that this structure continues to provide for the 'effective decentralization and co-ordination of community involvement', and takes up the recommendation from a study commissioned from AMREF that CBHC is the most effective approach for community involvement:

> The study recommends approaches that will empower communities to organise their health and health services within well defined Government administrative structures. It is recommended that the Government provides more support to CBHC activities since they benefit the majority of the population and represent the actual implementation of Primary Health Care.
>
> (Government of Tanzania, 1994, p. 67)

In reality, the implementation of CBHC remains predominantly an area of NGO, not government activity. This reveals how there may be constant contradictions between what a government says it will do, how it will do it, and its capacity to do so. Very often, the development of areas of activity is a process of interactions and emerging practice on the part of many actors. In the case of CBHC, if government is not undertaking its implementation directly, is it providing the 'well defined Government administrative structures', and are other actors using these?

The promotion of initiatives such as CBHC at the local level point to the positive stories of collaboration, where different groups, such as village committees, district governments and NGOs are able to come together and manage more participatory forms of co-ordination. At the same time, there are also substantial blockages to this kind of networking. In practice, local government staff may not be willing to support micro-level co-ordination activities on the part of community groups, having worked for many years in a top-down development mode. Even where they are willing, they may not have the resources to provide facilitation and support to these groups. In this respect, NGO programmes are not always realistic in their expectations of government. Interagency workshops and even committees may be established, but can flounder on questions of control, resource-access and commitment. The ongoing problem of limited information sharing can heighten mistrust and misunderstanding. In some cases, NGOs with adequate resources, or government staff who are managing donor-funded vertical health programmes, do not have any incentive to collaborate with others. In other cases, NGOs disengage from co-ordinative bodies when they sense that government departments or staff are seeking to control their activities. Even though the promotion of CBHC is now part of national health policy guidelines, the intersectoral and interagency action it promotes are never easily attained.

7.4 CONCLUSIONS

> The overall objective of the health policy of Tanzania is to improve the health and well-being of all Tanzanians, with a focus on those most at risk, and to encourage the health system to be more responsive to the needs of the people.
>
> (Government of Tanzania, 1994, p. 7)

There are two aspects of the 'what?' and 'how?' of state co-ordination touched on in this chapter, albeit of a different order. They could be termed the 'fundamental' and the 'pragmatic'. The statement from the Tanzanian Ministry of Health is a reminder of the fundamental – that there are distinctive reasons why 'the state' exists as a co-ordinating agency in national contexts. These reasons include the legitimacy and the scope to define national objectives and to guide action towards their achievement.

7.4.1 SOME FUNDAMENTALS OF STATE CO-ORDINATION

Whilst it is clear that individual states set about defining and meeting national objectives in a variety of ways, not all of which are deemed legitimate or sufficient by groups within or outside its boundaries, the idea and the reality of 'the state' remains vital in debates about tackling national and international development issues. For all the negative views of the state which have prompted various attacks on its role as co-ordinator in the 1980s, increasing recognition of the significance of this role has in recent years prompted more sophisticated discussion of state reform.

Whether the emphasis is on direct co-ordination, regulation or facilitation by the state, there are functions in economic, political and social life which only the state can provide, which are to do with its particular relationship to accountability, incentives and scale (as discussed by Chapter 2). However, the activities which the state undertakes in order to perform these functions, or the ways in which it approaches these, are not absolute givens. They vary across time and institutional context. They are constantly subject to challenge and change.

The 'ideal' which has dominated the international state reform agenda in the 1990s can be described as a liberal state based on representative democracy which is accountable through voting mechanisms to a universally-enfranchized electorate. It is this system of accountability which provides the liberal state with the legitimacy to define national objectives, and to provide the necessary incentives and sanctions through a regulatory framework which facilitates or enables actions by a plurality of 'private' organizations. These organizations can directly serve – whether through market or participatory mechanisms – a diversity of social and economic purposes more effectively and efficiently than the state. This is due to their smaller scale and relative autonomy, which leave them freer than the state to be flexible, innovative and responsive. Where these market or participatory mechanisms fail, there may also be a case for the liberal state to engage in direct provision of goods and services.

The World Development Report of 1997 discusses what is needed to build this kind of state:

> First, focus the state's activities to match its capability. Many states try to do too much with few resources and little capability. Getting governments better focused on the core public activities that are crucial to development will enhance their effectiveness.
>
> Second, over time, look for ways to improve the state's capability by reinvigorating public institutions. The Report puts particular emphasis on mechanisms that give public officials the incentive to do their jobs better and to be more flexible, but that also provide restraints to check arbitrary and corrupt behaviour.
>
> (World Bank, 1997a, foreword)

So the reforming state needs to review its activities and capacities, and to take action to clean itself up by building administrative capacity and virtuous bureaucratic behaviour.

However, this statement does not address the fact that determining what constitutes 'core public activities' and ensuring that these are acted upon, is not a matter of technocratic, state-centred decision-making. As the discussion of state management of non-state actors has shown, a variety of organizational forms are involved in a process of not just providing pre-determined services, but of simultaneously defining as well as meeting need. With a shift towards explicit promotion of a plurality of actors, and towards a facilitative role for the state, some of the existing challenges in managing diversity come into even sharper relief. The hope might be that:

> The role of various actors on the health care scene should be clearly defined to ensure compliance, co-ordination and efficiency. In this endeavour community participation/involvement and intersectoral/ multisectoral collaboration will feature prominently.
>
> (Government of Tanzania, 1994, p. 9)

But the achievement of such clarity and understanding of roles will depend upon the effective management of a dynamic and political process. The type of co-ordinative framework which the state provides will help to shape the incentives and sanctions which govern the arenas in which this process takes place. This has implications for the ways that government managers perceive and manage their roles, but also for the ways that other actors perceive the role of government.

Alongside the current agenda of state reform, runs another story, about the need for the active functioning of 'civil society'. This discourse contains various strands – about popular participation, about privatization – which reflect different views on what 'civil society' and its role is. For those who are thoroughly disenchanted with the role of the state in development, the active promotion of 'civil society' as a counterbalance to the state has become something of a panacea.

However, it should not be forgotten that 'civil society' encompasses those actors for which the state, according to the international reform agenda, is supposed to be providing an enabling environment. There are warnings from several quarters about an over-emphasis on civil society and non-state action, and that this is:

> ... not likely to add up to a meaningful intervention in the development process if it is not complemented by appropriate action to repair the state to enhance its capacity for development-oriented activity.
>
> (Agbaje, 1990)

'Civil society' needs the state. So state reform has implications for other actors (NGOs, for-profit companies, community organizations), which also need to look at their objectives, 'roles', and relationships. There is a fundamental interdependence between 'state' and 'civil society'.

The real issue for state co-ordination is how to structure the relationship between mutual dependence and independence – the extent to which the state seeks to coerce, control or co-opt actors which seek autonomy versus the extent to which the state creates boundaried spaces for independent actions which are coaxed or concerted towards certain outcomes.

7.4.2 PRAGMATISM AND STATE CO-ORDINATION

This is where the question of the 'pragmatism' of 'what?' and 'how?' becomes important. As a central state agency such as the Tanzanian Ministry of Health seeks to improve the health of *all* Tanzanians, but also recognizes that it is unable to directly provide for this itself, how can it ensure that this goal will be worked towards by other actors? Some of the answers to this question are indicated by the three arenas of activity described in this chapter. The discussion of NGO activity in health service provision points to a need for regulatory frameworks, but that these frameworks need to be based on full recognition and adequate knowledge of what NGOs (and other health actors) actually do, if they are to be effective. At the same time, some direct co-ordination mechanisms may continue to be important, as discussed in the case of decentralization. Again, however, the extent to which real powers are devolved, and to which state bodies at all levels open themselves to involvement with other actors, will have an impact on the effectiveness of direct co-ordination in achieving the aim of improved health for all. Finally, the example of CBHC is about ways that engagement between different actors can be facilitated, often pulling the actions of different groups together in more informal ways, but within the framework provided by direct co-ordination and regulation, which helps to set boundaries around this action. In this sense, this chapter provides a discussion of the need for all three approaches to co-ordination – a combination of vertical, horizontal and organic relationships.

At this level, co-ordination is also about direct relationships between groups, organizations and individuals, operating in close proximity, and even having face-to-face contact. As already indicated, perception and language play an important role. Differences of view derive not only from fundamental questions about who has a legitimate role in defining what constitutes overlap, duplication, or complementarity, but also from local histories and agendas, and the nature of the previous management of interaction. Have, for example, government managers approached the management of relationships with other organizations in a directly co-ordinative, regulatory or facilitative way? Have managers in other organizations responded positively or proactively to building relationships with government departments?

In part, some level of appreciation for the working realities and constraints which counterpart managers face in their own organizations can help to ease tensions in relationships. All too often, managers lack the space and time for thinking strategically:

> You know when you work with the government ... you can't concentrate ... sometimes ... I was co-ordinating UNICEF activities, sometimes World Bank activities ... You have to rush to workshops where you are told to do this ... and you don't have time to design interventions.
>
> (ex-government planner, Tanzania, 1998)

And in the pressure of operations, activities which are important for building and maintaining relationships, such as information-sharing, may be severely neglected. Without this sharing of information, the differences and similarities between organizations, the aspects of their agendas and approaches which can be used as the starting point for co-ordination, remain obscured, or are reduced to the most simplistic levels.

If, for example, one party (in this case government) is constructing the relationship between government, NGO and communities as follows:

> ... NGOs should do their work and should assist the community in accordance with the government policy ... the government is thinking of involving more people in their development by way of participation ... that it is the community itself who should think of what to do and implement their own activities, so we expect NGOs should take this role to create awareness [with] people so that they can identify their problems and plan for implementation.
>
> (Regional government planner, Tanzania, 1998)

Such an approach needs to be followed through with an assessment of the aims, experience, capacities and resources of the different parties. Only then will it become possible to realistically think in terms of effective co-ordination of this situation.

So what kind of co-ordinative function *should* the state provide? In many contexts, state co-ordination through direct control of the 'parts' is now considered impractical and ineffective – yet old habits die hard. Policymakers may talk of facilitation or 'enabling environments' at the same time as they seek direct control or standardization of emerging initiatives. New policy frameworks, new configurations of power and influence, and new practices challenge people's perceptions and management capacities. For many managers, whether government, NGO or other, the whole process of reform – from the redefinition of co-ordinative frameworks to day-to-day management – will often be experienced as friction, a sense of vulnerability, and misunderstanding. It is a fact of inter-organizational life that there will be persistent tensions. If existing inter-organizational relationships are not to be damaged and new relationships to be effectively forged, a real commitment to building the required mutual understanding, political will and requisite management skills is vital.

Ultimately then, the challenge of effectively co-ordinating in complex inter-organizational environments is how to build on existing relationships in ways which encourage collaboration rather than resistance. Of developing frameworks which provide some balance between establishing and enforcing central standards and allowing flexibility; between central control mechanisms and facilitated local action. It requires a good understanding of the nature of past, present and future interdependence. Such understanding will include appreciation of the need to allow for independence, to create spaces for responsible autonomous action, and a commitment to using those spaces responsibly, in the interest of effective collective outcomes.

8 INTER-AGENCY CO-ORDINATION IN EMERGENCIES

JON BENNETT

8.1 INTRODUCTION

Co-ordination is a value-laden concept. For some, experience teaches that co-ordination equals control, either in the form of an imposing authority or in the form of stifling bureaucracy. For others, co-ordination represents empowerment; it is a liberating ideal where mutual exchange and re-inforcement make the desire for co-operation self-evident. This chapter deals primarily with non-governmental organizations (NGOs), their relationships with each other, with governments and with the wider inter-national humanitarian community. In particular, it looks at co-ordination during humanitarian crises. These natural disasters and complex emerg-encies elicit responses from a wide array of organizations with different skills and, more often than not, from the relatively richer northern hemi-sphere. I will also examine how they relate to the growing number of indigenous 'Southern' NGOs and the United Nations system. Although all emergencies have unique political, economic and social characteristics, I suggest, drawing on case studies mainly from Asia and Africa, that the lessons learned in the last decade can be distilled into a set of key prin-ciples. I will further suggest that co-ordination is not only a matter of tem-porary pragmatic arrangements; rather, it is a process requiring specific professional skills. The manner in which co-ordination is carried out to a large extent determines the effectiveness of an inter-agency response to emergencies.

In the 1990s, much of the debate on the approaches to aid co-ordination concentrated on the acute phase of emergencies, the period when large scale external resources were brought through an internationally mobilized response to crises in countries such as Somalia, Sudan, Rwanda, Afghan-istan and Bosnia. However, in most cases an emergency is a protracted event. International agencies remain in a country long after the media has left, usually for many years into the rehabilitation and recovery phases of the emergency. It would be rather artificial to set up distinctions between approaches to co-ordination in emergency and non-emergency situations. It may be more useful to look at various phases which include: state col-lapse to re-establishment of government control; international intervention to withdrawal; autonomous NGO programmes to their integration in na-tional development plans; and economic collapse to re-investment.

Although the humanitarian machinery for emergencies is well rehearsed, surprisingly few lessons are learned from one emergency to another, as recent evaluations of international responses in Rwanda, Sudan and Bosnia have revealed (see, for example, DANIDA, 1996; Independent,1996). Often, issues of accountability are not dealt with until after the event.

During the acute phase of an emergency aid agencies are busy establishing a presence; it is rarely made clear where their responsibility ends and at what point specialized national organizations should come to the fore.

8.1.1 COMPLEX EMERGENCIES

The cause of much duplication and inter-agency tensions is found in the broader political context of the increasing number of 'complex' emergencies. The distinguishing feature of such emergencies is the collapse of a functioning national authority which traditionally might have provided a co-ordinating focus for international response. In post-adjustment states, humanitarian agencies sometimes find themselves without strong and consistent national counterparts and hence have difficulties functioning as mandated. In Africa in particular, aid agencies have entered an arena of political chaos in which competing parties, often in open conflict, claim various levels of geographical control and in which population displacement is not only a consequence of, but also in the strategic interest of, those same parties. Effective intervention and access to needy populations has depended on newly developed negotiating skills, security arrangements and risk assessment. A new humanitarian agenda has arisen, one in which state authority is no longer taken for granted. Donors increasingly use intermediary agencies for relief deliveries and expect these agencies to form their own modes of mutual co-operation.

In 1994, the scramble of organizations descending upon Central Africa left many wondering whether aid agencies would ever act in a co-ordinated fashion. The plethora of NGO placards lining the roads through refugee camps outside Goma left some observers lamenting the 'NGO supermarket'. Yet, elsewhere in the region, things were different. In Tanzania, the juxtaposition of an effective government, donor consensus and the designation of a lead UN agency facilitated impressive levels of co-ordination. ECHO (EC Humanitarian Office) and USAID decided to put all funding through UNHCR (United Nations High Commissioner for Refugees), the lead agency dealing with refugees. The Tanzanian government endorsed an arrangement where all contracts with partner NGOs were approved by UNHCR. About 40 NGOs were rejected; the successful agencies were unanimous that co-operation had never been better. Donor-led co-ordination is not without pitfalls, but at least in humanitarian emergencies many donors have developed their own field expertise and have become increasingly able to judge the competence of NGOs competing for funds.

8.1.2 'AID SHOCK'

Weak and ill-equipped governments emerging out of conflict are particularly vulnerable to 'aid shock' – the arrival and dispersal of hundreds of expatriates, vehicles and equipment backed by powerful donor interests. In Rwanda in August 1994, soon after the mass exodus of refugees fleeing genocide, more than 130 foreign NGOs arrived in the capital, Kigali, in a matter of days. By December the figure had risen to more than 200. There was no functioning government, no visas, no banks, no local markets. By the time the fledgling government established itself with relatively meagre resources, aid agencies were already entrenched with vehicles, computers, regular supply flights and many hundreds of expatriates. The onus of preventing duplication, improving access and rationalizing the division of labour among assistance givers had fallen squarely on the shoulders of either the UN or the NGOs themselves. The government barely had desks, let alone the necessary logistics capacity to deal with mass population movements and aid allocations. It was to take more than twelve months for the government to regain at least some of the initiative for national emergency planning. By then, a degree of resentment and distrust had set in. NGOs were accused (probably wrongly) by the government of unacceptably high percentages of administrative overheads and of bypassing skilled nationals in favour of expatriates. Although the charges were contested, the scene was set for uncompromising government regulations and from 1995 onwards a period of difficult relations between NGOs (and to a lesser extent the UN) and the Rwandan government.

How might such tensions have been reduced? I believe that in 1994 NGOs relied too heavily on the UN to co-ordinate activities on their behalf, rather than developing an autonomous NGO negotiating platform. The UN was already discredited in the eyes of the Rwandan government for its failure to respond effectively to the cataclysmic events of early 1994. Had the NGOs developed a collective and autonomous representational role for themselves from August 1994 onwards – while simultaneously helping to establish and liaise with HACU (the government's new Humanitarian Assistance Co-ordination Unit) – much misunderstanding might have been avoided. As it was, the NGO Co-ordination Committee was not set up until mid-1995, partly in response to the increased tensions with the government, though the damage had already been done.

8.2 TYPES OF NGO CO-ORDINATION

Before looking at specific examples of co-ordination, Box 8.1 briefly lists at least eight of the possible structures used to co-ordinate NGO activity. Despite the number of specific terms used to describe these different structures – consortia, councils, federations, umbrella agencies, networks, unions, co-ordination bodies – overall each group (or organization) requires:

- independence from government, though it may include government participation;
- the setting up of a secretariat, answerable to an elected executive committee, that takes responsibility for administering the day-to-day activities of a membership organization;
- a national perspective, i.e., it will usually cover more than just one sector (the exception being Group 2) and will take on some kind of representational role.

BOX 8.1 TYPOLOGY OF NGO CO-ORDINATION

A typology of this kind is useful only in a very general sense. Many 'umbrella' groups do not accept a co-ordination role as such, though invariably they facilitate co-ordination through information exchange. For example, a co-ordination mechanism initially set up to collect and disseminate development experiences could more recently have had to deal with issues relating to complex emergencies. In other cases, mechanisms set up initially under government direction have later attained a level of independence from the state. There are thus 'grey areas' and organizations can move from one category to another.

Group 1 *Umbrella organizations of NGOs*
Independent membership umbrella organizations of NGOs active at national or regional level. It would usually cover several sectors – health, agriculture, etc. It may comprise northern and southern NGOs together or may be set up exclusively for one or the other.

Group 2 *Umbrella organizations of NGOs for a single sector/issue*
Similar to Group 1 but specifically for one sector. This could also include groups which lobby on one specific issue. Can be either national or regional in scope.

Group 3 *Groups of grassroots organizations*
Federations, unions or networks of grassroots organizations. Includes human rights groups, women's groups, etc. Usually national in scope, though sometimes regional.

Group 4 *Consultative councils (government-NGO)*
NGO councils set up by the national government as part of a consultation process between itself and the NGO sector. In some cases it may be the only permitted co-ordination structure; in others it may be simply an irregular meeting point for government and NGOs.

Group 5 *Councils of social welfare or social services*
Mostly affiliated to the International Council on Social Welfare (ICSW). In Africa these are usually pre-independence institutions, mostly in Anglophile countries. Several have now changed their emphasis towards more general developmental activities, thus joining Group 1. In other cases the Council groups both government services and NGOs and receives a large proportion of its budget from the government.

Group 6 *International NGO consortia*
Consortia which bring together a number of northern and/or southern NGOs, combining financial and staff resources for a specific programme of activities. Often such consortia exist where it is more difficult for the individual members to operate alone.

> **Group 7** *Religious affiliation consortia*
> Consortia dealing with relief and development activities within par-
> ticular confessions (usually the Christian church, though also several
> Islamic consortia). Generally, these consortia bring together the de-
> velopment offices of national church/Islamic organizations. In rare
> cases, they represent an ecumenical inter-church alliance.
>
> **Group 8** *Sub-regional networks of NGOs*
> These may either be sector-specific or comprise members from other
> national/regional groupings (Groups 1-5).

8.3 NGO CO-ORDINATION

NGO approaches to co-ordination have one key characteristic in common:
they are *horizontal* organizational forms in contrast to vertical ones based
on hierarchical authority. They depend on the coexistence of autonomy
and interdependence. NGO co-ordination also requires a degree of informality and spontaneity. Though they may have a weak formal status in
international fora, they often have significant influence as the 'voice' of an
otherwise disparate group of agencies. By contrast, co-ordination within
United Nations organizations, though not necessarily hierarchical, nevertheless is often constrained and controlled by intergovernmental protocol
and accountability. This makes collaboration with others (whether governments or NGOs) more contractual than voluntary.

The juxtaposition of vertical and horizontal organizational forms, particularly in the relationship between NGOs and governments or NGOs and the
UN, may create conflict and competition. Very often the effectiveness of
these relationships depends upon a third relationship – that between NGOs
themselves. We will first look at the co-ordination approaches of international and indigenous NGOs and the dynamics between the two.

8.3.1 WHY CO-ORDINATE?

> Everyone is for co-ordination, but no one wishes to be co-
> ordinated, at least not just now.

As we have seen with the example from Rwanda in 1994, in complex emergencies the sheer number of NGOs, national as well as international, demands levels of co-ordination which, for some, becomes an unexpected
necessity. In a competitive funding environment, NGO project proposals
rarely, if ever, mention formal contact with other players on the ground.
Indeed, although lip service is given to inter-agency co-operation, the first
priority of any NGO in an emergency is to establish its own 'territory',
arguing for 'additionality' and some degree of exclusive proficiency. If
a formal co-ordination body, such as a field-based secretariat, is deemed
necessary, its activities are, at least initially, trimmed to the minimum; it is
a service provider, not a regulator. Its authority comes from collective con-

sensus within its membership; there is no hierarchical determination of authority.

This is not to say, however, that decision making is without unequal influence. Co-ordination is also about power – power to determine the allocation of resources, to exert influence over warring parties, governments and, let it be said, recipients. Most NGO co-ordination bodies comprise several dominant agencies who have a vested interest in using the body as a vehicle for pursuing policies complementary to their own programme. In the first year of its existence, NGO members of ACBAR (Agency Co-ordinating Body for Afghan Relief), set up in 1990 in Pakistan/Afghanistan, expended large amounts of energy and time on developing terms of reference for the agency which would not interfere with the autonomy of each member. To some extent, it was energy wasted, for the development of the Afghan war and the scale of resources channeled through NGOs subsequently forced a much broader representational and regulatory role for ACBAR as required by its donors. The Steering Committee for ACBAR (some 10 NGOs, mostly international) determined policy on behalf of 65 NGO members, including giving aid priority to certain areas in Afghanistan and negotiating a greater say in UN appeals and policy. With a secretariat staff of some 35, a resource centre, mapping service and consultancy division, ACBAR was by 1992 recognized as an influential platform for NGO concerns as well as a convenient focal point for donors who bilaterally funded it (Bennett, 1995).

An unusual, though instructive, example of NGO power relations can be found in the formation of the CRDA (Christian Relief and Development Association), set up in 1973 in Ethiopia. CRDA was to become a 'clearing house' for supplementary donor funds to its membership and, at one stage in its development, even an implemetor of its own projects. Through its control over the allocation of at least a proportion of relief resources, the CRDA was also able to act as a 'pool' for needs not met by existing NGO programmes. For example, the province of Wollo – one of the worst famine-stricken regions in the mid-1980s – was poorly supplied until the CRDA intervened in 1985. This was an unusual role for a co-ordination body but one determined by donor requirements and expectations of the Ethiopian government. By 1986, cash and in-kind assistance channeled through CRDA amounted to over $20 million, which included expenditure relating to its own 54-vehicle truck fleet used to service its 53 NGO members. Command of such resources gave CRDA significant influence and, arguably, enhanced its co-ordinating ability (Borton quoted, in Bennett, 1995).

Emergency relief inputs in Ethiopia in the mid-1980s were exceptional and the central role of the CRDA came at a time when international governments were looking for alternative channels to the government of Ethiopia through which to respond to needs. Apart from being politically expedient for donors, the CRDA also managed to increase the access of smaller, locally-based NGOs to donor resources and to facilitate a degree a decentralization of decision making from the head offices of donor organizations in Europe and north America. CRDA was, however, not without its critics. In the mid-1980s, the agency itself operated a string of feeding centres and, in doing so, competed for funds with its membership. Preferring it to be restricted to a purely consultative body, the membership handed over this project to other agencies after 2 years.

The dilemma was not so acutely felt in Lebanon where the Lebanese NGO Forum (LNF) has developed a number of advocacy, research and rehabilitation programmes for the displaced. The LNF is an indigenous consortium of 14 denominational groups, including those from mutually antagonistic communities during the Lebanese war. The unique cross-community role of the LNF, combined with its track record and legal expertise has given it the authority to undertake multi-funded projects in the name of the consortium. For example, with funds from the UN and various Nordic NGOs, it set up a legal advice and aid scheme for refugees and stateless persons in Lebanon which, through advocacy and detailed surveys, has provided a degree of protection for some 114,000 people without official residence status.

8.3.2 GENERAL PRINCIPLES OF NGO CO-ORDINATION BODIES

ACBAR, CRDA and LNF were created in protracted emergencies with a large number of resident NGOs. Similar, though mostly smaller, NGO co-ordination bodies have been created worldwide, usually emerging during a crisis, though adapting to the different requirements of relief and rehabilitation as time goes on. Two immutable principles repeated in various forms in the terms of reference for almost all NGO co-ordination bodies are

1   to minimize duplication and wastage through voluntary sharing of information and/or resources; and

2   to provide an independent forum through which the collective consensus of NGOs can be expressed to governments, donors and multilateral agencies.

If these are minimal requirements, there are also broader qualitative ambitions for a mature co-ordination structure. Among these are:

• the facilitation and encouragement of a tripartite division of labour between the UN/international donors, the host government and NGOs;

• the furtherance of debate and definition of 'civil society' though the creation of an independent, co-operative and productive environment for NGOs;

• advocacy for, and demonstration of, the comparative advantage of a buoyant NGO sector and guarding against either donor or government encroachment on this sector;

- acting as a reference point for smaller, less experienced NGOs wishing to engage more fully with the wider aid community;
- acting as a potential catalyst for NGO advancement through training and exchange with other NGOs;
- assisting national governments, donors and multilateral agencies in the identification of potential NGO partners through which to work;
- establishing operational guidelines and methodologies for good practice in the field.

A co-ordination body is usually set up in the capital or regional centre of the country in question. Often a 'lead agency' takes the initiative to gather NGOs and discuss a common programme of action for a particular problem facing the country. The Committee for Co-ordination of Services to Displaced Persons in Thailand (CCSDPT), for example, was set up to deal with NGO inputs into Cambodian refugee settlements in Thailand, though later they also co-ordinated NGO responses to Burmese and Vietnamese refugees. Here, as in other successful endeavours, a small secretariat was paid for by the members, with supplementary grants from bilateral government donors, independent foundations and the UN. Usually, a General Assembly of NGO members elects its own Executive Committee to oversee all aspects of the secretariat's work.

Traditionally, an NGO co-ordination body is primarily the centre for information exchange and the first point of contact for NGOs arriving in a country. More proactive organizations will attempt to map out needs in a particular area, persuade NGOs usefully to assign themselves different tasks and oversee the 'whole picture' of NGO intervention. As such, they have become increasingly important for the UN and others anxious not to have to deal individually with the multitude of NGOs, large and small, that arrive during a particular emergency. This intermediary role can be instrumental in ensuring that NGOs have a collective voice in formulating policies and priorities at a national level. In Mozambique, for instance, the LINK NGO Forum, set up in 1993, within two years had a seat on the national Humanitarian Assistance Committee, one of the various structures set up to implement the country's peace process. LINK also assisted the UN in its allocation of funds channeled through the Trust Fund for Humanitarian Assistance in Mozambique. LINK was also a vital channel through which Mozambican NGOs, represented on the Executive Board, could enhance their profile in a country which for many years had been dominated by foreign aid.

8.4 STATE-NGO RELATIONSHIPS

If complex emergencies in the 1990s were characterized by state disintegration, a new generation of aid personnel and agencies have, rightly or wrongly, perceived government itself as a problem. Some state authorities – ineffective in preventing mass suffering and sometimes even causing it – are for many development agencies an obstacle to the delivery of assistance. Other more effective and stable governments have not always escaped this perception of government as an obstacle to development. Debates on governance and conditionality have led donors to seek alternative routes to development funding through non-governmental structures. The process of 'rolling back the state' lays bare the issues of accountability (who does what and on behalf of whom), authority (who represents and regulates whom) and independence (who determines the freedom to join and form interest groups, the freedom to publish and advocate for change, etc.).

Statism traditionally implies a responsibility for the social welfare of the populous. Governments control the political framework in which people and their organizations have to operate and in which sustainable development is possible. The oft-expressed mission of NGOs is to foster appropriate and effective policy to the benefit of the poor and least powerful. They seek to support or influence governments to uphold a social contract (Edwards and Hulme, 1992). Governments have a tendency towards centralization and bureaucracy; by contrast, NGOs are perceived as small, flexible and innovative. The alignment of NGO goals and macro-political aspirations was plainly seen in the 1980s when donors began to attack the model of state-centered development in the south. Through structural adjustment packages, the IMF and World Bank demanded public sector reform and donors switched to NGOs to take over some state tasks (see, for example, Farrington and Bebbington, 1993).

If donor states and northern NGOs have recently entered a symbiotic relationship within the international aid system, what implications does this have for co-operation between NGOs and the State in which they operate? Some have argued that the increasing use of NGOs as public service contractors sets up an unhealthy relationship in which NGOs and the host government compete for scarce donor resources. Hanlon (Chapter 6) argues strongly that the Mozambican government's capacity was severely weakened over many years by the 'aid regime'. Others have noted with some alarm the increasing tendency towards stricter regulation of NGOs, both foreign and indigenous, as a 'reaction' against a perceived infringement of sovereignty. (Two recent studies by Adiin-Yaansah, 1995, and Bennett, 1997, look in depth at the issue of legislation and NGO-government relations.)

8.4.1 SRI LANKA: A STRONG GOVERNMENT AT WAR

Sovereignty and government responsibility has dominated the aid debate in Sri Lanka. In contrast to the 'collapsed government' scenario, Sri Lanka provides an example of a strong government able simultaneously to pursue political, military and humanitarian objectives in a protracted civil war. A special feature of Sri Lanka is that the government also provides a degree of humanitarian assistance in opposition controlled areas. From

1990 when the LTTE (Liberation Tigers of Tamil Eelam) gained control of most of the north, NGOs had some difficulty in arguing for access to these areas. The government, concerned that the LTTE would exploit the humanitarian argument (although the needs were palpably great), were particularly wary of 'partisan' NGO presence in contested areas. Two NGO co-ordination structures existed in Sri Lanka:

- the NGO Consortium on Relief and Rehabilitation; and
- the Interagency Emergency Group.

The former consisted of both international and national NGOs, a situation which was ultimately to weaken its impact. Sri Lankan agencies, fearing a backlash from the government, were unwilling to join in collective advocacy and representations, or to sign carefully worded press releases on issues of human rights violations. Yet it was precisely this role that was to strengthen NGO presence in the country, in particular with regard to the evolving crisis in the north. By contrast, the Interagency Emergency Group, consisting of eight larger international NGOs, insisted, as part of its mandate, on an ongoing dialogue with both the UN and the government about the meaning and nature of the humanitarian mandate. This was taking place at a time – the mid-1990s – when in many conflicts NGOs found it necessary to re-emphasize minimum humanitarian standards, opening the debate on neutrality and impartiality against a background of increased agency exposure to violence.

The formation of the Interagency Emergency Group as something more than an NGO information centre was an appropriate response to a highly politicized situation. Yet, there remained serious obstacles to effective co-ordination in Sri Lanka, both internal to the co-ordination bodies themselves and externally in relation to the war. The single most important impediment is the fact the government, and more particularly the military, retain the final authority, but do not invite close collaboration with aid agencies, keeping them outside their own intra-governmental co-ordination mechanisms. The significant government relief efforts are therefore planned separately from international efforts, engendering mutual suspicion and misinformation (Van Brabant, 1997).

8.4.2 AN IDEAL MODEL

Box 8.2 summarizes some of the strengths and weaknesses ascribed to an exclusively government-led co-ordination mechanism.

As we have seen in the case of Sri Lanka, military and security priorities will almost always dominate a government's agenda during complex political emergencies; and even in more stable situations the negotiation for humanitarian space is not always guaranteed. Nevertheless, it is instructive to look at an ideal model for NGO-government collaboration which recognizes complementarity rather than competition. Such a model might have the following components:

1   a recognition that the government sets out the broad national development agenda and strategic plans for a country and that NGOs reach out to communities with specific interventions;

2   NGOs communicate with the host government to fit their resources into existing national and local strategies and structures, usually through close liaison with line ministries;

3   NGOs and multilateral organizations consult each other to determine needs and resources, agree upon methods, and divide responsibilities and sites of operation;

4   based on this foregoing dialogue (items 2 and 3), each agency adapts its plans and strategy;

5   a co-ordination structure, ideally under the direction and authority of the host state and local administrations, is established with an effective communication system which enables feedback and a continuous adaptation to changing circumstances.

Setting up an ideal model is important for two reasons. Firstly, it provides a framework for comparative analysis of various forms of NGO-government co-operation over time and between countries. Secondly, it

BOX 8.2 GOVERNMENT-LED CO-ORDINATION

Examples
- Line ministry
- National or Regional construct (e.g. HACU in Rwanda)
- de facto government structure (e.g. ERA/REST in Ethiopia, SRRA in Sudan)

Strengths
- strengthen civil institutions
- ensure long term sustainability
- secure co-operation of local and regional government
- reduce duplication in national planning
- knowledge of local leadership structures

Weaknesses
- manipulate numbers/scale of 'the problem' for various reasons (political/financial)
- meager resources to sustain a long term structure
- often end up ceding control to external agents
- sometimes itself the cause of conflict-induced displacement
- can sometimes deny access to humanitarian agencies for political/military reasons

provides a crucial reference point for agencies working closely with government counterparts in post-emergency recovery – a reminder of how, and under what circumstances, NGOs (and their representational bodies) might strive to create a durable and non-threatening model of co-operation.

Where governments and NGOs have joint ventures these usually take three forms:

(a) the government sub-contracts the NGO;

(b) joint implementation; and

(c) government as financier of NGO projects.

The most common of these is the sub-contracting arrangement which often involves competitive bidding by NGOs. In Bangladesh, the General Education Project (GEP) is a donor financed, multi-year, multi-component project where the government has assigned the task of non-formal primary education to a coalition of NGOs under an umbrella named CAMPE (Campaign for Mass Primary Education). With government approval, CAMPE is 'self selecting' of its contributing NGOs; that is, the NGO membership sets criteria and assigns projects and geographical distribution according to capacity and proven track record. Bangladesh has one of the longest established records of NGO-government collaboration, with some of the largest indigenous NGOs in the world such as BRAC (Bangladesh Rural Advancement Committee) and Swanirvar being responsible for multi-million dollar integrated projects in close co-operation with the government's line ministries (World Bank, 1996).

Research has indicated that many examples of successful collaborative NGO-state projects are in non-traditional fields of regenerative or low external input sectors (agriculture, shelter, primary health care) where NGOs have absorbed new ideas and acquired new skills more rapidly than public sector agencies. Broadly speaking, the comparative advantage of NGOs has been in giving priority to process (or learning) goals rather than product goals in project design and implementation and in disseminating skills through non-formal networks and grassroots alliances (Wellard and Copestake, 1993).

8.4.3 NGO CO-ORDINATION IN THE 'NEW STATES'

The dismantling of the state, whether dramatically as in some Eastern European countries, or gradually and painfully in Africa and central Asia, has provoked a rapid reappraisal of the potential civic institutions have for providing the kind of services hitherto reserved exclusively for state authorities. Indigenous NGOs in particular have benefited from the increasing interest of northern donors to use them as channels for pursuing the democracy agenda. Aside from the funding implications this has for northern NGOs, there is the implicit assumption that responsibility for social welfare will gradually shift from top-down government structures backed by bilateral aid to that of the smaller, more flexible (and cheaper) indigenous NGOs. The privatization of aid places governments in more of a regulatory rather than implementation role while the demands of donor accountability are placed increasingly on the shoulders of the so-called 'third sector' (the NGO/voluntary sector). For example, in the newly independent states, the former Soviet state edifice is slowly being replaced by a pluralistic economy and social structure that will have profound effects on social welfare provision. Likewise, sweeping liberalization in some parts of Africa has put NGOs in direct competition with governments over scarce resources, the result sometimes being an entrenchment of prejudice towards NGOs and a recourse to strict regulatory controls (Adiin-Yaansah, 1995).

How might NGOs defend their position within this shifting political climate? Some have found the answer in greater collective, co-ordinated and policy-oriented action by the NGO sector as a whole; in particular, by creating a strong national association, council or collaborative network of NGOs. Creating the economic and political 'space' for the development of such structures requires the co-operation and encouragement of the 'visiting' aid community. Yet, particularly in disasters, scant attention is paid to the role, potential or real, that existing institutions play. Northern donors, NGOs and the UN are usually preoccupied with logistics – fast and efficient delivery systems backed by short term funds. Where local NGOs are promoted, they invariably provide extension services for the larger donors and are rarely given money even for administration, let alone capacity building. Outside of emergencies, indigenous NGOs, with a few notable exceptions, are poorly equipped in skills and in finance, to deal with the roles now being asked of them. The watchword for donors and NGOs alike is 'capacity building', with the role of international NGOs being increasingly consigned to that of an intermediary agency in the development of people skills (Bennett and Gibbs, 1995).

8.4.4 STATE REGULATION OF THE NGO SECTOR

National governments understandably use regulations and registration as their starting point in efforts to co-ordinate the NGO sector. Even when autonomous NGO co-ordination structures are in place, host governments invariably put demands on these structures to provide detailed information about each NGO registered as a member. This can invoke tensions over confidentiality, not least when details of national employees are requested, as was the case in Rwanda and Sri Lanka in 1995.

The thorny issue of NGO relations with national governments is further illustrated by what happened in Kenya in 1992. The Kenyan Government introduced the NGO Co-ordination Act which was to regulate and prioritize NGO inputs into the country at large in the wake of the Somali refugee crisis. At field level, UNHCR had already assigned NGO 'lead agencies' as their contractual partner for assistance to refugees, but the government was increasingly concerned about the autonomy enjoyed by the growing number of national and international NGOs setting up offices in the country. The NGO response to the Act was, not surprisingly, one of alarm. Backed by a powerful coterie of government and multilateral donors, they managed to delay – and in some cases cancel – certain provisions of the Act. Where NGO co-ordination had previously been poor, suddenly NGOs 'under attack' found very quickly a need for co-ordinated action. Interesting parallels can be drawn with security alerts in Afghanistan which have elicited impressive levels of NGO co-operation through the Agency Co-ordinating Body for Afghan Relief (ACBAR) in the last few years. A general threat to NGOs is not a prerequisite for co-ordination but it certainly helps.

8.5 NATIONAL NGO STRUCTURES

A discernible shift in favour of channeling funds through southern indigenous NGOs in recent years suggests that responsibility for social welfare will gradually shift from top-down government structures backed by bilateral aid to that of the smaller, more flexible (and cheaper) southern indigenous NGOs. For non-democratic regimes this may be an opportunity to invoke reactive legislation; for newly formed governments it is an opportunity to invest authority in previously discredited ministries. The rapidly growing NGO sector in Eastern Europe and the newly independent states, for example, is causing confusion for governments hitherto unused to dealing with large numbers of relatively autonomous agencies backed increasingly by northern capital.

Creating the economic and political 'space' for the development of indigenous NGO co-ordination structures will require the co-operation and encouragement of the northern aid community. Lack of financial capacity among local NGOs is frequently equated with a lack of overall capacity; skilled staff and local knowledge are thus ignored. Local NGOs, if they are engaged at all, become drawn into a spiral of contract service agreements which in themselves do not serve long-term organizational development. This is changing, however, as international donors increasingly look to indigenous NGOs to undertake more complex programmes and funds become more widely available for organizational development.

Tensions continue to exist between foreign NGOs and national NGOs and their respective umbrella groups. In spite of a conscious effort to accommodate and encourage national NGO participation, co-ordination bodies dominated by foreign NGOs in Afghanistan, Cambodia and Ethiopia, for instance, failed to attract smaller national NGOs as members, although several large multi-funded national NGOs have remained active members. In each of these three countries a parallel national NGO co-ordination structure was set up to deal with the particular aspirations and material requirements of a burgeoning local NGO community. Size and financial constraints may have been the initial reasons for a separatist approach but political, religious and cultural (notably language) differences also underlie the tendency to create breakaway groupings. In Mozambique the LINK NGO Forum offset some of these concerns by insisting that at least half of the Executive Committee and the Chair were from a national NGO, a formula that to date has proved successful.

In the rush to support local institutions, donors have not always appreciated local political and economic dynamics which often lead to abuse of NGO status. In Afghanistan and south Sudan, where prior to the onset of a humanitarian emergency there had been few, if any, indigenous NGOs, there are today in excess of 250 in each country. At best, they will become simple delivery agents for donors; at worst they may further erode genuine institutional development by setting themselves up as exclusive intermediaries. Moreover, in a phenomenon more frequent than is usually appreciated, government ministers themselves form NGOs to bypass official channels of assistance, using their government office to attract funds and minimize competition from elsewhere. These are the so-called GONGOS (government-owned NGOs).

Indigenous NGO co-ordinating bodies have often been ignored by international NGOs anxious to set up more 'efficient' structures during an emergency. The reaction against northern dominance may, in some cases, involve the setting up of an exclusively indigenous body. The Lebanese NGO Forum (LNF), for instance, is entirely managed by a consortium of 14 Lebanese NGO associations with a collective membership of hundreds of local community based organizations. Throughout the Lebanese war this loose coalition provided a counterbalance to the notion that sectarian groups were fundamentally irreconcilable. The LNF comprises Catholics, Muslims, Druzes and Orthodox groups with one common agenda: the provision of assistance to a population torn apart by war. In spite of its critics, the non-sectarian approach appears to have worked (Bennett, 1995).

8.6 CO-ORDINATION AS POLICY?

A major obstacle to effective field-based NGO co-ordination has been the tendency, particularly by large northern NGOs, to perceive co-ordination only in terms of self-interest. If ad hoc meetings with NGO colleagues suffice then why, they argue, should they invest time and money in setting up a co-ordination structure? The argument rests on the spurious notion that each NGO is at the same level of development with the same access to donors, governments, the UN and external resources. It neglects the fact that local NGOs in particular are empowered by collective representation and consensus; their working relationship with larger foreign NGOs is an important component of their institutional development. Moreover, if co-ordination is decentralized and local participation encouraged, such NGO collectives could become excellent vehicles for promoting conflict resolution and reconciliation. With such potential advantages – proven by field evidence in a number of recent studies – one would expect co-ordination to be highlighted as a policy priority to be encouraged (and financed) at all levels. However many northern NGOs have failed to do so, preferring simply to let already over-stretched field directors decide on how, when (or even if) they should co-ordinate with others (Bennett, 1995).

The dilemma is replicated at the level of international co-ordination where supra-national NGO consortia have been developed largely as single-sector advocacy groups, usually exclusively in the interest of the major international NGOs. There is a long history of NGO coalition building going back to the 19th century with international coalitions such as the World Alliance of Young Men's Christian Associations (founded in 1855) and the Caritas network (1924) (Ritchie, 1996). Today, the largest eight transnational NGOs command over 50% of all NGO resources worldwide, and more than 75% of emergency resource capacities (IFRC, 1997). These larger agencies, operating in several countries at once, provide a package of resources – investment funds, managerial, technical and entrepreneurial skills – and exert considerable political and economic leverage over southern labour and southern governments. Some, most notably World Vision and the International Save the Children Alliance (ISCA), have devolved responsibilities and associated authority to (semi)-autonomous organizations in the country of operation or to a 'lead' agency in a northern country. To ensure a common standard of service throughout, the ISCA, for example, has insisted on 'co-operation agreements' signed between SCF-US and the southern members (9 of the 24 affiliates of the alliance) (Smillie, 1995).

A notable exception to northern-dominated NGO coalitions is the Geneva-based International Council of Voluntary Agencies (ICVA), formed in 1965 as a lobbying platform for the relatively voiceless southern NGO sector. Uniquely, its membership comprises approximately two-thirds NGOs from developing countries. ICVA has struggled to support its management and finances against a drop in enthusiasm from the remaining one-third membership. It narrowly avoided closure in 1997. With the advent of very large 'multinational' NGOs – CARE, World Vision, Save the Children Alliance and the Lutheran World Federation – commanding collective resources estimated at $8 billion by the mid-1990s, the declining influence of broad-church co-ordination bodies like ICVA is perhaps inevitable. As one commentator suggests

> ... it is paradoxical that a process which owes so much to free-market ideology and to the notion that 'a hundred flowers should bloom' has resulted in a situation where the smaller actors, not to mention indigenous actors in Third World countries, are at a distinct disadvantage.
>
> (Donini, 1995)

8.7 CODES OF CONDUCT AND DISSEMINATION OF GOOD PRACTICE

The integrity of the humanitarian sector has been challenged in the 1990s as never before, and it is often external forces which act as an initial catalyst for organizational change. Donors, for example, are pressing aid agencies for greater accountability in the application of humanitarian assistance (ODI, 1998). There is competition from US and European military groups who have become increasingly active as alternative suppliers of relief assistance as depicted in the recent UK military recruitment slogan 'Their country needs you'. Although outside the scope of this chapter, Box 8.3 details some of the strengths and weaknesses of military-led co-ordination. Although many multilateral forces have developed humanitarian liaison units, their entry into the humanitarian field is still relatively new and only in extreme circumstances (for example siege conditions) do they act alone. Commercial contractors are also keen to become delivery agents, arguing that they are more flexible, focused and cost-effective (Crosslines, 1996).

BOX 8.3 MULTINATIONAL MILITARY FORCE

Examples

Use of force on humanitarian grounds under UN sanction used for the first time in Somalia (Operation Restore Hope, UNOSOM II), Iraq (Operation Provide Comfort), Liberia (ECOMOG), Rwanda (Operation Turquoise)

Strengths
- resources and institutional capacity to launch at short notice
- unequaled logistical capacity
- Security Council sanction

Weaknesses
- narrowly defined objectives, lacks flexibility
- reluctance of some civilians to co-operate
- poorly trained in humanitarian approaches
- intervention can exacerbate violence (e.g. increased polarization of warring factions in Somalia)
- often confounded by political inertia (e.g. UN Protection Force, UNPROFOR, in Bosnia)
- Cross-over from military to humanitarian roles can cause confusion and undermine NGO's neutrality

---

With so many different actors involved in development work the need for some common code of practice is greater than ever. The main impetus for change has come from within the NGO establishment itself. One of the first attempts at international consensus in the humanitarian field was begun in 1994 when eight non-governmental humanitarian agencies, including the International Committee of the Red Cross (ICRC), prepared and published a Code of Conduct for their work in disaster relief (ODI, 1994). Although the ten codes and three annexes were not binding, and no suggestions were made for monitoring and enforcing them, a number of operational principles were agreed upon. It will be many years before a professional body for relief workers is established and the principle of enforcement of codes of conduct is entered into. Meanwhile, the Code of Conduct at least provides a standard against which the behaviour of the signatory agencies is measured.

The Code recognizes the role played by other principle actors in the relief system – the governments of disaster affected countries, donor governments and intergovernmental organizations – and provides indicative guidelines for each. Self-regulation is imperative for several reasons: to reinforce and declare the superior standards of the more established non-governmental humanitarian agencies over those of the fly-by-night and less professional newcomers; to improve accountability to donors and to aid recipients; and to demonstrate professionalism to host governments.

The Code was the first step in what has more recently become a broader quest for minimum humanitarian standards. For example, the Sphere Project, begun in 1997 and led by a consortium of NGOs including the International Federation of the Red Cross, intends to promote and publish the consensual output of these minimum standards. And 1998 saw the launch of the Ombudsman Project, promoted through the British Red Cross and a committee of NGOs, an ambitious attempt at self regulation which foresees NGOs being answerable to complaints logged by recipients as well as donors. Essentially, they are a statement of humanitarian ethics and a reaffirmation that, at least within the NGO community, a commonly understood ethos exists. Whether this common ethos actually exists is a matter of debate (Lancaster, 1998). One thing is certain: the dissemination of such standards depends upon levels of policy coherence within and between NGOs (although not exclusive to NGOs). Co-ordination between NGOs is achieved at several levels – through international coalitions, networks and advocacy groups as well as regional and country level bodies. A main function of formal NGO coalitions is to develop or harmonize common positions on particular issues. At an international level, this can be done through, for example, bodies such as the International Council of Voluntary Agencies (ICVA) which addresses the Executive Committee of UNHCR each year; and EarthAction (one of the largest global NGO networks with over 700 member associations in about 125 countries) which puts forward views to the UN Commission on Global Governance.

In Afghanistan, ACBAR co-ordinated and published commonly-held standards and principles within the health and agricultural sectors and attempted to measure NGO performance against these standards. Adherence was voluntary and on several occasions consensus was not achieved due to adverse donor pressure. For example, CARE international was contracted by the US government to deliver food aid free of charge to certain areas inside Mujahidin-controlled areas at a time when the World Food Programme and its contracted NGOs preferred food-for-work in neighbouring areas. The disparity resulted in disputes and a temporary withdrawal of co-operation from Afghan recipients. This situation was never fully resolved due to policy being formulated in Washington without regard to local sensibilities. Above all, this was a reminder of the importance of linking local co-ordination decisions with international advocacy so that coherent policies could be pursued.

8.8 UN-NGO CO-ORDINATION

In an effort to improve their overall response to humanitarian crises the UN and its partner NGOs have found it useful to distinguish between two interrelated but distinct tasks:

- *strategic* co-ordination;
- *operational* co-ordination.

8.8.1 STRATEGIC CO-ORDINATION

Strategic co-ordination relates to the political and policy arena, and has traditionally been the primary responsibility of the UN. However, there are situations where a UN presence is either unwelcome or inappropriate. In such situations NGOs and/or the International Red Cross/Crescent become the lead agencies.

Strategic co-ordination can be divided into two analytically distinct components:

1 *Representational functions.* These are the functions for establishing consent or securing humanitarian space. For example: negotiated access; advocacy for respect of humanitarian principles; liaison with international military/political actors (including the UN system). Other representational functions include information management and effective use of the media.

2 *Policy functions.* These include setting overall direction and goals of a humanitarian programme; developing a strategic plan and allocating tasks/responsibilities; tracking and matching resource allocations; monitoring and evaluation.

Some analysts have challenged the idea that strategy is a function solely of external parties. They suggest rather that co-ordination is a function of interaction between the wider UN system (including member states, contracted NGOs and donors) and stakeholders on the ground. The members of this wider UN system are legally, morally and materially responsible for the welfare of an affected population, i.e. national governments, local governments, armies and, in some cases, rebel authorities. Local political and military authorities set the stage for strategic co-ordination through the provision (or not) of a 'framework of consent for humanitarian action' (Lautze *et al.*, 1998). The success of aid interventions in south Sudan, for instance, have depended on a delicate balance of interests between competing warring factions and the extent to which they have allowed the aid agenda to dominate activities on the ground at certain historical moments. More often than not, the dynamics of war sets the agenda rather than international humanitarian priorities.

8.8.2 OPERATIONAL CO-ORDINATION

Again, there are two analytically distinct components:

1 *Administrative*: e.g. providing common services for humanitarian actors, communications, security, common logistics systems. In August 1994, for example, the UN Rwanda Emergency Office (UNREO) provided a mapping and commodity tracking service, plus a sophisticated radio network for vehicles and field offices, also made available to NGOs.

2 *Substantive*: e.g. operational co-ordination in relation to specific sectors, geographical areas, or beneficiary groups. Most co-ordination bodies are organized in such a way that sectoral and/or geographical groups can meet to discuss their particular concerns, then report back to the general co-ordination meeting.

8.9 UN LED CO-ORDINATION

Although the main theme of this chapter has been inter-NGO co-ordination, it is important to remember the pivotal role played by the UN in complex emergencies. NGOs have, for instance, been increasingly invited to participate both as contracted implementers and as policy partners in the Consolidated Appeal process (CAP) where a UN-led strategic planning process across all sectors is required. Undertaking such a process through the UN lends authority and inter-governmental coherence to the co-ordination process as well as attracting funds.

Box 8.4 presents some of the strengths and weaknesses of UN-led co-ordination in emergencies (essentially a hierarchical mode of co-ordination).

Although the UN has developed increasingly sophisticated methods of negotiating access and promoting humanitarianism in war contexts, it is still beholden to the host government and cannot operate without invitation. Grave humanitarian situations in Burma, Turkey and East Timor, for example, have been entirely closed to UN intervention by the governments concerned. Even where the UN has access, confusions may occur

BOX 8.4 UN LED CO-ORDINATION

Examples

- UN Resident Co-ordinator
- Special Representative of the UN Secretary-General (link with political and military co-ordination)
- Lead Agency (e.g. UNHCR in Bosnia)
- Office of the Co-ordinator for Humanitarian Affairs (OCHA) (e.g. UNREO in Rwanda)

Strengths

- lend legitimacy
- attract funds (e.g. consolidated appeals)
- capable of multifaceted system-wide response
- mandated to negotiate cease-fires & ensure safe access
- UN buffer stocks of food, supplies, etc. can be used.

Weaknesses

- often paralyzed by state deterioration or by contested territory (e.g. Afghanistan)
- through its charter is biassed in favour of the incumbent government (e.g. little assistance to Renamo in Mozambique in 1980s; left Somalia at critical time in 1991)
- humanitarian concerns can be overridden by political/military considerations (e.g. confused mandates in Bosnia)
- when UN politicizes the context of humanitarian relief, NGOs begin to withdraw co-operation
- often ignores local resources and/or government structures

due to the various mandates of specialized agencies, ranging from political to humanitarian. In a multi-functional UN operation a controlling triumvirate might comprise the Special Representative of the Secretary-General (SRSG) and his secretariat, a UN-sanctioned military Force Commander and a UN Humanitarian Co-ordinator. The SRSG reports to the Secretary-General, the Force Commander to his national headquarters (or through NATO in some cases), and the Humanitarian Co-ordinator through the Office of the Co-ordinator for Humanitarian Affairs (OCHA).

Structures and processes in the UN as elsewhere depend for their success upon the skills and commitment of individuals. Simply appointing a 'co-ordinator' does not ensure success, particularly where there is a confusion between authority and facilitation. When the UN General Assembly adopted Resolution 46/182, which in 1991 formed a co-ordinating lead agency, the Department of Humanitarian Affairs (DHA), institutional jealousies soon followed. Part of the problem was the lack of training in co-ordination skills; the designated DHA field co-ordinator (or the appointed UN lead agency) lacked facilitation skills. The notable exceptions – Rwanda, for example, in the closing months of 1994, and Angola in 1995 – were due more to individual excellence than to any comprehensive staff training programme. Through in-house training, the situation is improving within the UN, though the process of designating a 'lead agency' in emergencies is still sometimes controversial (see also Chapter 9).

8.10 CONCLUSION

Finally, we return to the modalities of NGO co-ordination and a set of principles some of which are tantamount to common sense but which bear repeating:

- The primary objective of interagency co-ordination is to improve the efficiency and effectiveness of a joint response to identified needs.
- Co-ordination agencies and their individual participant agencies should understand the factors, barriers and dynamics which affect the success or otherwise of co-ordination modalities.
- Co-ordination mechanisms and roles must remain flexible and responsive to the changing contexts in which they operate.
- Participation and consensus are the basis of a working model for decision making, agenda setting and strategic planning.
- Interagency co-ordination should plan and implement strategies and programmes which build on and strengthen existing local institutions, develop local capacity and incorporate a phasing out of foreign-dominated assistance.

One would suppose that since senior aid agency staff spend a high percentage of their time in meetings, the basic rubric of conducting such meetings would have been decided long ago, but this is not the case. Democratic representation and efficient decision-making processes are skills to be learned and promoted. A poorly designed framework for co-ordination will simply fan the flames of competing egos. The mechanics of setting up an NGO co-ordination body and the comparative advantage such an organization has as a democratic representative of collective NGO views has been explored elsewhere (Bennett, 1997).

If NGOs as a community have something unique to offer, then a greater degree of NGO co-ordination at field level is crucial in realizing that potential. Accumulated experience must also be transferable. The inclusion of government structures and line ministry officials cannot be merely perfunctory; transparency, adaptability and reciprocity are crucial to the success of all co-ordination endeavours. The challenge is to design a structure conducive to strengthening co-operation without limiting the freedom of any one participant.

8.10.1 CHECKLIST OF CO-ORDINATION PRIORITIES FOR NGOS

General

Ensure that adequate senior staff time is allocated for regular co-ordination with government, UN and NGOs at national and regional levels.

Place priority on feedback mechanisms so that other staff are aware of activities within UN, government and other NGO circles.

Make provision for financial input into NGO co-ordination structures at field level; membership dues are the minimum requirement and are often supplemented by additional grants for activities undertaken by the co-ordination body.

Co-operation with national government

Identify and follow the procedures for information exchange and transparency required by government co-ordination and registration structures.

Apart from national multi-sectoral structures, identify sector-specific co-ordination mechanisms usually organized through line ministries.

If an NGO Protocol Agreement does not exist, or is in dispute, engage in dialogue with the government through an umbrella NGO mechanism. Avoid short-term ad hoc arrangements specific to your agency.

Where a national or regional NGO co-ordination structure exists, encourage invited participation by government officials.

Avoid any suggestion that a national co-ordination structure should 'vet' NGOs on behalf of the government. Suggest to the government that an NGO co-ordination structure is essentially an information clearing house and quality control mechanism; regulation, registration and sanction are beyond its mandate.

International NGO umbrella groups

Encourage the formation of a voluntary umbrella group of NGOs (preferably with a nationwide remit) to co-ordinate and represent them to the UN, government and donors.

Ensure that membership of this body is open to all – national and international NGOs. National NGOs should not, however, be discouraged from forming their own co-ordination body and should be allowed membership of both.

Promote and incorporate into organizational policy the following immutable principles of NGO co-ordination:

- that its prime purpose is to minimize duplication and wastage through voluntary sharing of information and/or resources;
- that it provides an independent forum through which the collective consensus of NGOs can be expressed to governments, donors and multilateral agencies;

- that it helps facilitate and encourage a tripartite division of labour between the UN/international donors, the host government and NGOs;
- that it promotes the furtherance of debate and definition of 'civil society' though the creation of an independent, co-operative and productive environment for NGOs;
- that it provides advocacy for, and a demonstration of, the comparative advantage of a buoyant NGO sector and guards against either donor or government encroachment on this sector;
- that it acts as a reference point for smaller, less experienced NGOs wishing to engage more fully with the wider aid community;
- that its acts as a potential catalyst for NGO advancement through training and exchange with other NGOs;
- that it assists national governments, donors and multilateral agencies in the identification of potential NGO partners through which to work;
- that it may establish operational guidelines and methodologies for good practice in the field;
- that it provides the possibility for two or more organizations to share resources in the field and thus cut operational costs.

Ensure that the membership of this structure determines, perhaps through an elected Steering Committee, the policy and limits of its mandate.

Actively participate in designing models for reaching consensus among members. Often, too much time is spent on discussing the parameters of co-ordination rather than designing simple models for decision making.

Encourage the formation of sectoral and/or geographical sub-groups within the larger NGO co-ordination structure which, where necessary, report back to the larger body.

Ensure that the Secretariat of the umbrella body is staffed with senior persons able to represent the sometimes delicate balance of views of the membership.

Ensure that those chairing co-ordination meetings (including sub-groups) receive minimum training in facilitation skills.

Suggest that the co-ordination body should develop and disseminate 'good practice' guidelines for all aspects of field operations.

National indigenous co-ordination structures

Encourage the formation of a national 'forum' or umbrella group for national NGOs, especially where their concerns are additional and different from international NGOs.

Where a national NGO co-ordination structure already exists, attempt to strengthen this rather than bypass it in the quest for 'efficiency', especially in emergencies.

Encourage partner agencies to join national or regional fora so that role of co-ordination is not dominated by urban elites.

Where community group attendance is not possible (usually due to geographic distance and cost), suggest and encourage a representational network of such groups with a designated (or revolving) delegate to attend national fora.

Do not assume that national NGOs will always wish to join a common platform with international NGOs; their level of development, capacity and concerns may require a different, though complementary, approach.

Insist upon equal participation of the national NGO co-ordination body at all national and international fora; for example, at UN inter-agency meetings, donors meetings, press briefings, etc.

Allocate finances to supporting national NGO co-ordination structures, either as a direct grant or as a percentage of project grants.

Encourage capacity building through training initiatives organized either locally or through the international NGO co-ordination structure; prioritize joint and complementary approaches to common concerns of the NGO community as a whole.

Ensure that internationally agreed 'good practice' guidelines (such as the NGO Code of Conduct) are disseminated through the co-ordination body and encourage the development of additional country-specific guidelines.

Share and develop a common constitution/charter for national and international NGO co-ordination structures so that each can defend and advocate for the other.

Assist the national body in fundraising from international donors and educate donors about the comparative advantage of an independent, autonomous national NGO co-ordination body.

The UN and donors

Remind donors that the key to successful co-operation and co-ordination at field level is complementarity and that therefore their full participation in the co-ordination process is essential if duplication and wastage are to be minimized.

Remind UN and intergovernmental agencies of the various international agreements that allow NGO access to policy dialogue as well as to operational modalities; ensure that national mechanisms are in place that reflect and feed into this dialogue.

9 CO-ORDINATION IN THE UN SYSTEM: THE REFORM PROCESS IN THE ECONOMIC AND SOCIAL ORGANIZATIONS OF THE UN

PAUL TAYLOR

9.1 INTRODUCTION

The 1990s has been a decade of huge changes in the economic, social and political map of the world. Hopes of a new world order, raised by the ending of the Cold War have not been fulfilled. It has also been a decade of increasing globalization – the effects of economic crisis or political instability are no longer confined to a single country or region. Problems or issues such as human rights or the environment are increasingly seen as global issues. High profile global conferences, such as that on the environment in Rio de Janeiro in 1992, have raised expectations about tackling such global problems. The United Nations (UN), as the international forum through which countries can respond to this changing world and its problems, has been both a source of hope and of bitter disappointment. In the aftermath of the Gulf War in 1991, praise for the UN's coherent response all too quickly turned to criticism for its perceived failures in the former Yugoslavia and in Somalia and other parts of Africa.

As the world adjusts to new political realities increasing emphasis is being placed on the economic and social work of the UN, especially as the increasing number of failing states threaten new kinds of international disorder. At a time when the UN is facing these increased demands, not only in the economic and social arena, but in its role as a peacekeeper, it has had to adjust to a decreasing budget. The main contributor states have been giving less and less – mostly well below the 0.7% of gross domestic product (GDP) promised as part of the UN's Development Decades agenda. In 1996 there was a crippling financial crisis in the regular Assessed Budget which pays for staffing and administration, and in the budget for peacekeeping operations. Criticism of the UN as expensive, ineffective and inefficient has also been rife. For example a recent report in the *Financial Times* claimed that millions of dollars donated by western governments to the United Nations High Commissioner for Refugees (UNHCR) had been wasted because of incompetent management, dubious accounting practices, etc.

This combination of increasing pressure to tackle global social and economic issues, budgetary constraints and associated criticisms of the effectiveness and efficiency of the UN, has been the driving force behind recent attempts at reform in the UN system. This chapter discusses these reforms with reference to the *mechanisms* for co-ordinating the economic and social work of the UN system; it does not deal with the impact of that system in the field.

9.2 THE UN SYSTEM

What is often referred to as 'the United Nations' has, in reality, always been a stubbornly polycentric system. Historically there has been no organization or agent within it which has been capable of co-ordinating and managing the wide range of economic and social activities which are carried out beneath its umbrella. The Economic and Social Council of the UN (ECOSOC) was intended to manage the system but it failed to live up to the expectations of its founders. In particular it failed to co-ordinate the activities of the Specialised Agencies, because it could not direct them, or require them to carry out their operations in concert with each other.

The Specialised Agencies, such as the as the Food and Agriculture Organiz- ation or the International Labour Office, are constitutionally independent of each other, and have been obliged only 'to report' to ECOSOC (Article 64 of the UN Charter). There is no central institution with legal authority over them. The Administrative Committee for Co-ordination (ACC) which was intended to function as the main co-ordinating mechanism has gener- ally failed, as its members, the Agency heads, used it to defend their territories rather than agree its management. It has been said that in prac- tice:

> There exists no means of harmonizing the thinking of executive heads and the senior staff of organs concerned with central policy issues, such as UNCTAD, UNIDO, UNDP, and directing it towards problems facing the international community and towards possible initiatives that the UN might usefully take.
>
> (Hill, 1978, p. 95)

The General Assembly, too, lacked the authority to instruct the Agencies, and though it could give advice and address recommendations to them, it lacked the means of effectively monitoring their performance. It had no way of checking the relationship between the Agencies' budgets and their programmes: it has been said that the General Assembly checked budgets in a vacuum. Its main watchdogs over the Agencies, the Advisory Committee on Administrative and Budgetary Questions, and the Joint Inspection Unit, though capable of providing good, hard-hitting reports, were essentially advisory. Equally, the General Assembly tended not to consult the Agencies when it considered economic and social proposals – an omission which might be considered extraordinary.

9.2.1 PAST ATTEMPTS AT IMPROVING CO-ORDINATION

In 1977, in an attempt to provide effective management and policy co-ordination, a new post of Director-General for Development and International Economic Co-operation (DGDIEC) was established, to ensure 'the coherence, co-ordination and efficient management of all activities in the economic and social fields' (General Assembly, A32/197, p. 127, para 64). The post proved to be largely ineffectual because in practice the Agencies refused to recognize his authority. He was not an elected officer, but was appointed by the Secretary-General, and ranked below the Agency heads in the hierarchy. The post was eventually absorbed in a major reorganization in 1991.

This experience was to a great extent repeated in that of the post of Under-Secretary which was created in 1992 to co-ordinate humanitarian assistance through the Department of Humanitarian Affairs (DHA). Jan Eliason, the first head of DHA, was suspected of wishing to impose a common framework of co-operation but this role was disputed by other organizations. There was also resistance in the United Nations High Commission for Refugees (UNHCR) and the World Food Programme (WFP) to allowing the DHA to take primary responsibility in crises such as that in Angola.

Jan Eliason seemed himself to be uncertain about how far the DHA should develop its own strong co-ordinating, as opposed to facilitating role. However, he strongly opposed the idea that one of the other organizations, such as UNHCR, should be the lead organization, because that would pre-empt a stronger role for the DHA. This left the DHA with the more modest role of encouraging co-ordination by providing high quality information and analysis, and a reasoned set of proposals for the differentiation of responsibilities. By 1997, however, the challenge to DHA had succeeded to the extent that the Secretary General Kofi Annan (UN, 1997) proposed that its operational responsibilities be transferred to other appropriate entities and that yet another attempt to 'intensify' inter-agency co-ordination should be made through a steering committee. Other responsibilities were taken over by a new Emergency Relief Co-ordinator and DHA was abolished.

9.2.2 WHY DID CO-ORDINATION FAIL?

There are some characteristic reasons which account for the failure of these various efforts at co-ordination:

- *Duplication.* There was an inherent tendency within the UN towards duplication, reflected in the number of entities in the UN system – such as ECOSOC and the ACC – which claimed to act as system managers and co-ordinators.
- *Reservation of roles.* There was a tendency to resist the concentration in the system of key functions, and there remained unresolved claims and counterclaims about where such functions should be performed. For example ACC generally took an unhelpful attitude towards strengthening central control, reflected in its unenthusiastic view of joint planning. There were numerous reports of squabbling between the ACC and the Committee on Programme Co-ordination (CPC) – reported as a sort of 'dialogue of the deaf' by Bertrand (UN-JIU, 1984, p.16, para 35), because neither had been willing to concede status to the other – and of only half-hearted attempts at improving matters.

The duplication and reservation of roles resulted in fragmentation. This was a reflection both of the play of 'normal' bureaucratic politics and the failure of member states to counter the problems inherent in the UN bureaucracy. These problems were reinforced by fierce disagreements between Member States on some matters. This led them actively to oppose change except on their own terms. The majority of international officials were hostile to anything which might weaken their particular organization or their role within it.

The interplay of bureaucratic politics and intergovernmental disagreement also explained the apparent increase in another form of duplication – a repetition of discussions about the same issues at various levels in the same institution, and in different institutions. ECOSOC too often went over the same ground as its own committees, and the General Assembly repeated the debates already conducted in main committees. A US Government official complained, acidly:

> Should we accept the continuation and repetition of the experience of the last eight months, for example, during which [of] the issues discussed at UNCTAD, six were reopened and repeated on at least three occasions?
>
> (Anon, 1984, Section 11, p.2)

Such duplication also arose because of the mistrust of governments towards each other: rationalization and specialization were seen as increasing the risk that a key function in the system would be 'captured' by a state or group of states of the 'wrong' persuasion. (For an account of the problems in the UN system see Taylor, 1993).

9.3 REFORM IN THE 1990S

As briefly discussed in the introduction, an important part of the background to the reforms in the 1990s are the changes that have taken place over the last decade or so which have reinforced determination to get something done.

9.3.1 A BRIEF BACKGROUND TO THE REFORMS

A number of Global Conferences took place (under the auspices of the UN) at which the pressing problems of the age were discussed, most recently

- environmental questions in Rio de Janeiro (1992);
- human rights in Vienna (1993);
- population questions in Cairo (1994);
- social development in Copenhagen (1995); and
- women's questions in Beijing (1995).

These Conferences each spawned a Commission – to carry forward the programme agreed at the conference itself. Such conferences represented a growing sense of the interdependence of the globe, and stimulated a renewed interest in translating such concerns – called by some a 'collective intentionality' (Ruggie, 1998, p.21) into more specific and more manageable programmes. Could the reforms of the 1990s be successful in doing this?

The increasing parsimony of states, especially reflected in the reluctance of the US to pay its dues, resulted in a shortage of funds. This added further impetus to the reform process and placed the heads of the big UN agencies under considerable pressure to undertake reforms and to improve their management and co-ordination.

The emergence, relatively recently, of the EU as a force prepared to push the reform agenda has added further impetus. It had been agreed in the Maastricht Treaty that the states would act together in the economic and social areas in the United Nations. A letter to the Secretary-General, sent by the Permanent Mission of Ireland to the United Nations from the EU Presidency in October 1996 clearly states their views of the time, namely that

> ... many UN Programmes and operations in the field were too often undermined by lack of adequate co-ordination, overlapping responsibilities and fragmentation of activities.
>
> (EU, 1996, para 12)

9.3.2 APPROACHES TO REFORM

In the mid-1990s there were three conceivable approaches to the reform of the economic and social arrangements of the UN system.

1 *Adopt a more supranational or managerial approach, by appointing a central manager.* This was not a promising route, the appointment of the DGDIEC in the 1970s used just such an approach. It had proved impossible to give such a manager the authority required to supervise the Agencies, and any efforts to introduce major changes into the Charter, in order to redistribute powers in favour of that officer, or a central organization like the General Assembly or ECOSOC, risked being protracted and bruising (see also Taylor and Groom, 1989, Chapter 1). A supranational or managerial approach seems doomed to failure – the system's multi-centred character has to be one of the givens of the situation.

2 *Scale down the UN's operations.* Turn the UN organizations into research institutes with no operational capacity (this is the approach recommended by Righter, 1995). The money which went to them should then be transferred to the World Bank, which had a reputation for

being more efficient, and, happily for those who held this view, was more generally disposed to favour right-wing economic principles. Such an approach was unlikely to appeal to the developing states themselves. They were generally suspicious of the Bretton Woods institutions, regarding them as being in the pockets of the developed states. Another consideration is that scaling down the presence of the UN actors in the developing states, could reduce the attention given by outsiders to their internal problems. Such a system would make it easier for funds to be syphoned off by beneficiary governments for illegitimate purposes.

3   *Entrenched multilateralism.* This would involve the strengthening of system norms within the existing structures, so that they were more likely to impose upon the participating actors. The relationship between the existing actors was to be altered within the present system so that the weight of the injunctions on their behaviour to conform with system rules was strengthened. Given the multi-centred nature of the UN system, and the fact that co-ordination mechanisms already existed (even if they were ineffective) this approach would seem to offer the greatest chance of success.

9.3.3 ENTRENCHED MULTILATERALISM

The meaning of 'entrenched multilateralism' is given in the inter-linked ideas of *regime theory,* and of *global governance.* The first of these postulates that there is a hierarchy of 'injunctions on behaviour, of greater or lesser specificity' (Keohane, 1984, p. 57), ranging from 'principles' and 'norms', which are less specific, through to 'formal institutions', which embody precisely defined decision-making procedures. 'Rules' come somewhere in-between, but they are of particular importance because they are the point in the hierarchy at which general impulses are translated into explicit constraints on behaviour. They are the specific instruments for realizing common purposes in a society – and can be applied without further interpretation. Principles and norms lack this specificity.

Global governance involves 'sets of rules that guide the behaviour of participants engaged in identifiable social practices' (Young, 1994) and can be distinguished from 'government' which requires formal institutions capable of authoritative allocation of values. 'Governance', then, as a form of rule-dominated, ordered society is appropriate to a multi-centric system, such as the UN system of states and organizations in which 'government' is of necessity excluded. Rules, however, may be generated through multilateral diplomacy even in the absence of government. They require adhesion by governments to a set of specific injunctions on behaviour which require no further interpretation, no further enactment, by courts or by other authorities. So 'entrenched multilateralism' arises when multilateral diplomacy is effective in generating rules.

Rules may be developed as a result of particular contingencies which arise in the process of multilateral diplomacy, including fixing the agenda, building supportive interests and empowering them, establishing 'knowledge clubs' (or epistemic communities). Put simply, entrenched multilaterism is the creation of circumstances during negotiation in which participants perceive that to opt out is more costly than to opt in. Negotiation has its own dynamic and tends to create commitments which give rise to a sort of self-fulfilling prophecy, especially when there is a rule of consensus, as applied in the EU and in decisions on UN reform issues. When multilateral diplomacy takes place in circumstances like these it becomes 'entrenched'.

The argument is illustrated in the history of the British response to the proposal for European Monetary Union. Even though the official position was that Britain retained the right to choose not to join, the British government insisted on participating in the negotiations about the arrangements for the proposed new single currency. The British government therefore (wittingly, or not) loaded the dice in favour of joining and of accepting the rules of Monetary Union. British diplomats sought to shape the arrangements to suit British interests, and financial institutions in the country inevitably made changes which they thought would be appropriate to membership, if that were to happen. Adjustments were made in matching technical arrangements within the member states, including Britain, in anticipation of a co-operative outcome. During negotiations there was a tendency for the advantages of participation to be upgraded at each further negotiating step, rather than downgraded. Regardless of the objective calculation of costs and benefits the latter all the time tended to become more evident. So though it was predicated upon the assumption of the right to opt out, multilateral diplomacy in fact shaped circumstances so that all were pushed towards opting in! The form of multilateralism became entrenched because the actors, though retaining the option of non-compliance, became subject to injunctions on behaviour that amounted to rules of the system. This process had two phases:

- A first stage of decisions to be in the negotiations because of the pattern of interests concerned. The British government decided that national interests dictated that it had to be involved in negotiations over European Monetary Union, even though it was uncommitted to the goal.

- A second stage of progressively entrenching multilateralism as a consequence of the negotiation process itself so that the specific goal was accepted.

How far has the diplomacy which has been going on over the reform of the economic and social arrangements of the UN system in the 1990s resembled this two-stage process?

9.4 THE REFORM PROCESS

In the 1990s the attempt to reform the UN's economic and social arrangements concentrated at two levels:

1 at the field or *country level* within the developing countries; and

2 at the general or *headquarters level*, especially as regards the role of the ECOSOC.

In both cases the reforms were included in a series of key resolutions approved by the General Assembly between 1992 and 1996, namely A147/ 199, A/48/162, A/50/120 and A/50/227. The origins of the new phase of reform may be traced further back to the Secretary-General's report on economic and social matters in 1990 (A/45/714), which followed the failure of the Special Commission on ECOSOC reform in 1987 and 1988 (Taylor, 1993, Chapter 5).

9.4.1 COUNTRY LEVEL

A key feature of the reforms at the field level was the adoption of Country Strategy Notes set out in Resolution A/47/199. These were statements about the development process tailored to the specific needs of individual countries and based on discussions between the Agencies, Funds and Programmes, donors and the host country. The UNDP played a key role in instigating the process of formulating the Country Strategy Note. This was identified as being the property of the host country, and had the obvious merit of setting out targets, roles and priorities.

At field level a central co-ordinating figure was necessary. Correcting the deficiencies in the existing system was chosen as the best option so the role of the UNDP Resident Co-ordinator as the responsible officer at the country level was reinforced. UNDP officers in the past had often not performed well so greater care was to be taken about the selection of officers, and with their training. This was another feature of the reform process reflecting increased concern for a more professional approach to the development process, in responses to humanitarian crises, and the management of peace keeping. The pace of change with regard to such reforms has accelerated remarkably quickly since the end of the Cold War in 1989 – moving away from the earnest amateurism of earlier generations. There was also an increasing professionalization of international governmental organizations (IGOs) which involved the agreement of performance standards and their monitoring. In this the continuing complaints of NGOs about poor IGO performance in the field had often been a powerful stimulus for reform (see Taylor, 1995).

In addition to the more professional approach, the UN officers were subject to a wider range of pressures to conform with system norms than before:

• field level Agency and Fund Officers were to be given enhanced authority, so that they could make decisions about the redeployment of Funds within a programme without reference to headquarters;

- a further attempt to introduce common information sharing and communication facilities was to be made. The various UN organizations involved were to be located in a single premises – bringing officers from different UN organizations together on a daily basis, hopefully improving inter-Agency communication and developing a sense of shared norms and goals. The money saved by this would be redirected to the development process;

- adopting an integrated Programmes approach, rather than having distinct projects organized by the various agencies (often in blissful ignorance of each other's presence in the same country!). Technical improvements, such as changes in information technology, made it unlikely that such 'stand alone' projects would continue as the norm.

There was also a decision to measure achievement through impact and sustainability rather than through the level of inputs of resources, technology, or personnel. The Advisory Committee on Co-ordination (ACC) co-operated with the Secretariat in setting up a number of Task Forces to promote more effective inter-Agency co-ordination at the country level. Task force members were chosen from the Agencies concerned with the programme selected. In implementing this the ACC had to work closely with ECOSOC, the Secretariat, or one of the major co-ordination committees of the Assembly such as the CPC. Furthermore Member States were to allocate funds to these Task Forces in response to approved plans and Programmes, which was itself an incentive to fit into the system at the country level.

Thanks to these changes, by the mid 1990s the task of the UNDP Resident Co-ordinator of promoting enhanced co-ordination between participating actors in countries had been made much easier. This, combined with better selection procedures and training for the officers themselves enhanced their effectiveness. There were numerous illustrations of the results of this: the UNDP Resident in Palestine had become a major channel for funding into the area, and the UNDP Capital Development Fund had been used by the World Bank as the pilot for larger scale investment; in Ghana UNDP administered a $50,000 project in local development which led to a successful large-scale tourism development programme. It was agreed, however, that UNDP needed to be involved operationally only to the extent necessary to get larger programmes off the ground. It should propose, work up and initiate programmes, but rely on those with the experience of large programmes, and matching resources, to carry these forward. Some thought this should be the model for the rest of the UN system!

9.4.2 HEADQUARTERS LEVEL

Reforms were also required at the general or headquarters level if the UN's role at the country level was to be effective. Attempts were focussed upon the reorganization and rationalization of the work of ECOSOC (Resolution A/50/227, section IV). The Council was to hold a single substantive session each year (meeting over a period of 4-5 weeks) and divided into four primary segments (Resolution A/45/264):

- High level
- General
- Co-ordination
- Operational

A fifth, Humanitarian segment was added later.

The 4 day *High level segment* was for discussion of general questions of policy at ministerial level, attended by senior government representatives and Agency heads who have authority to commit their governments and institutions to 'agreed conclusions' (or actions) in the chosen areas. Increasing public awareness of global problems, stimulated by the global conferences, makes it difficult for governments to ignore these meetings. The climate of opinion has changed with the climate!

However, the way topics were chosen for discussion at the meetings needed further consideration; there was scope for states and agencies to indulge in political manipulation in the preparatory meetings to choose 'easy' topics.

The *Co-ordination segment* looks at cross-sectoral and common themes in the work of so-called Functional Commissions, including those covered by global conferences. In July 1996 there were nine such Commissions, the membership chosen by the plenary meeting of ECOSOC and representatives of the various groupings of states.

Co-ordination efforts are based on the multi-annual Programmes of Work of the Commissions, derived in turn from the agreed conclusions of the global conferences. The Commissions also helped identify issues to be considered at the review conferences of each of the major global conferences.

Co-ordination between ECOSOC, the General Assembly and the Commissions

In 1996 further rationalization of the relationship between the General Assembly, the Functional Commissions and ECOSOC was agreed. The Commissions would concentrate upon their particular specialized sectors of activity, and eliminate overlaps or duplication in their areas of concern. The General Assembly was

> ... to consider and establish the broad policy framework; the Council was to integrate the work of its Functional Commissions, to provide guidance to the UN system on co-ordination issues, and to support the General Assembly in its policy role.
>
> (UN, 1996, para 6)

How was the Council to realize this laudable, if vague, ambition?

Programmes of work were central to promoting the rationalization of ECOSOC's role – the Council could integrate the work of the Commissions much more effectively if it could relate their agreed programmes to each other in advance and identify cross-cutting or common themes. A document produced in July 1996 identified such items and suggested Programmes on that basis for the ECOSOC co-ordination segment meetings over the next five years (UN, 1996, para 6).

With the Commissions adopting Programmes of work for the next four or five years, ECOSOC could then generate proposals which reflected cross-sector concerns. This process allowed proper preparation of studies and documents in advance, as well as ensuring the relevance of the work of ECOSOC to the work of the Commissions. (In 1996 the work of the co-ordination segment had been marred by inadequate document preparation.)

In July 1996 only four of the Commissions had a Programme of work agreed through until the year 2000 (UN, 1996). It was proposed that the others should do so promptly.

Relationship between the segments and other institutions linked to ECOSOC

The role of the ECOSOC substantive meeting was enhanced at the expense of the subordinate committees, which were subsumed in the plenary as of 1994 (Resolution A/48/162, Clause 17) and the relationship between ECOSOC and the General Assembly was made more specific including:

• strict injunctions not to repeat discussions in the various forums;

• plenary meetings must reach firm conclusions; and

• overlapping mandates of the General Assembly and of ECOSOC.

'... agreed conclusions containing specific recommendations to various parts of the UN system for their implementation' were to be reached in the High level segment which had quasi-legal status (Resolution A/48/162, Clause 2.12 2). The Secretary General was to inform the Council of steps taken to implement recommendations. The language used in the resolution was much closer to an assertion of the authority of ECOSOC than previously – itself a remarkable development.

These were further strengthened by a series of resolutions:

> ... the operational segment was to ensure that General Assembly policies were appropriately implemented on a system wide basis [and the outcomes of this segment were to be] reflected in the adoption of decisions and resolutions
>
> (Resolution A/48/162, Requirement 2.1.5)

The Council should fully implement its authority to take final decisions on the activities of its subsidiary bodies and on other matters relating to its system-wide co-ordination and overall guidance functions in the economic, social and related fields, as appropriate.

(Resolution A/50/227, para 37)

Resolutions, *decisions and agreed conclusions* should be implemented and followed up fully by all relevant parts of the United Nations System.

(Resolution A/50/227, para 44; emphasis added)

These powers are considerable in comparison to those attributed to the General Assembly and ECOSOC in the UN Charter, where they were only asked to issue recommendations and receive reports – which in practice were usually uninformative and banal.

Inter-Agency working groups were set up in the Operational segment to pursue more co-ordinated programmes in their allotted sectors. The Operational segment was also to monitor the division of labour between the Funds and Programmes and make recommendations on this as required to the General Assembly.

ECOSOC's greater assertiveness was also reflected in a new way of agreeing the respective agendas of ECOSOC and the General Assembly and its committees, especially the Second and Third Committees (the Economic and Financial Committee; and the Social, Humanitarian and Cultural Committee respectively):

1 Resolution 48/162 established a procedure for agreeing a draft Programme of work of the General Assembly's Second Committee with the assistance of the bureau of the Council (Annexe 2). Once agreed, this Programme 'should be changed only in extreme circumstances'.

2 The agendas of the Second and Third Committees of the General Assembly should have 'greater coherence and complementarity', a goal supported by the agreement that issues of a procedural nature should be taken by *decision* rather than resolution (paragraph 21-24 and Annex 11 of Resolution A/50/227).

ECOSOC had significantly increased its power over the agendas of the Second and indirectly of the Third Committees of the Assembly. The language used in Resolutions 48/162 and 50/127 is altogether more positive and authoritative than that in earlier resolutions, and, indeed, in the Charter. ECOSOC's leading role in the co-ordination of the system was asserted and it was correspondingly more assertive. There was evidence by the autumn of 1996 of a rapid increase in the number of conclusions in the form of *decisions* taken by ECOSOC which often linked with more concrete proposals.

External support for the reform process

In parallel with the internal pressures for reform which resulted in the restructuring detailed above the EU and the United States also pressed for adjustments in the divisions of the Secretariat concerned with economic and social work. At a G7 meeting during the Lyons summit in June 1996 they proposed the merger of the three existing divisions, Sustainable Development, Economic and Social Information and Analysis, and Development Support and Management Services. They also argued for placing this work in the charge of a new Under-Secretary General who would act as Executive Secretary of ECOSOC, and thus strengthen the Council's role of policy formulation and co-ordination. The new officer would also pursue the reform process in collaboration with the heads of Agencies, reducing overlap in mandates, abolishing redundant organizations, and generally enhancing effectiveness and efficiency. The outcome was the appointment of a new Deputy-Secretary in 1998. The appointment would also

> ... advance the rationalization of UN economic analysis and reporting and maintain a clear oversight in respect of UN Funds, Programmes and Agencies while respecting autonomies and competencies.
>
> (EU Presidency letter, 1996, p. 5)

The EU also backed the proposal made in Resolution 50/227 of 1 July 1996 to review the 'mandates, composition, functions and working methods of the Functional Commissions and expert groups and bodies with a view to ensuring more effective and co-ordinated discussions and outcomes of their work'.

9.5 REFORMS IN THE FUNDS AND PROGRAMMES: THE TRACK II PROCESS IN THE LATE 1990S

In July 1997, in response to the widespread criticisms of waste and inefficiency the new Secretary General promised to seek further savings in the UN budget by reducing the UN's administration and using the money saved for development purposes (UN, 1997). The General Assembly approved implementing legislation for this package of reforms (known as the Track II process) in September 1997 (Resolutions A/52/12 a & b). Future reforms and increased system-wide co-ordination became the responsibility of a new Deputy Secretary General (Suzanne Frechette). A new Strategic Planning section was to advise Frechette and the Secretary General on specific proposals to improve institutions and programmes. The reforms were in essence a parallel route to the those in ECOSOC (Section 9.4) and could replace or supplement them in the future. A further ambitious package of reforms were proposed but await approval by member countries.

9.5.1 CO-ORDINATING THE FUNDS AND PROGRAMMES

One area in which further reforms have taken place is in the development process work of the Funds and Programmes. Extensive changes could be made here by the Secretary General under his own authority as these were formally extensions of the Secretariat. In 1997 the big four Funds and Programmes, UNICEF, UNDP, UNFPA and WFP were joined together to set up a joint UN Development Group (UNDG). The idea was that the work of the Funds and Programmes would be more tightly integrated through the UNDG and their executive committees would hold frequent joint meetings (the first such took place in January 1998). The changes stopped short of fusing the Funds and Programmes into a single entity – a course favoured the EU and the Nordic countries. A joint secretariat with secondees from the participating organizations was set up – a remarkable development in view of the earlier resistance to even modest integration (Section 9.2.1). The new process was driven by the energetic head of UNDP, Gus Speth, who had been imaginative enough to allow the other organizations to fill roles previously only open to UNDP staff such as that of Resident Co-ordinators in developing countries. By 1998 UNICEF officers filled this post in five countries.

As well as bringing together the Funds and Programmes at headquarters level their staff were brought together at country level in what became known as UN Houses. Sixty or so had been set up by March 1998. This was an old idea, which, as already argued, had important implications for promoting savings and better, more co-ordinated management.

It was thought that working together on joint plans in this secretariat, and in the UN Houses in the beneficiary countries, would help to develop agreement between the partner organizations. They could command the development strategy of the United Nations through the UNDG, and create a common evaluation of what the UN could provide in relation to the target countries.

Under Speth the UNDP remained in charge of the grand strategy and determined the allocation of posts in the joint arrangements – it retained what was called a god-father role – and UNDP chaired the UNDG, and the Executive Committee. But the concessions made to the other Funds and Programmes to achieve greater efficiency obviously ran the risk of a declining UNDP role in the future.

The UNDG was tasked with producing the United Nations Development Assistance Frameworks (UNDAFs). One view of the country plans resulting from these was that they amounted to a supply-side view of development, whereas the country strategy notes represented the demand side. By March 1998 such frameworks had been agreed for 11 countries and the goal was to produce plans for all developing countries. The target states were then invited to accept the plans, not on a take it or leave it basis, but obviously in a context of pressure. The new plans were more specific with regard to policies and finance than the Country Strategy Notes: They were a further step towards more specific planning within the overarching framework of the Country Strategy Notes.

The UNDAFs drew on the work of the Global Conferences through the Functional Commissions, and aimed at agreeing cross-sector programmes in consultation with field level officials. UNDAFs were also likely to be considered by the operational and co-ordination segments of ECOSOC and through this to help shape future country strategy notes. This process also helped to reinforce the influence of the UNDG/UNDAF process on the Specialized Agencies and the member states. But very few Agencies had agreed to join the UNDG by the time of writing, March 1999. At that date the cohort of the latter was limited to UNIDO, though there was pressure on the other agencies from the Secretary-General and others to join. In late March 1998 a meeting of the Agencies' main co-ordination committee, the ACC, was to discuss their involvement and it was hoped that there would be a move in that direction. The hope was that this would contribute to the development of a collective sense of best development practice, drawing upon the Global Conference agendas and the related cross-sector programmes, which would become system wide to include Funds and Programmes, Agencies, donors and beneficiaries. One official argued that the way in which a collective view about population policy had emerged was the model: 'tremendous things are happening'.

The new development frameworks also reflected the new policy of linking development with a wider agenda of creating an enabling environment within which private investment in the developing countries would be encouraged. Like an increasing range of international organizational arrangements in the late 1990s, especially in the UN system and the EU, the new development plans included proposals for creating supporting infrastructures in the economic, social and political contexts. The range of these was wide and startlingly frank in its commitment to liberal pluralist arrangements: it encompassed the elements of a well founded civil society and democratization as well as such changes as improved credit and insurance arrangements. The significance of this should not be underestimated: for the first time in the history of the United Nations the organization was directly addressing core structures in the state and some argued that even in the difficult continent – Africa – illiberal practices were increasingly delegitimized. The head of UNDP stated that 40% of the resources of his organization now went on governance improving activities, which was a remarkable alteration in stress. UNICEF's strategy had also been reconsecrated: the new approach was to be 'rights based', meaning that it was to be derived from the Rights of the Child Convention. In the late 1990s another wind of change seemed to be blowing in the UN system: there was increasing perception of the need to give priority to a *strategy* of change in many areas – including human rights and development – rather than a policy of dealing with immediate pressing problems in ways which put the chances of long term improvement at risk.

For two years or so the donor countries had indicated their preparedness to work within the new framework in the OECD's Development Assistance Committee (DAC). The World Bank, a primary channel of influence for the donor countries, was also willing to link its own development planning process with that of the UNDAFs. The World Bank and the UNDG had worked together in developing the assistance strategy for Mali and Vietnam and the practice was likely to be repeated elsewhere. But predictably there was some uncertainty in the attitudes of both the target countries and of multinational companies. The former went along with the new approach reluctantly, seeing it as the only realistic option in the post Cold-War period. The latter were reluctant to see multiple conditionality get in the way of their untrammelled freedom to invest, which was implied in such texts as the proposed multilateral investment agreement, but were usually reluctant to come out publicly in favour of protecting social and political underdevelopment. The companies also found the shift in the ideology of development congenial: that one of the purposes of multi-lateral action was to facilitate enhanced private investment.

The UNDAFs were really enabling instruments, pushing democratization and an improved economic infrastructure, but intended through this to encourage private business to fill the gaps left by the retreat in the 1990s of official overseas development assistance, even of the more well disposed countries, such as the Scandinavians. In the longer term improvements in the target states could make it more politically acceptable in the richer states to return to higher levels of official bilateral aid, and to achieve the targets indicated in the UN Development Decade agreements. It would also make it more likely that the developing states would be able to help themselves.

In the debate to approve the new course in the General Assembly in December 1997 the G77 (a coalition of 132 nations in the developing world and China) had shown much unease. But the new instruments rested on a powerful coalition – the Funds and Programmes acting together with donor country support were hard to resist – and this was enough to convince a number of actors, including the main beneficiaries, that they needed to concur despite considerable initial opposition. The emerging arrangements reflected an increasing preparedness on the part of the developed world to put pressure on those in the developing world to put their house in order. But this fracture led to a much clearer identification of another: it had become evident by the late 1990s that the developing world, often referred to collectively as the G77, was itself divided between the more developed and the least developed. When the former insisted upon the unity of the whole they got in the way of special efforts to help the latter: there could be a beneficial fracturing of the G77 to make it easier for the richer to help the poorest states.

9.6 THE LOGIC OF REFORM: RELATING GLOBAL INTENTIONS TO COUNTRY PROGRAMMES

The essence of the problem was to relate global *intentions,* which were increasingly defined in Global Conferences which covered a particular sector of problems, to *Programmes* which were trans- or cross-sectoral. These Programmes represented the functional application of the global intentions in the field. Three developments were necessary to achieve this transfer of intentions to programmes. First was a reasonably simple way of transferring intentions to the different sectors through linked organizations. Second was a mechanism by which the sectoral intentions could be translated into cross- or trans-sectoral plans. Third was a place where the operational agencies could be subjected to pressures which bound them to these intentions, and which also committed them to pursuing the cross- or trans-sectoral plans.

9.6.1 THE LOGIC OF THE REFORMS

Since the late 1980s the number of Global Conferences has greatly increased, and they have become an accepted routine event of global importance and relevance. The conferences involve massive amounts of preparation, and are a focus of heroic effort by NGOs throughout the world. They also prompt intense interaction between the members of participating governments. The mandates they produce reflect compromises that are not always satisfactory, but they add something new to multilateral diplomacy: the identification of a core of agreed values and purposes, which forms the basis of special actions and programmes over a very wide range of human interests and needs. They have proven to be a remarkable contribution to the strengthening among diverse groups of human beings of a sense of common destiny.

The Conferences spawned two further institutions, the Functional Commissions, and follow-up conferences, normally held after 5 years. The Commissions are intended to work out the implications of the Conference conclusions and produce specific plans and costs. A feature of the Conferences in the 1990s compared with those of earlier periods was that their documentation and concluding statements more frequently included specific targets, timings and policy proposals.

ECOSOC was empowered to oversee the work of the Commissions and has authority to inspect and alter their mandates so that efficiency and effectiveness are enhanced. It also identifies cross-cutting and overlapping themes and translates plans evolved in particular Commissions, into proposals that are relevant to cross sectoral programmes – one of two key innovations of the reforms.

The second innovation (contained in Resolutions 48/162 and 50/227), was to bring the Heads of the Agencies and relevant officers into work centred in ECOSOC. This brings them under greater pressure to commit themselves to the specifics of programme activities, and fit their own plans into a common framework. Mandates concerning goals and resources have also been shaped in the presence of the representatives of donor countries. Field officers are brought into the centre where they can observe the behaviour of the executive more closely. This provides another element in a cluster of pressures upon Agencies to work within the new system – and it is also in their political and financial interest to do so.

There was a further set of interactions generating practical responses to broad intentions in the evolving relationship between the central mechanisms and field activities. Task Forces, which are interagency, receive a mandate informed by the cross-sector decisions of the Co-ordination Segment of ECOSOC. At the same time the Country Strategy Notes, and the greatly enhanced position of the UNDP Resident Co-ordinator on the ground, provide a machinery through which the programme-related cross-sectoral and common themes can be specified and operationalized. A number of developments have reinforced this tendency: the introduction of unified United Nations premises, which, though by no means universal, are now intended to be common, and the parallel reforms in the arrangements of the Funds and Programmes, encouraged the development of more co-ordinated cross-sector activities. In consequence, as already noted, in 1996 the number of 'stand-alone' projects (i.e. undertaken by Agencies acting alone) had been halved compared with 1991.

In sum, overall reorganization has meant that the two poles of the system – the end where *intentions* are formulated, and that where *programmes* are implemented, have become more rationally related. Operations at the programme end, the field level, are integrated to a greater extent than in the past, and field officers have been given enhanced discretion. At the other pole, the greater number of Global Conferences has encouraged a greater degree of agreement about what should be done, and the reform of ECOSOC has sharpened its capacity to shape these globally defined intentions, into cross-sectoral programmes with well-defined objectives. At the same time ECOSOC has acquired greater capacity to act as a conduit through which the results of field level monitoring can be conveyed upwards to the permanent representations of the Global Conferences, namely the Commissions. They, in turn, have become more capable of formulating well informed proposals for the consideration of the five-yearly Review meetings, and the successor conferences.

This process of reform through entrenched multilateralism has had various advantages. The procedures introduced have strengthened mutual obligations and respect for common rules with regard to the work of the Agencies. At the same time it has become more difficult for both agencies and states to opt out, because the system works in such a way that the benefits of compliance and the costs of non-compliance are continuously upgraded and there is no viable alternative. The system has become a forum of obligation.

States which flout the rules of the new regime run the risk of being identified as cheats, and of incurring the associated costs. The General Assembly reflected this in Resolution 50/227 when it concluded that

> Developing countries are responsible for their development
> processes and operational activities for development are a joint
> responsibility of all countries. Partnership between developed and
> developing countries should be based on agreed mandates,
> principles and priorities of the United Nations System in the
> development field. All countries should demonstrate their
> commitment to the Funds and Programmes.
>
> (Resolution, A/50/22 Annex 1, Clause 7)

9.7 CONCLUSIONS

With regard to interests, the agencies and the developing countries concurred that strengthening the co-ordination mechanisms – the route of co-operation – was the preferable course. It could lead to an increase in the level of funding, and at worst could help slow down the reduction in development resources. They expected to be worse off if such mechanisms were not introduced, or if they stayed outside the new system – hence the unenthusiastic acceptance by the G77 of the proposed changes. The donors for their part had an interest in the mechanisms because they promised greater efficiency in the use of development resources, and could weaken the case for a significant increase in development provision. For them opting out was likely to be the more costly option in terms of development, but also because of the other important agendas, especially democratization.

With regard to the consequences of being in the negotiations: the new mechanisms created two new kinds of rules: the progressively defined rules embodied in the new working arrangements; and the working decisions produced with regard to policy, programmes and finance in the new system. Entrenching multilateralism meant that throughout the system down to its lowest level, behaviour was more likely to be subject to system level rules because

1   finance was a reward for compliance with the new rules for Agencies, developing countries and Funds and Programmes;

2   the actors who were set up or empowered by the reforms were likely to be system supporters; the Task Forces, the Functional Commissions, the co-ordination segment of ECOSOC, the UNDG, the Agency and Funds and Programme officers grouped together at the country level in

UN premises – all were increasingly inter-linked. The weight of system-focussed activity generated by this increased range of actors was more difficult to resist.

3   actors within the developing states were likely to become system supporters, because they were empowered in the new arrangements through finance and function. Taking more decisions about the content and financing of programmes within local mechanisms, including national governmental and inter- and non-governmental organizations, created a system clientele. Bilateral providers, the states, were also now more likely to respond to this system, as they were required to refer to the Country Strategy Notes. They were also together in the key ECOSOC committees and exposed to socialization into system norms. Officials in provider ministries, like the ODA (later DFID) in Britain, were likely to be pushed toward support for system orientations. The alternative would imply a flat contradiction of the reforms to improve co-ordination, the case for which they had so often supported. Behaving badly remained an option – but any transgression would be far more public.

4   the juxtaposition of three key functions in a single unit, ECOSOC, created a powerful instrument:
   • the translation of sector proposals into integrated programmes which were more easily related to country plans;
   • the allocation of resources for programme implementation within countries; and
   • the monitoring of operational performance under the scrutiny of the main providers and programme formulators.

   Having these three functions in the same unit reinforced pressure towards system-orientated behaviour for policy formulators, donors, and programme implementers alike – all were locked into a way of working which supported system rules.

In sum once a pattern of interrelated interests existed, ensuing negotiations could lead to developments which trapped cautious and willing actors alike. They were pushed to compliance with system rules by: a fear of losing benefits by exclusion; an unwillingness to weaken a related existing regime which was regarded as beneficial; the creation and empowerment of new or existing actors who favoured co-operation; specifying sets of rules about co-operation, like the Country Strategy Notes, which could be evaded only by appearing to abandon the agreed concept, i.e. abandoning co-operation; and being involved in a forum where the only alternative to system compliance was marginalization. From the point of view of cautious actors they had to stay within the system because leaving would lead to even greater costs.

The way in which reform had been approached was consistent with the principles of the multi-centric system: it was evolutionary rather than revolutionary, which was usually the more difficult course to comprehend but at the same time the most practical. The changes involved something quite simple, making it less likely that the actors involved, which were both states and international institutions, would evade or wish to evade system rules. This effect was achieved by a combination of tangible incentives, and of less specific injunctions on behaviour. Most important, however, was modifying the perception of the self-interest of the actors. The negotiation process itself could generate a powerful self-fulfilling prophecy, in circumstances such as those which applied here, in which co-operation came to be seen as the right choice.

KEY CONCEPTS AND PRINCIPLES OF CO-ORDINATION

WHAT IS CO-ORDINATION?

Co-ordination is commonly associated with hierarchical management systems, or as Harriss writes in Chapter 10, with bureaucratic organization where the control mechanism is authority. The chapters in this section are about the existence (or non-existence) of such co-ordinative structures, but point to different forms of co-ordination which have different implications for the distribution of power and the organization of co-ordination. Bennett, for example, uses the term co-ordination in a generic sense, referring to *hierarchical* and *non-hierarchical* co-ordination. He identifies government, UN and military systems in emergency situations as hierarchical forms, and NGO structures as non-hierarchical. He suggests that where these two different forms of co-ordination come together, there can be conflict.

Whether or not you agree with the particular distinctions made here between, say, state and NGO forms of co-ordination, there is something important in the idea of different types of co-ordination. Different forms have different implications for process, inclusion, leadership, decision-making, and taking action. Non-hierarchical co-ordination does not mean that there is no form of leadership, but it does imply the voluntary coming together of equals, who collectively make decisions about who should have the mandate to lead, rather than having this imposed by a higher authority.

Robinson's discussion about *co-ordination, regulation* and *facilitation* is also about different approaches to co-ordination, reflecting on the ways in which the state can act upon its role as co-ordinator. At the facilitative end of the co-ordination spectrum lies Taylor's 'entrenched multilateralism', where control and authority is practised not simply through hierarchical organizational structures, but through the building of shared norms and practices.

So co-ordination is about control through authority, but this can be imposed or agreed. Leadership can be volunteered by one party and voluntarily accepted by others. Co-ordination mechanisms can emerge reflecting the capacities, legitimacy and expertise of the different parties involved, or they can be pre-designed and imposed

WHY CO-ORDINATE?

These chapters indicate that without co-ordination the outcomes of various actions may in fact be *less* than the sum of the parts. One of the most basic principles of co-ordination is that it will help to minimize duplication and wastage, or to rationalize the kind of situation which Bennett describes:

In an emergency, co-ordination is almost always linked to a desire to regulate what might otherwise be an anarchic and competitive environment in which NGOs in particular vie for money, attention and humanitarian 'space' in which to argue for their comparative advantage.

However, co-ordination is not just about creating relationships in a vacuum. These chapters indicate that in most contexts, various forms of co-ordination already exist. The issue is not simply building co-ordination, but building more effective and efficient forms of co-ordination to cope with new demands or changing realities. But what exactly does this mean? On the face of it, tackling duplication (Bennett) or fragmentation (Taylor) would seem to be the issue, and co-ordination is a 'good thing'. But is it that simple?

Part of the answer lies in the question 'why choose co-ordination?' (as opposed, for example, to competition). Thus, Taylor discusses certain 'bureaucratic pathologies' which help account for the failure of efforts to co-ordinate in the UN system. These pathologies include an inherent tendency to duplication (the UN system consists of a number of entities) and the reservation of roles (whereby units lay claim to functions, often in conflict with the claims of other units). One response to this fragmented competition might be to cut the bureaucracy, and to organize efforts at co-ordination in favour of a more healthy form of competition. Certainly, as Taylor writes, several ideas for ways of reforming the system have been mooted – including the appointment of a central manager to co-ordinate, and scaling-down UN functions and passing many of them over to a different sort of institution, such as the World Bank. What has been decided on is 'entrenched multilateralism'. The important point to note about this is that it is focused on working *within* existing structures. Rather than having units pull in different directions following the interests of the multiple centres of power that characterize the UN system or by having them controlled by one authority, the idea is that they can be encouraged to work more effectively together through the building of shared norms and rules in the system.

So the desirability of co-ordination cannot simply be explained in terms of efficiency in allocating resources in situations where signals for supply and demand are complex. Co-ordination is about trying to take a rational approach in situations where there are a number of centres (albeit different) of power. This is echoed by Robinson, suggesting that where there are many agendas, different concerns, and various ideas about appropriate action, 'public policy' and 'public interest' are in fact social and political constructions which emerge through a process of interaction between many sources of interest and power. It is appropriate that these interactions and ideas be co-ordinated. The danger however, may be that the approach taken towards co-ordination tends towards excessive control or even coercion. There are two levels at which this operates. At the macro level, there is the role of the co-ordinator (for example the state) in establishing its legit- imacy to co-ordinate, in providing the framework which will encourage those co-ordinated to 'behave' (through incentives and sanctions), and in ensuring the structures and systems through which organizations are held accountable. At the micro level, there is the behaviour of those organiz ations and individuals involved – an individual may attempt to coerce others, not co-ordinate.

There are a number of reasons for co-ordination, and these have their own implications for the form of co-ordination. These include a need to manage diversity of interest, capacity, and activity. In such situations, co- ordination may be primarily about gathering information in organization- ally complex settings; it may be about bringing organizations into relationships and discussions which generate innovative forms of action; it may be about building some shared meaning and constituencies for certain forms of action. So the approach taken to co-ordination depends upon what you are trying to achieve, and what the diversity of interests is. Achieving a 'rational' division of labour through co-ordination sounds like a techni- cal matter, and in some circumstances may be best thought of in that way. At times, it may be appropriate for co-ordination to be designed hierarchi- cally, whereby the power at the top makes decisions about what other parts of the system do. At others, a concern to draw together diverse organiz- ations and viewpoints with the intention of building consensus or constituency (such as allowing for the voice of 'civil society') may be more appropriately initiated as non-hierarchical co-ordination – leadership can be allowed to emerge through a process of interaction. As Bennett writes of NGO charters, these discuss ways of minimizing duplication through *sharing* information and resources, and promoting independent fora in which collective consensus can be expressed. This is not the same as directing resources of other organizations to be used in certain ways. There is a difference between voluntary codes of conduct, and more formal mech- anisms for enforcing rules. These types of co-ordination can be between organizations which feel themselves 'naturally' allied, such as Bennett's NGOs. It may be between organizations which come from even greater difference of perspective.

MANAGING MEANINGS

Meanings, and the management of meanings, is a strong theme in each of these chapters on co-ordination. They reflect on the importance to inter- organizational relationships of the ways in which organizations, and individuals and departments within organizations, perceive and represent themselves. They also reflect on the significance to the development of inter-organizational relationships, of the ways in which organizations, individuals and departments perceive and portray other organizations and players in the field.

The management of meaning therefore emerges as an important aspect of the building and management of inter-organizational relationships. Debates about what organizations are have moved over the years from the simple atomized unit notion of an organization – the boundaried entity which is distinct from other organizations and from its environment – towards an understanding of organizations as complex activity systems and social entities, interacting with other activity systems, and steeped in the norms, values and practices which permeate the wider society in which they are located.

But how is this emphasis on meanings relevant to the management of co-ordination? It appears in these three chapters that the 'stories' which organizations and groups of organizations tell about themselves and each other, have a significant impact on the way in which organizations engage with (and indeed, dinsengage from) each other. These are stories about roles, responsibilities and capacities.

Robinson, for example, refers to the 'public interest' story of the state: as modernizer and lead actor in development; as promoter and protector of the principles of universality, equity and access in the provision of social and development services. She also writes about the 'private interest' story of the state: as predatory and dominated by rent-seeking individuals. Against this is yet another story, about 'private' organizations (for-profit, NGO, and community-based organizations) as more effective and efficient service providers than the state. These stories are important because at different times, and in different places, they have provided agendas which have shaped public policies, funding and practice.

However, as Robinson's chapter shows, there are at least two sides to every story. For example, it is clear that each of these stories obscures important gaps between stated intention and practice, between rhetoric and reality. The ideas that 'private' organizations are filling gaps left by the state, or that they may offer more effective service provision than the state, may be based more on what is thought to be happening or what is felt should happen, than on what actually is happening. And these stories can be manipulated to serve the particular agenda. However, a cursory glance at what is happening begins to reveal a far more complex reality, in this case of a long history of interdependence between state and NGOs. In these relationships specific language has often emerged which enables the different parties to express their meanings, to negotiate their relative roles and responsibilities, and to manage their differences. At times these established meanings are unsettled, as for example, major reform programmes are initiated. These may introduce new language, such as 'contracts' in the case of current social sector reforms. This new language can create tensions as different organizations challenge or develop their interpretations of what this means for their roles and responsibilities.

It becomes evident therefore, that in order to build co-ordination it is not enough simply to identify the organizations and links between them. A map or diagram which does this may provide a starting point, but does not capture all the issues – the complex web of interdependence; the processes which are the substance of the relationships; or the shifting weight of power and influence to which relationships are sensitive. What is needed is something more than *identification* of organizations and relationships. Something more akin to *appreciation*.

This notion of appreciation has been put forward by Geoffrey Vickers in his writing about public management. Critical of 'target-setting' styles of public management, or approaches which focus simply on outputs, Vickers developed the ideas of regulation, appreciation, multi-valued choice and interdependence. His proposal was that in a world characterized by an 'increasingly complex net of interdependence', the task of public management needs to be understood as regulation. But this is not regulation in the strict rules and contract sense. Instead, regulation is about:

> ... maintaining through time a complex pattern of relationships in accordance with standards or within limits which have come to be set as governing relations. Its regulative function consists partly in maintaining the actual course of affairs in line with those governing relations as they happen to be at the time and partly in modifying these governing relations ... the goals we seek are changes in our relations or in our opportunities for relating: *but the bulk of our activity consists in the 'relating' itself.*

> (Vickers cited in Rhodes, 1995; emphasis added)

The significance of public managers focusing on the process of relating, not simply on outputs, lies in recognition of the fact that the management task is not merely a technical issue, but that the 'multi-valued choice [is] a central, inescapable, irreducible fact of life'. Rhodes (1995) uses Vickers' ideas to provide a critique of the New Public Management:

> By emulating private sector management, New Public Management plays down the importance of the multivalued choice because it seeks to depoliticise management of the public sector ... NPM is confined to the values enshrined in the '3Es' of economy, efficiency, and effectiveness, and does not encompass broader notions, such as the public interest and public accountability.

> (Rhodes, 1995)

Instead, for commentators such as Vickers, public management is about appreciation: a constant process of appreciating the state of the system (reality judgements) and the significance of these facts (value judgements).

Appreciation includes assessment of the language and meanings that individuals, departments and organizations employ to both identify themselves and to protect their roles, in very much the way that Taylor writes about the reservation of roles in the UN system. It also means understanding that 'reform' is not merely about a reallocation of activities or roles, but about changing established meanings. Appreciation of this fact helps to explain why building 'entrenched multilateralism' or an emphasis on systems which induce certain kinds of behaviour and shared meaning, was identified as a strategy for reforming the UN – to change global governance – and not just tinker with government mechanisms.

'DOING' INTER-ORGANIZATIONAL CO-ORDINATION: TURNING PRINCIPLES INTO ACTION

ORGANIZATIONS: BUILDING BLOCKS

> Everyone is for co-ordination but no one wants to be co-ordinated, at least not just now.

Bennett captures a basic problematic: that co-ordination is generally agreed to be desirable, but that many organizations do not really buy into it, or disengage from it. He goes on to propose that most relationships of co-ordination are short-term, based on self-interest, and ad hoc, with most of the agencies participating not thinking hard about the reasons for co-ordination or for going further. Even in state bureaucracies where co-ordination usually becomes successfully entrenched as the norm, one can still think of examples of groups and departments which at times attempt to pull out of aspects of the co-ordinative system. So the problem of co-ordination is that groups and organizations still want their autonomy and freedom to act as they choose.

This problem indicates that at the organizational level it is important that attention is paid to the roles and responsibilities that each organization might have towards the structures and processes of co-ordination. From the organizational to the inter-organizational there are important functions for individuals and groups. Feyerherm (1994) proposes that a key to successful inter-organizational action is leadership behaviour, based on an understanding that such leaders are 'managers of meaning'. As the contexts within which your organization is working evolve, as new guiding frameworks and new configurations of power emerge, then the role of managers, rather like the 'cosmopolite' leader mentioned in the previous section conclusion on competition, is one of looking outwards. But it is also one of building new forms of appreciation and understanding within and without the organization, which brings people and organizations together. This can be highly sensitive and political. As Bennett indicates: 'Weak and ill-equipped governments emerging out of conflict are particularly vulnerable to 'aid shock''. And it is often the case that the various organizations which might be part of a co-ordinative effort are relatively weak in terms of resource, power and capacities.

But the chapters also point to a number of strategies for building effective co-ordination. Taylor writes about some examples of initiatives to build 'entrenched multilateralism', which in the case of the UN were largely aimed at improving communication, and at bringing certain groups together to talk and decide, with the country strategy papers for example. Bennett talks about codes of conduct and dissemination of good practice as a means for bringing organizations together and 'co-ordinating' their behaviour. Unlike more coercive modes of co-ordination, these strategies require high levels of awareness, willingness to learn, and commitment to listen to and look at what others are doing.

WAYS OF ORGANIZING: INTERDEPENDENCE

If 'network agents' and individuals effectively become 'managers of meaning' in inter-organizational relationships, then it becomes important to think through the process through which co-ordination is managed – from structures, to power distribution, to mechanisms of control.

Although not writing about co-ordination specifically, Feyerherms' work on 'Multiple paths for organizational journeys' (1994) is useful because she reflects on ways of overcoming common difficulties encountered in building relationships. These include: (a) a lack of clear hierarchy and limited organizational structures; (b) organizations being brought together which usually have different backgrounds and language or jargon, and may have complex previous relationships which have involved conflict or lack of understanding; and (c) relationships tend to start with no initial common goal.

This is where leaders, as 'managers of meaning' come into their own. They can play a role both in illuminating the interests and positions of all the parties, and in helping to create new meanings (this is more akin to a facilitative approach to co-ordination).

Feyerherm (1994) proposes a framework which can be used in preparing for and managing negotiations between organizations:

- *Purpose:* What is the activity about?
- *Process:* What are the means for the discussion to proceed and for conflict to be resolved?
- *Characterization:* What is the perception of other people involved?
- *Interests:* What are the parties' interests?
- *Positions:* What are the parties' positions?
- *Stakes:* What is at stake for the parties?
- *Judgement basis:* What criteria will be used to judge a proposal as adequate?

The process of working through these questions is continuing. As soon as organizations agree on a common activity as the basis for co-ordination, and begin working on it, they are quickly faced, through the process of interaction, with the same questions again. In this way, they keep redefining the activity and their perceptions. This is a process which may lead to blockage and misunderstanding, or it may lead to a deepening of the relationship.

A vital issue in all inter-organizational relationships, but perhaps most apparent in this section on co-ordination, is the whole questions of governance. As indicated in both Bennett's and Robinson's chapters, as you move from the position that the state should co-ordinate towards other forms of co-ordination, then *accountability* (who does what for whom), *authority* (who represents and regulates whom) and *autonomy* (who determines the freedom to join and form groups for example) become more important issues. Any co-ordinative enterprise needs to look closely at these areas:

- Where does the form of co-ordination derive its legitimacy from?
- What mechanisms for sanction and control does it establish?
- How does it manage control and collectively defined priorities vis-à-vis the diverse perceptions and needs of the parties involved, their need for voice and exit opportunities, and their need for independence and choice?

As Taylor writes, these questions are not simply about government – or formal and identifiable organizational structures and systems – they are also about governance – the understandings, behaviours and practices which also shape participation and outcomes.

INSTITUTIONAL FRAMEWORK: THE RULES OF THE GAME

The institutional framework within which organizations are co-ordinating is important in terms of the incentives and also blockages it creates for effective co-ordination. In a highly centralized organizational culture, the non-hierarchical forms of co-ordination discussed by Bennett may be difficult to initiate, especially where there are significant contests over who is responsible for what. In many countries, governments are adjusting to the implications of organizational pluralism and diversity for development policy and practice, as described by Robinson. Very often, the spaces which other organizations have found to work in previously are being looked at by governments with an eye to regulation. The forms that such regulation take depend in large part on the philosophies and capacities of the organizations involved. The nature of the regulatory frameworks which are established will likewise play a significant role in the type of co-ordinative relationships which emerge.

What is clear from these chapters is the extent of existing organizational interdependence, and of potential interdependence in the future – inter-organizational relationships are not an occasional option. Organizations are already engaged in relationships, not just through simple linear links, such as between a government department and an NGO, but in interwoven, complex webs. These webs are important ways of mediating real politics, and of managing unspoken understandings of who is who. As Robinson indicates, whatever the diversity of social action which occurs around NGOs and communities, there is still a central role for a state as an actor with the mandate and legitimacy to work towards agendas such as the promotion of equity. Many organizations would seek to influence that central actor, and may well co-ordinate their efforts in a bid to do so. But none can perform that central co-ordinative role in quite the same way and with the same authority.

ENDNOTE: ORGANIZATIONAL LIFE AND DEATH

These chapters also touch in different ways on the question of organizational life and death. Bennett indicates that all too often co-ordination structures set up for managing relationships in emergency situations remain in place long after the emergency, having failed to start with a clear indication of where responsibilities end. A conclusion to draw from this is that once individuals and organizations become committed to a particular initiative, and organizing systems are developed around this, it can be difficult to disengage. This can be the result of reasons ranging from value commitment to the ability to keep generating the resources from willing sponsors. Such situations often result in an ineffective or inefficient use of resources – the 'ends' have been served but the 'means' have gained a life of their own.

Commonly, the approach taken to this kind of problem is reform. Taylor writes of the options facing the UN system, which included not only the building of entrenched multilateralism, but also the prospect of scaling-down the UN, or even of placing many of its responsibilities with another agency, such as the World Bank or IMF. Similarly, the reorientation of the role of the state discussed by Robinson is all about changing needs, capacities and roles in organizational life which require renegotiation and adaptation. Ultimately, it appears that once organizations develop the knack for survival, they become better at adapting than at dying off!

CO-OPERATION

10 WORKING TOGETHER: THE PRINCIPLES AND PRACTICE OF CO-OPERATION AND PARTNERSHIP

JOHN HARRISS

10.1 CO-OPERATION: THE THIRD IDEAL TYPE OF ORGANIZATION

The term *ideal type* was devised by the sociologist Max Weber to describe a theoretical construction which emphasizes certain traits of a given social item which do not necessarily exist in reality. 'Ideal', here, does not mean 'what is most desirable', but rather something like 'a pure form'. Thus, the economists' idea of 'the market' is an ideal type. We know that 'perfect competition' exists rarely, if at all, in reality, but the idea of it is useful theoretically and for empirical analysis. In the same way Weber's concept of bureaucracy is an ideal type (Giddens, 1989, pp. 278-279, p. 741).

This chapter is concerned with ideal types of 'ways of organizing' – that is, ways of establishing stable patterns of transactions between people. In practice these 'ways of organizing' are combined in all sorts of ways. For example, key actors in markets include firms, which are themselves very often organized hierarchically (i.e. bureaucratically). One of the trends in contemporary management thinking argues the virtues of 'organization-as-community', and of building greater degrees of co-operation into formal, bureaucratic organizations. Yet another urges the introduction of competitive, market principles into public management (so-called New Public Management, see Moore, 1992 and Chapter 5).

Competition, organized through impersonal market processes, and *co-ordination*, involving hierarchical control (as, classically, in a bureaucracy) are two of the most important 'ways of organizing'. They allow people, as individuals or groups, to reconcile the problems which arise from their different or only partially overlapping goals. But these are not the only ways of organizing. This chapter concentrates on the third ideal type of organization – *co-operation*.

Co-operation covers forms of organization such as those described as co-operative arrangements, partnerships, collaboration, coalitions, alliances or networks. I don't mean to imply that all these organizational forms are somehow the same, or that they are necessarily clearly distinct from markets and hierarchies. But I am suggesting that they have something in common which distinguishes them, as differing forms of another ideal type (i.e. co-operation), from those of 'market' (competition) and 'bureaucracy/ hierarchy' (co-ordination). Each of these ideal types involves specialized control mechanisms: that of price in the case of the market, and of authority in bureaucratic organization. So what controls relationships within the third ideal type?

> There exists ... a class of more general control mechanisms to which we can assign the label *trust* ... (meaning the expectation that one's exchange partner will not act opportunistically)'
>
> (Bradach and Eccles, 1989, p. 282)

The third ideal type therefore, is a form of organization in which the control of the relationships involved depends on the existence of trust. Another aspect of this ideal type is that it involves 'self-organization', in the sense of 'mutual adjustment of behaviour', over an extended period of time and in pursuit of a common goal. In the case of the market, organization results from the 'hidden hand' of competition, rather than from anybody's conscious decision; in that of bureaucracy it results from the exercise of authority through hierarchy. In the third ideal type, organization also results from consciously taken decision and action, but without involving hierarchy. Another way of putting it is to say that this way of organizing is more social, being dependent upon the existence of affectivity in relationships, mutual interests and reputations (or solidarity), and upon voluntary action, rather than on guidance by a formal structure of authority.

These core ideas – of an ideal type of 'co-operation' involving 'self-organization', dependent upon the existence of trust – are being talked about a great deal at the moment. The names for some of these forms of organization have clearly become buzz-words: 'partnership' and 'network' crop up continually in discussions of the business world, in government and in non-governmental organizations (NGOs).

10.1.1 CO-OPERATIVE ARRANGEMENTS

There is a sense in which all of the organizational forms which are discussed in this book have to do with establishing *co-operation*, for we defined management as 'the processes through which the co-operation which produces the goods and services which people need is organized'. Here the verb 'co-operate' means: 'to work together, act in conjunction with another person, or thing, to an end, or in a work' (Shorter Oxford English Dictionary). And 'co-operation' can be established, clearly, by the imposition of authority, or it may be the outcome of market competition. But there is also another, specific understanding of 'co-operation' as meaning people working together or acting in conjunction with others, for their mutual benefit, on a voluntary basis. It implies reciprocal sharing of rights and responsibilities (as amongst the members of 'co-operatives'). Co-operative relationships, in this sense, have also been defined (with particular reference to inter-organizational relationships) as 'socially contrived mechanisms for collective action, which are continually shaped and reconstructed by actions and symbolic interpretations of the parties involved' (Ring and Van den Ven, 1994). This resonates, clearly, with the suggestion which I made earlier about 'self-organization'.

Interpreting contemporary trends in business management, some argue that:

> Although co-operation has long been recognized as crucial to the success of enterprises, *there is evidence that its role will become even more important in the future.* In particular, the success of emerging structural forms, such as the self-managed task team, the horizontal organization, the network organization, the virtual corporation, and the international joint venture, rest largely on effective co-operation … Co-ordination stemming from co-operation seems particularly important in today's new organizational forms, where relationships are much more voluntary and self-defined than organizationally-mandated. If work is accomplished in a fluid, ever-changing pattern of relationships that cut across functional, hierarchical, and national boundaries, high levels of co-operation may allow for an efficient and harmonious combination of the parts leading to high performance.
>
> (Smith, Carroll and Ashford, 1995, pp. 9, 11, emphasis added; see also Castells, 1996, ch. 3)

The same authors argue that although research has identified a number of different conditions for the existence of co-operation, 'virtually all scholars have agreed that one especially immediate antecedent is trust' (Smith *et al.*, 1995, p. 10). So the co-operative arrangements which are seen as becoming of increasing importance in the business world (like partnerships amongst firms or between public and private sector agencies, as we shall see) seem to involve 'self-organization' among those involved. Relationships are 'much more voluntary and self-defined', as in 'self-managed task teams' or 'horizontal corporations', defined in part by 'flat hierarchy' and 'team management' (Castells, 1996, p. 164) and dependent upon the existence of trust as the key control mechanism.

10.1.2 PARTNERSHIP

'Partnership' is a term which has come to be used very loosely to refer to almost any kind of a relationship between individuals or groups. Thus straightforward contracting relationships are quite often described as 'partnerships'. For example those which sometimes exist between the Office of the United Nations High Commissioner for Refugees (UNHCR) and other agencies which supply particular services in refugee camps, or asymmetrical relationships between northern and southern NGOs, in which the language of partnership thinly veils power differences (see Chapter 1 for discussion of these examples). A rigorous definition, which also distinguishes the wider conception of 'partnership' from precise legal definitions, is the following, describing informal networks of sub-contracting in French industry:

> ... partnership entails a long-term commitment and reflects a condition of mutual dependency where both client and subcontractor are in a position to influence the other by their behaviour. Partnership is a set of normative rules, determining what behaviour is permissible and what constitutes a violation of trust. The rules are designed to facilitate exchange in a situation otherwise open to exploitation.
>
> (Lorenz, 1989, p. 189)

Compare also this statement from a discussion of highly successful value-adding partnerships (VAP) in industry and business:

> For a VAP to exist, its partners must adopt and adhere to a set of ground rules that generates trustworthy transactions.
>
> (Johnston and Lawrence, 1988, p. 201)

Another statement about partnership appears in a document of the Overseas Development Administration (as it then was) of the UK government:

> The term partnership is now widely used in the UK and European development, and increasingly in developing countries, to cover a partnership between public and private sector ... with 'the private sector' broadly defined to include business, local communities and NGOs, etc. Normally the term implies some joint working of the public and private sector towards a common goal shared by both parties.

Instances of this sort of partnership appear among rural development projects in the Netherlands which are being organized under the aegis of the Co-ordination Centre for Rural Development (CCRD) on which all three levels of Dutch government (central, provincial and local) are represented. The projects, in turn, involve 'joint working' across these different levels of government and with the private sector (banks and local businesses) as well as with voluntary organizations. The accent in these projects is on 'self-organization', 'mutual reinforcement' and 'co-operation between the various partners' (CCRD, 1997).

The ODA's statement about partnership is analytically much less comprehensive than Lorenz's, but the idea of 'some joint working ... towards a common goal' recalls his emphasis on 'mutual dependency'. And, certainly, the sorts of public sector/private sector relationships that are being described here – and which are represented by the Dutch rural development projects – are regulated neither by prices nor by authority. They involve, in the sense in which I have used this term, 'self-organization' and co-operation – which, as we have seen, depends to an important extent upon the existence of trust.

10.1.3 NETWORKS

'Network', like 'partnership', is one of the buzz-words of the moment. Several of the emerging forms of organization which I have referred to are seen as involving networks of relationships among the firms which are engaged in the production, distribution and use of goods and services. And:

> There is a division of work in a network that means that firms are dependent on each other. Therefore, their activities need to be co-ordinated. Co-ordination is not achieved through a central plan or an organizational hierarchy, nor does it take place through the price mechanism, as in the traditional market model. Instead, co-ordination takes place through interaction among firms in the network, in which price is just one of several influencing conditions.
>
> (Johanson and Mattsson, 1987, p. 256)

The same writers argue that industrial markets, in practice, are often characterized by lasting relationships between firms, because such relationships can reduce costs and promote knowledge development. These relationships, they argue, involve the 'mutual orientation' of firms towards each other (compare what Lorenz says about 'mutual dependency' in the relationships between firms in the partnerships he studied in French industry, cited earlier). The relationships develop through exchanges which are parts of 'a process in which the parties gradually build up a mutual trust in each other' (Johanson and Mattsson, 1987, p. 258; see also Chapter 3). Another writer says that:

> A basic assumption of network relations is that one party is dependent upon resources controlled by another, and that there are gains to be had by the pooling of resources. In essence, the parties to a network agree to forego the right to pursue their own interests at the expense of others.
>
> (Powell, 1990, p. 272)

In other words, networks depend upon the existence of trust.

In what are described as 'networks', therefore, we find again the essential traits which I have associated with the ideal type of co-operation as a mode of organization. Before we go on to consider where these traits come from it may be helpful to consider briefly another typology of ideal types of organizational forms, put forward by Ouchi (1980) in his influential paper 'Markets, bureaucracies and clans'. His argument is that:

> Transactions costs [may be seen as] a solution to the problem of co-operation in the realm of economic activity [if they are defined as] … any activity which is engaged in to satisfy each party to an exchange that the value given and received is in accord with his or her expectations.
>
> (Ouchi, 1980, p. 247)

Markets satisfy parties that exchanges are equitable through the price mecha-nism, in the context of a competitive market, and bureaucracies do so through the application of rules defined by legitimate authority. But there is another possibility:

> ... if the objectives of individuals are congruent then the conditions of reciprocity and equity can be met quite differently ... If the socialization of individuals into an organization is complete, then the basis of reciprocity can be changed.
>
> (Ouchi, 1980, p. 248)

In this 'clan' form of organization (as Ouchi calls it), socialization – so that there is a high degree of sharing of goals – is the principal mechanism of control. It is likely to be efficient, especially in circumstances in which there is ambiguity or difficulty over the measurement of individual per-formance (when the market mechanism doesn't work very well). Bureauc-racy will be the most efficient form of organization if the measurement of performance is difficult, and if there is not much congruence between the goals of the different parties. But according to Ouchi, 'When a bureauc-racy fails, due to excessively ambiguous performance evaluation, the sole form of mediation remaining is the clan, which relies upon creating goal congruence' (1980, p. 252). The argument is an important one, and useful in the present context for the following reasons:

1 Ouchi's third category, of 'clan', corresponds with the ideal type of 'co-operation', as it has been described here, and confirms that another trait which might be included within it is that of 'goal congruence'.

2 It offers an analytical argument about the conditions in which 'co-operation' is most efficient.

This ties up with empirical arguments about the reasons for the increasing development of forms of organization which involve a strong element of co-operation. These stress their value in circumstances in which, for example, there is exchange of knowledge, which is difficult to value. Thus Powell writes:

> Networks are especially useful for the exchange of commodities whose value is not easily measured. Such qualitative matters as know-how, technological capability ... (etc.) ... are not easily traded in markets nor communicated through a corporate hierarchy. The open-ended, relational features of networks [or, Ouchi's 'clans'], with their relative absence of explicit *quid pro quo* behaviour, greatly enhance the ability to transmit and learn new knowledge and skills.
>
> (Powell, 1990, p. 272).

Ouchi's argument has also suggested a possible distinction within the or-ganizational form that I have called 'co-operation'. He argues that 'clans may employ a system of legitimate authority (often the traditional rather than the rational-legal form) [though] … they differ fundamentally from bureaucracies in that they do not require explicit auditing and evaluation' (Ouchi, 1980, p. 252). This point has led Thompson to propose a typology of organizational forms (see Table 10.1), which distinguishes between 'network structures' and co-operative forms of organization which depend on the authority of tradition.

TABLE 10.1 A TYPOLOGY OF ORGANIZATIONAL FORMS			
		Approach to relationships	
		Competitive	Co-operative
Organizational form	Independent	Classic market	Network structure
	Hierarchical	Bureaucracy	Clan
(After Thompson, 1991, p. 244)			

But we should note, finally, that the categories which appear in these typological schemes all refer to 'ideal types', and that in reality an enormous range of plural forms occur (Bradach and Eccles, 1989).

10.2 THE BASIS OF 'SELF-ORGANIZATION'

A classic metaphor for the problems of collective action or 'working together' is that of 'the tragedy of the commons'. Where there is a common resource, such as grazing land or a fishery, it will be in the interest of each individual herder or fisherman to go on making use of the resource up to and beyond the point at which the grazing land becomes degraded, or the fishery is over-exploited.

> Each herder [for example] is motivated to add more and more animals because he receives the direct benefit of his own animals and bears only a share of the costs resulting from overgrazing.
>
> (Ostrom, 1990, p. 2)

There is thus a conflict between the interest of the individual (maximizing benefits from grazing or fishing, in the examples given), and that of the society or collectivity as a whole (the social interest is in sustaining the resource). At the heart of the 'tragedy', which illustrates the difficulties in bringing about collective action, is the *free-rider problem*: if parties cannot be excluded from obtaining the benefits of a collective good once it has been produced, then they have little incentive to contribute to its provision. It is part of our common experience that efforts at doing things together (a group of students running a reading room or small library, for example) often break down because people fail 'to do their bit', whilst still continuing to make use of the common good.

Garrett Hardin, who first elaborated 'the tragedy of the commons' argued that there are only two possible solutions:

1   for government to regulate access to the commons (the 'hierarchy' solution, in terms of the ideal types we have been discussing), and

2   to privatize – the argument being that those with secure individual property rights are likely to have a strong interest in maintaining their resources (the 'market' solution).

One or other of these courses of action has often been adopted in practice, with the intention of sustaining resource use. Thus forests which were held in common have been brought under the control of government departments (see, for example, Guha, 1991 on the forests of northern India), and common grazing land has been brought under government regulation or privatized (see, for an example, Drinkwater, 1991, writing on Zimbabwe). But people are now coming to the following conclusions:

(a)   Each of these solutions can be inefficient. In the case of government regulation this is often largely due to lack of good information or the costs of obtaining it (Drinkwater shows this very clearly in regard to the use of rangeland in Zimbabwe). In the case of privatization the inefficiency is due to socially sub-optimal results (for example, if rainfall varies across a rangeland, so that pasture is differentially available, then total production may well be lower if the range is divided into privately-owned lots, rather than being managed in common).

(b)   In practice, there are alternatives which often (*not* always) seem to work better. In these cases users of common resources have succeeded in establishing self-regulated systems for their management, without involving any external agency – 'self-organization', in short, in the sense in which the term has been used in this chapter. For example, it is now thought that in order for the common resource of water to be used efficiently and effectively in large-scale surface irrigation systems it is generally better to rely on local farmers' self-organization rather than expecting good results to be achieved by bureaucratic regulation (Wade, 1988, offers an analysis of one case of such successful self-organization at the local level in an irrigation system; see also Uphoff, 1992).

Elinor Ostrom (1990) has analysed the features of such long-enduring local institutions which have been successful in managing common-property resources, and cases, too, of failure. She argues that when individuals who set a high valuation on immediate returns, and who have little mutual trust

> ... act independently, without the capacity to communicate, to enter into binding agreements, and to arrange for monitoring and enforcing mechanisms, they are not likely to choose jointly beneficial strategies

> (Ostrom, 1990, p. 183)

But these are often *not* the circumstances of groups of users of relatively small-scale common property resources (CPR):

> In such situations, individuals repeatedly communicate and interact with one another in a localized physical setting. Thus, it is possible that they can learn whom to trust, what effects their actions will have on each other and on the CPR, and how to organize themselves to gain benefits and avoid harm. When individuals have lived in such circumstances for a substantial time and have developed shared norms and patterns of reciprocity, they possess social capital with which they can build institutional arrangements for resolving CPR dilemmas.
>
> (Ostrom, 1990, p. 184)

These institutional arrangements have some features in common, which include:

* *collective-choice arrangements*, which permit those affected by operational rules to participate in modifying them;
* *monitoring arrangements* in which those doing the monitoring are either accountable to the resource appropriators, or are the appropriators;
* *graduated sanctions*, against the violation of operational rules; and
* *conflict-resolution mechanisms* (Ostrom 1990, Table 3.1, p. 90).

For such arrangements to work there has to be a shared judgement that:

* the operational rules which are set up will be to the individual benefit, and that they will generally affect those involved in similar ways;
* individuals must value the continuation of activities based on the CPR; and
* the costs of obtaining information and of enforcing the rules have to be relatively low.

The sharing of generalized norms of reciprocity and trust is another condition, though one which Ostrom rates as being perhaps somewhat less important than the others. There are parts of the argument, however, as in the passage quoted above, in which there is a suggestion that much does depend, in the end, on the existence of extensive common knowledge and shared norms. And so the analysis might seem to come close to being circular: groups of people among whom there is already a good deal of collective action, and shared knowledge and expectations, are more likely to be able to manage resources collectively. The part of Ostrom's analysis which is particularly important for us, therefore, is that which concerns the *supply* of institutions of 'self-organization'.

Here she draws on studies of the development of private associations for the management of groundwater resources in California. It is an interesting example because it seems counter-intuitive to suppose that people who were unwilling to limit their pumping of groundwater in the first place should have been ready to invest in building up local organizations. What happened in this case was that modest local associations set up fora for discussion of problems, which led to the sharing of much information about others' activities and about the physical structure of the groundwater basins. Then:

> The private associations provided a mechanism for sharing the costs and the results of expensive technical studies ... By voluntarily sharing the costs of providing information – a public good – participants learned that it was possible to accomplish some joint objectives by voluntary, co-operative action.
>
> (Ostrom, 1990, p. 138)

What seems to have happened was that the modest step, involving very little cost for anybody, of taking part in discussion of problems, led to a *reframing* of them, as the understandings of all those concerned underwent change. One small step then led to another:

> Because the process was incremental and sequential, and early successes were achieved, intermediate benefits from the initial investments were realized before anyone needed to make larger investments. Each institutional change transformed the structure of incentives within which future strategic decisions would be made.
>
> (Ostrom, 1990, p. 137)

The other factor which Ostrom emphasizes is that the legal system of the state of California was, in various ways, supportive and conducive to investment in 'self-organization'. But the points that I want to emphasize for the present discussion of 'working together' are

1   the significance of the sharing of information, and of the 'reframing' of problems to which it gave rise, in this case; and

2   that institution building (here, the building of co-operation) is an incremental, sequential process which depends on learning (starting, here, with information sharing), and stimulates self-transformation of participants (starting with the reframing of problems as a result of that information sharing).

These may be necessary, though not sufficient, conditions for self-organization to develop. They certainly help us to understand how it is that successful co-operative relationships can develop between organizations – as we shall see.

A striking example from a developing country context of the development of co-operation, bearing out these points, is in Uphoff's account of the establishment of participatory water management in the Gal Oya scheme in south-eastern Sri Lanka (Uphoff, 1992; 1995, pp. 22-24). When Uphoff and his team from Cornell University and the Agrarian Research and Training Institute (ARTI) in Colombo started work in Gal Oya in 1981 it was an extremely run-down irrigation system, characterized by a history of violent conflict between cultivators over water use. Over a period of four years the team was instrumental in building up a participatory system of water management which has, reportedly, been sustained even after the end of the Cornell–ARTI project. In this case external facilitation was involved:

> The organizational effort in Gal Oya was 'catalysed' by a cadre of dedicated young organizers, and farmers insisted that they could not have established [the] new system of organization for themselves.
>
> (Uphoff, 1995, p. 23)

But Uphoff's account shows that the intervention of these organizers led to 'reframing' among cultivators within Gal Oya, and then to the institutionalized sharing of information among them through the hierarchy of committees (starting at the bottom with field channel groups) which were formed by farmers' representatives and which the project helped to establish. The approach taken was explicitly based on sequential learning (reflected in the phrase 'post-Newtonian social science', which appears in the title of Uphoff's book).

10.3 WHERE DOES TRUST COME FROM?

Some time ago the distinguished economist Kenneth Arrow wrote that: 'It can plausibly be argued that much of economic backwardness in the world can be explained by lack of mutual confidence' (cited by Putnam, 1993a). Under the assumptions of the economists' model of the perfectly competitive market, Arrow's statement wouldn't make much sense, because the model supposes that the economic system is transparent to all agents. If this were really the case then people wouldn't need to be concerned about whether or not they should have confidence in others. But in real world markets, economic transactions are influenced by the fact that

- agents have 'bounded rationality' (they cannot have complete or 'perfect' information); and
- (relatedly) that opportunism or 'malfeasance' (cheating) can occur.

These features of real-world transactions give rise to costs – what Ouchi (1980) and others, call 'transactions costs', i.e. the costs entailed in searching out information, of negotiating and securing contracts and then of monitoring compliance with them. But in the real world – as opposed to the ideal world of perfect competition – economic transactions generally involve wider social relationships; they don't just involve momentary contacts between completely anonymous people or agents. So it has come to be recognized (this is Arrow's point) that if these social relationships generate some degree of trust, then transactions costs can be lowered, so making for greater efficiency in the use of resources.

Trust, can be said to exist if a person is willing, in the course of doing something, to expose her/himself to the risk of opportunistic action by another. Or, as Gambetta puts it: 'Trusting a person means believing that when offered the chance s/he is not likely to behave in a way which is damaging to us' (1988, p. 219). Trust, in this sense, as I have argued, is an important element of the ideal type of co-operation as a mode of organization (see also, for example, Humphrey and Schmitz, 1996).

The question then arises as to where trust comes from, or what the bases of trust are. One position, reflected in some recent writing, is that some societies, or some sets of social relationships, are characterized by greater and some by lesser degrees of trust. This appears very clearly in an influential book by Robert Putnam, a political scientist, on Italian society and politics (called *Making Democracy Work*, 1993a). The book is based on a long-running study of regional governments in Italy, and Putnam shows that differences in their performance, and differences in levels of economic development between the regions, are most strongly explained by a factor which he refers to as 'civic engagement' or as 'social capital'. From his analysis it appears that those parts of Italy in which there is a long tradition of high levels of participation in voluntary associations of different kinds have done best, in terms of both economic and government performance – and that this 'civic engagement' has been the condition for high performance. In the Italian south, on the other hand, such civic engagement has generally been very limited, and in Putnam's account it seems that southern Italian society has for a long time been locked into a kind of a downward spiral in which the existence of mistrust has given rise to, or reproduces, social relationships which involve adaptation to the inability to trust people outside a small circle of kin. He says that 'Where norms and networks of civic engagement are lacking, the outlook for collective action appears bleak' (Putnam, 1993a, p. 183). So his argument is that some parts of Italy are characterized by much higher levels of trust than are others, and that this condition can be changed only with great difficulty.

But Putnam's argument is circular. He defines 'social capital' as 'features of social organization, such as networks, norms and trust, that facilitate co-ordination and co-operation for mutual benefit' (Putnam, 1993b). Then where does social capital come from? According to Putnam it is based in 'norms of generalized reciprocity' and 'networks of civic engagement'. But these are also the features of social capital! How is it that the problems of collective action (which, as we saw, have to do with free-riding, and which constrain reciprocity and 'civic engagement') are overcome in the first place? Implicitly Putnam's argument rests on the assumption that there are predispositions towards trust, or not, which are inherent in long-running cultural patterns. This is reflected in his blunt conclusion 'Them as has, gets' (Putnam, 1993b).

It is also the view of Francis Fukuyama, who argues that there are systematic differences in the ways in which capitalism is organized in the advanced industrial economies, which have to do with the varying extent (the 'radius', as he puts it) of trust within them – and also with cultural differences:

> China, France, Italy and South Korea [are 'familistic' societies]. In each, the family constitutes the basic unit of economic organization; each has experienced difficulties in creating large organizations that go beyond the family, and in each, consequently, the state has had to step in to promote durable, globally competitive firms … Japan and Germany, both high trust societies (on the other hand) have had a much easier time spawning large-scale firms not based on kinship.
>
> (Fukuyama, 1995, p. 12)

This kind of cultural determinism, I argued above, is also characteristic of Putnam's work. Though he himself has sought to refute the charge, other experts on Italian history and politics continue to challenge him (see the discussions by Tarrow, 1996, and the review of the concept of social capital and of Putnam's work in particular by Harriss and de Renzio, 1997). They believe that he:

- greatly underestimates the extent of association in southern Italy, for example the important graziers' association of Capitanata in Apulia, which was 'an indigenous invention to establish and enforce a set of norms to allow for continued economic co-operation among the pastoral population' (Marion, cited by Sabetti, 1996, p. 25);

- fails to take account of the effects on south Italian society of nineteenth century political developments, which destroyed such 'civic infrastructure' (Sabetti, 1996); and

- neglects the possible causal links between the establishment of progressive politics in some parts of the Italian north (notably the Po Valley) in the later nineteenth century, and both civic capacity and the performance of regional governments in the present (Tarrow, 1996).

The significance of these criticisms for this discussion is that they suggest it may, after all, be possible to create institutions which are conducive to the development of trust – or conversely to bring about the destruction of trust, where it existed before.

Zucker, a sociologist, who researched – as he puts it – 'the *production* of trust' in the United States between 1840 and 1920 came to the same conclusion:

> … disruption of trust through such factors as high rates of immigration, coupled with pressure to engage in transactions across group boundaries and geographic distance, caused the production of trust structures within and between firms.
>
> (Zucker, 1986, p. 54)

He suggests that there are, in general, three ways in which trust is produced:

1   *process-based trust*: tied to past or expected exchange, such as reputation or gift exchange;

2   *characteristic-based (or ascribed) trust*: tied to a person, depending on such characteristics as family background and ethnicity;

3   *institutional-based trust*: tied to formal societal structures (such as deliberately created rules, like those regulating banks or law firms).

Thus we may trust another because of:

(a) the experience of past transactions ('She has never let me down'); or

(b) our potential partner's personal characteristics ('She goes to the same church as me', or 'He is also a Bangladeshi from Sylhet' or perhaps because 'His accent shows that he is an educated man'); or

(c) institutions such as the codes of conduct which regulate, for example, the practices of solicitors, or accountants, or (even) motor-car dealers.

In the context of the present discussion the first two mechanisms of the creation of trust are particularly important. Ascribed trust is often very important, but it usually provides only a limited base for transactions, whereas process-based trust can extend much more widely. Humphrey and Schmitz offer a number of examples of how, through repeated transactions, enterprises build up trust in each other:

> To start a business in Singapore involves establishing credibility. Being of Chinese origin helps, but it is not enough ... small businessmen have to slowly build up a track record of trustworthiness through their performance. As they do so, the risks wholesalers are prepared to take increase.
>
> (Humphrey and Schmitz, 1996, p. 14)

This recalls Ostrom's argument about how self-organization develops through a series of small, incremental and sequential steps – and why she suggests that the existence of norms of generalized reciprocity and trust is not a necessary precondition for the development of local institutions capable of managing common resources effectively. It may well be that there are aspects of culture which assist, or which make it more difficult to establish relationships of trust, but both empirical evidence and argument show that trust can be built up.

An outstanding example of the building of trust comes from a study by Charles Sabel of the development of new forms of co-operation between enterprises in the old, and latterly declining, industrial areas of Pennsylvania, USA (Sabel, 1993). He points out that the burden of experience and reflection is that trust can be found but never created (which is rather the position which Putnam, and Fukuyama, take):

> ... co-operation is likely in two contrary and unusual
> circumstances. First, when exchanges are many and the gains from
> future dealings highly valued in relation to current ones, then it
> can well be more advantageous to risk betrayal in the end than to
> forgo the profits to be made in the meantime ... Second, [co-
> operation may come about] for reasons rooted in common
> history...
> ... Neither circumstance justifies the hope that trust can be created
> where it is needed.
>
> (Sabel, 1993, p. 105)

Yet Sabel is able to describe the revitalization of old industries, based on new patterns of co-operation among garments firms, plastics manufac- turers, tool- and die-makers and foundries 'in the heart of mass pro- duction, unrepentantly individualistic America – where theory and practice should rule it out' (p. 121).

The story Sabel tells is one of a situation in which there was a recognition of the existence of crisis, and in which all the four groups of industries concerned

> ... had had in the more or less recent past some experience of
> inter-firm or labor-management co-operation that, *together with
> their increasing awareness of the organizational basis of their
> foreign competitors' success*, made it plausible to think that each
> could benefit from rethinking its current forms of association.
>
> (Sabel, 1993, p. 129; emphasis added)

Economic development policies in Pennsylvania had previously included experiments with development banks, and then with extension services. It came to be realized that these had the effect in practice, no matter what the success or not of the programmes themselves, of creating informal networks between the business people, trades unionists, local government officials, bankers and educators involved 'who together discover ways to bring resources to bear efficiently on the problems to hand' (Sabel, 1993, p. 124). These networks were in fact an important means whereby the key actors came to define their own needs. It came to be recognized, then, that

> ... instead of trying to define programs directly ... state
> governments should try to design programs that encourage the
> actors to define their own needs. In so far as the definition of
> needs depends on the creation of certain types of local co-
> operative networks this means programs that encourage creation of
> the appropriate forms of co-operation among the actors in
> particular industries in particular locales.
>
> (Sabel, 1993, p. 125)

This recognition was achieved in Pennsylvania through the programmes of an organization called Manufacturing Innovation Networks (MAIN). It offered modest funding for proposals from groups of firms, with others such as unions or different public bodies, which included a strategic assessment of the state of their industry and of the possible usefulness of co-operative arrangements amongst themselves. Sabel argues that

> ... in coming to a common and generally surprising view of an economic situation that each thought it had fully understood, mutually suspicious groups [came to] redefine their relations and (prudently) began to construct communities of interest.
>
> (Sabel, 1993, p. 121)

Key players in the declining industries were encouraged to under take strategic audits, as a result of which they came up with many surprises, which in turn encouraged them to look for new possibilities. Sabel, again:

> Just as insomniacs can be led to forget their insomniacal thoughts and fall asleep by the request that they write down the symptoms of their insomnia, so the industry groups were invited, or invited themselves, to connive in a form of self-distraction that would allow them to catch sight of new possibilities. I call the kind of consensus and the associated forms of economic transactions that theoretically result from such a process *studied trust*.
>
> (Sabel, 1993, p. 130)

In short, just as happened with the California water users' associations, according to Ostrom's analysis, 'reframing', through the sharing of information, seems to have set in train a process of self-transformation, for, as Sabel puts it, a process of redefining collective identities ensued. And just as Ostrom shows that an incremental, sequential process of learning through small steps can then take place – in the course of which trust is gradually built up – so, in Pennsylvania, industry audits showed up consensus over the problem of training, which led to co-operative efforts in this limited field, and these in turn to co-operation across a wider front.

Sabel's notion of 'studied trust' is important. He points out that part of the problem with our understanding of trust is that so much of the literature portrays it in black and white, as either there or not there, whereas everyday language conveys some ambiguity about it. The phrases 'blind trust' or 'undying loyalty', for example, convey an idea of criticism, of the lack of calculation, or miscalculation, on the part of an individual or group, of the extent to which trust is justified in a particular case. Loyalty, in practice, can involve negotiation, and the line between trust and mistrust is actually much more blurred than the conventional social science theories suggest.

Sabel argues, then, that

> A community of self-reflexive selves is by definition both prudent and other-regarding. It can imagine a trusting world and imagine others imagining the same. It can also devise stratagems for testing and encouraging these beliefs.
>
> (Sabel, 1993, p. 113)

His observations amongst the variety of actors involved in the declining industries of Pennsylvania bear out this general proposition. Trust relations can be built up, or destroyed. These processes may be influenced by social values and norms which are part of the culture of a society, but they are not absolutely determined culturally. Uphoff's account of the development of effective participatory water management in the apparently unpropitious circumstances of the Gal Oya irrigation scheme in Sri Lanka points to the same conclusion. In this case, too, a vicious circle of mistrust seems first to have been broken by organizational innovations, and then replaced by the progressive building of relationships of trust (Uphoff, 1992; and see above).

10.4 CONCLUSION

In this chapter I have shown that 'market' and bureaucracy' or 'competition' and 'co-ordination' do not exhaust the possibilities whereby it is possible for people to establish the kind of co-operation and co-ordination which is necessary in social life. There is a whole range of other ways of organizing which correspond with the ideal type of 'co-operation', which involves 'self-organization' and in which the key control mechanism is trust. We have seen that, contrary to some powerful arguments in the social sciences, there are good reasons for believing that trust relationships can be built up, or broken down, by deliberate action. Trust is 'studied' or, in other words, negotiated, even if this occurs in ways of which the actors are hardly conscious. The construction of trust takes place together with the process of 'self-organization', which I have portrayed, following Elinor Ostrom and Charles Sabel, as a learning process in which self-transformation takes place (including in this the idea of 'redefinition of collective identities' – people arriving at new understandings of themselves, and of others with whom they interact). In practice the process involves a sequence of small steps, which are incremental, and is probably started off by events and/or by deliberate efforts which lead to a general 'reframing' (or reconceptualization) of problems. The next chapter looks in more detail at some examples of inter-organizational co-operation. But I will anticipate them, here, whilst also offering the last words for this chapter, by referring to the conclusion of two management experts who have made special studies of inter-organizational co-operation, which bear out the conclusions that I have drawn:

In practice, most co-operative inter-organizational relationships amongst strangers emerge incrementally and begin with small, informal deals that initially require little reliance on trust because they involve little risk. As these transactions are repeated through time, and meet basic norms of equity and efficiency, the parties may feel increasingly secure in committing more of their available resources and expectations ... what may start as a one-time solution to a specific problem may eventually become a long-term web of interdependent commitments to a co-operative inter-organizational relationship. Increases in trust between parties, which are produced through an accumulation of prior interactions that were judged by the parties as being efficient and equitable, increase the likelihood that parties may be willing to make more significant and risky investments in future transactions (so decreasing transactions costs and increasing managerial flexibility).

(Ring and Van den Ven, 1994, p. 101)

11 PARTNERSHIP

ANGELA PENROSE

11.1 INTRODUCTION

For most development agencies, particularly northern-based non-governmental organizations (NGOs), 'partnership' is not seen as an option but as an obligation. It has been Oxfam's policy, for example, to work through local partners wherever possible since the 1960s. It is assumed that local organizations representative of the local population are essential to the long term development process. In some emergencies where effective local organizations are weak and governments dysfunctional, international NGOs are still needed, providing water, distributing food and other material provision. However, an increasing number of international NGOs are signatories of the Code of Conduct for the International Red Cross and Red Crescent Movement and Non-Governmental Organizations in Disaster Relief. Signatories are committed to certain principles including attempts at 'building disaster response on local capacities' (Principle 6). In most situations, therefore, international NGOs work 'with' or 'through' partners; partnership becomes both a practical expression of organizational values and a pragmatic approach to fulfilling objectives and having greater impact and influence.

The aims and objectives which international NGOs believe they are fulfilling by working with and through local organizations include strengthening civil society, improving the sustainability of work as a result of the development of local structures, encouraging mutual learning through co-operative relationships, and encouraging participatory approaches through local organizations.

Many pragmatic reasons for working with local organizations can be added to the idealistic reasons for partnership. Local organizations are usually better acquainted with the programme/project areas. They usually maintain better relationships with the local communities and are more sensitive to local cultures and traditions. Often the involvement of two or more agencies can increase the power and creativity of the work. There are also issues of cost and of security in areas affected by armed conflict (D'Angelo, 1996). Box 11.1 lists six possible models of working together for NGOs.

A similar way of cutting the cake is adopted by Fowler (1997) who considers the spectrum of 'costs' to NGO autonomy, '… from complete sovereignty of decision-making and action to (self-) enforced constraint'. The NGO judges the trade-off between the benefits the organization will receive from collaboration against the limitations on its freedom.

BOX 11.1 MODELS OF COLLABORATION

A study by the Institute of Development Research, Boston, provides a framework that describes six models of international NGO (INGO)/ local NGO collaboration. It defines the different models of collaboration on the basis of shared governance. This is the extent to which decision-making authority, both formal and informal, is shared between the organizations. Each different model is appropriate to different circumstances.

1 *Contracting*: an INGO pays an independent NGO to provide a well-defined package of services under conditions largely established by the INGO.

2 *Dependent franchise*: a formally independent NGO functions as a field office of an INGO which undertakes most, or all, of its direction and functioning.

3 *Spin-off NGO*: a dependent franchise or INGO field office is expected over time to become organizationally and financially independent of the INGO.

4 *Visionary patronage*: an INGO and NGO with a shared vision of development jointly agree measures of outcomes and reporting requirements for a programme which the NGO implements and the INGO supports with funds and other resources.

5 *Collaborative operations*: the INGO and NGO share decision-making power over planning and implementation by the NGO with funding and technical support from the INGO.

6 *Mutual governance*: the INGO and the NGO each have decision-making power, or at least substantial influence, over each other's policies and practices at both the organizational and programme level.

(Adapted from SCF, 1994)

Fowler also identifies three levels of collaboration:

1 *Networks.* These are the loosest form of collaboration as members may be quite dissimilar, the primary function is information sharing.

2 *Alliances.* These take collaboration a step further providing greater benefits because participants synchronize their efforts and resources. Alliances tend to be functional and are increasing as NGOs actively seek to complement rather than compete with or duplicate the activities of others.

3 *Coalition and consortia.* These terms cover organizational entities which are 'constituted by and (are) the legal responsibility of the founding NGOs but (do) not have authority over them.' Coalitions tend to

provide increased profile and leverage, consortia usually provide increased access to, and application of resources. Coalitions usually require considerable investment of time and human resources from members but can result in greater strength when voicing shared positions.

There are also a growing number of international 'families' of NGOs which relate to each other according to a number of different models, some related to a form of federalism. One example is the International Save the Children Alliance described in Box 11.2. The statement suggests a commitment to a high level of partnership.

BOX 11.2 THE INTERNATIONAL SAVE THE CHILDREN ALLIANCE

The Save the Children International Union, an umbrella body which included Save the Children organizations from around the world was first organized by Eglantyne Jebb in Geneva in 1920. The connections were disrupted by the Second World War and not resumed until the formation of the International Save the Children Alliance in 1979.

The Alliance believes lasting benefits for children can only come about through changes in social values, public policy and practice. The Alliance is currently rebuilding itself in order to fulfill the following objectives and long-term goals.

- Lead through innovation and contribute knowledge and experience to a children's agenda for the new century.
- Promote a global commitment to children's rights through partnerships with national and international organizations and by drawing on public support.
- Demand recognition and action on behalf of the world's most vulnerable children, including victims of crisis.
- Contribute to the progressive realization of children's rights on the basis of the UN Convention on the Rights of the Child.

According to the new by-laws the members of the Alliance have decided that these objects can best be achieved by working in pursuit of common goals and developing joint strategies. In order to achieve that, when required, they have agreed to subordinate their individual ambitions to those collectively shared, and will commit the resources necessary.

The Alliance which currently has twenty-six members is extending its membership and hopes to have new members from each of the main regions across the world; members are required to 'have a nationwide basis in the sense that the organization is rooted and recognized in its own country as a contributor to the realization of children's rights'. The issue of membership has stimulated considerable debate as the existing members range from large international organizations with a head office in Europe and North America to single country organizations with relatively small programmes. The stated principle is that 'Save the Children believes in partnership and that partnership incorporates empowerment, trust, reciprocal accountability and mutual respect. These same principles govern relationships among its own members.' A clear vision exists but the existing organizations have evolved in different ways and operate in different cultures and contexts. This is seen positively and 'variety and diversity in membership' is seen as a resource. The challenge is to ensure that the common objectives enable the different members to work collaboratively at all levels.

The focus in this chapter is 'partnership' as a form of working together. It has already been noted (in Chapter 1) that the term partnership means different things to different people and that the language of partnerhsip can be used as a smokescreen to conceal differential power relations. Nevertheless, it is widely and increasingly used to describe – or at least to evoke – relationships between equals. It is also a preferred alternative to variations on the 'donor–recipient' or 'donor–beneficiary' relationship. I hope to show how the concept of partnership is increasingly recognized as central to the relationships which underpin development, but that it is not without problems as a term. Partnerships are rarely as straightforward in practice as the models might suggest. To the this end, the chapter is split roughly in two halves. The first discusses the ideal of partnership and the second, through two case studies, examines some of the practical difficulties of partnership.

11.2 TAKING PARTNERSHIP SERIOUSLY

Forming partnerships was originally the concern of northern and southern NGOs, as a concrete expression of international solidarity, official aid agencies, both bilateral donors and multilateral institutions have increasingly used the concept. During the consultation period for the UK Government's White Paper on International Co-operation, launched in November 1997, the Secretary of State for International Development (DFID), Clare Short, frequently referred to partnerships in the series of speeches she delivered on specific aspects of development co-operation.

> Our job is to transfer resources to enable states to deliver to their people. Ideally, our partnerships will be based on an open and agreed agenda involving government and civil society, as well as other donors.
>
> (Short, 1997b)

> The way in which my Department [Department for International Development] intends to take forward our development efforts is to work in partnership with developing countries who agree to make the focus of our collaboration the poverty elimination targets.
>
> (Short, 1997c)

The Green Paper on the future relations between the European Union (EU) and the African, Caribbean and Pacific (ACP) countries after the expiry of the Lomé Convention is subtitled 'Challenges and options for a new partnership' and states unequivocally that 'Partnership is undoubtedly still the ideal form for co-operation relations and any future agreement between the EU and the ACP States must endeavour to restore it'.

Aware of the danger of the term becoming a debased currency many have attempted to develop working definitions and typologies of the nature of 'partnerships'. The following was developed by Save the Children (SCF).

> Partnership is an approach to work which is an expression of the partner institutions' desire to work according to a set of values.
>
> A partnership should be an equitable, collaborative working partnership voluntarily entered into by two or more institutions (partners) which is characterized by mutual trust, respect, participation, commitment, learning, reciprocity, transparency and voluntaristic, negotiated decision-making. Partners should only ask of the other institution what they are prepared to do themselves.
>
> All partnerships should, therefore, be established through negotiation of the respective roles and contributions of each of the partners. This negotiated agreement should always be written down and should form part of the 'contract' between the partners.
>
> Partnerships should be viewed as dynamic relationships which can change over time. The early stage of a partnership may be more of an expression of commitment to work according to agreed values. As the relationship develops, these values *must* be reflected in the way the institutions work together. Partnership relationships should be regularly reviewed by the partner institutions to avoid the development of dependency.
>
> (Britton, 1994)

11.3 CRITERIA FOR SELECTING PARTNERS

The dual motivation of northern NGOs (NNGOs) and other agencies for working in partnership creates an inevitable tension. Respected NNGOs adhere to the principle of working through a local partner yet are also primarily seeking to realize their own organizational vision, mission, values, principles and goals. Whilst they subscribe to a belief in their interventions and assistance being 'demand' not 'supply-led' they are nevertheless accountable to funders and supporters calling ever-louder for measurable impact, cost-effectiveness and increased efficiency.

In seeking to prevent these tensions destroying or distorting partnerships NNGOs have attempted to regulate their partnerships by evolving criteria for successful partnership. A significant number of NNGOs have identified compatibility of values and mission as the most important criteria for developing a partnership relationship, from which they move on to more pragmatic criteria. The following suggestions were put forward as principles Save the Children should adhere to in developing partnerships with other institutions, irrespective of whom the potential partner is (SCF, 1994). Whilst the criteria developed are specific to Save the Children, the general principles they embody are widely applicable.

1 *Congruence of mission, values and operating principles*

The over-riding principle of developing partnerships for Save the Children should be that of shared or congruent values and principles and a shared or congruent mission with the partner agency. Partnership does not require identity of mission, principles and values, but it does require adequate levels of overlap to make the partnership meaningful, worthwhile and purposeful.

2 *Effectiveness*

Since Save the Children aims to achieve lasting benefits for children, potential partnerships should be assessed in terms of the likelihood of the partnership to achieve this. Assessments may be based on the previous 'track record' of the potential partner or on its institutional capacity to adapt and embrace this aim. Assessments should also be made of Save the Children's record of working successfully with certain types of partner.

Save the Children should aim to limit the number of its partnerships in the South to enable it to invest adequate levels of money and other types of support in these partnerships, in some cases in the longer term.

3 *Accountability*

Partners should be selected on the basis of an assessment of their current or potential degree of accountability at both functional and strategic levels.

Save the Children and its partners should be willing to monitor their accountabilities to each other, their constituencies, donors, trustees and supporters and to their host governments.

4 *Transparency*

Save the Children should nurture an atmosphere of openness concerning its finances, decision making, and negotiations with third parties.

Partner agencies should clarify and share their strategy, approach to development, areas of priority, funding sources (and reporting requirements).

Save the Children should provide access to the same forms of information as those which it requires from its partners.

5 *Mutuality*

Partnerships should be built on equality of commitment with a recognition that the contributions each partner makes to the relationship will be different but afforded equal respect.

We should always remember that choosing to enter a partnership should be a process of mutual selection. Save the Children should aim to make this process of mutual selection a reality by always developing a written partnership agreement.

Both parties should:

- respect and acknowledge the realities that impinge on each member of the partnership;
- mutually agree the parameters of success and the indicators for measuring these;
- agree the objectives and methodologies for specific projects or pieces of work.

6 *No hidden agendas*

Save the Children should not have any 'hidden agendas' concerning its work with partner agencies. For example, aims concerning the use of information gathered by and from partners for influence purposes should be made clear. At the same time, Save the Children should make it clear that it aims to maximize its impact and influence whilst retaining its independence as an NNGO.

7 *Sustainability*

Save the Children in its partnerships must strive to achieve sustainability; to strengthen the capacity of people (whether in community based organizations (CBOs), Southern NGOs (SNGOs), government or other groups, to further their own development.

Save the Children should:

- choose partners which share our definition of sustainability and which strive to achieve this in their work. With SNGOs we should take care that they do not confuse 'sustainability' with 'self perpetuation'.
- strive to diversify each of its partners so that they do not become a mere extension of SCF (avoiding the 'wholly owned subsidiary' syndrome).
- commit itself to the institutional strengthening and development of its partners and recognize that this may require long term working relationships.

8   *Minimizing demands*

Save the Children should aim to minimize its demands of partners, especially for written reporting and documentation. Reporting systems should enable transparency but should be designed with the partner so that they are realistic and achievable. Training, help with systems development and other forms of support should be made available.

Save the Children should be responsible for dealing with the paperwork requirements of its own funding sources and should not hand this over to its Southern partners.

9   *Maximizing distinctive competence*

In its choice of partners, Save the Children should aim to develop partnerships where its own and its partners' distinctive competencies are used to their maximum advantage. This will require open and honest assessments by both parties of their respective strengths and weaknesses and the development of mutually agreed strategies for building on strengths and overcoming weaknesses. It will also require the development of strategies which are consistent with the respective competencies of the partner agencies and which maximize the opportunity for synergy.

Save the Children should aim to maximize the opportunities for exchanging information with its partners so that the competence of each increases and develops.

10   *Timescales*

Funding commitments should be made on realistic timescales. It may not be desirable to talk, as USAID have done, of 'lifelong partnerships' but partnerships should be viewed within a longer term institutional-development perspective rather than merely shorter project-related terms whenever possible.

Save the Children should move towards funding arrangements which provide 'stability and predictability in the long term and timeliness and flexibility in the short term' (Van der Heijden, 1987). We should aim to avoid project-related funding arrangements except when these take place within the context of a wider institutional partnership agreement.

11.4 TENSIONS IN PARTNERSHIPS

Despite the ideals and aspirations of those seeking to form partnerships the problems encountered in forming equitable and effective relationships are well documented and the usefulness of the concept is being seriously questioned (Malhotra 1996, Muchunguzi and Milne, 1995).

Two types of problem bedevil 'partnership', differences of values and practical constraints. These reflect the normative and pragmatic reasons for seeking to develop partnership in the first instance.

11.4.1 VALUE INCOMPATIBILITIES

Perhaps the most fundamental issue is the fear that, despite formal agreements and attempts to develop different models, the donor–recipient relationship persists and characterizes most relationships between northern and southern partners, thus preventing equitable relationships (Fowler, 1997). Whilst the need to recognize complementary strengths and contributions is acknowledged often this is not reflected in practice.

A further constraint on the development of partnerships based on and driven by shared values is the incompatibility of the processes of human and organizational development with the dominant mode of project based development. Projects impose rigidities on schedules and activities which preclude the flexible and adaptive processes which are more likely to strengthen individual and organizational capacity – which is yet held as the overall objective (Fowler, 1997).

Ironically the criticisms by southern NGOs of northern NGOs reflect the criticisms by northern NGOs of multilateral institutions and bilateral donor governments: a lack of transparency and accountability, and non-reciprocity in relationships. Southern NGOs perceive the decision-making processes of northern NGOs as opaque or secretive, and issues around the constituency to which northern NGOs are accountable as complex. Northern NGOs are perceived to be accountable to members, supporters and donors in their own countries and all policy decisions appear to be made in the North. It is not clear where or how northern NGOs are accountable to their partners and local communities. Northern NGOs insist upon the financial accountability of their partners but do not open themselves up to financial investigation by their southern partners. There is no 'information accountability' allowing southern partners to check how information about them is used in the North. There are an enormous number of evaluations and visits from northern NGOs to southern partners. If the relationship is to be reciprocal then southern partners should be given more opportunities to visit and evaluate the work of northern NGOs in the countries in which they are based (Redd Barna, 1997).

11.4.2 PRACTICAL CONSTRAINTS

Many of the problems encountered, although related to and exacerbated by some of the intrinsic problems noted above are of a more practical nature. The case studies in Sections 11.5 and 11.6 which describe partnerships Save the Children engaged in (in Bangladesh and El Salvador) highlight some of these problems – and illustrate the gap that often exists between the theory and practice of partnership. Here, I list some of the most common constraints and then suggest one mechanism for improving the situation.

Governance and management: Lack of clarity over the rights, duties and roles of the two partners; difficulties in establishing relationships.

Financial management: Small NGOs – community based organizations, grassroots organizations, etc. – may find their internal management and accounting systems, originally based on informality and trust, coming under pressure as they grow and accept additional funding. In some cases inadequate accounting due to weak systems may appear to be hiding improprieties.

Reporting: Confusion over the type and value of reports partner organizations may be required to produce.

Practice: Significant differences in the understanding of best practice in implementation of development of technical policies.

Communications: Differences in style and language lead to misunderstandings especially in new partnerships when partners are worried about the others' intentions; delays in response to requests and lengthy decision-making chains cause inertia.

Problems of partnership must be tackled at many different levels. There are many practical ways which will strengthen partnerships – but basic assumptions, attitudes and behaviour need to be tackled as well.

A number of measures which broaden out the partnership relationship have been explored to overcome weaknesses including forming joint bodies to make decisions about operational activities or funding, establishing multiple-NGO fora to define agendas, engaging consultants to facilitate dialogue and undertaking 'reverse' evaluations of NNGOs by southern partners. A proposal to create an ombudsman has taken the idea of an objective third party, an adjudicator or mediator a step further.

To be effective in redressing the inequities and imbalances created by a fast globalizing world, development agencies will need to form alliances within and beyond the aid system which are equitable and mutually empowering. To help this happen, a case is made for creating a new development function – an ombudsman – whose role will be to act as mediator, initially between non government development organizations (NGDOs), when negotiating partnership issues or when significant problems arise in their relationships. The initiative would also be of use in strengthening relations between NGDOs and official aid agencies and, potentially, with the private sector.

11.5 PHASING OUT THROUGH PARTNERSHIP

The following case study illustrates how inexperience on both sides of a partnership led to difficulties.

11.5.1 BACKGROUND

Save the Children had run a project called the 'River Project' in northern Bangladesh for more than twenty years. Many very different projects had been implemented under this name. It had started as an emergency flood relief project but later phases had included health services, research and education. Although some of the work had been innovative and exciting, by the late 1980s it seemed that River Project's services represented an open-ended commitment to the community. Health and education work was phased out and a new credit and savings project was introduced. At the time (in the early 1990s) Save the Children believed that this would lead to more 'sustainable development'; reducing poverty was seen as a better way of tackling the community's health problems.

In 1994 an evaluation of SCF's operations in Bangladesh found a number of serious problems with the River Project. The credit and savings project compared very badly with other micro finance projects in the country. Its three thousand women members made it one of the smallest credit projects in the country – and its high annual running costs made its per capita costs the most expensive. There were other weaknesses besides cost. Its benefic-iaries were organized in five-member groups. Two members could take out a small loan each year and the savings of the other three members were seen as collateral for these loans. Most of the loan fund, meanwhile, languished in the bank. Most Bangladeshi micro finance projects demon-strated that it is safe to lend small amounts to all group members at the same time. Members repay loans because they value the opportunity of a further loan so highly. The evaluation also raised some fundamental questions about SCFs involvement in such a scheme including:

- its suitability for SCF to be involved in; hundreds of similar schemes are run by small local NGOs – was such a scheme the best use of the resources of a large international NGO?
- its effectiveness in benefitting children, their mother's and the commu-nity as a whole; such a scheme did not reach the poorest of the poor and an approach based solely on credit and savings seemed wasteful and achieved little.

The big problem, however, was the high annual cost for such a small, routine project. The project was limited to 3,000 members (the target group numbered 7,000) and required a large number of staff to run it.

11.5.2 SAVING THE PROJECT THROUGH PARTNERSHIP

Aware that the River Project was very inefficient in terms of use of resources Save the Children's management in Dhaka started to explore ways of saving the project without raising costs to its budget. Expanding the project to 4,000 beneficiaries and increasing the number of loans per group from two to four annually was quite possible with the existing loan fund and using the existing staff contingent. Doing this would raise quite a lot of revenue as the loan fund would then be bringing in a lot more in service charges. The project would still not compete very well with those run by local NGOs however, and would not be viable after the planned budget cuts.

The root of the problem was in the salaries that Save the Children paid to its field staff. These were some three times the local average. Save the Children decided to hand the project over to a neighbouring NGO – this seemed the only way to cut running costs sufficiently quickly (i.e. before the planned budget cuts). A neighbouring NGO was approached; it had little management experience, but it understood credit better than Save the Children did. It was already running a credit and savings project with 6,000 members and was doing this without receiving any funds from external sources. It borrowed money at one rate, lent it out at a higher rate (the same rate that SCF used) and paid for itself out of the difference. In negotiation the NGO agreed to run the River Project for half its current budget for the first year and to increase the membership to 6,000 during this period. In the second year it would need a very small budget but would need more money to increase the size of the loan fund. By the end of the third year it would be completely self-sufficient. The hand-over was completed within eight months of the original evaluation.

11.5.3 PROBLEMS ENCOUNTERED

The swiftness of the handover led to difficulties. Former SCF staff who had been retained by the local NGO felt deeply resentful and suspicious of their new employer. They were employed to do their old job – but for half the wages. Locally there was some resentment that recruitment was limited only to ex-SCF staff. The local NGO found itself embroiled in several disputes. The disputes caused tensions in the partnership as SCF field staff were perceived to be sympathetic to the disputants – their ex-employees.

Despite these problems the NGO easily achieved its targets and within eighteen months the River Project had 6,000 members and was paying for itself. By this time, however, the NGO's relationships with the local people and the project's staff were very poor. The NGO experienced a financial crisis within its 'home project' and its management decided to make up the shortfall with money from the River Project's group savings fund. Such a move caused further local resentment and after an assault on the NGO's project manager for the River Project, the NGO asked SCF to take the project back.

11.5.4 LEARNING THE LESSONS FOR FUTURE PARTNERSHIP

A new partner was sought and SCF staff entered into discussions – but conscious of the failures of their previous approach and conscious of the need for time to work out the nature of the relationship.

Their hurry had led them to neglect the basic principles, particularly taking time to develop a shared vision; in fact the long-term vision of either partner at the time of the handover was lacking. Whereas the stated objectives including 'developing new methods and sustainable structures to help people survive the continual cycle of disasters ...', the 'people' had been hardly involved. SCF's different interventions in the River Project had failed to build upon one another in ways which tackled the complex, long-term local problems. Thus SCF handed over without any clear identification of past problems or strategies for future direction. Not surprisingly the communities in the area of the River Project resented the behaviour of both partners.

Inadequate time was spent on participatory planning and management or of consulting on skills and human resource development. Whereas the objectives of the project were reformulated at the time of the handover to focus on management and advisory support to the partner little was done in practice to meet these objectives. However, this was not neglect as such. In many partnership relationships it is very difficult to determine the right balance between a welcome and acceptable level of involvement and an unacceptable level, perceived as surveillance. In this case SCF had considered that the partner, though small had been running an effective programme, and did not wish to appear too intrusive. At the point when it became clear to them that they should be more involved the problems had got out of hand.

11.6 THE IMPORTANCE OF SHARED VISION

This second case study demonstrates problems encountered when a group of European-based NGOs considered undertaking an evaluation of the work of a local NGO in Central America and the difficulties which occur when the 'process-based trust' (as discussed in Chapter 10) has not been built up. It demonstrates the need not only for 'shared mission, values and operating principles' but also the need for common understanding of the desired outcomes. In many instances a partnership is not a simple relationship between a 'northern' and 'southern' based NGO. It is common for indigenous NGOs to have several northern partners who may not necessarily have developed their approach towards partnership collaboratively.

11.6.1 BACKGROUND

In 1995, SCF(UK) joined a group of four European NGOs supporting the work of a well-known local NGO involved with street and working children in El Salvador. Of these, one, the largest and more important in the country, had been directly involved in the creation of the local NGO and provided almost half of its overall financial resources. The relationship amongst the European agencies, and between these and the local NGO, was therefore not horizontal or equitable.

It is the established practice of SCF in Central America to work with all partners on monitoring and evaluation processes, and this is built into partnership agreements.

In 1996, upon being informed by the other European agencies and the local NGO of the decision to engage in a medium-term strategic planning process (five years), SCF suggested that this be postponed until after a comprehensive evaluation of the work done during 13 years of uninterrupted activity. The medium-term strategic planning could then build on the lessons learned from the evaluation.

The local NGO had been running the project for all this time and their work had never been systematically assessed, despite the dramatic strategic changes which had understandably taken place over such a long period. Information that was available on the project – mainly from half-yearly and annual progress reports – was insufficient to explain the reasons underlying these changes.

The absence of an evaluation of the activities made it impossible to assess either the existence or magnitude of outcomes and impacts. This, together with the lack of a baseline study, made it impossible to determine whether the proposal was in fact relevant to the situation in which the project was intervening, whether its vision and general direction were adequate or if any changes were required.

It was also deemed necessary to make a cost-benefit analysis of the project, i.e. to assess its efficiency. The project involved the provision of supplementary school education and vocational training for street and working children in the central market area of San Salvador, as well as preventive health training and rehabilitation for child substance abusers, the work appeared costly (around £265,000 p.a.) given the small number of participants (475 children). Here the assessment of impact was essential, as the high costs could only be justified if the project's impacts were significant.

The project's cost-benefit analysis led to the assessment of the local NGO's internal organization, in order to determine whether its human resources were both quantitatively and qualitatively adequate for implementing the proposal; whether the distribution of roles and tasks was appropriate given the nature of the organizational intervention; whether operating costs were reasonable or should be rationalized; whether the monitoring mechanisms used were in fact producing relevant data on the implementation of activities and whether this was being duly recorded in ongoing reports.

The evaluation of the project's sustainability was considered from a number of different perspectives. The first approach focused on the sustainability of the actions carried out with the street and working children, their families and communities. This included the issues of participation by the local population, ownership of the proposal, empowerment and the target population's capacity to carry on with the work on their own. Technical sustainability was also an important issue, particularly whether the local NGO was capable of creating and maintaining their own working methodology. Finally, economic sustainability was measured by the implementing agency's capacity to generate their own funds, in order to reduce their reliance on external donor funding.

11.6.2 THE EVALUATION

The task of agreeing the terms and conditions of the evaluation with the donor agencies and the local NGO was not an easy one. Not all the parties involved were equally convinced of the need and relevance of the evaluation to enhance the local NGO's work and achieve, through learning, greater impacts on the participant population. There appeared to be a lack of an established practice of open and fluent exchange between the parties regarding the work of the local NGO and the role that should be played by the European agencies. The evaluation showed that there were important conceptual differences between the parties which had never been addressed, let alone agreed upon, on a collective basis.

11.6.3 THE DONOR AGENCIES

The evaluation showed a lack of common vision amongst the donor agencies regarding the work of the local NGO and the ways of addressing the problems faced by the project. To a certain extent this was inevitably the result of their different visions, missions, objectives and strategies. However, beyond significant differences in terms of institutional culture, the lack of permanent dialogue among them made it impossible to arrive at even minimal agreements regarding the use of the evaluation's results and their future feeding into the local NGO's strategic planning. The evaluation found serious shortcomings, including:

- the impact of the work upon the living conditions of the target population was negligible;
- participation by the local population in project design and management was minimal, particularly among the working children's families, whose involvement was constrained to being passive supports rather than active subjects;
- the total lack of sustainability of the activities, both economically and in terms of their continuation by the local population itself;
- the project's high costs in relation to the small number of beneficiaries and the modest impacts achieved;
- the large number of staff in relation to the limited number and size of activities carried out.

There was no tradition of dialogue and discussion about the running of the project amongst the donor agencies, or between these and the local NGO. The donor agencies had never systematically accompanied the work. Not all of them were equally interested in starting a process of reflection about the results of the evaluation or reaching any agreements about them – let alone including these in a realistic plan, to be translated later into strategic changes to the project. In these circumstances, the evaluation turned out to be a purely academic exercise, thus failing to seize an opportunity to learn from experience and feed these lessons into the local NGO's policy and practice.

11.6.4 THE LOCAL NGO

The local NGO agreed to participate in the evaluation mainly because it was requested to do so by the donor agencies, rather than out of a genuine belief that useful lessons could be learned from the exercise for their own organizational work. After long years of considering the project's activities as ends in themselves – supported by the donor agencies, whose sole concern was the achievement of goals – they never regarded the cycle of a project as a learning process both for their own work and for the participant population. Thus, the local NGO expressed from the beginning its desire to carry on with the strategic planning process as originally agreed. This explains the staff's marginal involvement in the writing of the terms of reference for the evaluation, as well as in the selection of external evaluators.

11.6.5 THE OUTCOME

SCF's position became very difficult; it was the only agency insisting on the need to use the results of the evaluation. SCF's repeated efforts to persuade the other parties were unsuccessful, and it soon became clear that SCF's involvement in the project would only bring about further disagreement. It was in these circumstances that the local NGO, most probably with the approval of representatives from the donor agencies, suggested terminating the co-operation relationship with SCF based on 'essential differences' about the project.

11.6.7 THE LESSONS

A number of sharp lessons can be learnt from the above experience:

1 The complexity of a partnership relationship inevitably increases when more than one donor agency is involved. Efforts should therefore be made to establish a practice of horizontal, transparent and regular dialogue at two levels:

   (a) among donor agencies themselves, to harmonize criteria, expectations and requirements vis-à-vis the local partner;

   (b) between donor agencies and the local partner, to decide the nature and precise forms of involvement of the former in the latter's implementation of the work.

2 A 'shared vision' should not be accepted at too simplistic a level at the point at which partners select each other if methodologies and approaches are not compatible.

3   Whilst northern partners may be perceived as behaving in unnecessarily dominant ways they are accountable to a number of stakeholders including those who provide their funds and the ultimate recipients.

4   Partnership is a process of permanent negotiation which demands acknowledgement of and respect for the *differences*, as well as a strong belief in the need to reach specific agreements based on the higher concern of achieving maximum impact for the local population.

5   Agencies should not only fund the work of local organizations and demand different requirements 'from outside' such as reports, strategic planning, systematizations, evaluations, etc. They should *accompany* the process of project implementation at all stages under terms and conditions expressly agreed by all sides involved. The aim is not a desire to control or impose policies or practices. On the contrary, it is to *facilitate* the local partner's work, i.e., to ensure that the donor agencies' resources and/or services help improve the project's efficiency, effectiveness, sustainability and impact. This involvement in the partner's work as *facilitators* of the implementation process will enable donor agencies to gain insight into the work 'from within'. In this way a genuine co-operative relationship can develop based on the principles of equity, respect, reciprocity and companionship, and on the progressive discovery of the synergy and mutual advantages which can emerge from a relationship in which difficulties and achievements, risks and opportunities, are continuously shared. It must be recognized that building a mutual vision can take time.

11.7   WHAT LESSONS HAVE BEEN LEARNED?

Despite intense questioning of their value and effectiveness both northern and southern NGOs continue to form partnerships. In Alan Fowler's view this is not a waste of time:

> ... for authentic partnership 'new-style', understood as mutually enabling, interdependent intervention interaction with shared intentions is still very much needed for two reasons. First, politically, this quality of national and international NGDO relations contributes to the 'social capital' which enables civil society to better deal with states and markets at all levels of their co-operation ... A second reason for being serious about partnerships and building social capital within the NGDO community is economic. In the language of economists, authentic partnerships can reduce transaction costs within the NGDO system which leads to greater cost-effectiveness.
>
> (Fowler, 1997, pp. 107-8)

Box 11.3 gives some advice on partnerships for southern NGOs (or NGDOs as Fowler calls them).

BOX 11.3   REACHING REAL PARTNERSHIPS

- be sure of yourself, who you are and what you stand for, because 'good donors do not like to be donor driven';
- be credible by being competent – show results;
- have information at your fingertips;
- be transparent in your external dealings – don't hide failure when it occurs;
- demonstrate that you are learning from what you are doing, then challenge donors to do the same.

The hardest challenge for Northern NGDOs who dare to use the term partnership will be to:

- move to measures of joint performance;
- exercise trust within performance agreements;
- move to partner-based, impact oriented financing;
- share aspects of governance which affect both parties;
- seek partner concurrence with messages and positions adopted on their behalf;
- open up decision making processes to partner scrutiny.

(Fowler, 1997, p. 110)

Northern NGOs are under increasing scrutiny and pressure but if they can adapt their behaviour in response to criticism and the changing environment they do have a role as intermediary. Increasing emphasis needs to be placed on the influencing, lobbying and education activities of northern NGOs in their *own* countries in order to increase public support for development. Different approaches need to be developed to ensure an educated and aware constituency which provides a guarantee of voluntary income and also brings pressure on bilateral donors. Complementary roles with southern NGOs in terms of policy development, advocacy and lobbying are now being developed which have progressed from the former emphasis on 'speaking on behalf of ...' to collaboration at international level. This is based on international NGOs disseminating and synthesizing information, facilitating access and providing training and support in different skills. If both northern and southern NGOs can learn from past experiences - and follow the advice given in Box 11.3 – true partnerships may be forged and the reality of partnership may come closer to the rhetoric.

HELENA DOLNY

12.1 INTRODUCTION

In May 1997, I was appointed managing director of the Land Bank in South Africa, an institution with 1,300 employees. In April 1997 its senior management comprised seventy-one persons, all white, all Afrikaner, and all, except two, were men. There was no Communications Department, no Human Resources department. These gaps presented the newly appointed managing director with an opportunity to recruit new staff, pursuing a pro-active race and gender approach. By the following year there had been a flattening of the management structures. The Senior Executive now comprised 42 persons. The 25 branch managers were all men, but there were six women among the 17 members of the Senior Executive located at Head Office, well placed to influence the process of reshaping the organization.

This chapter is a reflection on that reshaping, or 'transformation'. It is about the fundamental redesigning of an organization – of its structures, processes and behaviours – in the name of new values and objectives, and of producing effective outcomes. It is a story about the process of building new relationships and forms of trust within an organization. It is also a story about the creation of new relationships and forms of trust outside the organization, with external stakeholders both old and new. And it is a story of transformation taking place in a radically changing and challenging institutional context.

12.2 INSTITUTIONAL TRANSFORMATION

> One case in the board minutes was a case of discrimination where the woman was an applicant and it was decided that she wasn't a proper farmer since she was only a part-time farmer and her husband was only a part-time farmer – he had another job as well. This is so foolish in this day and age. This guy had another job as well as farming and his wife applied for the loan and it was refused.
>
> (Helena Dolny, 1998, interview)

In the new South Africa, the Land Bank has been presented with the challenge of institutional transformation:

> The bank needs to turn around, both to prosper as a business and to fulfil its new mandate to serve the previously disadvantaged.
>
> (Land Bank, Prospectus 1999, p. 1)

Institutional transformation means different things to different people. There are many examples of institutional re-structuring occurring in South Africa, in all sectors – private, parastatal and state. Many of them get described as institutional transformation, a catchall phrase which can be misleading however. The term institutional transformation can be used to encompass three extremely different approaches:

- down-sizing;
- reformation (restructuring); and
- transformation.

The old management of the Land Bank claimed it had started its 'transformation' process in 1995, but what they talked about as transformation, we would describe as reformation. It is important to be clear about these terms, because in their differences lie the defining essentials. What kind of change is implied – real or cosmetic, superficial or deep? Do the proposed changes set out at heart to achieve some of the goals held dear by the social architects of a new South Africa – black empowerment, gender justice, and work-place democratization?

12.2.1 DOWN-SIZING

'Business Process Re-engineering' (BPR) exercises have characterized many private sector initiatives for change, which are limited to restructuring and modernization of technological processes in the workplace. These are often linked to 'down-sizing', or 'right-sizing' to use the gentler term. They may make a modest attempt to recruit a number of black staff, but forthcoming legislation on workplace representation will be needed before these businesses bite the bullet of more far-reaching change.

12.2.2 REFORMATION

The approach adopted by some liberal private sector and parastatal institutions even prior to the 1994 election period, the Basuto Hat model, advocates an uneven representation of blacks in the different managerial and staffing levels of the institution. This exemplifies reformist change initiatives which have enabled white management to take some action whilst retaining its sense of comfort.

The Basuto Hat model provides a modestly incremental plan whereby top business managers of historically white organizations accept a gradual 'colouring' through the appointment of black persons to different managerial and technical levels. Often, the new black staff are recruited into 'soft skill' areas, such as Human Resources, Public Relations, and Communication. If criticized, such management has often been defensive, saying that change must not come too quickly, because if it is too fast and radical, the white senior and middle management will be alienated and eventually lost, as white technical staff no longer see a career paths for themselves.

At the Land Bank, 'transformation' translated itself as the recruitment of black persons with technical qualifications. This was the first time in the bank's history that blacks had been recruited for posts other than sundry positions. However, the recruitment drive concentrated at the junior technical level only. In the Auditor General's Performance Report of June 1997 it was noted that this strategy of recruitment implied that there would be no significant change in race representation at senior and middle management levels for at least fifteen years.

12.2.3 TRANSFORMATION: TRYING FOR THE REAL THING?

Since 1997 and the appointment of the new Board of Directors and Managing Director, the Land Bank has rejected the reform path in favour of a more thorough approach to institutional transformation. This approach sets out to address and make significant changes on three fronts:

- black empowerment;
- gender justice;
- workplace democratization.

We feel that the word 'transformation' embodies the idea of holistic metamorphosis. When we talk of a person as being 'transformed', we acknowledge that the essence of the person remains, but that something fundamental has happened, something which has affected the whole person. We chose the 'everlasting flower' as the symbol of our transformation process, because its reproductive and survival process involves traumatic exposure to heat and smoke to ensure germination. At the Land Bank, the transformation process we are in the midst of has involved us in a holistic trauma – both exciting and terrifying.

Gender justice is one of our overarching aims; both for ourselves as employees and for the many rural women who we hope will become out clients. We see ourselves achieving gender justice through a many-pronged and holistic process. It is not a marginal activity to be undertaken by a specialized gender desk – although the existence of such a catalyst may be necessary.

The four main components of our transformation strategy have been and continue to be:

1 A top-down, bottom-up, inside-out extensive consultation process, involving both employees and external stakeholders.

2 Developing a shared acceptance of the need for change based on the social imperative, the business imperative, and the imperative of the new mandate.

3 Gaining a shared vision.

4 Setting in place goals which can be acted on pro-actively by both employees and clients.

12.3 THE TRANSFORMATION PROCESS

12.3.1 CONSULTATION

A new Board of Directors was appointed to the Land Bank in April 1998. They held a 'bosberaad' in June, and one of their objectives was to orient the transformation initiative about to be unleashed. They requested a brainstorming workshop to come up with a process design for transformation. They also drew up a list of principles for guidance:

- vision-led;
- through consultation;
- sustainable transformation;
- transparency;
- personal choice;
- fairness and justice;
- gender affirmation;
- affirmative action;
- inclusivity;
- empowerment.

The Board also gave a directive to staff '… and it must be fun!' – some of it has been, but not always!

12.3.2 THE NEED FOR AN INTEGRATED PROCESS

From the very beginning one thing was clear, the Land Bank had no internal culture of organizational development. If the guiding principles laid down by the Board of Directors were to be adhered to, we would need access to external expertise. But we wanted more than to contract in facilitators. We wanted an organizational development group which had a track record of engagement in institutional transformation, using a workshop style which would maximize participation, and develop common values and ideas about what constituted desirable and desired outcomes.

We began an extended working relationship with the guild of RGA (Reconstruction, Growth and Alignment) as organizational development consulting partners. Their accumulated years of experience of working with organizations undertaking institutional restructuring, underscored by an ethos of transformation, have been of great benefit to the bank. RGA emphasized the need for a consultative stakeholder approach, and especially on drawing in external stakeholders – the current business clients, the potential civil servants, and so on. Our consultative workshops were saved over and over again from lapsing into internal navel gazing through this emphasis, which helped redirect staff to focus on the essential, in other words, 'you exist as staff members because we exist as clients'.

12.3.3 THE PROCESS MAP AND TIME-TABLE

To initiate the process following the Board of Director's orientation, we brought together a group of Land Bank employees from various departments, various branches, and from different staff and managerial levels.

We mapped out a process which involved different task teams working on different business topics, such as a Human Resource Task team, a Communications Task team, and a timetable of consultation with our Board of Directors and Trade Unions.

We have learnt that timetabling and complementarity between activities is paramount. Communication also needs to be continuous, be it to Board, staff, unions, clients or investors. Hiccups in the transformation process may lead to industrial unrest, and if you are not in close communication with your investors, the business consequences may be drastic.

Our new task team working on the development of new products displayed maverick tendencies. Whilst these may be advantageous in the search for new products to suit client needs, there also needs to be regular liaison to enable continued focus on their absorption into mainstream operations, otherwise there might be resistance from various quarters when it comes to implementation. The Human Resource Task team had far-reaching consequences in recommending more appropriate conditions of service and a trimming down of the management layers. Negotiations needed to take place, and we have learnt that it is advisable to have a labour lawyer involved as early as possible.

12.3.4 THE PROCESS IN THE PROVINCES

Every one of the 25 branches of the Land Bank held two workshops. One was for staff only, and the other was a consultation with stakeholders. These were run by members of Head Office who had volunteered for the Communications Task team, and by branch level 'change agents' trained by RGA.

Each province then held a provincial workshop which mapped out the vision, mission and organizational culture of the institution. External stakeholders were represented in these workshops, and one of their products was the 'stakeholder scorecard'. The stakeholders selected various topics, such as: Land Bank customer service; interest rates; marketing; range of financial products; speed; flexibility and so on. They not only designed the score card but also filled it in, often using two columns, one for commercial farmers, the other for the historically disadvantaged. These scorecards have provided the Land Bank with baseline information against which to measure and evaluate its progress.

The impact of consultation with our stakeholders was tremendous. Stakeholders themselves were amazed that their inputs were being solicited, and that they were being listened to. On the part of the Land Bank, it provided a wake-up call. In other words, the realization that we will continue to lose market share if we do not work with our clients and design products that better meet their needs.

One of the criticisms also voiced by the stakeholders at the provincial consultative workshops was that they were wary of a Land Bank board which did not have 'constituency' representation. In these instances, we shared a review of the current Land Bank board, which described the skills they shared between them, the rationale behind the government (at Cabinet level) having final approval on board members, and how this secured a board that would seriously undertake the guardianship of an institutional transformation process. However, the inputs of the provincial stakeholders was recognized as a valuable resource that the Land Bank should not overlook when there was willingness to contribute the time. The external stakeholders came up with the idea of Provincial Advisory Forums. When this was raised at the Land Bank's National Consolidation Conference (the culmination of the consultative workshops), it was not only applauded as a positive idea to be adopted. It was also proposed that a Board member should be allocated to each one of the provincial fora to help ensure the flow of ideas and information directly back to the Board.

12.4 THE EMERGING OUTCOMES OF TRANSFORMATION

12.4.1 REDESIGNING PRODUCTS TO RESPOND TO CLIENTS NEEDS

External stakeholders made many suggestions on an improved range of products which would better cater to their needs. However, the biggest challenge to the bank will be to prove that it can cater for the needs of female clients and make them feel welcome in the bank.

The presidential commission on rural financial services, the Strauss Commission noted how intimidating and alienating it is for black rural women to walk through the glass swing doors of commercial banks, probably to receive poor treatment. One prominent banker has described such clients as 'high volume, low value, nuisance transactions'.

However, we have found that even white women complain about the patriarchy of the Land Bank. One woman explained that she and her husband had different skills – he did the practical farm management whilst she did the financial planning and accounting. They travelled together to their nearest Land Bank branch. Despite the fact that her husband insisted that she present the financial facts, with which she was most familiar, the loan's officer at the bank was unable to address himself to the woman. He sub-consciously refused to engage with her, and persisted in directing his questions to the husband, who persisted in redirecting them to his business partner wife.

In the redesign of our financial products we are trying to create those which will appropriately benefit rural women. In April 1998, we have launched a micro-lending product called 'Step-up' which allows a person to borrow small amounts and to establish a formal track record which qualifies them to borrow larger amounts. The first few months were to be a pilot to test whether the programme might be successful. Many people believed we would not get our money back. Our first few months experience seems to be proving them wrong. In the first eight months 14,000 people have taken Step-up loans; some are already on their second or third cycle of loan and repayment. Our current repayment rate is an amazing 92%.

In our design of Step-up we tried to take into account rural women who need small sums of money for inputs into their business. However, many rural women are farm-workers and often suffer under working conditions which do not comply with the labour law. The Land Bank would in future like to use its position to leverage improvements in farm-worker conditions through financial incentives.

12.4.2 SHARED ACCEPTANCE OF THE NEED TO CHANGE

This has been the most difficult challenge at the Land Bank. Early in the transformation process a consultant observed that 'most staff saw change at the bank as politically motivated and failed to understand the business imperative for change'. There has been a steady, albeit uneven acceptance of the need for change, which has been developed around two ongoing discussions and through the continued sharing of information:

The 'speak bitterness' session: Where are we coming from?
At each one of the provincial workshops there was a 'history' session planned into the agenda. The participation in these was uneven and on more than one occasion it was necessary not only to break up into small groups, but to separate people into black, women, and white men. Only then did people begin to speak more freely. There were many dissatisfactions which reveal that we are only at the beginning of tackling our apartheid inheritance, which was based not only on racial social engineering, but also on patriarchy and repression. There were complaints about the custom of calling black staff by their first names, whilst some managers insisted that male white staff be addressed as 'Meneer'. Black field officers complained that they had to spend a year at the branch before being allowed to do field trips, whereas newly appointed white field officers started field trips immediately. In one office, the black field officer (with a Master's degree) dealt only with black clients, and the white field officers with white clients only. There were other complaints about some managers insistence on a church testimonial as a pre-condition of employment. Muslim staff enquired why it was not acceptable to wear their customary dress for work, why the bank's uniform was not designed to cater for religious and cultural diversity.

A new mandate in a new South Africa
The old Land Bank had served the white commercial farming sector. The Strauss Commission argued for the continuation of the Land Bank. Rather than advocate privatization, the Commission argued for a Land Bank which not only extended improved services to its current clientele, but that the professional skills amongst it staff should provide the basis for the bank to extend its services for the benefit of the previously disadvantaged – especially rural women.

The *de facto* imposition of this mandate has been accepted by the majority of bank staff, although some voice their hesitation about the capability of the bank to respond on the basis that this is an unfamiliar segment of the market, and the majority of staff members to not speak African languages.

While many staff are supportive, and even enthusiastic about the challenge of the new mandate, the fact that it was externally given does allow some staff to ignore the imperatives for change, and to just argue that its all to do with politics.

12.4.3 TAKING FORWARD A SHARED VISION

The 'history' session, the business analysis, followed up by the work on a vision statement, turned out to be very rewarding. People want to feel proud of the place they work in. They want to feel that they are part of a 'world class' organization whose professional and human resources practices rank among the world's best, albeit with South African characteristics. Land Bank staff produced nine mission statements in the nine provincial workshops. These were inspiring exercises.

The discussions about mission statements and shared vision highlighted four areas which staff felt to be important to the transformation of the Land Bank.

1 Organizational culture

Land Bank staff drew up a charter of their desired organizational culture, which included effective communication, understanding and empathy for cultural diversity, multi-skilling through training, knowledge and empowerment, a team-based approach to focus and motivate staff and maximize potential, and professionalism based on pride and integrity.

2 Workplace democratization

This recognition of the importance of a different organizational culture gave impetus to changes being undertaken to improve workplace democratization. Each one of the twenty five branches has undertaken its own week-long redesign exercise. The objective was to begin the move away from the sectionalized, supervisory model, towards a team-based management concept. The teams have put themselves together ensuring that they share between them a complement of skills that are necessary to complete the task in hand. They aim for self-management, self-discipline with quality control, exercised on a collegiate basis. They offer fundamental opportunities to women and people of colour to proceed on the fast-track towards acquiring their professional skills. A delighted woman employee said: 'I have been a typist for eighteen years. I never wanted to be a typist for eighteen years. I am now being offered a new opportunity in the bank, and I am definitely going to make the most of it'.

3 Desired leadership culture

The Land Bank's charter of desired leadership characteristics includes:

- People-centred, emphasising reliability, empowerment, team-work, accessibility, and transparency.

- By example, demonstrating integrity, confidentiality, participation and determination.
- Visionary, pioneering, dynamic, innovative and open-minded.
- Customer-focused, characterized by two-way feedback, accessibility, flexibility, adaptability, and market responsiveness.
- Professional, driven by results, continuous improvement, a business orientation and accountability.

It should be noted that there is no mention of black empowerment and gender justice. It may have been that by the time we arrived at the National Consolidation workshop in December 1997, there had been so much emphasis on the participation of women and black staff that perhaps the working group drafting the leadership statement took this for granted.

4 Aligned leadership
What we have learned at the Bank is the importance of leadership. The senior team will be working on its leadership charter. We have also learnt that we are a team of strong, talented individuals, with strengths and weaknesses. Without alignment there is a danger that we charge towards our goals, veering in different directions. It is clear that transformation cannot take place unless you have a committed and aligned leadership.

12.5 CONCLUSION: THE CONTINUING TRANSFORMATION PROCESS
The story of the Land Bank and its current process of transformation is a story of the total reorientation of an organization's purpose, of its activities and processes for achieving that purpose, and of its indicators of effectiveness in achieving that purpose. It is about building an effective organization in a climate which is increasingly competitive:

> It was when we began the transformation that we started to see the fragility of the bank. It does make money on it's wholesale finance, but there is a lot more competition around ... 160 foreign banks have come into the country in the last three years, and the co-operatives themselves are becoming financially more sophisticated in their own management skills.

> (Helena Dolny, 1998, interview)

The process of building that effective organization has not been simply a matter of introducing 'hard' organizational technologies, such as designing systems to transform the bureaucratic 'paper trail', but of developing 'soft' organizational technologies – creating space to talk, active consultation, emphasizing continued communication. The process has been about maintaining and building trust between an array of stakeholders; creating a more effective and competitive organization through co-operative action. In the first brainstorming session, Dolny remembers that people were asked to draw their experiences of the Land Bank:

One drew an ostrich. Another drew a tortoise – slow, narrow-visioned, anti-social.

(Helena Dolny, 1998, interview)

More recently, it has been said:

'What changes I have seen' – This is the Land Bank's UBUNTU. Ubuntu means: I am the Land Bank and the Land Bank is me. I saw a lot of personnel taking responsibility with real commitment and energy and there is still a lot of unreleased energy that can have a positive effect on the whole transformation process that we are busy with. The participation process that we have done – I think it will only contribute to the Land Bank's future and well-being.

(Land Bank, Prospectus 1999, introductory page)

We feel at the Land Bank that we have put in place a holistic and coherent process that is creating the enabling conditions for transformation, a transformation based on black empowerment, gender justice, and workplace democratization. However, it is not enough to design an enabling process. We have learned that we need constant vigilance, and that we need to dedicate a special budget to conscientization. We have learned that the conditioning vis-à-vis race, gender and authority, reaches very deep within our psyche.

At a recent re-design workshop, sociologists from Witswatersrand university carried out a 'socio-gram' of participation. They found that the small group discussions were still 90% male-dominated, and almost 90% dominated by white Afrikaners. Senior managers were recently requested to propose branch staff who would participate in a workshop on remuneration strategy. Their proposal was 100% white Afrikaner male. Staff were asked to make proposals on branch staff to be trained in a particular work methodology. There were several proposals for women candidates which were put down on the basis of the women not being strong enough. How do women become strong when continuously denied the opportunity?

There has been a question asked – is the Land Bank different because it has a female managing director? It would seem that the issue is more complex than that. There have been women world leaders who have acted as if they were honorary men, and there has been no advance in gender justice. There have been instances where governments comprising an overwhelming male majority have responded positively to lobbying on gender justice. We are finding the same in the Land Bank. With everything we do, we need to review the group composition – its race and gender composition. Unless it is spelt out, people tend to slip into the comfort zones that they have been conditioned to. And we, the entire leadership of the Bank, have to be aligned and charged to create a level of sustained discomfort in the pursuit of empowerment, justice and workplace democracy.

KEY CONCEPTS AND PRINCIPLES OF CO-OPERATION

WHAT IS CO-OPERATION?

Harriss describes co-operative relationships as those based on trust and self-organization. Trust is fundamental to the idea of co-operation because while price is the control mechanism in the market, and authority in a bureaucratic organization, *trust* is the mechanism through which co-operative relationships are controlled.

Co-operation based on trust, or the confidence that partners will not act opportunistically, is also associated with the idea of people and organizations working together voluntarily and for mutual benefit. In other words, their motives are not shaped simply by ideas of material gain (the premise of market organization) or coercion (the premise of hierarchical organization) but by a sense of common purpose.

This difference in motivation allows for the possibility of *self-organization*, namely relationships which are 'more voluntary and self-defined than organizationally-mandated'. This conveys a sense of co-operative relationships being those which emerge over time through regular interactions and detailed knowledge of all parties. This has to be the case since such relationships require trust, joint working and some common goals. But the term self-organization should not be read as less organization! It refers to the motives for, and quality of the organization of relationships, not on the degree of organization involved. In fact, in many respects, co-operative relationships, relying as they do on mutual understanding and trust, require very high levels of organization.

Harriss indicates that trust and self-organization are the principles of the ideal type 'co-operation'. However, reality is more complex, and different forms of co-operation exist. In part these arise from different types of trust. Harriss refers to process-, characteristic- and institution-based trust. Each form of trust enables a slightly different form of transaction between co-operating partners – and requires a slightly different starting point.

As noted in Chapter 1, the terms 'partnership' and 'co-operation' are commonly used together. In practice, many so-called partnerships are far from the type of co-operation described by Harriss, but they are often an expression of a desire to co-operate more effectively. The question then becomes, why?

WHY CO-OPERATE?

The answer to this question takes us back to the same broad answer given to 'why compete?' and 'why co-ordinate?', namely to ensure a more effective allocation of resources than would otherwise be the case. However, what is it about co-operation which might produce a more effective alloc-ation than say competition or co-ordination?

Harriss describes the debate surrounding the idea of the 'tragedy of the commons'. Whilst collective goods might be managed either by turning them over to government regulation or by privatizing them, there are significant downsides to both of these strategies. Thus it is proposed that self-regulation by those commonly bound to those resources can overcome such problems.

As already noted there are very different types of co-operation, which relate to Harriss' different forms of trust. These might be aptly, though simplistically, captured by the words 'camaraderie' and 'collaboration'. The former refers to a form of co-operation based on solidarity, or alliances which are more fundamental and strategic, between those who share the same values, goals and ways of working. The latter refers to more tactical relationships, between those who see an advantage in co-operating, perhaps for the purpose of building constituencies, influence or new forms of resource, but who do not necessarily share the same values, goals and ways of working. Implied in each of these forms of co-operation is a different underlying rationale for co-operating. The example of the transformation of the Land Bank points to efforts to build both forms of co-operation: a fundamental process within the organization to build a shared vision which will guide the way the Bank works; and a tactical process of co-operating with existing and potential stakeholders outside the organiz-ation in order to ensure that the Bank becomes more relevant and competitive in the market-place.

MANAGING 'PARTNERSHIP': AN INCREMENTAL PROCESS

Building co-operative institutions is an incremental process which depends on learning and stimulates self-transformation (starting with re-framing through information-sharing).

(adapted from Harriss, this volume, p. 234)

Harris writes about an idea of co-operation, which more overtly than discussions about competition and co-ordination, draws you into the behavioural aspects of relating. Organizational structures and processes remain important, but behaviour, and expectations about the behaviour of others, are key to understanding and building co-operation.

In this sense, co-operative relationships are about sharing values and visions. For example, the transformation of the Land Bank in South Africa has been based on efforts to build a strong stated commitment to new values – black empowerment, gender justice and work-place democratiz-ation. The focus then becomes how to do this – how to build shared commitment amongst a range of interests and long-entrenched norms and behaviours?

The other chapters in this section echo Harriss' discussion that co-operation is about iterative processes, information-sharing and reframing, and a commitment to learning.

Thus one of the main themes of this section is the importance of iterative process. In other words, of the continued space for interaction between parties which both allows for learning, adaptation and innovation – helping to develop and maintain some of the fundamentals which allow for close and long-term relationships to work effectively.

TAKING ACTION: TURNING PRINCIPLES INTO PRACTICE

WAYS OF ORGANIZING: INTERDEPENDENCE

There are many configurations of inter-organizational relationships which are commonly referred to as 'co-operation'. These include partnership, collaboration, coalition, alliance and network. Whichever configuration you feel most aptly describes a particular co-operative endeavour, it is clear that these relationships are at the 'high' end of the spectrum in terms of the application of organizational 'ways of organizing', resources and capacities. In the case of the Land Bank, the process of transformation has been based on the ethos of maximizing participation, and indeed this is all part of building process-based trust. But the use of a consultative stakeholder approach, drawing in not just staff but a range of external stakeholders such as business clients, civil servants, and customers, has required a huge investment of people's time.

Whether your objective in co-operating is strategic or tactical, this investment in terms of time remains key to successful relationships, and cannot be half-hearted. It is not simply a question of bringing in stakeholders to a process, but of how you bring them in and use their input. We suspect that a number of co-operative initiatives collapse in their infancy because individuals and groups become frustrated by the lack of immediate and apparent tangible outputs! This process of building a common understanding, shared commitments, and even visions is vital, because what mediates the co-operative enterprise is not a clear mechanism of control, but joint agreements, both explicit and implicit.

ORGANIZATIONS: THE BUILDING BLOCKS

At the organizational level the implication of these two rationales for co-operation are that not all relationships are equally important, and that different strategies and forms of co-operation will be developed by the organization.

These different strategies in turn have implications for the type of management approaches that the organizations encourages or needs to encourage. As Dolny shows in the case of the Land Bank, moving from centralization, over-supervision and hierarchy, towards a flatter structure based on multi-skilled, self-managing work teams requires some major changes in approach. It has necessitated an emphasis on the development of an internal culture of organizational development and learning, and on communication.

INSTITUTIONAL FRAMEWORKS: THE RULES OF THE GAME

Levels of trust and self-organization in any context are strongly influenced by the incentives and opportunities created by the prevailing institutional frameworks. As Harriss writes, institutional-based trust, or the existence of societal structures, rules and regulations, shapes the kind of co-operation which emerges. Therefore the nature of regulatory frameworks; of incentives and sanctions which encourage transparency and accountability; of supportive institutions promoting and valuing innovation and learning; and of the availability of opportunities to lever resources or power, or to make more of an initiative through additionality, will all influence the level and type of co-operation which prevails.

When Dolny writes about the forms of 'institutional transformation' being attempted in the new South Africa, they make the point that most businesses will not individually move towards greater inclusivity and workplace democracy unless provided with the incentive to do so through relevant legislation. Similarly, the fundamental change in South Africa's institutional context, in the form of new values being articulated and applied to the whole of society, has created the space for the Land Bank's own transformation.

ENDNOTE: ON ORGANIZATIONAL LIFE AND DEATH

Penrose writes about 'phasing out through partnership'. The idea as it is discussed here is that northern NGOs can change the nature of their organizational involvement in development activities by partnering organizations such as NGO and CBOs in the South. But, this raises another question. Whether intervention and processes of organizational interaction always need to leave behind an organizational structure? When does a network, or a partnership just die off? As Harriss points out, co-operative relationships are good for organizing the exchange of commodities whose values are not easily measured. It is this difficulty in measuring value, and the high level of human interface involved, which can make it difficult for 'partners' to disband.

Another perspective is provided by Dolny. Writing about institutional transformation she discusses the different organizational strategies this term might encompass – from down-sizing, to reformation to transformation. All strategies for organizational survival!

13 ROYDS REGENERATION PROGRAMME: A CASE STUDY IN INTER-ORGANIZATIONAL RELATIONSHIPS

GORDON WILSON

13.1 INTRODUCTION

This chapter is about how a range of actors, including the state, voluntary organizations, grassroots organizations and private commercial agencies came together to manipulate the public environment (Mackintosh, 1992) in a development intervention. It shows how their inter-organizational relationships have been managed in practice and to what extent these are enabling desired outcomes to be realized from the intervention.

The story concerns 'The Royds', three predominantly local-authority-run (Council) estates in Bradford, a large industrial city in northern England. One day, in 1994, the Royds woke up to find that it had 'won' £31 million from the UK government's Single Regeneration Budget (SRB) in order to regenerate the three estates, physically, socially and economically. Why and how did this happen?

> Public action is not … just a question of public delivery and state initiative. It is also a matter of participation by the public in a process of social change.
>
> (Drèze and Sen, 1989)
>
> How can relationships between organizations be managed so as to build the public action outcomes desired of development management?
>
> (Chapter 1, p.14)

Interesting as the question is, answering it is only a small part of the story. Most people know that throwing money at something is usually not sufficient to realize desired outcomes. *How* that money is managed and used is crucial. And there are always differing views on how money should be managed and used, especially large sums of money.

The principal characters of this drama are:
- Royds Community Association, a grassroots organization representing the residents of the three estates;
- Bradford Metropolitan District Council – the local authority;
- the voluntary sector, including a housing association and the church;
- the private sector, comprising the main firm contracted to undertake physical rehabilitation work of the estates.

These organizations comprise the 'Royds Board', which is serviced by a further important set of players – paid professionals covering all aspects of the regeneration. The 22-strong Board membership has an in-built majority of 12 Community Association resident-directors, directly elected by the residents and representing each of the three estates. The chair of the Board is constitutionally a resident director.

There are other players, outside of the formal structure of the Royds Board, but nevertheless having an important impact on its work. These include the local police, schools and shops, social workers who are grappling especially with drug abuse problems on the estates, and, lest we forget, the ordinary residents themselves going about their daily lives.

13.1.1 THE VISION

The Royds will be a self-sustaining community where local residents are actively involved in participating in and identifying their needs and implementing the means to achieve their goals.

In and around the area there will be opportunities for employment, access to training, good quality social services and facilities for recreation and leisure.

Within the area there will be three clearly identifiable communities with a balance of tenure, good quality houses to meet all needs and sense of community identity and ownership.

(Royds Single Regeneration Budget Bid, 3rd September 1994)

The quote above is the vision or mission statement for the area, jointly agreed by 'the partners' who comprised: 'the residents through the Royds Community Association, Bradford MDC [Metropolitan District Council], Keepmoat Construction Ltd. [a property developer] and Brunel Family Housing Association'. However, behind the vision lies a story of a shifting institutional landscape, from welfarism to self-sufficiency; from state-led to resident-led development; from local government to local governance; from fragmented development to holistic development; from fragmented, sometimes antagonistic, actors to partnerships.

These institutional shifts summarize a history, the fairy tale version of which runs as follows:

Once upon a time the physical and social welfare of the Royds estates were seen as the responsibility of the local state authority or council (as were similar council-run housing estates throughout the UK). Such a view amounted to a paternalistic ideology (the 'nanny' state), because, not only was it widespread, it was also the prevalent view of the recipients of welfarism – the residents of the estates.

Times changed. Throughout the 1980s there was a concerted attack on such ideology from a right-wing government that believed that the state should be 'rolled back'. This attack complemented minority left-wing criticisms of welfarism: that local councils often did not do a very good job on the estates. Such left-wing critics had argued for many years in favour of community development, where estate residents would be better able to hold the councils to account.

The right-wing-dominated attacks led to private and fragmented responses, as the state steadily retreated and left a vacuum. Then entered a magic missing ingredient: *governance*, where multiple actors representing the state, the private sector and civil society come together in a synergistic relationship to meet society's needs, and where everyone lives happily ever after.

Fairy tales are fun to listen to, but seldom true. Synergistic relationships between organizations do not come about with a wave of a magic wand (even £31 millions worth!). They have to be worked at, hard.

This is where our story truly starts. It is about:

- why the different groups and organizations in the area came together and what the incentives were;
- how they achieved a broad legitimacy by becoming accountable;
- how, through continuing motivation, commitment and effort they maintain and build social capital and relationships with one another, and the importance of this relationship for realizing the Royds vision;
- the institutional sustainability of what they are doing.

13.1.2   LIFE BEFORE £31 MILLIONS

The Bradford Metropolitan area lies within the county of West Yorkshire, UK, and has a population of approximately 450,000 (1991 census data). The city grew rapidly during the industrial revolution to become the centre of the wool processing industry, but the virtual disappearance of this industry during the last quarter of the 20th century has resulted in entrenched social and economic problems. Economic regeneration has not been helped by the city's proximity to the larger city and regional capital of Leeds (10 miles, 16 km away) where industry has been more diversified and which has taken the lion's share of the new service industries.

In common with all British cities that grew rapidly as a result of the industrial revolution, the inner areas of Bradford contained vast swathes of 'slum' housing with poor public health facilities. These were the subject of mass clearance programmes through at least the first six decades of the 20th century, their residents being rehoused in specially created large housing estates, built mainly on the fringes of the cities. Apart from pockets of privately owned houses, the ownership and management of the new estates became entirely the province of the local urban authorities or councils, giving rise to the terms 'council houses' and 'council tenants' (i.e. the people who live in the council houses).

The three estates of Royds – Buttershaw, Delph Hill and Woodside – fall into this general pattern. Building started in 1949 and was continued into the 1950s. The population was, and still is, predominantly white and working class. The current population of the three estates is approximately 12,000, with Buttershaw being the largest by a wide margin.

Although created as the answer to slum housing, it became increasingly obvious throughout the 1970s that Royds and similar estates nationally were themselves suffering from acute problems. Their often marginal locations away from shopping, leisure and health facilities, high unemployment among their inhabitants and deteriorating physical condition of the houses and immediate environment, led to vicious circles of decline. In addition it was claimed that a 'dependency culture' had set in among the residents who were quick to complain when the local council did not fulfil adequately its obligations as owner and manager of the houses, but who showed little initiative in trying to deal with the problems themselves. In short, this dependency culture bred apathy.

One way of looking at these vicious circles of decline is to examine them in terms of institutional failure. The market economy had failed to provide local jobs; the National Health Service and other social institutions were inadequate to local needs. Above all, government, or at least local government, was failing the 'council house tenants'. This sense of collective failure resulted in a breakdown of legitimacy of these institutions among significant sections of the estate populations. In other words, the validity of their 'rules, norms and values' (Fowler et al., 1992, p. 14) were being questioned.

The breakdown of legitimacy manifested itself on the estates in rising crime, vandalism and other anti-social behaviour, including an alarming rise in hard drug abuse. Table 13.1 provides some basic indicators for the Buttershaw estate.

The figures for owner occupancy in Table 13.1 might seem surprising because, as mentioned earlier, these council estates were predominantly owned and run by the local authorities when they were created. The right-wing (Conservative) governments of Margaret Thatcher in the 1980s, however, led a concerted attack on the very concept of council housing and granted tenants the 'right to buy'. This was partly a response to the 'dependency culture' and the philosophy of these governments was towards greater individual responsibility. It was also part of a concerted attack on the power of the local authorities, many of which were controlled by the socialist opposition party (Labour).

Whatever else it did, the right to buy certainly did not solve the problems on the estates. Thus, various schemes using public funds were attempted throughout the 1980s and 1990s to address these problems, partly prompted by further breakdown in public order on some of the estates that culminated in riots.

TABLE 13.1 SOME BASIC INDICATORS FOR THE BUTTERSHAW ESTATE		
	Buttershaw	Bradford District
Unemployment (%)	23.2	11.1
Unemployed aged 16-24 (%)	33.5	17.2
Lone parent households (%)	8.3	4.6
Households with no car (%)	47.7	40.9
Owner occupation (%)	58.8	71.1
Overall crime rate (crimes per 1000 dwellings)*	160	145[†]
Burglaries (per 1000 dwellings)	125	75[†]
Criminal damage (per square km)	120	75[†]

*The overall crime rate is a composite of: assault, burglary, criminal damage, theft from cars, theft of cars.

[†] These figures are for the Bradford South area (of which Buttershaw and Royds are part) rather than for the whole district. Figures for the latter are likely to be lower.

(Buttershaw Neighbourhood Forum Profile, Bradford Metropolitan District Council, based on 1991 census data)

The latest of these initiatives is the 'Single Regeneration Budget' (SRB), which came into being in the early 1990s. The idea behind the SRB is that problems of unemployment, poor social conditions and poor physical condition of housing stock are inter-linked and have to be dealt with in a single, holistic package. In that the initiative for any bid is supposed to come from the tenants of the estates and bring in the private sector as a partner, it also represents a reversal of earlier approaches to urban renewal, which had mainly been top-down in conception and implementation. At the time of its conception, the SRB again fitted well with the Conservative government's (now under John Major) philosophy of greater individual responsibility. It is also fair to say that the SRB sits comfortably with the mission of the New Labour Government (since May 1997) under Tony Blair, of creating a 'stakeholder society' which involves responsibilities as well as rights.

13.2 THE SRB AND ROYDS: INCENTIVES

The UK Government of the early 1990s dangled the incentive of a hefty prize in front of those who might be tempted to make a bid to the Single Regeneration Budget. £31 millions was a considerable sum. It is also interesting that the government initiative that formed the late 1980s fore-runner to the SRB was called 'City Challenge', containing within the title an explicit reference to the competitive nature of these bidding processes. In other words, the government did not have a bottomless pit overflowing with funds. Local communities had to work hard and bid for money from it, implicitly against each other. This was bare-faced prize competition in the sense of Chapter 5, although it might also be viewed as 'contracting' – where local communities take over from the local authorities the responsibility for their own welfare.

The trigger incentive for the Royds SRB bid was, in fact, a successful City Challenge bid made by another large estate in the city. Tony Dylak, the general manager for the Royds Community Association worked for Bradford Council at the time and describes the competitive response to this success. It drew, he says:

> ... a very predictable response from other council estates throughout the city who said, 'Hang on a minute, we're all deprived, why did that estate get chosen, not ours?'. Wherever I was involved I explained the reason so that, in effect, a challenge was put down to estates like the three in Royds to do the same. [I told them ...] 'Spend a couple of years identifying your problems, identifying your way out, identifying what kind of partnerships you might wish to set up to address those problems, and get yourself a high profile.'
>
> Royds did do that and had the Minister for Housing up and other people who came for individual projects but got a feel for what was happening in the field and that the [SRB] plan was being put together. Through the partners that were involved, the Royds Programme ensured that it (a) had a very feasible business plan ... and (b) that it had a quickly rising national profile so that when it was raised down in London people said, 'Oh, we've heard of that scheme', or 'So and so's been to visit that and said it was an interesting scheme'.

A more general incentive was that, as Table 1 hints, life is a struggle on the Royds estates and here was an opportunity to 'play the game' to different rules, backed by hard cash, which would hopefully improve life and con ditions. But seizing such an opportunity is not easy and requires a high degree of motivation which Royds amply demonstrated. This might seem surprising when examining Table 1, but to paint a picture of the Royds estates depicting widespread apathy, crime, drug-taking, unemployment and other negative images would be misleading. The bid in 1994 for SRB money did not come out of thin air and the bid document made a virtue out of there being on each estate 'committed groups of local people prepared to work for change'. In other words, there was a wealth of social capital as the document made clear:

> The residents of the area have been highly active. They produced the GBH (Greater Buttershaw Heritage) report in 1992 and the Woodside survey which brought the problems and issues of the area to the attention of the various public authorities. It is the strength of

their commitment which has ensured the co-operation of the Local Authority and other agencies ... and has led to the development of the SRB bid.

(Royds Single Regeneration Budget Bid, 3rd September 1994)

GBH is also a common acronym in the UK for the form of criminal assault known as 'grievous bodily harm'! At the time of the Greater Buttershaw Heritage report a popular political thriller about local government was being televised under the title GBH (involving further double meanings). In the Buttershaw context, GBH has also been decoded colloquially to mean 'Get Buttershaw heard'!

Steve Crossley, who was the chair of the Royds Board in 1997/98 and a resident-director for the Woodside estate, became involved initially because he was 'one of the local activists on the estate', where he was heavily involved with children's groups. Tina Belt and Maureen Hall are resident directors on the Royds Board from the Buttershaw and Delph Hill estates respectively. Tina was involved in the report referred to above and the subsequent Royds bid from the start. And it turns out that the GBH report did much more than simply highlight the estate's problems:

> There was a group of us and we started a drama group. We had a few people involved – residents, children as well, and we all had a say on what we'd like on the estate. [We produced from this] a play and there were over three hundred people came to watch us on stage, and they swear that this is where Buttershaw first started with Royds. Then we fetched the other estates in with us and made it one big thing.
>
> (Tina Belt)

Delph Hill estate joined the Royds scheme at a comparatively late stage. Despite being generally thought of as the 'worst' of the three estates, even here residents' groups were active. Maureen, for example, was active in the residents' group for the part of the estate where she lives. It was because the group 'seemed to be in limbo' and 'wasn't getting anywhere' that it decided to join Royds.

Royds showed, therefore, that prize incentives are closely related to motivation (see Chapter 2), and also to the social capital from which motivation can draw its strength. The resident motivation continues to be a source of strength and it is catching, because another feature of the Royds Regeneration Programme is the commitment of the paid officers. General manager, Tony Dylak, is quite explicit about this when he says:

> I worked for the local authority for 15 years. Every job I've had has been involved in working with the community. When this scheme came up I think I saw what I'd been looking for all those years. This scheme was genuine – it wasn't a group of professionals

saying we've got a good idea here, let's go and talk to the chair of the community association and then we can say we've got the residents involved, which is the traditional way of doing it, this was something quite different. That led me to make quite a big decision. I have left a permanent job to take a temporary contract to work here. I don't regret that decision at all, I love this job …

Incentives for other stakeholders seem more straightforward. Private building firms engage in tender competition for Royds contracts. The voluntary sector have their own objectives to fulfil. In general, stakeholders have their own agendas, and the extent to which incentives that stem from these agendas can translate into commitment to Royds is a continuing insti tutional issue for the Programme. Much of the brokering in Royds has been about forging such joint commitment out of individual stakeholder agendas, or, as Hanlon (Chapter 6) puts it in the very different context of Mozambique, getting to know each other's goals and bottom line.

13.3 THE SRB AND ROYDS: ACCOUNTABILITY

One argument for SRBs is that they make development interventions in the UK more accountable to the people they are supposed to serve, the residents on the estates, by virtue of being 'bottom-up' and by being closer to them. Indeed great claims have been made for Royds that it is genuinely 'resident-led'.

There seem to be three mechanisms by which accountability towards the Royds residents is enacted:

- the resident-directors on the Royds Board in their formal role;
- the resident-directors informally as part of everyday life;
- the public consultation 'roadshows'.

13.3.1 RESIDENT-DIRECTORS: FORMAL ROLE

The accountable body for Royds is the Royds Board. Given that this is chaired by a resident-director and that resident-directors (four from each of the three estates, giving a total of 12) have a majority on the Board, their role is crucial.

The legitimacy of this arrangement has had to be worked at; it has not been easy for those partners who would see themselves as more 'natural' candidates for the lead role, whether they are in the private, public or voluntary sectors, to accept it.

Thus, General Manager, Tony Dylak refers to initial local authority antagonism and how this has been steered:

That the accountable body status should be with the residents, with the [Royds] Board, did cause some problems. The local authority felt that it was more in their remit to be the accountable body and that did create some antagonism and it resulted perhaps in a lot of time-wasting, some of which hasn't gone away ... but the mark of a good democratic organization is that people can accept these tensions, can accept the differences, and can agree a common way forward, even if they personally are not happy with it.

Danny Mangham is an elected City Councillor for the area that includes Royds and one of three Bradford Council representatives on the Royds Board. He speaks of his initial personal unease:

I had concerns about it ... I told them, as a ward councillor when they were thinking about Royds, I wasn't really happy about giving that amount of money to people who'd not been used to handling that amount of money ... I was wrong, it's worked out. It was a bit dodgy at first but gradually they've come to realise that the money has to be spread out and has to be used properly. I've no problems with it at all now.

And Ian Taylor of Brunel Housing Association tells of how he and colleagues had the novel experience of being interviewed in order to become a partner:

For myself and the chief executives [of the housing association] who were actually interviewed it was a bit of a novel experience, because, normally when we've entered these special regeneration-type schemes, it's been led by the professionals, rather than by the local community.

Gradually, sceptical stakeholders have 'come round' to recognizing that the resident-directors are good guardians of the public purse, that they have developed the necessary skills, and most importantly, that they genuinely represent the Royds residents, thus conferring the programme with a broad legitimacy. The other initial fear, moreover, that the resident-directors would not recognize the legitimate agendas of other partners has similarly been overcome. Ex-chair, Steve Crossley, explains with respect to the private sector:

If somebody's honest enough to come to you and say, 'Look, our aims and objectives are to build this and we need to make this percentage', you can live with that, because they have to take on board your goals as well, and you both achieve the same. They get their percentage, build the building, but you get a good facility. Everybody's happy.

The resident-directors are elected by private ballot on each estate and there are regular elections. There are inevitable tensions between their role as representatives of those who have elected them and of the 'general good' of the project. This is essentially the background to the initial fear of Danny Mangham, expressed above, that the money has to be used properly, and the tension still surfaces. At one Board meeting attended by the author, for example, it became clear that the Buttershaw resident-directors felt that their estate was being 'left out' after plans to replace a dilapidated shopping parade with a 'village centre' comprising shops and social facilities were shelved because of difficulties in obtaining private sector support.

13.3.2 RESIDENT-DIRECTORS: INFORMAL ROLE

The resident-directors can be held to account by not being re-elected, but it is essentially in their everyday lives that real accountability to the Royds residents lies. This view is forcibly expressed by the ex-chair:

> ... you need people involved who live in the estates because, at the end of the day, the professionals, the people employed, all get in their cars, or catch a bus, and go home, and it's the residents who live there who are left to deal with a lot of issues. Now, because we live here ... if something goes wrong the residents come to us, so we get involved with the various agencies. And we get it resolved today.

Rosalind Jenkinson and Barry Schofield, resident directors for the Buttershaw and Woodside estates respectively, also speak of this informal accountability to the residents and the pressures it brings. Rosalind:

> It really is amazing how people [on the estate] recognize you. I hope I can carry on being recognized as somebody that's doing some good ... Sometimes [when residents contact me], it's nothing to do with Royds [Programme]. One of the elderly people had her windows broken and it was Council property, but because she knew I'm from Royds [Programme], she thought that maybe I could help her to get it sorted because it had been like that for about six weeks. I got in touch with the Council and next morning the windows were mended ...

Barry:

> You go out of your house and you want to go shopping. You think, 'I'll just go into the local shop, it will take me 15 minutes.' ... As you're walking along, somebody will stop you and say, 'The lights are out on this street, can you get them fixed?' ... You finish up [spending] two hours because people are stopping you as you're going around your daily business.

It is probable that this informal and very immediate contact with residents around concrete (very) local issues makes the Royds resident-directors more accountable than it is ever possible for the elected Council representatives to be. They might not be able to exert an 'exit' option, but, in terms of 'voice', the residents are able to exert a loud one (Chapter 2). Their loyalty is also key, both in the formal sense of electing the resident-directors and in the informal support (or not) that they give to the directors.

13.3.3 THE PUBLIC CONSULTATION ROADSHOWS

The third mechanism by which accountability to the residents is exercised is by public consultation roadshows. This involves taking a travelling display with support staff and resident-directors to a particular part of Royds where a new project has been proposed. Often this display will park alongside an estate shopping parade for several hours and discuss with residents a proposal. Some residents will come especially (leaflets publicizing the event will have been delivered to residents' homes a few days earlier), others will be passing shoppers. If attendance is poor, the workers and resident-directors present will knock on doors to pull people in.

This process of formally involving the public is preferred to holding public meetings in church halls or schools. Tony Dylak outlines the reasons at the end of one roadshow:

> The traditional way to do consultation is to hold public meetings, and we do hold public meetings, but my experience is that you often only get the activists at those meetings … So we thought we wanted to do something quite different … Yesterday we were outside a school and when the school finished and the parents came to pick their kids up, we got practically all the parents, most of whom would say that they don't have time to go to a meeting. So we're doing it the other way round – we're not asking people to give up their time to come to us, we're giving our time to go to them.

The results of each consultation exercise are collated into a report of residents' views that is presented to the next meeting of the Royds Board. The crucial question, however, is the extent to which the roadshows give local residents, who are going to have to live with the various projects, a real say in their conception, design and implementation. Take, for example, the following dialogue between the Royds Project Development Officer, Raj Panesar, and a local small shopkeeper at a roadshow consultation on the proposed village centre for Buttershaw (before it was shelved), where part of the plan was to have a greatly enlarged 'Co-op' supermarket. The Co-operative Society was originally set up in the UK in the 19th Century, with the premise that its services were run for the benefit of its users. Today it operate a range of services including a supermarket chain. The 'Co-op' is the largest retail outfit on the Buttershaw estate.

> *Shopkeeper*: How can a small shopkeeper compete with the Co-op? This is the biggest question, because they're on a bigger scale.
>
> *Raj Panesar*: We can talk to the Co-op about it because we don't want the Co-op monopolizing the retail outlets in the area and I'm sure that they don't either … So we will talk to the Co-op but, at the end of the day, we can only ask them, we can't dictate to them.
>
> *Shopkeeper*: You haven't got any power really to pressurize them, you know.

Raj Panesar: We can probably bring pressure to bear from the community, and I'm sure the Co-op will be as amenable as they can, but they're not coming here to invest for humanitarian reasons, they're coming here to make money ... But we will certainly talk to them and we'll work with you to make sure you can continue offering a service to these residents as you've been doing for the last six years ... you've got my assurance that we will do whatever is within our power to make sure that you have a part to play in this.

Raj Panesar went on to say that without the Co-op on board the village centre project would not be viable. Other groups would only participate and put money in if they saw a major retail outlet doing so and ultimately, the concerns of the small shopkeeper above were secondary to this. It is pertinent that the later postponement of the village centre, announced at the Royds Board, was not because of small shopkeeper objections, but because the big private players – the developers – refused to pay for the necessary infrastructure changes.

On other occasions, however, the public consultation does result in changes to Royds projects. This is particularly the case when the consultation relates to matters of design and implementation, rather than conception. Barry Schofield:

I think at the last roadshow we held, at the bottom of the Woodside estate, we had actually suggested that there was some build of new houses, and the people living down there didn't want [this]. So, in actual fact, immediately, those houses were struck off and are not going to be built ...We always try and find alternatives.

13.3.4 OTHER ACCOUNTABILITIES

So far we have examined accountability of the Royds Community Association to the residents and small shopkeepers. But the Community Association has other accountabilities, to partner organizations and, ultimately, to the Government paymasters. By and large, these other partners are able to exert an 'exit' option, and this is particularly true of the private sector. The simplest manifestation of this is when developers refuse to pay some of the costs of the Programme which they do not see to be their responsibility, as with the proposed Buttershaw village centre above.

At times, of course, there are clashes between the different accountabilities. The residents, who have to rely on 'voice', were also vocal in connection with a drug rehabilitation unit that was proposed as part of the Buttershaw village centre. Yvonne Troy, a local community development worker, describes graphically the residents' reaction to having any form of formal drug-abuse help on the estate:

From my coming into post, everyone has come to me and said, 'When are you going to do something about the drugs problem' ...

So, as soon as you start to tackle it, then it's 'not in my back yard'. We had some really terrible things said about drug dependants on the estate at a public meeting, people shouting things like, 'We didn't ask them to do it, why should we do anything for them?' The fact is that they are members of this community ... [drug abuse is] a societal problem ... and people need help and treatment, and it can only benefit the community.

The message from many residents to the community association trying to 'sell' a drugs rehabilitation unit as part of the village centre is pretty clear. But Royds Community Association is also accountable to Bradford Health Authority which is a partner in both the establishment of the drugs rehabilitation unit and a conventional health centre in the area. Accommodating the different interests on a topic such as this, which stirs strong emotions, is no easy matter.

13.4 DILEMMAS OF GOVERNANCE

Reading the discussion in the last section raises the question of whether, by virtue of its greater accountability, the Royds Community Association has become a surrogate city council. Is it the legitimate authority on the estates in the eyes of the local residents, rather than Bradford Council? It is true, that the Community Association has in a sense been sub-contracted to manage some of the physical and social services that were once the province of the Council, but the question of legitimacy goes somewhat beyond these formal arrangements, as the quotation from Rosalind Jenkinson above about her informal role reveals. It is as if the Community Association has insinuated itself into every aspect of life on the estates.

If this is the case, a further question then becomes, drawing on Moore (Chapter 5): 'Does Royds perform the public sector management basics of discipline, honesty, accountability, predictability and coherence?' I have argued above that the Community Association is certainly accountable and this is why it is seen to be replacing the City Council in many aspects. Many of the quotations above also suggest that, despite initial misgivings, it is disciplined, recognizing the agendas of different partners and accommodating these.

With respect to honesty, it is a pointless exercise to try and prove that each individual involved will always act completely honestly. More to the point, there are mechanisms for dealing with dishonesty within the Community Association when it surfaces and these have been enacted on occasion. In general, the overall accountability of resident-directors to the residents, and of the different partners to each other, maintains a high level of honesty.

There may be difficulties, however, over predictability and coherence of response because the boundary between Council and Community Association responsibility is not precisely agreed, as the ex-chair illustrates with respect to Royds physical rehabilitation work on houses owned by the Council:

> At the end of the day, the local authority get all their housing stock brought up to a decent standard [by the Royds Programme]. Now the local authority should be doing that, not the Royds, but we do it.

This lack of precise boundary is bound to cause difficulties. Rosalind Jenkinson might take up problems with the Council on behalf of residents, but it is not her job to do so, and others, particularly if hard-pressed, might refuse. This is the danger when some actions are voluntary — the response cannot be guaranteed to be either predictable or coherent. It also raises other issues such as eventual 'burn-out' of over-committed people and the need to negotiate norms and practices that make it clear where obligations start and end

13.4.1 RELATIONSHIPS BETWEEN THE COMMUNITY ASSOCIATION AND BRADFORD COUNCIL (THE LOCAL STATE)

Governance is predicated in a major way on the government sharing some of its power with 'partners'. In other words, government's traditional monopoly is broken and to suggest that this can happen without tension is untrue.

There can be no doubt that the Single Regeneration Budget bid could not have been made and certainly would not have been won if it had not received the full backing of Bradford Council. Peter Eccles, current chair of the Royds Board, is both blunt and generous on this point: 'Without the local authority initially, it wouldn't have got started'.

But the change in attitudes required from local state politicians should not be under-estimated. I alluded above to some of the early reservations expressed by Councillor Danny Mangham. Keith Thompson, another City Councillor who sits on the Royds Board gives a further perspective on his current role:

> [The SRB partnership] is breaking new ground ... the Council is not used to taking ... a minority seat in decision-making ... and one of the more interesting areas and difficulties is the role that the [Bradford] Council directors have. Quite often there are tensions because, technically as a Council director on the [Royds] Board, we represent the interests of the Council ... But that conflicts quite often with the role that we might have as a local ward councillor, because as a local ward councillor ... you also work quite often as an advocate for local people and local groups ... and you would quite often be critical of the Council's performance because that's your role in terms of the way you were elected by people to represent them in this area ...

What emerges is that Royds Community Association has had to earn its respect from the City Council. The commitment, emerging capacity and confidence among the resident-directors is one major factor in this respect, although it should be borne in mind that any initial reticence shown by Bradford Council about the project was partly to do with the political context of the time and had little to do with the residents. It is a Labour-controlled council, and the SRB was conceived by a central Conservative Government as part of a strategy of 'rolling back the state', a strategy it applied to both local and central government. It is inconceivable that such 'rolling back' could occur without a struggle by the many opposing elements within the state apparatus, including the predominately Labour, urban, local councils.

Nevertheless, 'rolling back' did occur at Royds, where Bradford Council's role in the SRB bid became, in the language of Chapter 7, that of a facilitator. The Council still has an ongoing role as provider of funds and owner of many of the houses on the estates and it is, as we have seen, formally represented on the Royds Board. It cannot, however, in any sense be described as a co-ordinator of the Programme implementation; that is firmly the role of the Board on which the Council representatives are a small minority compared to the resident-directors.

Inevitably there are still ongoing disagreements about the wholeheartedness of the Council's acceptance of its role, yet Peter Eccles is positive about the Council-directors on the Board:

> On the Board of directors there are three local councillors, two of whom represent wards in our constituency. Both of them do a tremendous amount of work on behalf of Royds. They have to wear two hats of course. They come to a Royds meeting and if it's something that concerns the [Bradford] Council, they have to put their Council hats on, obviously … But we get good representation … [They] do a damn good job frankly, a damn good job.

Tony Dylak is also positive, but with some reservations and he alludes to institutional Council fears:

> The local authority as a partner is committed to the overall vision of improving the quality of life on the estates, but there are elements of it that they're less comfortable with. For example, there are great fears that one of the outcomes of this scheme may well be that property is transferred to the Royds Community Association. That isn't a current plan but it could well be a plan in the future.

Others, such as the ex-chair of the Royds Board, are much less charitable altogether:

> … to be quite honest with you, if somebody says, 'Partnership works', I would like to see that. I've been involved with Royds now for five years and one of our key and main partners [Bradford

Council], that are putting £14 million into the Programme, causes a tremendous deal of problems, which must be hard for our ward councillors.

As in any relationship, perceptions of each other are often based on historical assumptions which then translate into fears (Chapter 7). Thus, the Labour Council is sometimes accused of failing to understand the validity of private sector agendas. The Council, for its part, has been wary of the residents' capacity and capability to do the job. These assumptions stem from complex previous relationships, for example from when the Council claimed to be 'socialist' and the sole definer and defender of the local public interest. How to manage, and ultimately transcend this history, is an important challenge for developing relationships between the Community Association and Council.

One clue to meeting this challenge is perhaps provided by the relationship between the local authority and Royds Community Association. To the extent that the relationship does work, it appears due to the fact that the two Bradford Council representatives on the Royds Board – Danny Mangham and Keith Thompson – are, like the resident directors, deeply embedded within the local community. Keith Thompson is a local ex-headmaster. Danny Mangham was a Union man in the Bradford textile industry. Yet, at the same time, the Royds Board has a certain autonomy with respect to local politics as the SRB is a central government initiative, and constitutionally it can act independently of the local authority. Although there are undoubted tensions between being embedded and being autonomous, as many of the previous quotations testify, it seems that a good mix of the two can be creative in fostering relationships and overcoming predilections (Harriss, 1999).

13.4.2 CO-ORDINATION BETWEEN THE PLAYERS

The formal co-ordinating body, the Royds Board, is an example of 'governance' in action, where different stakeholders in the Programme come together to decide priorities, make decisions over implementation and learn from what they are doing.

Although Paul Taylor in Chapter 9 is writing about a completely different scenario (humanitarian aid) and co-ordination among a completely different set of institutions (United Nations institutions), in many respects the Royds experience reflects what he calls 'entrenched multilateralism'. As with increasing co-ordination efforts among the UN actors that Taylor describes, different stakeholders at Royds initially opted in because the costs of not doing so were perceived to be greater. Tony Dylak:

> The old adage that money attracts money is quite definitely true. If one agency [the Government] is prepared to commit £31 million to an area then, almost by default, other people come forward and offer their money in order to get a bit of that. So, in effect, you build up the £31 million quite quickly simply by people seeing it as an opportunity for themselves to benefit.

The Royds bid is an interesting example where the 'prize' in 'prize competition' was of sufficient value to draw in the private property sector for the obvious reason that some of the 'prize' would filter to it through contracts in an econmically depressed area. Some of the other stakeholders have also brought resource with them (Bradford Council alone has put in £14 millions, as mentioned above), so that the original £31 millions SRB is now well in excess of £100 million.

One of the estates with no financial resources to bring, Delph Hill, was not part of the original plan. It opted in because it felt that this was the only way to gain a slice of the action. Delph Hill resident-director, Maureen Hall:

> The [Delph Hill] residents' group seemed to be in limbo. We weren't getting anywhere, so we decided that the best course of action would be to join Royds. So that's when we decided, through the constitution, that one of us should stand as a Royds director.

By joining in, these actors accepted the broad Royds mission and, with the formation of the Royds Board, the 'rules of the game', which included a resident-majority on the Board (again reminiscent of Taylor's entrenched multilateralism, see Chapter 9). Thus, general, vague exhortations that started with the national government of the early 1990s became accepted and translated into operational rules and procedures, in other words they became institutionalized in the Royds project.

This isn't to say that the Royds mission and agendas of the different stakeholders do not clash from time to time. This was vividly shown when the private sector refused to accept the burden of providing the infrastructure of the Buttershaw village centre. In that the Royds Board cannot force the private sector to accept this burden, it can be argued that an over-arching 'rule of the game' is the supremacy of the market as a social institution and that the resident majority does not carry much weight in such circumstances. But there is space to 'push' the private sector a little harder because there are costs to it exhibiting the 'exit' option – goodwill from a range of actors, from the Government to the residents, will be lost. It is just, as Tony Dylak explained, that the sector was pushed too far over the village centre proposal:

> It might be perfectly possible for the private sector to throw a bit of tarmac down outside somebody's house because it makes it easier, but if you want the whole road making up for free the private sector will say, 'Hang on a minute, partnership goes so far, but somebody needs to pay us for this', and that creates tensions, I suppose, that means the vision gets diluted.

Balancing this, there are some impressive examples of co-ordination. Because of the Royds Regeneration Programme a co-ordinated education policy for the area is emerging. Andy Barnett is headmaster of a local primary school:

> I think the first thing that Royds did was bring together the schools in the area. There are eight schools physically within the Royds boundary. Incredibly, even though we're only a few hundred yards apart, we had never actually sat down, the eight heads of these schools, and talked to one another before Royds got us together. Over the initial period we were able to look at a strategy for education from five to 18 within this area. We were then able to plan things like the *Reading Support Programme* that Royds are financing, instead of just throwing some money into school, and saying, 'Here you are, try and use this to develop and improve reading standards.' ... that has had a really significant input. Within my school, the money in the first and second years was targeted at children at Year 1 and when we tested those children at the end of last academic year, we had 85% of those children ... scoring above their age, which, for our school in our community, is a very significant mark.
>
> We've been able to pull a lot of adults into school through different programmes and that is beginning to have an effect. Those same adults are now training to be volunteer reader-helpers, and that's sustainability for the whole Royds project ... We're working on people's confidence in basic literacy skills, basic numeracy skills, parenting skills, as we believe that's the only way we're going to lift the whole project.

Thus, both adult (within a wider remit of increasing confidence) and children's literacy are being addressed. Danny Mangham is enthusiastic especially about the latter:

> We've done more for children than I thought possible. In fact, the biggest success for me is that we've put money into the local schools ... I think, if we did nothing else right in Royds, that's been worth it.

Another example of co-ordination is in tackling the problem of youth crime. Chris Graham is the community police constable for the area:

> One of the initiatives we've got going, the police alongside Royds, is the FOCUS initiative which develops young people who sometimes are disaffected ... we're trying to give them an alternative ... by offering constructive activities like climbing, or arts and craft, football ... That's one of the ways that we have brought down [very significantly] the crime figures within Royds. Now, it's not just the police, it's Royds as well, it's the residents within Royds and it's the Royds Community Association that have helped to do this. They've funded it.

The FOCUS initiative described here is particularly interesting because it involves co-ordination between Royds and an institution that is not represented on the Board – the police. The sustainability of the scheme depends as much on continuing support of the latter as it does on the Royds Board. Chris Graham has the backing of his local command, and claims a lot of support within the police force generally, but is not clear as to whether this can continue when performance indicators for police are normally biased towards number of crimes solved rather than social preventative work.

13.4.3 CO-OPERATION AND PARTNERSHIP

Paul Taylor's notion of entrenched multilateralism in Chapter 9 has the initially negative connotation that organizations 'opt in' to mutual relationships through which co-ordination might take place, because the costs of not doing so are greater. But is there more to the co-ordination role of the Royds Board than this? It is useful, when considering this question, to take another cut across the stakeholder relationships, and ask whether they are based on the positive connotation of voluntary co-operation for mutual benefit, as John Harriss describes in Chapter 10.

Co-operation, according to Harriss, is founded on the mechanism of 'trust'. Harriss, however, is particularly interested in what he terms 'process-based trust' which is 'tied to past exchange, such as reputation or gift exchange'. He argues that such trust can be built, or 'studied', in contrast to other forms that might be determined by common family background, ethnicity or pre-disposition through prior stock of social capital.

Royds offers a good illustration of his argument. There was a process of building trust, involving the initial coming together of the stakeholders and the ensuing institutionalization of values and practices within the Board. Thus, the Royds stakeholders came together initially because of a common issue or problem that seemed impossible to resolve individually (or where it seemed more important to be 'in' rather than 'out'). This led to reframing of the problem and relations between actors who were hitherto lacking in mutual trust (and who may have been antagonistic towards each other).

Again, it is easy to find examples in Royds where problems have not been reframed. Many residents still appear hostile, for example, to any new approaches to the drugs problem. The private sector makes it clear that its primary concern is to make a profit. On the other side, the efforts made at reducing youth crime and the literacy efforts in schools represent areas where problems have been reframed. The wider notion that this is a holistic programme, integrating physical, social and economic renewal is itself a reframing of earlier fragmented approaches.

From reframing problems one can proceed to constructing shared intentions among stakeholders, which builds trust up to another level. In other words, first you agree what the problem is; then you decide what you are going to do about it. This moreover is the essence of partnership as formulated especially by Angela Penrose in Chapter 11. Thus, she quotes Alan Fowler on partnership: 'mutually enabling, interdependent intervention interaction with shared intentions.' 'Partners' and 'partnership' unsurprisingly feature strongly in the Royds vocabulary:

> Ours is a very active partnership, but what makes our scheme unique is the fact that the residents' involvement is significantly different to many other partnerships.
>
> (Tony Dylak)

> I'm the project development officer and the main aspect of my position here with Royds is to bring in external funding [with] any funding agency out there that is prepared to work with Royds in partnership, ...
>
> (Raj Panesar)

> The Royds Drug Initiative (RDI) is another excellent illustration of partnership work within Royds. It is not the Council leading ... it is the Community Association lead ... You've got membership [on the RDI Board] from the Community Association, from the voluntary sector, from the Church, from the youth and community, and also the police. We get together around a table at least once a month and talk about what we're doing.'
>
> (Chris Graham, community constable)

> By and large they [the developers] work well together with us. Obviously it's a partnership. I'm a married man, me and my wife's a partnership. We fall out, we argue, and so we do with our partners. We pull together, we solve whatever problems there are. By and large the partnerships work exceedingly well ... There are still certain agencies that don't work with us as well, but they'll come together eventually. They've got to, for the benefit, not only of Royds, but for the better deal of Bradford. The Council are beginning to understand that, so that's a partnership that's working. Obviously the developers are in this partnership to make money, otherwise they would go out of business. But there's ways of doing business where they can work closely with the community.
>
> (Peter Eccles)

These statements, however, suggest different emphases as to what partnership means. Tony Dylak emphasizes the active involvement of a frequently excluded group – the 'beneficiaries' of a programme – for whom, from other comments recorded in this chapter, there does not appear to be a trouble-free process of building mutual trust. For Raj Panesar, partnership could mean a straightforward contracting partnership (Harriss, Chapter 10). Chris Graham's example, however, does seen to accord with Alan

Fowler's view above. Finallly, Peter Eccles suggests that the stakeholders are together for better or ill. They may disagree, but they are too far in to be able to pull out, so accommodations of each other's interests are necessary. A whiff of entrenched multilateralism again?

13.5 INSTITUTIONAL SUSTAINABILITY AND LEARNING FROM ROYDS

Both a major concern, and an aim, at Royds is to build institutional arrangements that will ensure that the Programme more than outlasts its funding. The following quotations have the common theme of 'sustainability':

> There are plenty of examples of heavily-funded Government-sponsored Programmes that run for [up to] seven years, but when the money runs out the whole thing grinds to a terrible halt and people are almost left in a worse situation than they were before, because they've been given the impression that money is easy to get hold of, that projects can easily be funded ... In terms of social development it seems to me that we can either pay an organization to fund community workers and then we have to say what happens when that money runs out, or we can pay to support existing organizations such as churches, 'Help the Aged', local schools, who are involved in community development work and work with them on the basis that they will still be here when the money runs out. That's what the Board understands by sustainability ... and that's really how the Board is looking at a sustainable future for Royds.
>
> (Tony Dylak)

> The one thing I've been hammering home ... is, if we can't make whatever we're doing, if we can't see it paying its way when the SRB runs out, we shouldn't start ... And that's what we're trying to do on Royds, everything we set up we're trying to make it pay its way.
>
> (Danny Mangham)

> All the community want is to have a say in what goes on in their estate, and to take ownership, because at the end of the day that's sustainability ...
>
> (Steve Crossley, ex-chair)

> 'One of the other things that we're finding at Royds is that we're getting new groups starting. We actually have a literary group, which was something you would never have thought about on the Royds 18 months ago. A group of people have actually received a grant to write books and poetry ... On Buttershaw they've now started their new group for young families ... We're actually beginning to see people socializing again ...

... One of the things that we're trying to get across now is that any new group really must ensure that they are going to be sustainable at the end of the Royds [Programme]. If a new group is formed, one of the questions we are saying to them is, 'How are you going to sustain yourself beyond the year 2002?' We're getting people to look at how things are going to be continuing after the money has dried up.

(Barry Schofield)

Most of the things we're trying to do, we are trying to set up so they are sustainable – things like the motor education project where we are training volunteer mechanics, so they can carry on working with young people after the money runs out.

(Andy Barnett)

Barry Schofield and Andy Barnett emphasize ongoing social capital development, Tony Dylak the existing institutions such as the church and schools. Steve Crossley's concern is that the residents themselves should always have a major stake and this can only be achieved by resident primacy over other partners. Danny Mangham's concern is that the Board is able to make 'sustainable' decisions on how to spend the money.

All of these quotations assume, however, that development on the estates will continue to involve a multiplicity of organizations and agencies, each with their own agendas. The relationships between these organizations and agencies are therefore both crucial *and part of* the institutional development. Institutional sustainability is what matters here, which relates both to the sustainability of the regeneration of the estates beyond when the money runs out, and to the sustainability of the inter-organizational relationships between the Community Association, Bradford Council, and the private and voluntary sectors.

One question of course is: 'How did these organizations and agencies at Royds come together in the first place?' It seems that a joint pre-requisite is a wider political context that is 'pushing governance' as a good thing, together with a grassroots 'pull' for public action in the social arena. Both were much in evidence during the early 1990s, with the government pushing nationally for what it envisaged largely as public-private partnerships plus resident self-sufficiency, and the Royds residents themselves making strong demands for improvements in their lives. But a grassroots demand is itself predicated on the existence of a certain level of social capital, and it is clear that this was also present in Royds from the start; indeed, the SRB bid made a feature of it.

Political push relates roughly to the first trend identified by Hewitt in Chapter 3, that inter-organizational relationships are the result of forced interactions brought about by neo-liberal governments taking a hierarchical co-ordination role. As Hewitt points out, however, this is an inadequate specification. In Royds, for example, the private sector has responded to the political push, but there is also a strong element of the second trend identified by Hewitt: that is the private sector has entered into voluntary association with the local state, the voluntary sector and the residents for business reasons – to give itself a niche and to enhance its reputation, not to mention its profits.

In this way, private sector involvement in Royds is a departure from the 'ideal' of pure competition between atomized firms, which raises a tension with respect to the ethics of business dealings. On the one hand, the private sector has a formal representation on the Royds Board, which is the forum for explicit inter-organizational relationships, and it also engages in discussion on the design of projects. On the other, individual firms are required to compete for Royds contracts by secret tender, where any relationship between the Community Association and the firms would potentially open up a pejorative discourse of 'cronyism' and even 'corruption'.

Grassroots pull also does not map easily onto either of the trends identified by Hewitt, or rather one can again see strong elements of both. Certainly the political context was favourable to forming relationships with other organizations, especially the private sector. But part of the 'pull' was not just about gaining resources in order to help the estates, it was also about process, to be involved in the running of their estates as Steve Crossley suggests in his quotation above. In this sense, the residents themselves demanded at least equal relationships with other state and private actors.

It is important here to realize that, as Hewitt again points out, inter-organizational relationships have a history, and this is certainly true of the relationships between Royds residents and Bradford Council. This history pre-dates the SRB bid and some of it involves mutual suspicion between Council and residents, as earlier pages of this chapter testify, but it has its positive side too. Thus, Bradford Council and estate residents used to meet periodically through a Council-run consultative forum known as Bradford South Area Panel. Tony Dylak worked for the Council at that time and attended those meetings on its behalf. It is there that he talked about making a Single Regeneration Budget bid; it is there that he forged relationships with many of those at the forefront of the community association today; it is there that the seeds of trust were sown.

Political-push, grassroots-pull and a private sector with an eye for business can create 'impulses' for coming together, for co-operating and a willingness to take part in co-ordinated action. But much hard work is required before these impulses can be translated into values, rules and practices, in other words, before they become entrenched in the Taylor (Chapter 9) sense.

Tony Dylak emphasizes the initial role and importance of 'champions':

> I think there has to be a key person who can say, 'This is going to be my scheme and I'm going to batter every door I can find and I'm going to work 25 hours a day to make this happen' ... In some cases it's a local authority worker, in some cases it might be a councillor, in some cases it's a voluntary or charity worker. It could just be a local resident ... If you haven't got the individual that's prepared to invest that time and effort, it's unlikely to happen ...

> In the early days of Royds, a lot of this campaigning work was done by a worker who worked for one of the local organizations, a chap called Martin Drury who spent all his time persuading residents that they didn't need to live in this situation, that they could do something. He spent his time knocking on the Council's doors saying, 'Don't just ignore us, don't pretend that I'm just an idiot because I'm from one of the estates.' And he did speak plainly and frankly to private sector partners and say, 'Come on, dip your hand in your pocket. We know you're out to make a profit but lay a bit out here.' All those things can be done if you've got the right individual there and I don't think you necessarily need to have the big amount of money as a carrot, but it does help.

One can add to the individual champion two other pre-conditions for setting the inter-organizational process on its way. Both are highlighted by Hewitt (Chapter 3). The first is to have organizational capacity in the first place, and this chapter has provided evidence of this on several counts: the SRB bid document highlighted the ability of the residents to produce reports about their estates and other residents have talked of being involved in children's and drama groups on the estates before the bid was made. The second is for the different parties to have a clear idea of what they want and to be prepared to invest resources into achieving that. Of the main players at Royds this has been certainly true of the community association and the private sector, although one can be less sure of Bradford Council. It could be that some of the partnership problems with the Council that have been hinted at from time to time have emanated from the latter not being totally clear about what it wants.

Beyond these pre-conditions, however, there is a long process, part of which consists of building multiple accountabilities among the stakeholders, where each has at least the option of exhibiting voice, exit, or removal of loyalty. Given that beneficiaries of social development interventions rarely have the exit option, this means establishing both formal and informal means for democratic accountability to them so that voice is given force. A second part of the process concerns building trust between partners so that norms of mutually beneficial, voluntary co-operation can be established. Such trust-building is best started around concrete issues that everyone is concerned about: education and crime reduction campaigns being prime examples on Royds. It then needs to move on to institutionalizing the basis of the trust, which involves establishing reciprocal rights and obligations among the players (Chapter 3). Thus, the Royds Community Association, by virtue of its majority on the Board, has the right to spend the money, but it also has an obligation to spend it in appropriate and responsible ways that have to be negotiated. Bradford Council has a right to indicate how the money should be spent, but also an obligation not to be obstructive. The private sector has a right to make a profit, but also an obligation to give something back to the estates in return

A third aspect concerns ongoing social capital development, as suggested in the quotations from Andy Barnett and Peter Eccles above. Maureen Hall introduces the advocacy aspects of this development when she talks of the newly-formed residents' group on Delph Hill:

> We started off with a group of ten women and eventually the membership's up to 80, although the committee is still quite small. We're here basically to help the people of the estate, make the estate better for them. If they have a problem they want to air, they can come to the residents' group, which is people they know, and the residents' group can take it on for them at a higher power ... There's power in numbers, isn't there? United we stand.

Initial champions, followed by an ongoing process of developing accountabilities, trust and social capital – in the final analysis, we are talking about establishing the legitimacy of a set of relationships that are inclusive, enabling and learning and which can carry on over time. The challenge appears formidable, but Royds, Bradford, UK shows that it can be done.

14 PUTTING INTER-ORGANIZATIONAL IDEAS INTO PRACTICE

TOM HEWITT AND DORCAS ROBINSON

14.1 INTRODUCTION

We know more than we can tell.

(Polanyi, 1966)

The last chapter about the Royds Regeneration Project gives us a rich often messy picture of what building inter-organizational relationships can be like. Many of the themes of the preceding chapters can be found here in the flesh – whether expressed in the apparently abstract notions about institutionalization of norms and values or in the practical difficulties of building trust and accountability. Listening to these people's experiences leaves us admiring of their determination and motivation to make changes for the better against the odds. We were also struck by how things got done – flexibility, thinking on your feet, common sense and learning as you go along – all seemed to have their place. Yet this was all achieved without losing sight of *why* things were being done – using tactics, yes, but also having a strategy and goals to aim for. The strategy in the case of Royds was urban regeneration of a sort that would create self-sustaining and participatory communities. There are no fixed ways of attaining such goals, thus the tactics used to get there were varied and negotiated in real time.

In this chapter we will discuss some of the practical ways that may help you in building such relationships. However we don't have a special package of tools labelled 'building inter-organizational relationships'. Many of the techniques and practices discussed here are not necessarily any different from those that you would bring to bear on problem-solving and decision making *inside* your own organization. They may however be used in slightly different ways.

The practical measures discussed here relate to the progression of ideas built up in the book, particularly in the three section conclusions. In these we stressed the importance of moving from appreciation of a situation, to an analysis of that situation and then to strategic engagement in the situation. Our choice of 'skills' in this chapter reflects this progression. They are a way of trying to grasp the big picture or, in Senge's words, of thinking beyond 'the illusion that the world is created of separate, unrelated forces' (Senge, 1990, p. 3).

Thus the tools discussed here lend themselves to ways of thinking about the whole situation and push us in the direction of appreciation, reframing and learning – all recurrent themes in this book – in ways that other more orthodox tools (such as framework planning) do not. The techniques chosen also highlight organizational interdependencies, another strong theme of the book.

In short, this chapter is a reflection on practical means for building, or helping to build inter-organizational relationships. Polanyi's words at the top of the page are apposite. He is talking about tacit knowledge as opposed to skills. 'Skills implies knowing how to make something happen, it involves cognition but also other aspects such as manual dexterity or sensory ability' (Senker, 1995, p. 101). Tacit knowledge is this and more. It is the accumulated learning and experience we bring to skills; it is the things that we know work although we can't really explain why – like riding a bicycle. It is the combination of skills and tacit knowledge that we might call 'expertise' (Senker, 1995, p. 102).

We want you to bring your expertise to bear on the practical dimensions of building inter-organizational relationships discussed in the chapter. The discussion is a reflection on practice rather than a 'how-to' manual. Wherever possible, we refer to the materials already presented in the book by way of illustration. We hope that much of what is said strikes you as common sense – and it encourages you to apply some of the techniques to your own work.

Some techniques will work better for you than others – and anyone familiar with even only a small sample of management literature will know that there is no shortage of techniques. The only way to find out what works for you is by trying things out. (Further reading at the end of this chapter provides useful sources of more detailed information on some of the techniques discussed.).

14.2 FROM APPRECIATION TO ENGAGEMENT

Its not unusual to feel like a drop in the ocean when confronted with the many organizations involved in any particular field of work. We sometimes feel this in our work (in higher education). How can we have any impact on what goes on? We do not have a great deal of influence but over the last ten years or so our experiences have given us a better sense of the shape and behaviour of the higher education sector. This appreciation, in turn, gives us a stronger sense of how to engage with our organization and with others to pursue what we and our colleagues deem to be important in our work.

One colleague in particular has long held the habit of jumping up during meetings to write down the elements of the discussion on the whiteboard, ordering the component parts, labeling clusters of ideas, pointing out links with arrows and so on. This has always been useful, even as a distraction when the meeting became tedious. After a while though, we realized that these doodlings were helping us to build our own mental maps of situations in a more organized fashion. Since then, we have started to use such maps in order to better understand or appreciate inter-organizational relationships.

14.2.1 APPRECIATING INTER-ORGANIZATIONAL RELATIONSHIPS THROUGH MAPPING

Gaining an appreciation of other organizations – whether in your own 'sector' or across public, private and civil society sectors – is important for understanding the non-cash resource contributions that each might make to a relationship. Such resources might be: people, expertise, information or physical (Tennyson, 1998, p. 17). Now you do not have to make a map to appreciate a given situation. Listening to people, observing, taking notes, reading documents and mentally absorbing information gleaned are all perfectly acceptable means of building understanding.

So first we had better explain why we think mapping is particularly useful for building up an appreciation of inter-organizational relationships – the first step, we have argued, in being able to make strategic choices.

One strong message from this book is that organizations have quite permeable boundaries, particularly those organizations that have multiple interdependencies. Grasping the threads of these interconnections can be an elusive task since they are often informal arrangements and they frequently change their configuration.

We think that mapping can be helpful in these situations in the following way. First of all, mapping can help to construct a framework for how your own organization (you and your colleagues) relate to an issue. Similarly, mapping can help you in constructing a framework of how other organizations might relate to the issue.

Combining these two can help you to develop an agenda for negotiation with others. And from here the different organizations can attempt to construct a shared map. This is turn forms the basis of what different organizations would jointly like to see happen. In this way, the mapping has assisted in moving from appreciation to action.

Maps can play an important role in this process because:

- they can be shared, discussed, argued over and modified with others;
- they bring out issues of ownership of problems and issues, particularly if mapping is carried out as a group exercise;
- they are immediate, in that they represent the situation as the parties involved perceive them and, often, in the words that participants use to describe a situation. Compare this to some of the rather abstract checklists presented in Chapter 3 and elsewhere in this book;

- they can be used to inform modelling exercises in quite a straightforward way. For example, a map of a situation as perceived by one person or group can be annotated by another to show up similarities or differences in the way that the latter perceive things.

In this mapping as a tool can help us to build trust by clarifying (mis)understandings and can help to reframe problems. Both these issues are taken up later in the chapter.

14.2.2 MAKING CONNECTIONS – SOME EXAMPLES

For now, let us look at a few examples of mapping as a tool. We have already seen some earlier in the book.

Chapter 2 contains three simple maps (Figures 2.1, 2.2 and 2.3) which have been used to summarize Section 2.2. These 'concept maps' as we would call them, represent elements of market, state and civil society. They are a way of taking notes, picking out key concepts and making connections. It is unlikely that we would have made these connections if we had written the notes in a linear fashion. The maps make explicit some interconnections which are only implicit in the text itself.

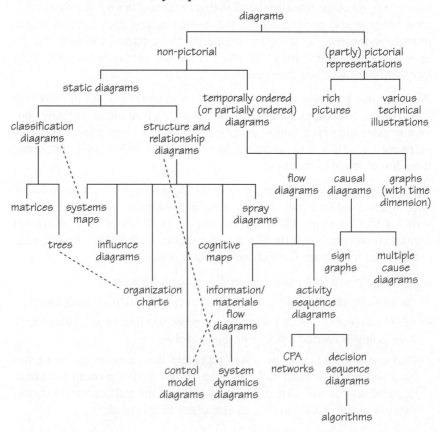

Figure 14.1 Some common diagramming and mapping techniques

Maps come in all shapes and sizes. Figure 14.1 – itself a kind of map – gives some of the more common types of diagrams or maps. Different kinds of mapping are useful for different purposes as the following examples show.

Multiple cause diagrams

The purpose of different kinds of map is to allow you to make sense of a situation for yourself and/or for others. The former may appear easier, but the latter is probably more useful. To explain something to others we need to understand it ourselves. Testing our understanding on others is a good way of focusing the mind. To illustrate this we have used a multiple cause diagram to try and understand the interconnections in the story told by Joe Hanlon in Chapter 6 on health services in Mozambique.

As its name implies, a multiple cause diagram can be used to explore why a given set of events happened. It doesn't predict behaviour but can help in identifying the factors to bear in mind when trying to explain a situation. They are also useful for finding out why something went wrong so that it can be avoided in the future.

The case study in Chapter 6 gives us a clear picture of the way competition for resources and for ideas between organizations produces (often unwanted) effects. This is an extreme (but not unusual) example in as much as the context is one of war.

Figure 14.2 gives a sample diagram of the situation. It highlights the atomized and fragmented responses of different organizations. Little interaction takes place between organizations – particularly the government and NGOs (and their external donors) – that appear to be in competition with each other. The reasons for this appears to be lack of information or poor information flows, competition over limited resources, tensions over roles, 'gap-filling' and so on.

Our diagram only shows part of this picture and we think we would have to have a second shot at it to get more detail. However, what it does show is the interesting (and tragic) relation between the strategy of Renamo to attack government health provision, the reaction of the population to migrate (internally and externally) as a result and the strategy of donors to target specific parts of the population. Donor support for the victims of Renamo's strategy and the neglect of the government's health priorities for all seems to have prolonged not shortened the destruction associated with the war.

The multiple cause diagram helped us in this instance to start thinking not only about the 'multiple causes' of the demise of the national health care programme in Mozambique but also about some of the consequences of multiple actors/organizations' involvement without co-ordination or co-operation. In short, the diagram has helped to identify some of the possibly unintended outcomes of development policy.

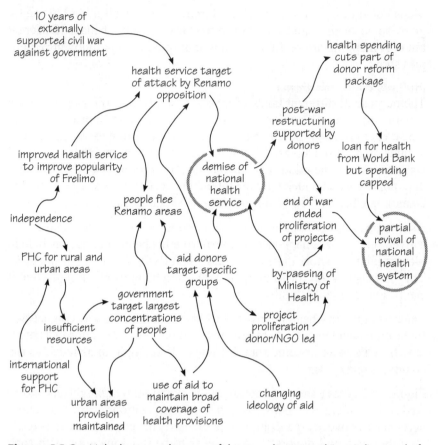

Figure 14.2 Multiple cause diagram of the rise, demise and (partial) revival of Mozambique's national health system; PHC is primary health care

The only other point we would like to make about this diagram is that it is tracking a series of events and causes along a time line (from independence to civil war to reconstruction). Multiple cause diagrams are useful for depicting chains of events over time. Broad sweeps of history help our understanding of how a situation got to be the way it is, but most of us are working in the midst of this history and need a more detailed appreciation of the here and now. Two useful techniques for this kind of appreciation we have found are systems maps and influence maps. A more powerful tool still is cognitive mapping.

Systems maps

Systems maps give a graphical snapshot of a set of inter-relationships. Devising such maps encourages you to structure a situation and its component parts and, in addition, makes you set the boundaries to the system (or sub-system) of components you are examining. In this way, a quite complex picture can be built up. Depending on where you place the boundary to the system, some revealing insights can be found. For

example, in an analysis of a multi-organization refugee education programme in Bhutan, our systems map revealed the recipients of the
programme – the refugees – to be outside the boundaries of the system.
This, it transpired, was the source of severe tensions and conflict in the
management of the programme leading to a withdrawal of some the
principal agencies involved.

Influence maps

These are similar in form to the systems maps but with an added dimension: lines of influence between the components of the system or
sub-systems. Adding such lines can elucidate multiple sets of relationships
between organizations, concepts, actions and events. Having a better sense
of what is influencing what, puts us in a stronger position of knowing where
things might be changed for the better, or the route the repercussions might
take if we were to intervene in a certain part of the system.

Cognitive maps

This is a more powerful mapping tool for understanding problems and it is
also a technique that can be used for decision making. As the name
suggests, cognitive mapping is based on your understanding or cognition
of a problem or issue. The technique can aid your own thought processes
by laying out the logic of how you think and feel, your assumptions, etc.
Cognitive mapping can also be done as a group activity with a facilitator
who helps lay out the logic of others' thinking, assumptions, values etc.
and can then use this to show differences, build on commonalities, generate group maps, etc. Cognitive mapping can be used as an interviewing
technique, as a group activity, as a way of reading (gutting) documents, or
as a way of clarifying agendas for further meetings.

However the real strength of cognitive mapping is as a decision-making
tool. We can illustrate this by way of the example shown in Figure 14.3. To
structure a map, start with a statement or phrase about the problem or issue
(clarifying its meaning by stating what its opposite or converse is). Then
extend arrows from this (and subsequent statements or phrases) by stating
what it leads to (and its converse). Working back from your original statement ask what led to this problem or issue and have arrows leading from
this *into* your original statement. As you can see in Figure 14.3 the components of the problem or issue are arranged hierarchically with

- broad *goals* at the top of the map; then
- *strategic directions*: actions which require resources, may be long term,
  are costly, irreversible, may require a change in culture and need a portfolio of actions to bring them about; and at the bottom
- *potential options*: the specific actions required.

Here arrows of causation are such that options lead to (cause) desired strategic directions, which in turn 'lead to' goals.

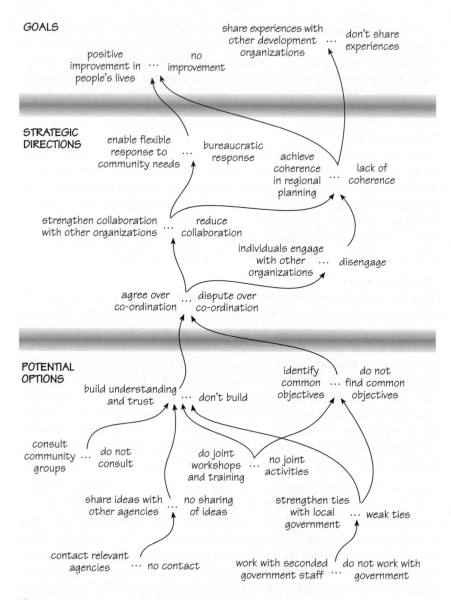

Figure 14.3 Fragment of a cognitive map

Figure 14.3 shows a fragment of a cognitive map drawn by an NGO staff member exploring the problems of relating to other development organizations working in the area. The NGO's stated goals were achieving improvement in people's lives through its work and the desire to share experience with other agencies in the region. These goals appear at the top of the map. In the middle of the map, strategic directions involved, for example, building trust and collaboration with different agencies. The options (actions) needed to meet these are below (for example, contacting agencies, doing joint activities and so on).

The problem was that tensions and misunderstandings between the different parties led to their disengagement with each other. The map maker thought that if some joint training needs could be discussed and agreed on, this would be an important step in bringing the organizations closer together. A second line of reasoning was that lack of inter-organizational relationships induced a lack of coherence in regional planning and, in turn resulted in bureaucratic responses to situations. This in turn fed into the growing tensions between the parties.

Such mapping is quite straightforward on a small scale, as with our example above. However, building more complex maps and/or working with a group turns cognitive mapping into a powerful decision-making tool.

Further reading on the mapping techniques described above (and others) can be found at the end of the chapter. It may not be immediately apparent how such techniques could help you with specific problems. You will need to try them out for yourself. The NGO manager with whom we worked on the above extract of a cognitive map had these comments to make on the exercise:

> I use this type of approach in my head anyway, having had some systems training. I think it is useful, unlike the problem tree which is too simple. That does things like identifies 'lack of trust' and then just says turn it into an opportunity and build trust. But how? You need to adopt an incremental approach, and recognize that these tools are not going to solve problems just help you analyse them.

> It is like a jigsaw puzzle. To do a jigsaw you have to have all the pieces, but in these cases you only have bits. You have to make a big picture with only some pieces. The map helps you to identify bits and start to see the connections. This can help you make decisions about action, but it doesn't in itself lead to solutions – it just lays issues out on the board.

> The problem I used in the map is quite specific and tight, but these cases, like this problem are multi-cultural, complex, characterized by poor communication, politics/economics/social issues interlinked. Every aspect of the problem is part of a complex environment.

> When I was younger, I would have stood up and told the committee they were wrong. I have learnt the hard way. This type of tool is useful in training people and giving them an ability to be proactive and ahead of the game (most NGOs are reactive). This can help stop panic and crisis management – it encourages you to look at different options.

14.3 ENGAGING STRATEGICALLY

> Think of a game of chess. Bad players (who may be crafty or cunning in details) play chess without a sense of strategy. They move pieces in terms of immediate opportunities or dangers, but fail to develop a campaign plan (a strategy) which structures their game as a whole. Good players do just that: they position pieces in view of a broader strategy and their tactics become an instrument of this strategy.
>
> (Wuyts, quoted in The Open University, U208, 1999, p. 108)

Appreciating a situation gets us beyond coping (usually) to being able to think more strategically about how to act. Cognitive mapping certainly helps in identifying what might be strategic options to consider.

Understanding your own and others' organizations is the important first step towards identifying and devising action points for building inter-organizational relationships. In the real world, with all its attendant pressures and time constraints, the temptation is often to try things and see what happens, without much preparation. In fact, we often have no alternative to relating with other organizations than on this basis. For example, the requirements of accountability to donors which face recipient organizations are often on terms not devised by the recipient. In any inter-organizational arrangement, whether between two organizations or involving many, issues of relative power and control of, and access to, resources, come into play significantly.

Being prepared – having a strategy – does not necessarily change power relations or inadequate resources but it can enable an organization to get the most out of their relationships with other organizations.

It is important, therefore when possible, to plan and resource inter-organizational relationships so that you have an idea of:

- what you are letting yourself in for;
- what might be of benefit to you; and
- what might be the value-added benefits for all the parties involved.

In brief, strategy is about being proactive. So how do you decide to act proactively in a given situation? How does strategy come about? One important clue to this is to recognize how other organizations tend to act and to be able to identify the kinds of strategies which are the outcome of such behaviour.

But is any particular strategy appropriate or obviously related to a particular institutional framework and way of organizing? A range of types of strategy suggested by Mintzberg and Waters (1998, p.31) are listed in Table 14.1. They are ideal types but give an idea of the ways in which strategy can be thought about and how strategy emerges. Comments from one of us are given in the right hand column of Table 14.1. (You might want to think about which ones would be particularly applicable to the way you work.)

TABLE 14.1 MINTZBERG AND WATERS' SUMMARY DESCRIPTION OF TYPES OF STRATEGIES (1998, P. 31)

Strategy	Major features	Our comments
Planned	Strategies originate in formal plans; precise intentions exist, formulated and articulated by central leadership, backed up by formal controls to ensure surprise-free implementation in benign, controllable or predictable environment; strategies most deliberate.	I think of co-ordination in the sense of the welfare state, with top-down planning and control.
Entrepreneurial	Strategies originate in central vision; intentions exist as personal, unarticulated vision of single leader, and so adaptable to new opportunities; organization under personal control of leader and located in protected niche in environment strategies relatively deliberate but can emerge.	This reminds me of ideas to do with winning, the individual engaged in competitive activity, although it also contains a strong hint of co-ordination, from the top in a hierarchy.
Ideological	Strategies originate in shared beliefs; intentions exist as collective vision of all actors, in inspirational form and relatively immutable, controlled normatively through indoctrination and/or socialization often proactive vis-à-vis environment; strategies rather deliberate.	As soon as anyone mentions shared beliefs I automatically think of co-operative action, tending to associate beliefs with values with voluntarism. In fact, once beyond that initial reaction, I realized that this description of strategy could apply to any type of organiz-ation driven by any particular ideal form, including those based on competitive principles. This type of strategy is based on the joint vision of actors within the organization, regardless of what type of organization it is.
Umbrella	Strategies originate in constraints; leadership, in partial control of organizational actions, defines strategic boundaries or targets within which other actors respond to own forces or to complex, perhaps also unpredictable environment; strategies partly deliberate, partly emergent and deliberately emergent.	Again, the word 'umbrella' immediately conjured up visions of co-operative ways of organizing. However, this is not what this type of strategy necessarily means. Instead it encompasses the idea that 'strategy originates in constraints'. In other words, there is no vision or plan providing strategic direction, rather a range of boundaries which are set, within which organizational actors operate. These, one assumes, define the limits of strategic action.

Process	Strategies originate in process; leadership controls process aspects of strategy (hiring, structure, etc.), leaving content aspects to other actors; strategies partly deliberate, partly emergent (and, again, deliberately emergent).	In the description of this type of strategy, I was left thinking about business organization, particularly multi-national companies which have a head office which determines overarching issues, but then country offices which develop their own plans relevant to their specific context. Thinking harder about it though, this is the kind of model of strategy that many international NGOs are ostensibly pursuing, setting broad value concerns and objectives through headquarters or international committees, and then leaving specifics to field offices, programmes or the independent units which make up a federal organizational model.
Unconnected	Strategies originate in enclaves; actor(s) loosely coupled to rest of organization produce(s) patterns in own actions in absence of, or in direct contradiction to central or common intentions; strategies organizationally emergent whether or not deliberate for actor(s).	This is resonant of rather fragmented, unhealthy forms of competition. A classic example being pretty much any development scenario where there are commonly many agencies with different agendas failing to talk to each other. However, the model of market competition would not describe strategy as developing in unconnected ways, since the price mechanism and attendant competitive forces would in fact provide a means through which organizations determine their strategy and its outcomes are then in some sense connected.
Consensus	Strategies originate in consensus; through mutual adjustment, actors converge on patterns that become pervasive in absence of central or common intentions; strategies rather emergent.	This makes me think of co-operative forms, again the assumption being that groups can only develop consensus through co-operation. But is there some inherent reason why organizations or groups organized around the principle of competition can't also effectively develop patterns based on mutual adjustment and emerging consensus?

| Imposed | Strategies originate in environment; environment dictates patterns in actions either through direct imposition or through implicitly pre-empting or bounding organizational choice; strategies mostly emergent, although may be internalized by organization and made deliberate. | The whole idea of imposition immediately conjures up images of state control through imposed co-ordination. But in the description of this strategy, Mintzberg and Waters are referring really to constraints or directions imposed by the environment. That may include government policy and action, but environment can also refer to other factors, such as technological or financial limitations and so on. |

It is useful to think about the descriptions and try to relate them to each of the ideal forms. It makes us think harder about what strategy actually means and how it comes about. It is clear that an organization's strategy is not simply about explicit planning, but is probably an ongoing process in which a number of factors play a role – environmental, organizational, individual and so on. In addition, any strategy adopted will have both intended and unintended consequences, or, in the words of Mintzberg and Waters, who distinguish '*deliberate* strategies — realized as intended – from *emergent* strategies – patterns or consistencies realized despite, or in the absence of, intentions' (1998, p. 20). As you read above, one manager described strategic thinking as 'being like doing a jigsaw puzzle for which you never have all the pieces'. You can piece some parts together and possibilities emerge, although others may not be clear, or only emerge later, if at all.

Relating the descriptions to each of the ideal forms also makes explicit a lot of the implicit assumptions we make about what different types of institutional framework, ways of organizing and organizations are – their assumed qualities and ways of operating. For example, that competitive organizations do not work on co-operative lines.

It is important to note that no single type of strategy is necessarily associated with a particular type of organization or way of organizing. Different ways of thinking about strategy, and of developing strategy, are available to all of us. No one approach, or one institutional form exists in a pure form, untouched by other forms and approaches. Thus, an organization which develops on competitive principles may adopt a consensus approach to strategy.

It is one thing to recognize the kind of strategy that your or others' organizations are involved in. This helps you to decide how to approach others. But we still need a basis from which to embark on these strategic directions.

Three broad strategies for inter-organizational relationships, identified by Hudson (1993), are for us a useful starting point for taking decisions on how to relate to other organizations. They involve recognition of the rules of the game with which one is going to have to contend. They are:

1 *Co-operative strategies*, key here will be engagement with processes of negotiation and exchange (of information, resources, etc);

2 *Incentive-based strategies*, where one is exploiting the institutional incentives that exist;

3 *Authoritative strategies*, where direction/co-ordination is through vertical or horizontal links.

Tennyson (1998) provides some useful guidelines on practical steps for planning and resourcing a relationship, particularly for co-operative strategies or partnerships. The steps include:

- *Decide* what you want to do. It seems obvious, but it is important that the relationship has a purpose!

- *Identify* partners who will best fit that purpose. Here your appreciation of other organizations will be invaluable in identifying the track record and resources of other organizations as well as the expertise and experience of their staff (with whom you will have to work).

- *Agree* core principles. These are often based on *equity* (measured by the value of each organization's knowledge, skills and representativeness), *transparency* (openness and honesty in transactions from which trust can grow), and *mutual benefit* (think back, for example, to the mutual benefits gained in Royds between community, private business and local government).

- *Formalize*, at least to some degree, the relationship (even if only in a Memorandum of Understanding in the first instance).

- *Set* objectives, possibly quite broad to begin with and then becoming more concrete as the relationship develops.

- *Engage* with stakeholders. Consult and act on this engagement. Again, think back to the Royds consultations and the compromises made as a result.

- *Mobilize* resources. As already mentioned, non-cash resources are particularly important. Expertise, labour, equipment, accommodation and supplies are as important as cash.

14.4 BUILDING TRUST, REFRAMING AND NETWORKS

For sustained relationships between organizations, trust as a control mechanism crops up constantly as a theme in this book. Trust is also an important term for this chapter since it is something that we as individuals can contribute towards directly through our own voluntary action, rather than something imposed by the disciplines of market or hierarchy.

14.4.1   TRUST

How is trust built? This is a question addressed by John Harriss in Chapter 10. First of all Harriss is quick to point out that cooperation based on trust in the real world is a messy and rather unpredictable process. So there are no quick, automatic or easy answers to the question of how to build trust. It is a process not a blueprint. Nor, we should add, is building trust a question of paying lip service to process, for example, through the mechanical use of participatory methods which nonetheless fail to win over the participation or trust of participants.

Thus Harriss is able to dismiss arguments which imply trust is merely a cultural predisposition. Instead he emphasizes other aspects (echoing Ebers 1997a, cited in Chapter 3) amongst which we find:

* positive experience of past transactions;
* personal and mutually 'approved' characteristics of potential co-operators (i.e. similar values);
* institutional rules and norms which regulate the behaviours of defined professions, business, etc.

The first of these, in particular when based on a series of small, incremental and sequential steps not only strengthens trust but can also create trust where none previously existed (or that had been destroyed earlier). Quoting the work of Sabel, Harriss goes on to point out how informal networks of individuals from different organizations are able to define their own needs in a particular context, very much along the lines described in the Royds programme in Chapter 13.

A very good example of a conscious decision to build trust in a different situation altogether is the one we find in Chapter 12 on the transformations taking place in South Africa's Land Bank. Here, as the chapter title suggest is a process of trust building going on in a context of wide-ranging institutional transformation both within and outside the bank. That this appears to be taking place in the context of co-ordinated (i.e. hierarchical – leadership is important here) change is even more compelling. Being competitive, just to round off the picture, is a key element for the future of the Land Bank

14.4.2   REFRAMING

The second key aspect or outcome of trust raised in Chapter 10 (p. 234) is the idea of reframing problems. Reframing is an expertise based on a combination of skill and tacit knowledge as we mentioned at the start of the chapter. It also has an 'unexpected' quality about it well described by Sabel. That is not to say that reframing automatically occurs. It comes about from looking at problems from different angles – through talking to different people and organizations with an open mind – trying to understand their meanings and not your assumptions. Reframing also comes about through putting together different 'configurations' of resources as discussed in Chapter 3. What comes through clearly from the Royds and Land Bank experiences is that reframing occurs through having the determination to make change happen.

14.4.3 NETWORK AGENTS

A rather specific aspect of inter-organizational relationships, but one which can act as a stimulus to trust and reframing is to be found in the notion of 'network agents' (Inskip, 1994). These are 'middle-level organizations that connect policy and services planning and development by facilitating communications between the macro (government generally) and micro (community groups or individuals) levels of governance' (Inskip, 1994). Such agents may be organizations or individuals. They are a resource that can be applied to making collaboration more viable by investing the necessary time and resources.

14.5 THE CONDITIONS FOR COLLABORATION

If an organization's strategy is to enter collaborative relations with other organizations, how do you go about it? The Wilder Foundation (Mattessich and Monsey, 1992) has identified 19 factors (under six broad headings) which are key to collaborative success. These factors were derived from a review of the US literature concerning collaboration in social services.

It is important first to note what the authors of the study define as collaboration. For them the term connotes more pervasive and durable relationships, bringing previously separated organizations into a new structure with full commitment to a common mission where authority is determined by the collaborative structure and resources are pooled and products shared. This definition corresponds most closely with co-operation as it has been defined in this book. However, the existence of these factors is also key in many other situations, even where durability or resource-pooling are not sought.

We asked the author of the last chapter – Gordon Wilson – to comment on this checklist in the light of his research in Royds. He said that although there were seldom clear-cut responses to many of the factors, he found them relevant and answerable in some way. The 19 factors, under their headings and Gordon Wilson's comments are reproduced in Table 14.2.

TABLE 14.2 THE ROYDS REGENERATION PROJECT AND THE WILDER FOUNDATION'S 'KEYS TO COLLABORATIVE SUCCESS'

Factor (Mattessich and Monsey, 1992)	Comments on these factors in Royds (Gordon Wilson)
ENVIRONMENTAL	
History of collaboration in the community	No particular instances of historical collaboration prior to Royds. There was a local authority-run 'Bradford South Area Panel' which enabled tenants on the estates to air grievances; also there were tenants'/residents' associations prior to Royds which agitated for better conditions on the estates.
Collaborative group seen as a leader in the community	This seems to be the case; in fact it appears that Royds is in some ways seen as the local government. Resident directors on the Board are stopped in the street, pub, etc. and often asked to sort out matters that strictly are Bradford Council's responsibility.
Political/ social climate favourable	The Single Regeneration Budget (SRB) was a UK Conservative (political right) government strategy for addressing urban regeneration. It fitted in with their ideas of moving from dependency to self-sufficiency, hence the emphasis on the regeneration being resident-led and economic regeneration (training, business start-up grants – an estate of entrepreneurs?) as well as social and physical regeneration. The aims also fit with the New Labour (political left) ideas on partnership between private and social sectors, the stakeholder society, and the holistic attack on social exclusion.
MEMBERSHIP CHARACTERISTICS	
Mutual respect, understanding, and trust	This hasn't always been present. The local authority was originally suspicious that the resident-majority Board could cope with the large sums of money involved, but the local authority representatives have come round (whether the Council as an institution has come round is a different matter). Similarly, Housing Association, police, churches have been impressed.
Appropriate cross-section of members	Royds Board has 22 members – 12 of whom (i.e. the majority) are resident directors (including the chair), three are local authority representatives (two Labour, one Conservative), one housing association, one from the Bradford council of churches, one from the main developer, the rest from Bradford's 'great and good'.
Members see collaboration as in their self-interest	Little directly on this, but implicitly it is obviously the case. Royds Community Association is at pains to stress partnership with private business, and the chair respects the private business ethos of being clear about what the objectives are.

Ability to compromise	My impression is that most compromises are with the private sector and those who hold the purse strings. Some compromises with residents on details of proposals, but not that much is changed as a result of consultation with residents. I discussed different accountabilities at length in my interview with the general manager.

PROCESS/STRUCTURE

Members share a stake in both process and outcome	I'm not so sure that private sector is that bothered [concerned with the project]. It is present in Royds because money has been pumped there, but it would be no great loss to the private sector if Royds folded. The Board meeting, however, did give a sense of shared process and outcome.
Multiple layers of decision-making	There are sub-groups representing the different facets of regeneration – economic, physical, social. Final decisions go to the Board.
Flexibility	Board meetings are run quite autocratically. Chair obviously has a clear view. But there is a general flexibility towards different stakeholder interests.
Development of clear roles and policy guidelines	The aims and objectives of Royds are pretty clear.
Adaptability	The Board does adapt to constraints, especially constraints that arise from private sector involvement. e.g. because a new 'village' centre for the Buttershaw estate had to be shelved because the private sector would not pay for infrastructure, the debate moved on to providing several smaller satellite facilities rather than large centralized ones.

COMMUNICATION

Open and frequent communication/ Established informal and formal communication links	There are complaints from resident directors of Buttershaw estate at the Board meeting that they had not been consulted over some new plans. Also, general complaints that important background papers are not always available prior to Board meetings. At the informal level on the estates, resident-directors are at the 'beck and call' of residents who frequently stop them in the streets, pubs, etc. Formally, there are the public consultation roadshows.

PURPOSE

Concrete, attainable goals and objectives	One criticism is that goals and objectives are too easily attained as they relate only to inputs (how many people on a training course, etc.). Suggestion by general manager that goals and objectives should be more related to quality of inputs and to outputs (how many trained people get jobs, for example).
Shared vision	General view that there is a shared vision although the chair hinted darkly that the local authority does not always share the vision when we interviewed him.

Unique purpose (goals unique to individual organization in group)	It is difficult to say whether the broad social goals of Royds differ from, for example, the goals of the private developers. Perhaps the latter only go along with the social goals insofar as they don't clash with their bottom-line, profit goals.
RESOURCES	
Sufficient funds	The SRB amounted to £31m, and this has immediately attracted more money ('when you have that sort of money, others immediately come forward'). It is estimated that Royds now has over £100m to use. Is this sufficient? The more you do, the more you need. The length of the piece of string cannot be measured.
Skilled convenor	Some had doubts about the chair of Royds at the start, but all have come round and think that he's very good. He has a good knack of grasping and explaining in straight language many of the complex issues. He was particularly impressive at the Board meeting.

What the assessment of the Royds estate in Table 14.2 suggests is that many of the factors necessary for successful collaboration are in place at this point in time. This augurs well for continued and effective action. However, over time, certain factors may change (for example, the level of resourcing, or the chair may be replaced). What strikes us though, based on the information in the table and Chapter 13, is that processes and a history of interaction have been developed which should allow for adjustments to be made for change. Even if this particular initiative falls apart in the future, the process has helped to develop the 'social capital' which will emerge in other forms of action.

So, we understand a situation better through developing our appreciation. We may have taken strategic decisions as a result on how to collaborate and we know the factors that need to be in place for a collaboration to have a chance of success. What do we do next? Inskip's (1994) framework for the process that network agents could perform is applicable to any inter-organizational relationship (a similar checklist can be found in Tennyson, 1998, p. 67). The suggested steps are:

1 scan the contextual environment;
2 identify and communicate the problem;
3 identify potential network participants who share the problem;
4 mobilize networks of appropriate network participants;
5 learn continuously about the problem in inductive and iterative inter-actions with network participants;

6   build a consensus of values about the problem and about its potential solutions;

7   work on power relationships among participants;

8   negotiate conflicts among participants;

9   agree on long term goals for the resolution of the problem;

10 develop action plans to solve the problems;

11 potentially develop organizations to manage the problem on a long term basis.

This might appear rather mechanical and abstract but, adapted to specific circumstances, it can be useful as a set of 'actions' that need to be taken. However, it doesn't answer the question of how certain problems are resolved. For example, 'learn continuously ...', 'build a consensus ...', 'work on power relations ...', 'negotiate conflicts ...' and so on are all big and tricky issues.

14.5.1   OVERCOMING OBSTACLES

There is a tendency to overlook the political problems and barriers in discussions of inter-organizational relationships. Nowhere is this more apparent than in the areas of organizational autonomy and power relations. For example, how does an organization retain its autonomy whilst working jointly with other organizations? As we have said elsewhere, this is a question of being clear about what all parties want from collaboration, as well as being clear that any loss of autonomy and of resources invested in collaboration will have a pay-off. Hence the importance of engaging *strategically*. In this way, it should be possible to maintain your organization's agenda or goals and at the same time avoid pointless conflict or replication of effort.

There are practical steps which can be taken to help overcome impediments to successful inter-organizational relationships, the most important of which is to be open about acknowledging their existence and to confront them directly. Tennyson (1998), again, has some useful common sense tips here, for which the mapping techniques discussed in Section 14.2 may come in very useful:

1   *Identify the obstacle(s)*. They may be several but can include such things as:

- *confused or conflicting priorities* (e.g. overemphasis on money, different priorities and hidden agendas, absence of shared goals, cross-cultural or cross-sectoral intolerance etc.);

- *people limitations* (e.g. competition between strong personalities, lack of leadership, lack of appropriate skills, lack of staff confidence etc.);

- *process frustrations* (e.g. conflicts with pre-existing hierarchical organizational structure, over-lengthy consultation without action, loss
  of focus, failure to carry out agreed action, low commitment etc.).
  In addition, there may be external, institutional obstacles that need
  to be identified.

2 *Meet the 'challenge'* (often used as the opposite pole to 'obstacles',
   much as one might use in cognitive mapping). This might involve:

   - developing better skills (see, for example, Section 14.6 on
     win-win negotiation);

   - widening the expertise base by including others;

   - stepping back to think strategically rather than just tactically (as in
     Section 14.2);

   - responding positively to difficulties;

   - modifying your behaviour to unlock a tense situation etc.

3 *The option to say 'no'* if problems persist (or others may say 'no' to
   you). Overcoming obstacles, however, may have positive and
   unexpected outcomes: new ideas, greater commitment or greater
   impact etc.

14.6 OTHER PRACTICES FOR INTER-ORGANIZATIONAL RELA-TIONSHIPS

There are a number of other areas of expertise which are helpful in developing inter-organizational relationships which this section provides a brief
introduction to.

14.6.1 TYPOLOGIES AND MODELS OF PARTNERSHIP

As with the business literature surveyed in Chapter 3, there are numerous
models, typologies and criteria for networks and partnerships in the development business. See for example, Chapter 8 by John Bennett and Chapter
11 by Angela Penrose in this volume, Tennyson (1998, Appendix B) and
Fowler (1997). These have a useful function – as we have seen in the Royds
example in Section 14.5 – but they can only have real relevance when
applied and adjusted to specific circumstances.

14.6.2 PROCESS AND GETTING TO KNOW PEOPLE

As was discussed in Chapter 3 where the 'long-term and socially embedded nature of inter-organizational relationships' was stressed, process is
key in building inter-organizational relationships. This is reiterated in other
chapters in the way that trust is build up incrementally and over time.

The experience of the Land Bank in Chapter 12 is a good example. In the
process of transformation – institutional and organizational – Helena Dolny
noted that consultation had positive results:

The impact of consultation with our stakeholders was tremendous. Stakeholders themselves were amazed that their inputs were being solicited, and that they were being listened to … (p.265)

The process of building that effective organization has not been simply a matter of introducing 'hard' organizational technologies … but of developing 'soft' organizational technologies – creating space to talk, active consultation, emphasizing continued communication. The process has been about maintaining and building trust between an array of stakeholders; creating a more effective and competitive organization through co-operative action. (p. 269)

14.6.3 DOING RESEARCH

Sources of knowledge are diverse. Ways of getting that knowledge are multiple. For us finding out just about anything counts as research – from someone's phone number, to compiling the data for the next World Development Report, to learning the expressed needs of a community of refugees, or of the Royds estates' residents.

In working with inter-organizational relationships, sometimes the only way to find out if collaboration is on the cards is to broach the subject by going to talk to other organizations. But there is always merit in finding out as much as you can from other sources too.

Such finding out is part of the appreciation discussed earlier. But research doesn't stop there. Inter-organizational relationships are not automatic nor costless. They have to be nurtured and invested in. An important component of this is researching how the process is going and to use this as a feedback mechanism for keeping the relationship on track and/or adjusting the process to ensure that mutually beneficial outcomes do indeed occur. That is partly a process of learning (of which more below).

To achieve this, it is probably inadequate simply to research *on* something. It becomes necessary to be part of the process; to participate in what some call action research where all who participate are co-learners – including the researcher. Because of the long-term nature of inter-organizational relationships, 'snapshot' results seldom give an accurate enough picture of what is really happening (over time) nor, therefore, what adjustments might need to be made over the life of the relationship.

Some sources of useful discussion and guidelines for choosing methodologies and carrying out research are given under further reading at the end of this chapter.

14.6.4 REPLICATING LEARNING

Working as a 'learning organization' is one the many buzz words current in management. One thing is clear, there are no blueprints for building inter-organizational relationships. Replicating others' experiences can only be achieved with a sharp eye to the particularities of any situation and set of relationships. But learning can take place both from others and one's own experiences.

Ross *et al.* (1994) define learning in organizations as 'the continuous testing of experience, and the transformation of that experience into knowledge – accessible to the whole organization and relevant to its core purpose' (p. 49). This principle can be applied to inter-organizational learning as well as internal learning. Information exchange is a key component of such learning.

A singular contribution to the challenge of developing relationships can be found in Chambers (1997). Here he writes about changing institutions and challenges the managerial professionalism of the development business. It also introduces strategies for building relationships through 'reversals' of assumptions.

Chambers argues strongly against hierarchies of control and co-ordination. Indeed he argues that in an ideal world hierarchies need to be reversed – putting the last first. As he says:

> ... the institutional challenge for all development agencies is to become learning organizations: to flatten and soften hierarchy, to develop a culture of participatory management, to recruit a gender and disciplinary mix of staff committed to people, and to adopt and promote procedures, norms and rewards which permit and encourage more open-ended participation at all levels.
>
> (Chambers, 1997, p. 224).

The strategies (and tactics) that Chambers recommends for such changes to take place in learning organizations are:

- commit with continuity;
- network with allies;
- start small and slow;
- fund flexibly;
- train, support and encourage grass roots staff;
- build out and up from grass roots success.

Idealistic? Chambers thinks not. A major bottleneck to change, according to him, is what he calls 'normal professionalism – the ideas, values, methods and behaviours accepted and dominant in professions and disciplines'.

In fact, we often need to learn to learn. There are different ways in which learning can take place – through participant observation, study visits, exchange visits, internship, secondment, etc. – but a common feature is interaction. Learning which benefits an organization or several rather than an individual needs to be communicated and shared. That way, learning can be translated in action to improve inter-organizational relationships and learning also becomes institutionalized.

The implications of Chambers' (and others') work is that one of the greatest challenges in inter-organizational relationships is to put aside our preconceived notions about others and be open to new ideas and new ways of doing things. This is the gist of the next section which introduces negotiation and brokering.

14.7 NEGOTIATING AND BROKERING INTER-ORGANIZATIONAL RELATIONSHIPS

Negotiation and brokering permeate all aspects of inter-organizational relationships and therefore we will end this chapter with a short discussion of some of the basic approaches in this area. First, we briefly consider the traditional approach to negotiation and then four principles useful for creating 'win-win' negotiations. The principles of negotiation and brokering sketched here act as a useful reminder that building inter-organizational relationships is not merely a technical issue about resources or contracts. It is a very human and social activity where success comes down to your and others' ability to work together to reach mutually beneficial goals.

14.7.1 POSITIONAL BARGAINING

Negotiating and bargaining have commonly been perceived as some sort of haggling over different positions, for example arguing over the price of something, reacting to a set of trade union demands or trying to get a larger grant from the local authority. These are all forms of positional bargaining; that is, each of the parties has a particular position which it seeks to advance in the face of what are seen as the opposing and incompatible positions and demands of other parties. The assumptions are of the 'win-lose' type. Such positional bargaining may be quite 'hard line' or may have a superficial friendly or 'soft' aspect to it, but this softness belies the underlying 'win-lose' nature. Indeed, it may be a deliberate tactic to gain advantage.

Voluntary and non-profit organizations are not immune from the pressures to adopt a positional approach. 'Sticking to our principles', 'protecting our clients', 'asserting our right to autonomy' – all these sorts of commitment can lead to a sense of internal and external negotiations as 'win-lose', positional affairs. Yet, the limitations of such a confrontational approach are such that a better way needs to be found if at all possible.

14.7.2 FOUR CONSTRUCTIVE APPROACHES TO NEGOTIATING

Fisher and Urry (1986) advocate four basic approaches to negotiation which begin to overcome the problems, limitations and impasses of positional bargaining.

Separate the people from the problem

All negotiations involve two elements: the substantive issue over which you are negotiating and your relationship with other people involved in the negotiation process. One of the recurring problems in negotiations is that these become hopelessly intertwined. Taking the sort of approach which separates the issues from the personalities requires a conscious effort from you to consistently make that separation. Practical steps towards this are to

- ask people what their intentions are – instead of just assuming them;
- be open about your perceptions;
- avoid ascribing motives and feelings to the other party.

A consistently positive approach to the other people helps make this separation. In terms of the issues, it is wise to develop options that give them a stake in the outcome and to develop proposals which they can accept without loss of face.

Focus on interests, not positions
It is important to get behind specific positions to address the more general interests and concerns of the various parties in a negotiation. Once into this area, rather than the specific positions adopted, it may be that there is more scope for compatibility than at first appeared possible. The fact that all parties have multiple interests extends the scope of what is possible. Such an approach helps the people involved to focus attention primarily on the problem rather than on their respective solutions.

Invent options for mutual gain
Given the complexity of even the smallest organizations, there is unlikely to be a single 'right' solution to an organizational issue. The positional assumption of a single 'win-lose' solution is not really valid. The negotiation process does not have to be a limited trade-off between a fixed set of options. A search for alternatives and for mutually advantageous outcomes is possible within the framework of a negotiation. This requires being prepared to develop and explore innovative options, suspending judgement till much later in the process.

Insist on objective criteria
Talk of 'win-win' outcomes should not, of course, conceal the fact that interests do conflict and that deals have to be struck. What this approach is about is seeking to ensure that the eventual agreement is underpinned by reference to a set of agreed principles or a formula which all participants recognize as valid. Thus, it is important that the outcome is not dependent on the wills of the parties alone. Rather, the questions this approach would prompt you to ask (depending on the context) would be things like:

- What is the basis on which you would find a solution acceptable?
- What specific standards of care are needed for the performance of this unit to be seen as acceptable again?
- What are the standards by which you would assess whether or not our operation is environmentally acceptable?

Whilst such principles and criteria may be subject to renegotiations later, since circumstances and standards change over time, it is important that negotiated agreements reinforce the basic coherence and reasoned justification that are essential organizational life.

14.8 CONCLUSIONS

Perhaps you have found this an idiosyncratic mix of practical ideas of developing inter-organizational relationships – we hope so. There are too many contexts and too many techniques out there to hope to be comprehensive. We do also hope, however, that we have raised some possibilities for combining ways of organizing for you too. For us the most compelling examples of such possibilities have been related in the experiences of the Land Bank in South Africa, the Royds programme in the UK and the story recounted from Sabel in Chapter 10. No doubt you will have found other useful tips in other chapters of the book.

If there is one message that we would like to end with, it is this: contingency, flexibility and your own imagination are the only limiting factors to developing inter-organizational relationships for mutual benefit whatever your field of work. Use whatever tools you feel most comfortable with. That way they will work.

FURTHER READING

The following are useful sources of further information for some of the techniques, concepts and ideas briefly introduced in this chapter. Sources referenced directly in the chapter are included in the references at the end of this book.

Choosing methodologies and carrying out research

Bell, J. (1993) *Doing your research project: A guide for first time researchers in education and social science*, second edition, Buckingham, Open University Press.

Hewitt, T. and Johnson, H. (eds.) (1999) 'Special issue on Development Management in Practice', *Development in Practice*, vol. 9, nos. 1 and 2.

Pratt, B. and Loizos, P. (1992) *Choosing Research Methods: An Oxfam Development Guideline*, Oxford, Oxfam, 128pp.

Thomas, A., Chataway, J. and Wuyts, M. (1998) *Finding Out Fast: Investigative Skills for Policy and Development*, Sage Publications in association with The Open University, London, 376 pp.

Tennyson, R. (1998) Chapter 7 of *Managing partnerships: tools for mobilising the public sector, business and civil society as partners in development*, London, The Prince of Wales Business Leaders Forum.

Yin, R. (1984) *Case Study Research: Design and Methods*, Sage Publications, London, Thousand Oaks and New Delhi.

Learning

Chambers (1997) *Whose Reality Counts? Putting the First Last*, London, Intermediate Technology Publications.

Eden, C. and Huxham, C. (1996) 'Action research for the study of organizations', in S. Clegg, C. Hardy and W. Nord (eds.), *Handbook of Organization Studies*, Beverly Hills, Sage.

Eden, C. and Ackermann, F. (1998) *Making Strategy: the Journey of Strategic Management*, London, Sage.

Senge, P., Kleiner, A., Roberts, C., Ross, R.B. and Smith, B.J. (1994) *The Fifth Discipline Fieldbook: Strategies and Tools for Building a Learning Organization*, London, Nicholas Brearley Publishing Ltd.

Tennyson (1998) Chapter 4 of *Managing Partnerships: Tools for Mobilising the Public Sector, Business and Civil Society as Partners in Development*, London, The Prince of Wales Business Leaders Forum.

Mapping

Ackermann, F., Eden, C. and Cropper, S. *Decision Explorer: Getting Started with Mapping* [online], Management Science, University of Strathclyde. Available from http://www.banxia.com/depaper.html [Accessed May 24 1999]

Carter, R.B., Martin, J.N.T., Mayblin, W. and Munday, M. (1984) *Systems Management and Change: a graphic guide*, London, Harper and Row.

Giles, K. and Hedge, N. (1998) *The Manager's Good Study Guide*, Milton Keynes, The Open University.

Jenkins, M. (1998) 'The theory and practice of comparing causal maps' in C. Eden and J.-C. Spender (eds.), *Managerial and Organizational Cognition: Theory, Methods and Research*, London, Sage.

Laukkanen, M. (1998) 'Conducting causal mapping research: opportunities and challenges' in C. Eden and J.-C. Spender (eds.), *Managerial and Organizational Cognition: Theory, Methods and Research*, London, Sage.

Martin, J. (1997) B882 *Creative Management* Block 2 *Techniques*, Milton Keynes, Open University.

Practicalities of negotiation and brokering

Lane, A. (2000) T552 *Systems Thinking and Practice: Diagramming*, Milton Keynes, Open University.

Nierenberg (1991) *The Complete Negotiator: The Step-by-Step Plan used by Top Professionals across the Country*, New York, Berkley Books.

REFERENCES

Abrahamsson, H. and Nilsson, A. (1995) *Mozambique: The Troubled Transition*, London, Zed Books.

Adiin-Yaansah, E. (1995) *An Analysis of Domestic Legislation to Regulate the Activities of Local and Foreign NGOs in Croatia, Kenya, Rwanda and Uganda*, Refugee Studies Programme and the Centre for Socio-Legal Studies, Oxford University.

Agbaje, A. (1990) 'In search of building blocks: The state, civil society, voluntary action and grassroots development in Africa', *Africa Quarterly*, vol. 30, pp. 24-40.

Ake, C. (1978) *Revolutionary Pressures in Africa*, London, Zed Press Ltd.

Alter, C. and Hage, J. (1993) *Organisations Working Together*, Newbury Park CA, Sage Publications.

Angell, A. (1996) 'Improving the Quality and Equity of Education in Chile: The Programa 900 Escuelas and The MECE-Basica', in Silva, A. (ed.) *Implementing Policy Innovations in Latin America. Politics, Economics and Techniques*, Washington DC, Inter-American Development Bank.

Anon (1984) *North/South Dialogue and UNCTAD*, an anonymous internal US administrative document, dated Feb.16.

Bennett, J. (1995) *Meeting Needs: NGO Co-ordination in Practice*, London, Earthscan Publications Ltd.

Bennett, J. (1997) *NGO Co-ordination at Field Level: A Handbook*, Oxford, ICVA/INTRAC, new edition, first published 1994.

Bennett, J. and Gibbs, S. (1996) *NGO Funding Strategies: An Introduction for Southern and Eastern NGOs*, Oxford, ICVA/INTRAC.

Beres, Z. and Wilson, G. (1997) 'Essential emotions: the place of passion in a feminist network', *Nonprofit Management and Leadership*, vol. 8, no. 2, pp. 171-188.

Bessant, J. and Francis, D. (1999) 'Policy initiatives in transitional environments – Using learning networks to help improve manufacturing competitiveness', *Technovation*, vol. 19, no. 6/7, pp. 373-381.

Bradach, J. and Eccles, R. (1989) 'Price, authority and trust: from ideal types to plural forms', *Annual Review of Sociology*, pp.97-118 [page references relate to the abridged version published in Thompson, G. *et al.* (eds.), 1991].

Brett, E.A. (1993) 'Voluntary agencies as development organisations: theorizing the problem of efficiency and accountability', *Development and Change*, vol. 24, no. 2, pp. 269-303.

Brett, E.A. (1995) 'Institutional theory and social change in Uganda', in Harriss, J., Hunter, J. and Lewis, C. (eds.) *The New Institutional Economics and Third World Development*, London, Routledge.

Brett, E.A. (1996) 'The participatory principle in development projects: the costs and benefits of cooperation', *Public Administration and Development*, vol. 16, no. 1, pp. 5-19.

Britton, B. (1994) 'Partnership in South Asia', *SARO Discussion Paper* no. 1, Save the Children (UK) South Asia Regional Office, Kathmandu, October.

Burawoy, M. (1996) 'The state and economic involution: Russia through a China lens', *World Development*, vol. 24, no. 6, pp.1105-1118.

Cannon, C. (1996) 'The NGO-government relationship: A case study from Uganda', unpublished paper, Nuffield College, Oxford.

Castells, M. (1996) *The Information Age: Economy Society and Culture. Volume 1: The Rise of the Network Society*, Oxford, Blackwell.

CCRD (1997) *New Opportunities for Regions: 15 Examples of Rural Development*, The Hague, Co-ordination Centre for Rural Development.

Chambers, R. (1997) *Whose Reality Counts? Putting the First Last*, London, Intermediate Technology Publications.

Chandler, A.D. (1977) *The Visible Hand: the Managerial Revolution in American Business*, Cambridge MA, Harvard University Press.

Chataway, J. (1998) 'Building capacity in biotechnology: The role of networks and partnerships', UNCTAD Conference on Partnerships and Networks in Energy and Biotechnology in Developing Countries, Malta, September.

Chisholm, D. (1989) *Coordination without Hierarchy. Informal Structures in Multiorganizational Systems*, Berkeley, Los Angeles and London, University of California Press.

Clark, J. (1991) *Democratizing Development: The Role of Voluntary Organizations*, London, Earthscan Publications Ltd.

Coulson, A. (1982) *Tanzania: A Political Economy*, Oxford, Clarendon Press.

Crosslines (1996) 'WorldAid '96', a special supplement of *Crosslines Global Report*, Geneva, International Centre for Humanitarian Reporting, September.

D'Angelo, G. (1996) *Working with Partners*, discussion paper from Training Workshop of El Zamorano, Honduras, August.

DANIDA (1996) *The International Response to Conflict and Genocide: Lessons from the Rwanda Experience*, Copenhagen, DANIDA, March.

Deakin, S. and Wilkinson, F. (1997) 'What makes markets work?', *New Economy*, vol. 4, no. 3, pp. 155-158.

DeBresson, C. and Amesse, F. (1991) 'Networks of innovators: a review and introduction to the issue', *Research Policy*, vol. 20, no. 5, pp. 363-379.

DeJong, J. (1991) 'Non-governmental organisations and health delivery in Sub-Saharan Africa', WPS708, Population and Human Resources Department, World Bank.

Deutsch, M. (1985) *Distributive Justice: A Social Psychological Perspective*, New Haven, Yale University Press.

DFID (1997) *Eliminating World Poverty: A Challenge for the 21st Century*, White Paper on International Development, Department for International Development, London, HMSO.

Doner, R. F. and Ramsay, A. (1997) 'Competitive clientelism and economic governance: the case of Thailand', in Maxfield, S. and Schneider, B.R. (eds.) *Business and the State in Developing Countries*, Ithaca and London, Cornell University Press.

Donini, A. (1995) 'Surfing the crest of the wave until it crashes: intervention in the South', *Journal of Humanitarian Assistance*, http://www-jha.sps.cam.ac.uk/a/a009.htm, posted on 3 October 1995.

Dosi, G. (1988) 'The nature of the innovative process', in Dosi, G., Freeman, C., Nelson, R., Silverberg, G. and Soete, L. (eds.) *Technical Change and Economic Theory*, London, Pinter Publishers.

Drèze, J. and Sen, A. (1989) *Hunger and Public Action*, Oxford, Clarendon Press.

Drinkwater, M. (1991) *The State and Agrarian Change in Zimbabwe's Communal Areas*, London, Macmillan.

Durkheim, E. (1964) *The Division of Labour in Society*, New York, Free Press.

Easton, G. (1996) 'Review article: only connect: networks and organizations', *Organization*, vol. 3, no. 2, pp. 291-310.

Ebers, M. (1997a) 'Explaining inter-organizational network formation' in Ebers, M. (ed.) *The Formation of Inter-organizational Networks*, New York, Oxford University Press.

Ebers, M. (ed.) (1997b) *The Formation of Inter-organizational Networks*, New York, Oxford University Press.

Edwards, M. and Hulme, D. (eds.) (1992) *Making A Difference: NGOs and Development in a Changing World*, London, Earthscan Publications Ltd.

Eisenhardt, K.M. and Schoonhoven, C.B. (1996) 'Resource-based view of strategic alliance formation: strategic and social effects in entrepreneurial firms' *Organization Studies*, vol. 7, no. 7, pp. 136-150.

Elkington, J. and Burke, T. (1987) *The Green Capitalists*, London, Gollancz.

EU (1996) European Union Presidency letter to the Secretary-General, Permanent Mission of Ireland to the United Nations, 16th October 1996.

Evans, P. (1996) 'Government action, social capital and development: Reviewing the evidence on synergy', *World Development*, no. 24, vol. 6, pp. 1119-1132.

Farrington, J. and Bebbinton, A. (1993) *Reluctant Partners? Non-governmental Organizations, the State and Sustainable Agricultural Development*, Routledge, London and New York.

Fayol, H. (1916) *General and Industrial Management*, original published in French; translated 1949, London, Pitman Publishing.

Feyerherm, A. (1994) 'Multiple paths for inter-organizational journeys', paper prepared for the Workshop on Multi-organisational Partnerships: Working Together across Organisational Boundaries, European Institute for Advanced Studies in Management, Brussels, September 19-20.

Fisher, R. and Urry, W. (1986) *Getting to YES*, London, London Business Books Ltd.

Forsgren, M., Hagg, I., Hakansson, H., Johanson, J. and Mattsson, L.-G. (1995) 'Firms in networks: A new perspective on competitive power', *Studia Oeconomiae Negitorium* no. 38, Uppsala, Acta Universtatis Upsaliensis.

Fowler A. (1997) *Striking a Balance: A Guide to Enhancing the Effectiveness of Non-governmental Organizations in International Development*, London INTRAC/Earthscan Publications Ltd.

Fowler, A., Campbell, P. and Pratt, B. (1992) *Institutional Development and NGOs In Africa: Policy Perspectives for European Development Agencies*, International NGO Training and Research Centre and Novib, Oxford and The Hague.

Fox, J. (1994) 'The difficult transition from clientelism to citizenship', *World Politics*, vol. 46, no 2. pp. 151-184.

Friedman, M. (1962) *Capitalism and Freedom*, Chicago, Chicago University Press.

Fukuyama, F. (1995) *Trust: the Social Virtues and Creation of Prosperity*, London, Penguin Books.

Gambetta, D. (1988) 'Can we trust trust?', in Gambetta, D. (ed.) *Trust: Making and Breaking of Co-operative Relationships*, Oxford, Blackwell, 295p.

Gibbons, M., Limoges, C., Nowotny, H., Schwartzman, S., Scott, P. and Trow, M. (1994) *The New Production of Knowledge: The Dynamics of Science and Research in Contemporary Societies*, London, Sage Publications.

Gibson, J.G. (1990) 'Bureaucratic power and public policies: a critique of a test of the rational staff maximization hypothesis', *Political Studies*, vol. 38, no. 2, pp. 330-334.

Giddens, A. (1989) *Sociology*, Cambridge, Polity Press.

Gilson, L., Sen, P.D., Mohammed, S. and Mujinja, P. (1994) 'The potential of health sector non-governmental organisations: policy options', *Health Policy and Planning*, vol. 9, no. 1, pp. 14-24.

Government of Tanzania (1994) *Proposals for Health Sector Reform*, Dar es Salaam, Ministry of Health, Government of Tanzania.

Government of Tanzania (1995) *National District Health Planning Guidelines*, Version 1.0, Dar es Salaam, Ministry of Health, Government of Tanzania.

Government of Tanzania (1996) *Health Sector Reform Plan of Action (1996-1999)*, May/Revision 1, Dar es Salaam, Ministry of Health, Government of Tanzania.

Grandori, A. (1997) 'An organizational assessment of interfirm co-ordination modes', *Organization Studies*, vol. 18, no. 6, pp. 897-926.

Grandori, A. and Soda, G. (1995) 'Inter-firm networks: antecedents, mechanisms and forms', *Organization Studies*, vol. 16, no. 2, pp. 183-214.

Granovetter, M. (1973) 'The strength of weak ties', *American Journal of Sociology*, vol. 78, no. 6, pp. 1360-1380.

Granovetter, M. (1985) 'Economic action and social structure: the problem of embeddedness', *American Journal of Sociology* no. 91; reprinted in Granovetter, M. and Swedberg, R. (eds.) (1992) *The Sociology of Economic Life*, Boulder, Westview Press.

Green, A. and Matthias, A. (1994) 'Government and NGO roles and relationships in policy making: The health sector in Zimbabwe', paper presented at 'NGOs and Development: Performance and Accountability in the New World Order', International Development and Public Management, University of Manchester, UK.

Guha, R. (1991) *The Unquiet Woods: Ecological Change and Peasant Resistance in the Himalaya*, Delhi, Oxford University Press.

Hakansson, H. and Snehota, I. (1994) *Developing Relationships in Business Networks*, London, Routledge.

Handy, C. (1995) *The Empty Raincoat*, London, Arrow Business Books.

Hanlon, J. (1984) *Mozambique: The Revolution Under Fire*, London, Zed Books.

Hanlon, J. (1991) *Mozambique: Who Calls the Shots*, London, James Currey.

Hanlon, J. (1996) *Peace Without Profit*, London, James Currey.

Hanlon, J. (1997) 'It's the IMF that runs Mozambique' in Sogge, D. (ed.) *Mozambique Perspectives on Aid and Civil Sector,* Oegsteest (Netherlands), Gemeenschappelijk Overleg Medefinanciering.

Harriss, J. (1999) 'Social capital', guest lecture given at Open University residential school for TU872 *Institutional Development: Conflicts, Values and Meanings*, Loughborough, 8th February 1999.

Harriss, J. and De Renzio, P. (1997) "Missing link' or analytically missing?: The concept of social capital', *Journal of International Development*, vol. 9, no. 6.

Held, D. (1987) *Models of Democracy*, Cambridge, Polity Press.

Hewitt, T. (1999) 'Institutional tensions and private sector promotion in Tanzania: Whose agenda?', *Technovation*, vol. 19, nos. 6/7, pp. 383-391.

Hewitt, T. and Wield, D. (1997) 'Networks in Tanzanian industrialisation.' *Science and Public Policy*, vol. 24, no. 6, pp. 395-404.

Hill, M. (1978) *The United Nations System: Coordinating its Economic and Social Work*, Cambridge, Cambridge University Press.

Hirschman, A.O. (1970) *Exit, Voice and Loyalty: Responses to Decline in Firms, Organizations and States*, Cambridge MA, Harvard University Press.

Hood, C. (1991) 'A public administration for all seasons?', *Public Administration*, vol. 69, no. 1, pp. 3-19.

Hood, C. (1996) 'Control over bureaucracy: cultural theory and institutional variety', *Journal of Public Policy*, vol. 15, no. 3, pp. 207-30.

Hudson, B. (1993) 'Collaboration in social welfare: A framework for analysis', in Hill, M. (ed.) *The Policy Process: A Reader*, New York and London, Harvester Wheatsheaf, pp. 362-376.

Hudson, B. (1993) 'Collaboration in social welfare: a framework for analysis', in Hill, M. (ed.) *The Policy Process: A Reader*, New York and London, Harvester Wheatsheaf.

Hughes, O.E. (1994) *Public Management and Administration. An Introduction*, London, Macmillan.

Humphrey, J. and Schmitz, H. (1996) 'Trust and Economic Development', *Discussion Paper* no. 355, Institute of Development Studies.

IFRC (1997) *World Disaster Report 1997*, International Federation of Red Cross and Red Crescent Societies, Oxford, Oxford University Press.

Independent (1996) *Operation Lifeline Sudan: A Review*, Independent (supported administratively by UN-DHA), July.

Inskip, (1994) 'Network agents: organisations as special facilitators of early stages of interorganisational development', paper prepared for the Workshop on Multi-organisational Partnerships: Working Together across Organisational Boundaries, European Institute for Advanced Studies in Management, Brussels, September 19-20.

Johanson, J. and Mattisson, L.-G. (1987) 'Inter-organizational relations in industrial systems: a network approach compared with the transactions-costs approach', *International Studies of Management and Organization*, vol. 17, no. 1, pp.34-48 [page references relate to the abridged version published in Thompson, G. *et al.* (eds), 1991].

Johnston, R. and Lawrence, P. (1988) 'Beyond vertical integration – the rise of the value-adding partnership', *Harvard Business Review*, July-August, pp. 94-101 [page references relate to the abridged version published in Thompson, G. *et al.* (eds), 1991].

Jonsson, U. (1986) 'Ideological framework and health development in Tanzania 1961-2000', *Social Science and Medicine*, vol. 22, no. 7, pp. 745-753.

Kahama, C. (1995) *Tanzania into the 21st Century,* Dar es Salaam, Tema Publishers Company Ltd.

Kanter, R. (1972) *Commitment and Community: Communes and Utopia in Sociological Perspective*, Cambridge MA, Harvard University Press.

Keohane, R.O. (1984) *After Hegemony: Cooperation and Discord in the World Political Economy*, Princeton NY, Princeton University Press.

Kickert, J.M., Klijn, E., and Koppenjan, J. (1997) *Managing Complex Networks: Strategies for the Public Sector*, London, Sage Publications.

Klitgaard, R. (1989) 'Incentive myopia', *World Development*, vol. 17, no. 4, pp. 447-59.

Knight, J. (1992) *Institutions and Social Conflict*, Cambridge, Cambridge University Press.

Knoke, D. and Kuklinski, J.H. (1991) 'Network analysis: basic concepts', in Thompson, G., Frances, J., Levacic, R. and Mitchell, J. (eds.) (1991) *Markets, Hierarchies and Networks: The Coordination of Social Life*, London, Sage Publications.

Lal, D. (1984) *The Poverty of Development Economics*, London, Institute of Economic Affairs.

Lancaster, W. (1998) 'The Code of Conduct: whose code, whose conduct?', *Journal of Humanitarian Response*, http://www-jha.sps.cam.ac.uk/a/a645.htm posted on 18 April 1998.

Lane, J.-E. (1995) *The Public Sector: Concepts, Models and Approaches*, 2nd. edition, London, Newbury Park and New Delhi, Sage Publications.

Larranaga, O. (1997) 'Chile: a hybrid approach', in Zuckerman, E. and de Kadt, E. (eds.) *The Public-Private Mix in Social Services*, Washington DC, Inter-American Development Bank.

Larsson, R., Bengtsson, L., Henriksson, K. and Sparks, J. (1998) 'The interorganizational learning dilemma: collective knowledge development in strategic alliances', *Organization Science*, vol. 9, no. 3, pp. 285-305.

Lautze, S., Jones, B. and Duffield, M. (1998) *Strategic Humanitarian Co-ordination in the Great Lakes Region, 1996-1997*, an independent study for the UN Inter-Agency Standing Committee, OCHA, United Nations, New York, March.

Liebeskind, J.P., Oliver, A.L., Zucker, L. and Brewer, M. (1996) 'Social networks, learning, and flexibility: sourcing scientific knowledge in new biotechnology firms', *Organization Science*, vol. 7, no. 2, pp. 428-443.

Lipnack, J. and Stamps, J. (1994) *The Age of The Network: Organizing Principles for the 21st Century*, New York, John Wiley.

Lorenz, E. (1989) 'Neither friends nor strangers: informal networks of sub-contracting in French industry', in Gambetta, D. (ed.) *Trust: Making and Breaking of Co-operative Relationships*, Oxford, Blackwell, pp.194-210 [page references relate to the abridged version published in Thompson, G. *et al.* (eds.), 1991].

Lowndes, V., Nanton, P., McCabe, A. and Skelcher, C. (1997) 'Networks, partnerships and urban regeneration', *Local Economy*, vol. 11, no. 4, pp. 333-342.

Lutz, S. (1997) 'Learning through intermediaries: The case of inter-firm research collaborations', in Ebers, M. (ed.) *The Formation of Inter-organizational Networks*, New York, Oxford University Press.

Mackintosh, M. (1992a) 'Introduction', in Wuyts, M., Mackintosh, M. and Hewitt, T. (eds.) *Development Policy and Public Action*, Oxford, Oxford University Press in association with with the Open University.

Mackintosh, M. (1992b) 'Questioning the State', in Wuyts, M., Mackintosh, M. and Hewitt, T. (eds.) *Development Policy and Public Action*, Oxford, Oxford University Press in association with The Open University.

Macpherson, C.B. (1962) *The Political Theory of Possessive Individualism*, Oxford, Clarendon Press.

Macpherson, C.B. (1973) *Democratic Theory*, Oxford, Clarendon Press.

Malhotra K. (1996) *A Southern Perspective on Partnership for Development: Some Lessons from Experience*, Bangkok, October.

Marschak, T. and Reichelstein, S. (1998) 'Network mechanisms, informational efficiency, and hierarchies', *Journal of Economic Theory*, vol. 79, no. 1, pp. 106-141.

Mattessich, P. and Monsey, B. (1992) *Collaboration: What makes it work?*, St. Paul, Amhurst H. Wilder Foundation.

Mill, J.S. (1910) *Utilitarianism, Liberty, and Representative Government*, London, J.M.Dent and New York, E.P. Dutton.

Miller, G.J. (1992) *Managerial Dilemmas: The Political Economy of Hierarchy*, Cambridge, Cambridge University Press.

Mills, A. (1994) 'Decentralisation and accountability in the health sector from an international persepctive: what are the choices?', *Public Administration and Development*, vol. 14, no. 3, pp. 281-92.

Milne, S. (1997) *Making Markets Work: Contracts, Competition and Co-operation*, London, Birkbeck College, University of London [pamphlet produced to report on research under the ESRC's Contracts and Competition Programme, directed by Jonathan Michie, University of London], December.

Mintzberg, H. and Waters, J.A. (1998) 'Of strategies, deliberate and emergent', in Segal-Horn, S. (ed.) *The Strategy Reader*, Oxford, Blackwell Publishers Ltd. in association with The Open University; reprinted from Mintzberg, H. and Waters, J.A. (1985) 'Of strategies deliberate and emergent', *Strategic Management Journal*, 6, pp. 252-272.

Moe, T.M. (1984) 'The New Economics of Organization', *American Journal of Political Science*, vol. 28, no. 4, pp. 739-77.

Monekosso, G.L. (1994) *A Framework for Health for All Beyond The Year 2000: Effective and Efficient Management of District Health Systems*, World Health Organisation, Regional Office for Africa.

Moore, M. (1992) 'Competition and Pluralism in Public Bureaucracies', *IDS Bulletin*, vol. 23, no. 4, pp. 65-77.

Muchunguzi, D. and Scott, M. (1995) *Perspectives From The South: A Study on Partnership*, AFREDA (African Relief and Development Consultancy Association) and CIDA (Canada).

Mujinja, P., Urassa, D. and Mnyika, K. (1993) 'The Tanzanian public/private mix in national health care', paper prepared for Conference on the Public-Private split in health, London School of Hygiene and Tropical Medicine.

Munishi, G. (1995) 'Social services provision in Tanzania: The relationship between political development strategies and NGO participation', in Semboja, J. and Therkildsen, O. (eds.) *Service Provision under Stress in East Africa*, Copenhagen, Centre for Development Research.

Murray, R. (1992) 'Towards a flexible state', *IDS Bulletin*, vol. 23, no. 4, pp. 78-88.

Murray, R. (1993) 'CITER', in Rush, H. *et al.* (eds.) *Background/Benchmark Study for Venezuelan Institute of Engineering*, Brighton, CENTRIM, University of Brighton.

North, D. (1981) *Structure and Change in Economic History*, New York, Norton.

North, D. (1990) *Institutions, Institutional Change and Economic Performance*, Cambridge University Press, Cambridge.

ODA (1996) *Mechanisms for Private Sector Support. Supplement A to Technical Note 11: Private Sector Development*, London, Overseas Development Agency.

ODI (1994) *Relief and Rehabilitation Network Paper 7*, Overseas Development Institute, London, September 1994.

ODI (1998) *Briefing Paper*, Overseas Development Institute, London, March.

OECD (1996) *Shaping the 21st Century: The Contribution of Development Co-operation*, London, Development Assistance Committee, Organization for Economic Co-operation and Development.

OECD (1997) *Geographical Distribution of Financial Flows to Aid Recipients. Disbursements, Commitments, Country Indicators*, Paris, Development Assistance Committee, Organization for Economic Co-operation and Development.

Oliver, C. (1990) 'Determinants of inter-organizational relationships: integration and future directions', *Academy of Management Review*, no. 15, pp. 241-65.

Osborne, D. and Gaebler, T. (1992) *Reinventing Government: How the Entrepreneurial Spirit is Transforming the Public Sector*, Reading, MA, Addison-Wesley.

Ostrom, E. (1990) *Governing the Commons: The Evolution of Institutions for Collective Action,* Cambridge, Cambridge University Press.

Ostrom, E., Schroeder, L.D. and Wynne, S.G. (1993) *Institutional Incentives and Sustainable Development: Infrastructure Policies in Perspective*, Boulder, Westview Press.

Ouchi, W. (1980) 'Markets, bureaucracies and clans', *Administrative Science Quarterly*, vol. 25, pp.129-141 [page references relate to the abridged version published in Thompson, G. *et al.* (eds.), 1991].

Park, S.H. (1996) 'Managing an interorganizational network: a framework of the institutional mechanism for network control', *Organization Studies*, vol. 17, no. 5, pp. 795-824.

Pinheiro, J. (1997) Opening Address to the UK consultation on the EC's Green Paper on the future of EU–ACP relations, June 1997.

Piore, M. and Sabel, C. (1982) *The Second Industrial Divide*, New York, Basic Books.

Polanyi, M. (1966) *The Tacit Dimension*, London, Routledge and Kegan Paul.

Powell, W. (1990) 'Neither market nor hierarchy: network forms of organization', *Research in Organizational Behaviour*, vol.12, pp.295-336 [page references relate to the abridged version published in Thompson, G. *et al.* (eds.), 1991].

Putnam, R. (1993a) *Making Democracy Work: Civic Traditions in Modern Italy*, Princeton NJ, Princeton University Press.

Putnam, R. (1993b) 'The prosperous community: social capital and public life', *The American Prospect*, no. 13.

PWBLF (1996) *Business as Partners in Development. Creating Wealth for Countries, Companies and Communities*, London, Prince of Wales Business Leaders Forum in collaboration with The World Bank and The United Nations.

Rawls, J. (1972) *A Theory of Justice*, Oxford, Oxford University Press.

Redd Barna (1997) *Partnership – Redd Barna policy for co-operation with partners*, [quoted from Asia Regional Meeting, Thailand 1996], Bangkok, Redd Barna.

Rhodes (1995) 'Foreword' in Blunden, M. and Dando, M. *Rethinking Public Policy-Making: Questioning Assumptions, Challenging Beliefs: Essays in Honour of Sir Geoffrey Vickers on his Centenary*, London and Thousand Oaks CA, Sage Publications.

Righter, R. (1995) *Utopia Lost: The United Nations and World Order*, New York, Twentieth Century Fund Press.

Ring, P. and Van den Van, A. (1994) 'Developmental processes of co-operative inter-organizational relationships', *Academy of Management Review*, no. 19, pp. 90-118.

Ring, P.S. (1996) 'Networked organization: a resource based perspective', *Studia Oeconomiae Negitorium*, no. 39, Uppsala, Acta Universtatis Upsaliensis.

Ring, P.S. (1997) 'Processes facilitating reliance in trust in inter-organizational networks', in Ebers, M. (ed.) *The Formation of Inter-organizational Networks*, New York, Oxford University Press.

Ritchie, C. (1996) 'Co-ordinate? Cooperate? Harmonize? NGO policy and operational coalitions', in Weiss, T. and Gordenker, L. (eds.) *NGOs, the UN and Global Governance,* Boulder, Lynne Reinner Publishers.

Robinson, D. (1999) 'The development management task and reform of "public" social services', *Development in Practice*, vol. 9, nos. 1/2, pp. 78-87.

Rondinelli, D., McCullough, J. and Johnson, R. (1989) 'Analysing decentralization policies in development countries: a political economy perspective', *Development and Change*, vol. 20, pp. 57-87.

Ross, R., Smith, B., Roberts, C. and Kleiner, A. (1994) 'Core concepts about learning in organizations', in Senge, P.M., Kleiner, A., Roberts, C., Ross, R.B. and Smith, B.J. (eds.) *The Fifth Discipline Fieldbook: Strategies and Tools for Building a learning Organization*, London, Nicholas Brearley Publishing Ltd.

Rounds Parry, T. (1997) 'Achieving balance in decentralization: a case study of education decentralization in Chile', *World Development*, vol. 25, no. 2, pp. 211-226.

Ruggie, J.G. (1998) *Constructing The World Polity: Essays on International Institutionalization*, Routledge, London and New York.

Sabel, C. (1993) 'Studied trust: building new forms of co-operation in a volatile economy', in Swedberg, R. (ed.) *Explorations in Economic Sociology*, New York, Russell Sage Foundation.

Sabetti, F. (1996) 'Path dependency and civic culture: some lessons from Italy about interpreting social experiments', *Politics and Society*, vol. 24, no. 1, pp. 19-44.

Salancik, G.R. (1995) 'Wanted: a good network theory of organization' *Administrative Science Quarterly*, vol. 40, no. 2, pp. 345-349.

SCF (1994) *Indian Partnership Study for Plan International Region of South Asia*, London, Save the Children.

Schick, A. (1996) *The Spirit of Reform. Managing the New Zealand State Sector in a Time of Change*, Wellington, State Services Commission.

Schmitz, H. (1995) 'Collective efficiency: Growth path for small firms', *Journal of Development Studies*, vol. 31, no. 4.

Schmitz, H. (1997) 'Collective efficiency and increasing returns', *Working Paper* no. 50, Institute of Development Studies, University of Sussex.

Sen, A. (1990) 'Development as capability expansion', in Griffin, K. and Knight, J. (eds.) *Human Development and the International Strategy for the 1990's*, London, Macmillan.

Senge, P.M. (1990) *The Fifth Discipline: The Art and Practice of the Learning Organisation'*, reprinted 1997, London, Century Business.

Senge, P.M., Kleiner, A., Roberts, C., Ross, R.B. and Smith, B.J. (1990) *The Fifth Discipline Fieldbook: Strategies and Tools for Building a learning Organization*, London, Nicholas Brearley Publishing Ltd.

Senker, J (1995) 'Networks and tacit knowledge in innovation', *Economies et Societes*, vol. XXIX, no. 9, pp. 99-118.

Shirley, M.M. and Xu, L.C. (1997) 'Information, incentives, and commitment. An empirical analysis of contracts between government and state enterprises', *Policy Research Working Paper* no. 1769, Washington DC, World Bank.

Short, C. (1997a) Speech given at the School of Oriental and African Studies, London, May 1997.

Short C. (1997b) 'Development and the Private Sector: a Partnership for Change', speech given at the Institute of Directors, London, 8 July 1997.

Short, C. (1997c) 'Democracy, Human Rights and Governance', speech given at University of Manchester 30th June 1997.

Simon, H. (1957) *Administrative Behaviour*, 2nd edition, New York, Macmillan.

Sivalon, J. (1995) 'The Catholic church and the Tanzanian state in the provision of social services', in Semboja, J. and Therkildsen, O. (eds.) *Service Provision under Stress in East Africa*, Copenhagen, Centre for Development Research.

Smillie, I. (1995) *The Alms Bazaar: Altruism under Fire – Non-profit Organizations and International Development*, London, Intermediate Technology Publications.

Smith, K., Carroll, S. and Ashford, S. (1995) 'Intra- and inter-organizational co-operation: towards a research agenda', *Academy of Management Journal*, vol. 38, no. 1, pp. 7-23.

Tandon, Y. (1990) cited in 'Critical Choices for the NGO Community: African Development in the 1990s' (Proceedings of a conference at the Centre for African Studies, University of Edinburgh, May 1990), Edinburgh, Centre for African Studies.

Tarrow, S. (1996) 'Making social science work across space and time: a critical reflection on Robert Putnam's Making Democracy Work', *American Political Science Review*, vol. 90, no. 2, pp. 389-397.

Taylor, P. (1993) *International Organization in the Modern World: the Regional and the Global Pattern*, London, Pinter Publishers.

Taylor, P. (1995) 'Options for the reform of the international system for humanitarian assistance', in Harriss, J. (ed.) *The Politics of Humanitarian Intervention*, London, Pinter and Save the Children.

Taylor, P. and Groom, A.J.R. (eds.) (1989) *Global Issues in the United Nations' Framework,* Basingstoke, Macmillan.

Tendler, J. (1993) *New Lessons from Old Projects: The Workings of Rural Development in Northeast Brazil*, Washington, Operations Evaluation Department, World Bank.

Tendler, J. and Freedheim, S. (1994) 'Trust in a rent-seeking world: health and government transformed in northeast Brazil', *World Development*, vol. 22, no. 12, pp. 1771-1791.

Tennyson, R. (1998) *Managing Partnerships: Tools for Mobilising the Public Sector, Business and Civil Society as Partners in Development*, London, The Prince of Wales Business Leaders Forum.

Thomas, A. (1996) 'What is Development Management?', *Journal of International Development*, vol. 8, no. 1, pp. 95-110.

Thompson, G. (1991) 'Introduction', in Thompson, G., Frances, J., Levacic, R. and Mitchell, J. (eds.) *Markets, Hierarchies and Networks: The Coordination of Social Life*, London, Sage Publications in association with The Open University.

Thompson, G., Frances, J., Levacic, R. and Mitchell, J. (1991) *Markets, Hierarchies and Networks: the Coordination of Social Life*, London, Sage Publications in association with The Open University.

Thorp, R. (1996) 'The reform of the tax administration in Peru', in Silva, A. (ed.) *Implementing Policy Innovations in Latin America*, Washington DC, Social Agenda Policy Group, Inter-American Development Bank.

Tullock, G. (1987) *The Politics of Bureaucracy*, New York, University Press of America.

UN (1996) *Background Paper on the Harmonization and Coordination of the Agendas and Multi-Year Programmes of Work of Functional Commissions of ECOSOC*, E/1996/CRP.4, 10 July 1996, Geneva, Economic and Social Council, General Segment.

UN (1997) *Renewing The United Nations: A Programme for Reform: Report of The Secretary-General*, A/51/950, New York, United Nations.

UNDP (1993) *Human Development Report*, New York, Oxford University Press.

UNDP (1997) *Human Development Report*, Oxford, Oxford University Press and United Nations Development Programme.

UN-JIU (1984) *Report to the Economic and Social Council*, JIU/REP/84/7, prepared by Maurice Bertrand, Geneva, United Nations Joint Inspection Unit.

Uphoff, N. (1992) *Learning from Gal Oya: Possibilities for Participatory Development and Post-Newtonian Social Science*, Ithaca NY, Cornell University Press.

Uphoff, N. (1995) 'Why NGOs are not a third sector: a sectoral analysis with some thoughts on accountability, sustainability and evaluation', in Edwards, M. and Hulme, D. (eds.) *Non-Governmental Organizations –*

Performance and Accountability. Beyond the Magic Bullet, London, Earthscan Publications Ltd, pp. 2-30.

USAID (1987) 'A section plan for financial year 1989', Maputo, USAID.

Van Brabant, K. (1997) 'The co-ordination of humanitarian action: the case of Sri Lanka', *Network Paper* no. 23, London, Relief and Rehabilitation Network, Overseas Development Institute.

Wade, R. (1988) *Village Republics: Economic Conditions for Collective Action in South India*, Cambridge, Cambridge University Press.

Wade, R. (1990) *Governing the Market, Economic Theory and the Role of Government in East Asian Industrialisation*, Princeton, Princeton University Press.

Walt, G. (1983) 'The Evolution of Health Policy' in Walt, G. and Melamed, A. (eds.) *Mozambique: Toward a People's Health Service*, London, Zed Books.

Weber, M. (1968) *Economy and Society*, 2 vols., Berkeley, California University Press.

Welford, R. (1995) *Environmental Strategy and Sustainable Development. The Corporate Challenge for the 21st Century*, London, Routledge.

Wellard, K. and Copestake, J. (1993) *Non-Governmental Organizations and the State in Africa: Rethinking Roles in Sustainable Agricultural Development*, Routledge, London.

White, G. (1993) 'Towards a political analysis of markets', *IDS Bulletin*, vol. 24, no. 3.

Wield, D. (1997) 'Coordination of donors in African Universities', *Higher Education Policy*, vol. 10, no. 1, pp. 41-54.

Williamson, O.E. (1985) *The Economic Institutions of Capitalism*, New York, Free Press.

Williamson, O.E. (1979) 'Transaction cost economics: the governance of contractual relations', *Journal of Law and Economics*, no. 22, pp. 233-261.

Williamson, O.E. (1985) *The Economic Institutions of Capitalism: Firms, Markets, Relational Contracts*, New York, Free Press.

Wilson, L. (1993) 'Kenyanization and African Capacity 'Shuffling'', *Public Administration and Development*, vol. 13, no. pp. 489-499.

Womack, J., Jones, D.T. and Roos, D. (1990) *The Machine that Changed the World*, New York, Rawson Associates.

World Bank (1981) *Accelerated Development in Sub-Saharan Africa*, Washington, World Bank.

World Bank (1989) 'Public Expenditure Review', vol. II 7615-MOZ, Washington DC, World Bank, 6 April.

World Bank (1993) *Investing in Health*, World Development Report, Washington DC, World Bank.

World Bank (1994) *The World Bank and Participation*, Washington, World Bank.

World Bank (1995a) 'Health Sector Recovery Program', 14373-MOZ, Washington DC, World Bank.

World Bank (1995b) 'Country Assistance Strategy', 15067-MOZ, Washington DC, World Bank.

World Bank (1996) *Pursuing Common Goals: Strengthening Relations Between Government and Development NGOs*, World Bank Resident Mission, Bangladesh.

World Bank (1997a) *The State in a Changing World*, World Development Report, Washington DC, World Bank.

World Bank (1997b) 'Mozambique Country Assistance Review', Washington DC, World Bank, 2 December 1997.

World Bank (1999) *World Development Report 1998/99: Knowledge for Development*, World Bank, Washington, DC.

World Bank and International Money Fund (1988) 'Mozambique final document on the initiative for Heavily Indebted Poor Countries (HIPC)', Washington DC, 31 March.

Wuyts, M. (1992) 'Conclusion', in Wuyts, M., Mackintosh, M. and Hewitt, T. (eds.) *Development Policy and Public Action*, Oxford, Oxford University Press in association with the Open University.

Wuyts, M. (1995) *Negotiating and Managing Public Expenditures*, Institute of Social Studies, The Hague, April.

Wuyts, M. (1999) *Residential School Handbook*, U208 *Third World Development*, Milton Keynes, The Open University.

Young, O. (1994) *International Governance: Protecting the Environment in a Stateless Society*, Ithaca NY, Cornell University Press.

Zucker, L. (1986) 'Production of trust: institutional sources of economic structure, 1840-1920', *Research in Organizational Behaviour*, vol. 8, pp. 53-111.

ACKNOWLEDGEMENTS

Grateful acknowledgement is made to the following sources for permission to reproduce material in this book:

TEXT

Various extracts from Nelson, J. (1996) *Business as Partners in Development*, The Prince of Wales Business Leaders Forum;

FIGURES

Figure 4.1: JSB (1996) *The Presenter's Guide*, JSB Training: Needs assessment exercise of medium sized firms in Poland, Segal Quince and Wicksteed Ltd;

TABLES

Table 10.1: Reprinted by permission of Sage Publications Ltd from Thompson, G., Frances, J., Levacic, R. and Mitchell, J. (eds.) (1991) *Markets, Hierarchies and Networks*, Copyright © 1991 Sage Publications Ltd; *Table 14.1:* adapted from Mintzberg and Waters (1985) 'Of strategies, deliberate and emergent', *Strategic Management Journal*, 6. Copyright © 1985 by John Wiley & Sons Limited;

INDEX